T0336779

Solutions for Sustaining Scalability in Internet Growth

Mohamed Boucadair
France Telecom, France

David Binet
France Telecom, France

A volume in the Advances in Web Technologies and Engineering (AWTE) Book Series

An Imprint of IGI Global

Managing Director:	Lindsay Johnston
Editorial Director:	Joel Gamon
Production Manager:	Jennifer Yoder
Publishing Systems Analyst:	Adrienne Freeland
Development Editor:	Monica Speca
Acquisitions Editor:	Kayla Wolfe
Typesetter:	Erin O'Dea
Cover Design:	Jason Mull

Published in the United States of America by
Information Science Reference (an imprint of IGI Global)
701 E. Chocolate Avenue
Hershey PA 17033
Tel: 717-533-8845
Fax: 717-533-8661
E-mail: cust@igi-global.com
Web site: http://www.igi-global.com

Library of Congress Cataloging-in-Publication Data

Solutions for sustaining scalability in Internet growth / Mohamed Boucadair and David Binet, editors.
     pages cm
 Includes bibliographical references and index.
 Summary: "This book investigates current issues impeding the growth of information architecture and explores methods for developing a wider-reaching and ever-evolving internet"--Provided by publisher.
  ISBN 978-1-4666-4305-5 (hardcover) -- ISBN 978-1-4666-4306-2 (ebook) -- ISBN 978-1-4666-4307-9 (print & perpetual access) 1. Internet. 2. Computer network architectures. I. Boucadair, Mohamed. II. Binet, David, 1969-
 TK5105.875.I57S6676 2013
 004.67'8--dc23
                                        2013011324

This book is published in the IGI Global book series Advances in Web Technologies and Engineering (AWTE) (ISSN: Pending; eISSN: pending)

British Cataloguing in Publication Data
A Cataloguing in Publication record for this book is available from the British Library.

All work contributed to this book is new, previously-unpublished material. The views expressed in this book are those of the authors, but not necessarily of the publisher.

Advances in Web Technologies and Engineering (AWTE)

Ghazi I. Alkhatib
Princess Sumaya University for Technology, Jordan

David C. Rine
George Mason University, USA

ISSN: Pending
EISSN: Pending

MISSION

The **Advances in Web Technologies and Engineering (AWTE) Book Series** aims to provide a platform for research in the area of Information Technology (IT) concepts, tools, methodologies, and ethnography, in the contexts of global communication systems and Web engineered applications. Organizations are continuously overwhelmed by a variety of new information technologies, many are Web based. These new technologies are capitalizing on the widespread use of network and communication technologies for seamless integration of various issues in information and knowledge sharing within and among organizations. This emphasis on integrated approaches is unique to this book series and dictates cross platform and multidisciplinary strategy to research and practice.

The **Advances in Web Technologies and Engineering (AWTE) Book Series** seeks to create a stage where comprehensive publications are distributed for the objective of bettering and expanding the field of web systems, knowledge capture, and communication technologies. The series will provide researchers and practitioners with solutions for improving how technology is utilized for the purpose of a growing awareness of the importance of web applications and engineering.

COVERAGE

- Case Studies Validating Web-Based IT Solutions
- Data Analytics for Business and Government Organizations
- Human Factors and Cultural Impact of IT-Based Systems
- Knowledge Structure, Classification and Search Algorithms or Engines
- Mobile, Location-Aware, and Ubiquitous Computing
- Ontology and Semantic Web Studies
- Security, Integrity, Privacy and Policy Issues
- Software Agent-Based Applications
- Strategies for Linking Business Needs and IT
- Web Systems Engineering Design

IGI Global is currently accepting manuscripts for publication within this series. To submit a proposal for a volume in this series, please contact our Acquisition Editors at Acquisitions@igi-global.com or visit: http://www.igi-global.com/publish/.

Titles in this Series

For a list of additional titles in this series, please visit: www.igi-global.com

Solutions for Sustaining Scalability in Internet Growth
Mohamed Boucadair (France Telecom, France) and David Binet (France Telecom, France)
Information Science Reference • copyright 2014 • 310pp • H/C (ISBN: 9781466643055) • US $190.00 (our price)

Adaptive Web Services for Modular and Reusable Software Development Tactics and Solutions
Guadalupe Ortiz (University of Cádiz, Spain) and Javier Cubo (University of Málaga, Spain)
Information Science Reference • copyright 2013 • 415pp • H/C (ISBN: 9781466620896) • US $195.00 (our price)

Public Service, Governance and Web 2.0 Technologies Future Trends in Social Media
Ed Downey (State University of New York, College at Brockport, USA) and Matthew A. Jones (Portland State University, USA)
Information Science Reference • copyright 2012 • 369pp • H/C (ISBN: 9781466600713) • US $190.00 (our price)

Performance and Dependability in Service Computing Concepts, Techniques and Research Directions
Valeria Cardellini (Universita di Roma, Italy) Emiliano Casalicchio (Universita di Roma, Italy) Kalinka Regina Lucas Jaquie Castelo Branco (Universidade de São Paulo, Brazil) Júlio Cezar Estrella (Universidade de São Paulo, Brazil) and Francisco José Monaco (Universidade de São Paulo, Brazil)
Information Science Reference • copyright 2012 • 477pp • H/C (ISBN: 9781609607944) • US $195.00 (our price)

E-Activity and Intelligent Web Construction Effects of Social Design
Tokuro Matsuo (Yamagata University, Japan) and Takayuki Fujimoto (Toyo University, Japan)
Information Science Reference • copyright 2011 • 284pp • H/C (ISBN: 9781615208715) • US $180.00 (our price)

Engineering Reliable Service Oriented Architecture Managing Complexity and Service Level Agreements
Nikola Milanovic (Model Labs - Berlin, Germany)
Information Science Reference • copyright 2011 • 420pp • H/C (ISBN: 9781609604936) • US $180.00 (our price)

Developing Advanced Web Services through P2P Computing and Autonomous Agents Trends and Innovations
Khaled Ragab (King Faisal University, Saudi Arabia) Tarek Helmy (King Fahd University of Petroleum and Minerals, Saudi Arabia) and Aboul Ella Hassanien (Kuwait University, Kuwait)
Information Science Reference • copyright 2010 • 284pp • H/C (ISBN: 9781615209736) • US $180.00 (our price)

Integrating Usability Engineering for Designing the Web Experience Methodologies and Principles
Tasos Spiliotopoulos (National and Kapodistrian University of Athens, Greece) Panagiota Papadopoulou (University of Athens, Greece) Drakoulis Martakos (National and Kapodistrian University of Athens, Greece) and Georgios Kouroupetroglou (National and Kapodistrian University of Athens, Greece)
Information Science Reference • copyright 2010 • 440pp • H/C (ISBN: 9781605668963) • US $180.00 (our price)

www.igi-global.com

701 E. Chocolate Ave., Hershey, PA 17033
Order online at www.igi-global.com or call 717-533-8845 x100
To place a standing order for titles released in this series, contact: cust@igi-global.com
Mon-Fri 8:00 am - 5:00 pm (est) or fax 24 hours a day 717-533-8661

Table of Contents

Section 1
Issues and Design Principles

Mohamed Boucadair, France Telecom, France
David Binet, France Telecom, France

Section 2
Scalable Routing and Forwarding Architectures

Rolf Winter, University of Applied Sciences Augsburg, Germany
Iljitsch van Beijnum, Institute IMDEA Networks, Spain & Universidad Carlos III de Madrid, Spain

Yaoqing Liu, University of Memphis, USA
Xin Zhao, Google, USA
Lan Wang, University of Memphis, USA
Beichuan Zhang, University of Arizona, USA

Section 3
Advanced Features

Chapter 10
Waveband Switching: A Scalable and Cost Efficient Solution for the Internet Backbone 195
Yang Wang, Georgia State University, USA
Vishal Anand, The College at Brockport, USA
Xiaojun Cao, Georgia State University, USA

Detailed Table of Contents

Section 1
Issues and Design Principles

Chapter 1

Mohamed Boucadair, France Telecom, France
David Binet, France Telecom, France

It is commonly agreed that the continuous increase of routing and forwarding tables (Huston, 2001; Meyer, Zhang, & Fall, 2007) is a sensitive issue which may question the growth of the overall Internet. Some technical practices such as multi-homing using Provider Independent (PI) prefixes and shrinking advertised prefixes to support advanced inbound traffic engineering policies exacerbate the increase of inter-domain routing tables (Narten, 2010). This chapter synthesizes routing and forwarding issues encountered by current Internet routing architecture and provides an overview of analyzed solutions.

Section 2
Scalable Routing and Forwarding Architectures

Chapter 2

Rolf Winter, University of Applied Sciences Augsburg, Germany
Iljitsch van Beijnum, Institute IMDEA Networks, Spain & Universidad Carlos III de Madrid, Spain

Inter-domain Traffic Engineering (TE) is an important aspect of network operation both technically and economically. Outbound Traffic Engineering is less problematic as routers under the control of the network operator are responsible for the way traffic leaves the network. The inbound direction is considerably harder as the way traffic enters a network is based on routing decisions in other networks. There are very few mechanisms available today that facilitate inter-domain inbound traffic engineering, such as prefix deaggregation (i.e., advertise more specific prefixes), AS path prepending and systems based on BGP communities. These mechanisms have severe drawbacks such as exacerbating the increase of the size of global routing table or providing only coarse-grained control. In this chapter, an alternative mechanism is described and evaluated. The proposed solution does not increase the size of the global routing table, is easy to configure through a simple numeric value and provides a finer-grained control compared to currently used mechanisms that also do not add additional prefixes to the global routing table.

Yaoqing Liu, University of Memphis, USA
Xin Zhao, Google, USA
Lan Wang, University of Memphis, USA
Beichuan Zhang, University of Arizona, USA

In this book chapter, the authors first present Optimal Routing Table Constructor (ORTC), an optimal one-time FIB aggregation algorithm that preserves strong forwarding correctness. The authors then present four-level FIB aggregation algorithm(s) that can handle dynamic routing updates while maintaining forwarding correctness. Afterwards, the authors evaluate our algorithms using routing tables from RouteViews, and compare the algorithms with ORTC using routing tables from a Tier-1 ISP. The authors found that ORTC's aggregation ratio is better than the Level-1, Level-2 and Level-3 algorithms, but the Level-4 algorithm has better aggregation ratio than ORTC as they relax the requirement of forwarding correctness. Finally, the authors evaluate the potential impact of introducing extra routable space in the Level-4 algorithm and discuss how to limit such negative impact.

Dan Jen, Center for Naval Analyses, USA
Michael Meisel, ThousandEyes, USA
Daniel Massey, Colorado State University, USA
Lan Wang, The University of Memphis, USA
Beichuan Zhang, The University of Arizona, USA
Lixia Zhang, University of California, Los Angeles, USA

The global routing system has seen a rapid increase in table size and routing changes in recent years, mostly driven by the growth of edge networks. This growth reflects two major limitations in the current architecture: (a) the conflict between provider-based addressing and edge networks' need for multihoming, and (b) flat routing's inability to provide isolation from edge dynamics. In order to address these limitations, we propose A Practical Tunneling Architecture (APT), a routing architecture that enables the Internet routing system to scale independently from edge growth. APT partitions the Internet address space in two, one for the transit core and one for edge networks, allowing edge addresses to be removed from the routing table in the transit core. Packets between edge networks are tunneled through the transit core. In order to automatically tunnel the packets, APT provides a mapping service between edge addresses and the addresses of their transit-core attachment points. We conducted an extensive performance evaluation of APT using trace data collected from routers at two major service providers. Our results show that APT can tunnel packets through the transit core by incurring extra delay on up to 0.8% of all packets at the cost of introducing only one or a few new or repurposed devices per AS.

This chapter describes a new Identifier/Locator split architecture, referred to as Routing Architecture for the Next Generation Internet (RANGI), which aims to deal with the routing scalability issues. Similar to the Host Identity Protocol (HIP) architecture, RANGI also introduces a host identifier (ID) layer between the IPv6 network layer and the transport layer and hence the transport-layer associations (e.g., TCP connections) are no longer bound to IP addresses, but to the host IDs. The major difference from the HIP architecture is that RANGI adopts hierarchical and cryptographic host IDs which have delegation-oriented structure. The corresponding ID to locator mapping system in RANGI is designed to preserve a "reasonable" business model and clear trust boundaries. In addition, RANGI uses special IPv4-embedded IPv6 addresses as locators and hence site-controllable traffic-engineering and simplified renumbering can be easily achieved while the deployment cost of such new architecture is reduced greatly.

TARA (Topology Aggregating Routing Architecture) is a novel architecture which allows to generate a map of the Internet. TARA allows to maintain and compute a precise topology of the near surrounding and lesser zoomed topologies the more remote they are. In the context of TARA, nodes are identified with "locators" which are derived from longitude/latitude degrees/minutes/seconds. TARA is designed to satisfy advanced traffic engineering such as computing QoS-inferred paths or non congested paths. TARA achieves these goals without requiring an increase of RIBs an FIBs. TARA solves also the issues of dynamic update churn as currently experienced in BGP-based Internet. TARA is also designed with mobility requirements in mind. Indeed, Mobility is supported without requiring dependency on home agents or care-of-address servers.. Note, the Time-To-Live mechanism is neither needed nor used in TARA-forwarding. TARA supports various multicast, broadcast, MP2P (multipoint-to-point), anycast and MP2MP (multipoint-to-multipoint) communication schemes. In particular a stateless concept for multicast is outlined; this concept may serve as a pattern for anycast and MP2MP applications. TARA is fully prepared to cope with the IPv4-unicast address depletion issue.

Section 3
Advanced Features

The routing architecture of today's Internet is facing scalability problems. Multi-homing, traffic engineering, suboptimal address allocations are making the Forwarding Information Base (FIB) of the Default Free Zone (DFZ) growing at a nonlinear rate. Such scalability problems are mainly caused by the overloading of the IP address semantics. That is, an IP address represents not only the location but also the identity of a host. To address the scalability problem, Identifier Network, as a novel proposed network architecture, separates the identifier and locator roles of IP addresses into two evolving spaces: Accessing Identifier (AID) and Routing Identifier (RID) by Identifier/Locator separation mechanism. Such separation provides opportunities to reconsider routing optimization for inter-domain Traffic Engineering, as which is a main contribution to the Border Gateway Protocol (BGP) routing table growth. Based on Identifier Network, we propose a solution for traffic engineering, which can be divided into two distinct parts: End-to-End traffic engineering and Neighbor-to-Neighbor traffic engineering. For each scenario, we develop a routing decision method for both routers and other network entities, such as IDMS (Identifier Mapping Server in Identifier Network). To analyze the feasibility of the solution, we collect Routeviews data set and the results show that the scheme proposed could reduce the burden of the core routing table.

Chapter 8

Damien Saucez, Inria Sophia Antipolis, France

Luigi Iannone, Telecom ParisTech, France

Olivier Bonaventure, Université catholique de Louvain, Belgium

Internet lacks of strong security mechanisms, opening the way to a plethora of different manners in which integrity and availability can be compromised by malicious activities. Furthermore, the trend shows an increase of security threats, at least in the foreseeable future. Despite such situation, new proposals for Future Internet architectures mostly aiming at solving scalability issues do rather neglect security aspects. Among candidate Future Internet architectures, the ones based on the Locator/Identifier separation paradigm has been largely explored, but security had no major role in these research activities. We present a security threats analysis of such approach using the Locator/Identifier Separation Protocol (LISP) as a running example. The chapter does not overview the merits of the Locator/Identifier separation paradigm. Rather, the aim is to provide a thorough analysis of the security aspects, assessing the security level of the architecture and providing recommendations on possible practices to improve it.

Chapter 9

Shankar Raman, Indian Institute of Technology Madras, India

Balaji Venkat, Indian Institute of Technology Madras, India

Gaurav Raina, Indian Institute of Technology Madras, India

The authors present a metric-based hierarchical approach to reduce power consumption in core and edge networks. The proposal considers both unicast and the multicast cases. For unicast, the metric used is consumed-power to available-bandwidth and for multicast the metric is consumed-power to available-replication-capacity. With unicast, the metric is used to determine a low-power path between sources and destinations. The source and destination entities could be attached to Autonomous Systems (ASes) or to routing areas within the Autonomous System. Determining a low-power path within an Autonomous System provides a unique challenge as the topology of the constituent areas may not be known. To that end, we propose the use of a selective leak technique for disclosing low-power paths. Additionally, the proposed method can also be used to determine disjoint or redundant paths for load-balancing or fault tolerance. With multicast, the metric serves the twin purpose of finding low-power multicast paths as well as multicast replication points. Once low-power paths in either the unicast or the multicast cases are identified, then currently available traffic engineering techniques could be used to route the data packets.

Chapter 10

Yang Wang, Georgia State University, USA
Vishal Anand, The College at Brockport, USA
Xiaojun Cao, Georgia State University, USA

In this chapter, the authors describe and review some of the recent research on WBS, including Multi-Granular optical cross-connect (MG-OXC) architectures that can switch traffic at different granularities. The authors focus on the dynamic online WBS problem, and describe and analyze two reconfigurable MG-OXC architectures in terms of their port count and blocking probabilities. Based on the analyses, the authors then propose a novel dynamic graph-based waveband assignment algorithm in conjunction with adaptive routing. The proposed algorithm employs ant optimization techniques to reduce ports and blocking probability in the network with online traffic in a distributed manner. The authors use simulation experiments to evaluate the effectiveness of the authors' approach under various parameters such as varying number of ants, varying the number of routes and the wavelength assignment algorithm. The authors' simulation results show that their graph-based waveband assignment algorithm combined with adaptive routing can achieve a superior performance when compared to other schemes. Furthermore, the authors' studies shows that even with limited resources, WBS can achieve a low blocking probability and port savings.

Preface

INTRODUCTION

The Internet is suffering from a wide range of complications which may impact its evolution. Some of these complications alter the growth of the Internet while other issues induce more complexity to introduce innovative services in the Internet at large scale. Particularly, the continuous increase of routing and forwarding tables is a sensitive issue which may question the growth of the overall Internet and therefore would complicate the delivery of advanced services by network and service providers with a global reachability scope. Some technical practices, such as multi-homing using Provider Independent (PI) prefixes and shrinking advertised prefixes to support advanced inbound traffic engineering policies, exacerbate the increase of inter-domain routing tables. Routers have to process more and more information and the growth of routing and forwarding tables to be managed may not be (only) satisfied by router technology evolution. Furthermore, such routing capabilities requirements dramatically impact routers' power consumption.

Solving the various encountered complications can not be easily achieved because of the Internet's anarchical nature: there is no central entity controlling and managing the Internet. Nevertheless, some of the problems can be mitigated owing to an architectural re-design, the deployment of new protocols, and the enforcement of appropriate operational guidelines.

Designing a scalable, robust, predictable, and stable routing system to sustain the growth of the Internet should be seriously tackled by Internet actors. Concrete actions to avoid the potential failure of the deployed Internet routing architecture, and therefore avoid the emergence of a fragmented Internet, should be adopted. Because the Internet is de-centralized, introducing new tools won't be shipped overnight. To be successful, making evolving Internet Routing Architecture requires the involvement and coordination of several actors.

Deploying new innovative tools to mitigate Internet routing issues may take a long time before being adopted at large, but it should not be considered as a "pretext" to delay introducing the proposed new schemes, and to cease investigating efficient solutions. This should be even used as an opportunity to better design, specify and assess the validity of the efficiency of the proposed innovative solutions. If no particular action is conducted to soften (and even overcome) issues encountered by the Internet routing architecture, serious risks for a fragmented Internet with non-global reachability will be faced.

CONTRIBUTIONS FROM THIS BOOK

This book aims to offer a detailed view of issues as currently met by the Internet architecture and a comprehensive overview on the recent advances in exploring viable and promising solutions for expanding the scalability limits of routing and forwarding tables. Towards this end, the book includes chapters describing new ideas and proposals on relevant techniques for designing and deploying a scalable Internet Routing Architecture. Individual chapters included in this book offer recently proposed solutions in multiple and complementary dimensions of the overall Internet routing puzzle.

HOW THIS BOOK IS STRUCTURED?

We aim to provide in this book an overview of the specific issues and proposed solutions dealing with Internet Routing Architectures. The book is organized into three parts:

- Section 1 provides an overview on encountered issues in current Internet.
- Section 2 presents a set of solutions to mitigate some of the issues discussed in Part 1. The solutions we selected to be listed in this part are complementary. Indeed, this part includes both evolutionary and disruptive solutions. It also includes solutions requiring some changes in the host side and other solutions which do not require such changes. Some of these solutions can be deployed in the short term without requiring any interaction with adjacent domains while other solutions do require interaction with external parties. Other solutions require some levels of coordination with adjacent domains.
- Part 3 focuses on advanced features such as the support of Traffic Engineering (TE) in the context of Locator/Identifier separation. This part discusses also security-related considerations which are valid for Map and Encap solutions. Another important item discussed in this part is power consumption and how advanced metrics can be defined to tweak the forwarding engine in order to optimize the overall network power consumption. Note the concepts of Locator/Identifier separation and Map and Encap are both introduced in Part 1.

Hereafter we provide a brief summary on each chapter that has been included in this book.

- Section 1 "Issues and Design Principles" is structured as follows:
  - The chapter "Issues with Current Internet Architecture" aims to describe the issues encountered in current Internet Architectures. The chapter includes also a brief overview of initiatives conducted within the IETF (Internet Engineering Task Force) to mitigate these issues. To solve the remaining issues, the chapter lists some requirements and design goals to take into considerations when designing solutions. The chapter introduces two classes of solutions: CEE (Core Edge Elimination) and CES (Core Edge Separation). A brief comparison between CEE and CES is included in this chapter.
- Section 2 "Scalable Routing and Forwarding Architectures" includes the following chapters:
  - The chapter "Inter-Domain Traffic Engineering Using the Origin Preference Attribute" advocates for an alternative mechanism to achieve inter-domain traffic engineering. Concretely, this chapter proposes a new BGP (Border Gateway Protocol) attribute called: Origin Preference Attribute (OPA). In this chapter, OPA is defined as a way to indicate an origin's relative preference for a given prefix announcement as seen through a particular AS path route. The proposed design assumes OPA is set by the origin AS (Autonomous System) and is not changed by any intermediate AS. To achieve its goals, the chapter includes an in-depth discussion on how BGP route selection process has to be updated to take into account OPA. The chapter discusses also some deployment considerations such as the combination with

AS path pre-pending. The validity of the proposed approach and obtained gains are detailed in this chapter.

○ The chapter "On the Aggregatability of Router Forwarding Tables" presents an approach to achieve FIB (Forwarding Information Base) aggregation. This approach relies on combining multiple entries in the forwarding table without changing the next hops for data forwarding. The proposed approach can be achieved with software updates. One of the main characteristics of this approach is that it does not require changes to routing protocols. The proposed approach can be implemented in a given domain without requiring any actions to be enforced in adjacent domains. This approach can be seen as a short-term remedy to solve the increase of routing table. In order to assess the viability of the proposed design, the chapter includes the specification and the evaluation of five algorithms at different aggregation levels. The results show a reduction of the FIB size up to 70%.

○ The chapter "APT: A Practical Tunneling Architecture for Routing Scalability" presents an architecture called APT (A Practical Tunneling architecture). The proposed architecture belongs to the Map & Encap solution scheme. Note Map & Encap concept is introduced in Part 1. The proposed approach relies on a hybrid Push/Pull model to distribute mapping information, a data-driven notification mechanism to handle physical failures between edge sites and their providers, and a public-key distribution mechanism for cryptographic protection of control messages. The chapter claims APT can be incrementally deployed with minor changes and marginal impact on the delay to be experienced by forwarded packets. According to this chapter, no more than 0.8% of all packets will be observed with an extra delay.

○ The chapter "Routing Architecture for the Next-Generation Internet (RANGI)" presents a new Identifier/Locator split architecture, referred to as Routing Architecture for the Next Generation Internet (RANGI). The proposed approach is similar to the Host Identity Protocol (HIP) architecture. Indeed, RANGI introduces a Host Identifier (ID) layer between the IPv6 network layer and the transport layer. This chapter describes the rationale adopted by RANGI to assign and to manage Identifiers. The chapter provides more detail about RANGI implementation.

○ The chapter "Topology Aggregating Routing Architecture (TARA): A Concept for Scalable and Efficient Routing" describes a novel approach to mitigate the issues encountered in current Internet Routing Architectures. This chapter describes how TARA is used to generate a map of the Internet using a completely innovative new concept. The chapter adopts an original approach which assumes nodes are identified with "locators" derived from longitude/latitude. The chapter specifies how TARA satisfies advanced traffic engineering objectives such as computing QoS-inferred paths, compute non-congested paths, etc. This chapter discusses also how TARA fulfills multicast and mobility requirements.

• Section 3 "Advanced Features" contains the following chapters:

○ The chapter "Routing Optimization for Inter-Domain Traffic Engineering under Identifier Network" defines the concept of Identifier Network and discusses a solution to achieve traffic engineering in such context. The chapter distinguishes End-to-End (E2E) traffic engineering from Neighbor-to-Neighbor Traffic Engineering. The chapter describes a routing decision scheme which is designed to reduce the size of the core routing tables. The chapter elaborates also on the feasibility of the proposed approach.

○ The chapter "The Map-and-Encap Locator/Identifier Separation Paradigm: A Security Analysis" presents an in-depth analysis of security-related threats encountered in Map&Encap

schemes with a particular focus on LISP (Locator/Identifier Separation Protocol). LISP is an experimental protocol currently specified within IETF (Internet Engineering Task Force). LISP defines two distinct namespaces: non-globally routeable Endpoint Identifiers (EIDs) and to routeable Routing Locators (RLOCs). LISP defines also functions for mapping between the two namespaces and for encapsulating traffic issued from hosts identified with EIDs across a network that forwards using RLOCs. The chapter claims, except for the LISP specific header, the main functioning of the protocol is valid for any other Map&Encap solution.

○ The chapter "A Hierarchical Approach to Reduce Power Consumption in Core and Edge Networks: A Metric-Based Proposal" proposes a metric-based hierarchical approach to reduce power consumption in core and edge networks. The chapter covers both unicast and the multicast forwarding schemes and proposes distinct metrics for each scheme. For unicast forwarding scheme, the proposed metric is consumed power to available bandwidth and for multicast forwarding scheme the metric is consumed power to available replication capacity. The chapter proposes also a selective leak technique for disclosing low power paths. This method can be used in particular to determine disjoint (or redundant) paths for load-balancing or fault tolerance purposes. The chapter discusses also multicast-related considerations such as how to use the proposed power metric to determine low power multicast paths and multicast replication points.

○ The chapter "Waveband Switching: A Scalable and Cost Efficient Solution for the Internet Backbone" focuses on another important topic: Waveband Switching in optical networks. This chapter provides a review of the challenges in designing Waveband Switching in optical networks. The chapter describes an approach for designing Multi-Granular Optical cross-connect architectures and algorithms for Waveband Switching to accommodate dynamic traffic demands. Both mathematical analyses and bounds on the number of required ports and blocking probabilities of various Waveband Switching algorithms and architectures are discussed in this chapter. The chapter describes also the proposed architectures and algorithms for dynamic Waveband Switching to decrease the blocking probability of dynamic traffic. It includes the results of the simulation experiments conducted to evaluate the effectiveness of the proposed approach. These results show that (1) Waveband Switching can achieve a low blocking probability and port savings even with limited resources and (2) the proposed graph-based waveband assignment algorithm combined with adaptive routing can achieve a superior performance.

○ The Glossary, at the end of the book, is a set of terms used within the book. These terms are common to all chapters.

Mohamed Boucadair
France Telecom, France

David Binet
France Telecom, France

Acknowledgment

Many thanks to Christian Jacquenet, Davide Cuda, Edoardo Bonetto, Esther Le Rouzic, Fred Templin, Ning Wang and Panos Georgatsos for their careful review and help.

Mohamed Boucadair
France Telecom, France

David Binet
France Telecom, France

Section 1
Issues and Design Principles

Chapter 1
Issues with Current Internet Architecture

Mohamed Boucadair
France Telecom, France

David Binet
France Telecom, France

ABSTRACT

It is commonly agreed that the continuous increase of routing and forwarding tables (Huston, 2001; Meyer, Zhang, & Fall, 2007) is a sensitive issue which may question the growth of the overall Internet. Some technical practices such as multi-homing using Provider Independent (PI) prefixes and shrinking advertised prefixes to support advanced inbound traffic engineering policies exacerbate the increase of inter-domain routing tables (Narten, 2010). This chapter synthesizes routing and forwarding issues encountered by current Internet routing architecture and provides an overview of analyzed solutions.

Internet actors should work on an action plan to mitigate the increase of Routing Information Base (RIB) and Forwarding Information Base (FIB) table sizes and the load induced by routing updates churn (BGP Instability Report, n.d.).

PROBLEMS TO BE SOLVED

Simplicity, flexibility and extensibility were the main characteristics of the Internet architecture [Clark, RFC1958, RFC3426, RFC3439], but unfortunately these design principles are not the actual characteristics of the Internet. More precisely, the Internet is suffering from a wide range of complications which may impact its evolution.

Examples illustrating encountered complications include:

- **IPv4 address shortage:** Both the run out of Class B addresses and the whole IPv4 address space were a concern for the Internet community as soon as the early 90's. In 2011, the exhaustion of public IPv4 addresses has become a con-

DOI: 10.4018/978-1-4666-4305-5.ch001

crete concern for Fixed and Mobile IP Connectivity Providers. Both backward (e.g., The Extended Internet Protocol (EIP, [RFC1335, RFC1385])) and disruptive proposals (e.g., (Ullmann, 1993)) have been considered in the past to solve IPv4 address depletion.

- **Emergence of middleboxes such as CGNs (Carrier Grade NATs), firewalls and DPI (Deep Packet Inspection):** It has been reported recently that some enterprise networks contain as many middleboxes as routers (Bonaventure, 2011); as such, packets are altered in the forwarding path without any notification to the sender or the receiver.

- **Inability to extend protocols which are part of Internet foundations such as IP and TCP:** These protocols were designed to support options but in practice these options are "not anymore an option" (Fonseca et al., 2005) or their use is not reliable (Honda et al., 2011). This issue is likely to be encountered by IPv6 extension headers. The review of Internet's history shows, as documented in (Handley, 2006), two evolution periods: period of fundamental changes (1970-1993) and a second period of failures (1993 to the present).

- **Inability to introduce new transport protocols at large, e.g., SCTP (Stream Control Transmission Protocol, (Stewart, 2007)) or DCCP (Datagram Congestion Control Protocol, (Kohler, Handley, & Floyd, 2006)):** This is a direct consequence of the massive deployment of middleboxes which break the end-to-end principle.

- **Restriction of reachability to some protocols:** Only TCP/UDP, and in some cases only HTTP, is accepted. This was a driver for several solutions that suggest to de-velop layer applications over HTTP (or in DNS) [RFC3205, RFC3426].

- Brokenness of bi-directional communications because reachability is not symmetric due to the presence of NAT and tunnels (e.g., If "A" can reach "B," this does not mean "B" can reach "A"). The reachability asymmetry is now part of the "new" characteristics of Internet just like path asymmetry. Applications should be designed to accommodate this new constraint.

- Brokenness of applications which make wrong assumptions based on the IP address (Ford et al., 2011). A non-exhaustive list of these issues is provided below:
  - Incoming port negotiation mechanisms may fail
  - Incoming connections to Assigned Ports will not work
  - Port discovery mechanisms will not work
  - Some applications will fail to operate
  - Parallel/serial connections may fail
  - TCP control block sharing will be affected
  - Reverse DNS will be affected
  - Inbound ICMP will fail in many cases
  - Amplification of security issues
  - Fragmentation will require special handling
  - Port randomization will be affected
  - Penalty boxes will no longer work
  - SPAM blacklisting will be affected
  - Geo-location services will be impacted
  - Geo-proximity mechanisms will be impacted
  - Load balancing algorithms may be impacted
  - Authentication mechanisms may be impacted

- ○ Traceability of network usage and abusage will be affected
- ○ Frequent keep-alives reduce battery life
- ○ Service usage monitoring and abuse logging will be impacted for all elements in the chain between service provider and content provider

- **Increase of routing and forwarding tables:** The analysis of inter-domain routing tables shows several evolution phases which are listed hereafter [Growth, Flat, RFC4632]:
  - ○ An exponential growth from 1980 to 1994 with an acceleration of the exponential trend in late 1993: in that period, Transit IP Connectivity Providers were unable to aggregate routes.
  - ○ This alarming increase has been solved with the advent of BGP (Border Gateway Protocol, RFC 1654) in 1994. Indeed, BGP has facilitated the aggregation capability for the sake of inter-domain routing optimization.
  - ○ A linear growth from mid-1994 to 1999.
  - ○ An exponential growth from 1999 to 2001.
  - ○ A flattening growth in 2001.
  - ○ A linear growth from 2002 to 2003.
  - ○ Another exponential growth beginning 2004.
  - ○ Linear increase between 2009 and 2011: According to (Hutson, 2011b), the IPv4 prefix count growth in 2010 is 9% compared to 14% in 2011. As for IPv6 BGP table increase, the prefix count growth in 2010 is 70% compared to 104% in 2011.

- **Instability of core routing tables induced by few edge networks (BGP Instability Report, n.d.):** (Pelsser et al., 2011) reports only 3% of the prefixes are responsible for 36% of the BGP (Rekhter, Li, & Hares, 2006) messages. (Hutson, 2011a) revealed the increase of the inter-domain routing tables from 2007 to 2011 is about 73% while the growth of unstable prefixes is only 25%. (Hutson, 2011a) showed also the AS path density is almost constant for more than 10 years while the number of routing entries has increased from 50000 to 300000. The instability issue can be mitigated if BGP includes a notion of scope to restrict the propagation of BGP Update messages (Huston, 2001). RFD (Route Flap Damping, (Villamizar, Chandra, & Govindan, 1998)) has been proposed as a solution to the inter-domain routing instability, but it turned out RFD is harmful (RIPE, 2006). Recently, a study ((Pelsser et al., 2011)) claimed RFD can be safely deployed to reduce BGP updates churn by appropriately configuring the RFD algorithm constants.

- **Lack of deterministic tools to achieve (inter-domain) inbound traffic engineering:** Current practice relies upon the injection of more specific routes, which aggravates the growth of inter-domain routing tables, or by prepending AS numbers for multi-homed networks. AS prepending is not deterministic because it depends on the policies enforced by remote ASes.

- **Lack of efficient means to support prefix portability for multi-homed or re-homed networks:** The current practice to achieve prefix portability, and therefore to avoid renumbering for a re-homed network, is to use PI (Provider Independent) addresses. Because these addresses can not be aggregated by Transit IP Connectivity Providers, advertising these addresses in the inter-domain routing leads to the increase of the inter-domain routing tables. More discussion on multi-homing practices, their limitations and renumbering are documented in [RFC4116, RFC5887].

- **Prefix hijacking:** To soften the impact of prefix hijacking, some networks advertise more specific prefixes in the inter-domain routing. This practice exacerbates the growth of inter-domain routing tables.
- **Rapid shuffling of prefixes:** Some networks change their route advertisements frequently to better control the utilization of their interconnection resources. This practice has a severe impact on the instability of the inter-domain routing tables (especially the DFZ).
- **Unbalanced cost and benefit:** Some edge networks inject their prefixes in the inter-domain routing tables to achieve some engineering goals (e.g., bound traffic addressed to a set of destinations to a given interconnection link, load balance the traffic between several interconnection links, optimize interconnection costs, better react when a failure occurs, etc.). The action of injecting specific routes has a cost on the routers involved in the DFZ while only edge networks benefit from this practice (see *Table 1*). This unbalanced alignment between the cost and the benefit may have some drastic impact on the quality level of some delivered services if Transit IP Connectivity Providers decide to not upgrade their infrastructure to meet the continuous increase of control plane load.

Further technical challenges such as the following ones are also to be considered when designing Internet Routing Architectures alternatives:

1. Simplify architectural design of nodes involved in core networks owing to the use of OPS (Optical Packet Switching), OBS (Optical Burst Switching) or "multipaths" techniques (Cuda et al., 2011);
2. Reduce power consumption in both edge and core transit networks [Power, Yoo];
3. Offload control plane capabilities from routers to dedicated nodes (e.g., Routing Control Platforms (Feamster et al., 2004));
4. Relying on the AS number instead of the IP prefix to achieve inter-domain route aggregation [Compact, Hybrid].

Solving all the aforementioned complications can not be easily achieved because of the Internet's anarchy nature (there is no central entity controlling and managing the Internet) (Carpenter, 1996). Nevertheless, some of these problems can be mitigated owing to an architectural re-design and the enforcement of appropriate operational guidelines. A more detailed description of encountered routing issues and design goals for alternatives solutions are documented in [Narten, RFC1752, RFC4984, RFC6115].

FORMER PALLIATIVES

The Internet community has been mobilized in the past to agree on a strategy for the evolution of the Internet and its associated IP model [Model, RFC6250]. An effort, called Internet "Architecture Retreat," has been initiated in the early 90's by the IAB (Internet Architecture Board) and IESG (Internet Engineering Steering Group) to investigate issues met by the Internet. A set of recommendations "towards the future Internet architecture" have been drawn (Clark et al., 1991). At that time, although it may be seen as a nonsense today, the Internet community faced a dilemma of choosing between accepting either limiting the growth on Internet or disruption the network to new techniques. In addition to the need to support real-time services, (Clark et al., 1991) acknowledged routing information explosion and address space consumption were the most urgent problems to solve. Given small changes may require a long time to be effective, (Clark et al., 1991) advocated for a long term action plan to preserve the architectural principles of Internet instead of implementing small changes.

Then, a group called ROAD (Gross & Almquist, 1992) has been formed to structure the problem space and to propose some directions for future Internet. ROAD and (Clark et al., 1991) have inspired IAB to propose a plan of action to overcome the dangerous decrease of IP address pools and the growth of routing tables (IAB, 1992). Concretely, IAB recommended:

- To deprecate the Class A/B/C address taxonomy,
- To enforce CIDR (Classless Inter-domain Routing)(Fuller & Li, 2006) as a short term solution,
- Prepare for the introduction of "IP version 7" (not to confuse with (Ullmann, 1993)) in a mid and long term,
- Once the address shortage is solved, design a routing architecture which does not assume any dependency between addresses and the underlying routing topology.

Later, the IETF (Internet Engineering Task Force) has adopted the strategy proposed by the IAB but it has objected some technical choice. Particularly, the IETF rejected the recommendation on IPv7 in favor of IPv6.

As an input to its decision-making process, the IETF formed a working group called Address Lifetime Estimation (ALE) to estimate the IPv4 address depletion date and to implicitly qualify the level of urgency to specify an alternative scheme to IPv4 addressing. For the record, ALE estimated the IPv4 address depletion date between 2005 and 2011 (Bradner & Mankin, 1995); this projection has been confirmed by recent announcements of IANA about the depletion of IPv4 addresses. The IETF community has then dedicated tremendous resources to solve IP address depletion (i.e., IPv6 specification) and to document operational guidelines for short and mid-term solutions to shape the growth of global inter-domain routing tables (i.e., CIDR). The IETF has also anticipated the depletion of AS (Autonomous System) numbers by extending BGP to support 4-byte encoded AS numbers (i.e., AS numbers pool is expanded to 2^{16} instead of 65535) (Vohra & Chen, 2007).

The actions conducted by the IETF answered to a subset of issues experienced by the Internet architecture (e.g., run out of Class B IPv4 addresses, run out of overall IPv4 address space, slow down the growth of inter-domain routing tables and depletion of AS numbers). Effectively, at early stages of CIDR deployment, the increase of routing tables followed a linear increase but an exponential increase has been observed again early 1999 and beginning 2004. The growth of routing tables motivates the need to revive initial plans documented in (Clark et al., 1991): re-design the Internet routing architecture.

Revisit the Internet routing architecture is not exclusively motivated by scalability concerns; additional technical challenges such as the lack of deterministic tools to enforce advanced traffic engineering policies are to be taken into account [RFC6227, Narten]. An effort in this direction has been recently launched by the IRTF (Internet Research Task Force) through a dedicated working group called RRG (Routing Research Group) (RRG, n.d.). Like ROAD, RRG failed to reach a consensus on the recommended solution for routing and forwarding issues; only the IRTF RRG WG chairs recommendations have been documented (Li, 2011a).

SOLUTION SPACE: FOCUS ON ROUTING AND FORWARDING

Despite the effort conducted within IETF, designing a scalable, robust, predictable and stable routing system to sustain the growth of the Internet should be continuously tackled by Internet actors (including IETF, regulatory bodies and IP Connectivity Providers). Particularly, IP Connectivity Providers should undertake concrete actions to anticipate potential failure of deployed Internet routing architecture. Obviously, a companion effort to define enhancements to maintain current routing and forwarding system is required but Internet actors should prepare the introduction of complementary tools to solve all or the majority of the issues discussed in "*Problems to be Solved*" Section.

Because the Internet is de-centralized (Carpenter, 1996), introducing these new tools won't be shipped over the night. To be successful, the involvement of several actors and coordination of their effort will be required. Evidently, deploying these complementary tools may take a long time before being adopted at large, but it should not be considered as a pretext to delay introducing the proposed new scheme, and to cease investigating efficient solutions. If no particular action is conducted to mitigate issues encountered by the Internet routing architecture, serious risks for emerging a fragmented Internet with non-global reachability will be faced.

Alternative routing and forwarding system(s) should be seen as an overlay infrastructure plugged over the existing BGP-based routing system. Integrating these tools and interaction with existing functional elements should not induce much trouble. Specifically, the activation of these tools should not impact the stability of "legacy" inter-domain routing system (Floyd, 2002). By no means, the new routing and forwarding system must not interfere with the introduction of IPv6; the new system must be IPv6-compatible.

The efficiency of the new routing and forwarding system should not require upgrading existing networks. Early networks participating into the new routing and forwarding scheme should perceive immediate benefits. Deploying complementary tools to solve Internet routing and forwarding issues is not only motivated by technical considerations but should be seen as a new business opportunity (e.g., some of the solutions discussed in "*Solution Space: Focus on Routing and Forwarding*" Section may require a new business role) and therefore a new source of revenue. Early adopters of CES solution are likely to be involved in the "heart" of Future Internet and will contribute to expand the scalability limits of Future Internet.

The re-design of the Internet routing architecture is an opportunity for IP Connectivity Providers to offer new differentiated services; early IP Connectivity Providers are likely to be involved in the hearth of the Future Internet system and as such may benefit from new business opportunities. It is worth noting that a re-design of Internet routing architecture does not require to deprecate BGP. Indeed, three options can be envisaged: replace BGP, modify BGP or add an overlay layer over BGP-based infrastructures.

Internet actors should not wait until current BGP-only inter-domain routing fails, then it will be too late to remedy the problem and to try new alternatives. Adding new changes to existing Internet routing architecture is a realistic goal, especially in the light of past Internet experience which has shown that (1) changes are still possible to be added to Internet by defining new "pieces" fitting existing voids (e.g., MPLS), (2) modifying the transport layer has failed during the last three decades (e.g., congestion notification) and (3) changes to Internet infrastructure are driven by money-based decision-making process. Plugging a new Internet routing architecture over the existing one does not require modifications to the transport layer and, as mentioned above, may be an opportunity to develop a new business value.

REQUIREMENTS AND DESIGN PRINCIPLES

A List of Requirements

This section lists the main design objectives to be met by any candidate solution to overcome routing issues discussed in *"Problems to be Solved"* Section. This objectives list is used as selection criteria to privilege one or few solution proposed solutions:

- **Alignment of cost and benefits:** As illustrated in *Table 1*, edge networks are used to enforce some engineering policies to achieve their local objectives but the cost of these practices are on the core transit networks side. Proposed solutions should correct this cost/benefit misalignment issue otherwise it will be a strong barrier for introducing a new routing architecture.
- **Scalable routing:** Any proposed routing architecture must scale independently of the growth of connected networks (and connected users population). The proposed solution must reduce both the growth rate of inter-domain routing tables and also the update churn rate. Proposed solutions should support path diversity without altering the overall scalability of the routing system.
- **Scalable support for traffic engineering which preserves the stability of the inter-domain routing system:** Stub-

networks must be able to enforce deterministic inbound and outbound traffic engineering policies. This requirement must be met without impacting the scalability of the inter-domain routing system and without introducing traffic churn on the control plane. Practices such injecting specific routes in the inter-domain routing and rapid shuffling of prefixes must be avoided.

- **Scalable support for multi-homing:** Multi-homing is generally a requirement for enterprise networks which are used to be assigned with PI addresses. For example, in light of some "simplistic" forecasts 10 million PI prefixes will be needed. Injecting this amount of PI prefixes into global inter-domain routing is likely to impact the scalability of inter-domain routing system. Consequently, proposed solutions must provide means to support scalable multi-homing. This is doable if global inter-domain routing tables carry only PA prefixes; announcing PI prefixes in the global inter-domain routing must not be allowed. Proposed solutions should allow networks to easily multi-home (e.g., add new interconnection links, be connected to more than one IP Connectivity Provider) and to re-home (i.e., networks in process to change their transit IP Connectivity Provider).
- **Portability support:** This is a critical requirement for re-homed networks. Stable identifiers independent of the underlying topology should be preferred.
- **Improved routing security and quality:** Proposed solutions must not induce a path's stretch and must not impact the convergence of the inter-domain routing system. Moreover, better security should be offered (e.g., prefix authentication, ori-

gin AS authentication, etc.). This requirement, would mitigate the issue of shrinking prefixes into small ones to avoid prefix hijacking.

- **Scalable support for mobility:** When IP network mobility will be deployed at large, no session failure should be observed if a mobile network changes its attachment to Internet. This requirement should be supported at the routing level especially because transport protocols use the IP address to bind the transport session and also to compute the checksum. A companion solution to routing is to update operating systems and APIs to avoid binding a transport session to an IP address and use an "Identifier" instead (e.g., stable name).

Additional deployment-specific requirements are listed in *Table 2*. Given only one billion of users are connected to Internet worldwide while the world population is estimated to 7 billions, disruptive solutions may emerge. For this reason, we tagged "Incremental deployment" as "Desired" and not "Strongly Desired" (inspired from RFC6227).

Design Principles

Below are listed some design principles which, if followed, would help in designing solutions meeting the requirements discussed in the previous sub-section:

1. **Modularity:** The new proposed inter-domain routing system should be decomposed into simple and extensible subsystems. Loose interaction between these subsystems is encouraged. Interdependency between these subsystems should be avoided.
2. **Locator/Identifier Separation:** The new proposed inter-domain routing architecture should adopt a clear separation between the

naming and routing namespaces: "Identifier" and "Locator." Separating naming and addressing is also recommended.

As a reminder, Identifier is a topology-independent object bound to a node, one of the node's interfaces or even a software instance. An "Identifier" is generally structured as a "name," e.g., FQDN (Fully Qualified Domain Name) or URI (Unique Resource Identifier). "Identifier" objects must not be used for forwarding purposes. (Shoch, 1978) precises: "name" (i.e., "Identifier") of a resource indicates "what" we seek, an "address" indicates "where" it is, and a "route" tells us "how to get there." While Locator is a topology-dependent object used to identify a topological attachment of a "Host" or an interface belonging to a "Host." A "Locator" is also referred to as host attachment information. A "Host" identified by an "Identifier" can be reached using a "Locator" as input to invoke the underlying IP transfer capabilities.

SOLUTION SPACE: FOCUS ON ROUTING AND FORWARDING

A large list of candidate solutions have been proposed in the past to mitigate all or part of the issues encountered by the current Internet routing architecture and detailed in previous sections. Examples of these candidates include: hIPv4 (Hierarchical IPv4 Framework, (Frejborg, 2011)), LISP (Locator/Identifier Separation Protocol, (Farinacci et al., 2010)), Ivip (Internet Vastly Improved Plumbing Architecture, (Whittle, 2010)), AIS (Aggregation with Increasing Scope, (Khare et al., 2009)), TIDR (Tunneled Inter-domain Routing, (Adan, 2006)), NPTv6 (Network Prefix Translation for IPv6, (Wasserman & Baker, 2011)), GSE (Global, Site, and End-system address elements, (O'Dell, 1997)) RANGI (Routing Architecture for the Next Generation Internet, (Xu, 2010)), RANGER (Routing and Addressing in Networks with Global Enterprise Recursion, (Templin, 2010)), IRON (Internet Routing Overlay Network, (Templin, 2011)), TARA (Topology Aggregating Routing Architecture, (Heiner, 2010)), SixOne (Vogt, 2008), Name-based Sockets (Vogt, 2009), ILNP (Identifier/Locator Networking Protocol, (Atkinson, 2011)), Nimrod architecture (Chiappa, 1991), TP/IX (Ullmann, 1993), etc.

This list is not exhaustive. Some of these solutions have been abandoned (e.g., Nimrod) because at that time (i.e., early 90's) the Internet community concluded that the introduction of such architectures is questionable and further research effort is required to freeze the specification of a viable alternative routing architecture (Bradner & Mankin, 1995). Some of these solutions share the same design principles but differ in technical details and subtleties (e.g., LISP and Ivip). Not all the aforementioned solutions share the same assumptions: for instance some of these solutions assume that by the time of deployment, only PA (Provider Assigned) prefixes would be injected in the core routing while PI (Provider Independent) won't be leaked in the DFZ.

Except AIS which is an evolution-based solution, all proposed solutions can be organized into two categories:

1. Core-Edge Elimination (CEE) or Locator/ Identifier Separation solutions.
2. Core-Edge Separation (CES) solutions (Jen et al., 2008).

CORE-EDGE ELIMINATION (CEE)

To solve the growth of the global inter-domain routing table, the Core-Edge Elimination (CEE) approach advocates for eliminating PI prefixes in favor of PA which will be the only prefixes to be advertised in the inter-domain routing. CEE does not require any change to the current Internet routing architecture but instead CEE defines two distinct namespaces: one for identification (called "Identifier") and another one for routing purposes (called "Locator").

When CEE is widely deployed, only routes towards "Locators" will be instantiated in the inter-domain routing tables. This is likely to enhance the efficiency of aggregation in transit routers.

Figure 1 illustrates a simplified overview of the CEE approach. "S" and "D" are assigned with an "Identifier" and a "Locator." A mapping between the "Identifier" and "Locator" is advertised by each "Host" ("S" and "D") in a Rendezvous service

Figure 1. CEE overview

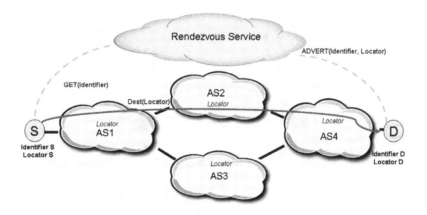

Figure 2. Identifier/locator separation

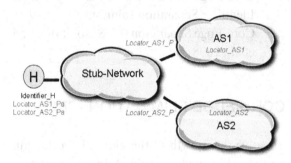

(e.g., DNS). Routes to "Locator" are exchanged in the underlying inter-domain routing. In order to establish a communication between two "Hosts" supporting the "Identifier"/"Locator" separation, the initiating party ("S") is supposed to know the "Identifier" of the remote party ("D"). This information is then used as a key to retrieve, from the Rendezvous service, one or more "Locators" associated with the "Identifier" of the remote party. Once retrieved, the initiating party, sends its packets to the IP address returned from the Rendezvous service. These packets are then forwarded until being delivered to their ultimate destination.

When a "Host" gets a new "Locator," it must update its records in the Rendezvous service.

A "Host" connected to a stub network (also denoted as edge network) is assigned with both an "Identifier" and one or more "Locators." As shown in *Figure 2*, a host "H" is connected to a multi-homed network (to "AS1" and "AS2"). "H" is therefore configured with two "Locators": "Locator_AS1_Pa" and "Locator_AS2_Pa." "Locator_AS1_Pa" is an address belonging to the "Locator_AS1_P" prefix assigned by "AS1" while "Locator_AS2_Pa" is an address belonging to the "Locator_AS2_P" prefix assigned by "AS2." "H" must be upgraded to be able to select the appropriate "Locator" to use in the context of a given session.

ILNP (Atkinson, 2011), RANGI (Xu, 2010) and Name-based sockets (Vogt, 2009) are examples of CEE solutions.

CORE-EDGE SEPARATION (CES)

The CES approach assumes networks are organized into two categories: edge networks (or stub networks) and core networks. A typical example of core networks are networks operated by transit IP Connectivity Providers; such networks are composed of DFZ routers. Edge networks are stub networks which acquire global reachability via one or several transit IP Connectivity Providers. Within CES, hosts connected to edge networks are assigned with "normal" IP addresses; no new namespace is required to be created.

Figure 3. CES overview

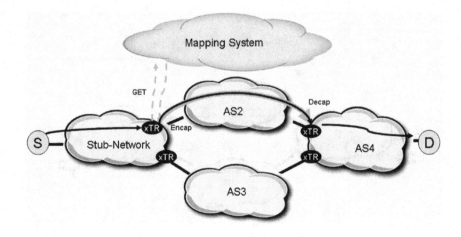

Overview

To mitigate the issues listed in *"Problems to be Solved"* Section, CES suggests to not leak endpoint addresses (i.e., addresses used in edge networks) in the global Internet routing; edge network prefixes are eliminated from the DFZ table. Because CES removes the constraint of PA prefixes on the growth of routing table sizes, the growth of edge networks is not reflected anymore in the core routing table size and moreover, unstable edge networks do not flood the DFZ with their updates.

One important characteristic of CES is that it does no place any new requirement on the "Host" side. "Some" dedicated intermediary nodes will implement new functions described below.

Just like today's Internet, CES assumes hosts are assigned with IP addresses. These addresses may be PI or PA but only PA aggregates are advertised in the global Internet routing. To do so, a redirection is introduced using a mapping system between the IP address assigned in the edge networks and one or several routing addresses (denoted in some proposals as RLOC (Routing Locator)).

A realization example of the CES has been first described in (Deering, 1996). Later, more proposals have been made, e.g., LISP (Farinacci et al., 2010), Ivip (Whittle, 2010), IRON (Templin, 2011), hIPv4 (Frejborg, 2011) and TIDR (Adan, 2006).

CES operations can be decomposed into three functions described in the following sub-sections.

Maintain the Mapping

This is typically a "Push" operation to instantiate a mapping record or to update an existing record. A mapping refers to an association between an EID (Endpoint Identifier) and an RLOC. This step is a prerequisite before forwarding occurs. Several implementation options can be envisaged for implementing the mapping system:

1. Each ITR maintains the full mapping database.
2. A copy of the full mapping database is maintained in each domain hosting an ITR.
3. The mapping database is fully distributed. No device stores a complete copy of the full mapping database. An overlay infrastructure is used to retrieve the appropriate mapping. Just like DNS, authoritative mapping servers may be defined for this purpose.

Discover a Mapping

This function is invoked because indirection is needed. When a packet is received at the boundaries of the originating stub network, the forwarding process requires to be provided with the corresponding RLOC. This can be achieved in various ways:

1. By querying a local cache of the full mapping database maintained by the ITR.
2. By querying a local Mapping Query Server maintaining the full mapping database. Each

Table 1. Summary of inter-domain routing issues and impacted networks

Technical Concern	Impacted Networks
Increase of routing and forwarding tables	Transit Networks
Instability of core routing tables induced by few edge networks	Transit Networks
Lack of deterministic tools to achieve inbound traffic engineering	Transit Networks
Lack of efficient means to support prefix portability for multi-homed or re-homed networks	Transit Networks
Prefix hijacking	Transit Networks
Rapid shuffling of prefixes	Transit Networks
IPv4 address depletion and need for dual plane routing	Transit Networks

Table 2. Deployment considerations

Requirement	Priority
Offer new business opportunities	Desired
Do not require a universal agreement among all interconnected ASes	Strongly Desired
Support Incremental deployment	Desired
Do not impact session establishment; session failure are not to be experienced	Strongly Desired
Do not interfere with IPv6 introduction	Strongly Desired

ITR is configured with one or several local Mapping Servers to contact.

3. By querying a default Mapping Server which will relay the request to the authoritative Mapping Query Server.

Encapsulate and Decapsulate

This function refers to the process of using the retrieved mapping record to forward the packet. Technically, this is achieved using encapsulation/de-capsulation (e.g., (Deering, 1996)) or address re-writing (e.g., (Whittle, 2010) supports ETR Address Forwarding (EAF) for IPv4 and Prefix Label Forwarding (PLF) for IPv6).

Illustration Example

An overview of CES architecture is depicted in *Figure 3*. A host "S" is connected to a stub net-work; as such, it acquires an IP address. This IP address is used by "S" to connect to the Internet and to be reached by remote hosts. When "S" sends an IP packet to a given destination located in the Internet, this packet is forwarded in the stub-network using legacy IP transfer capabilities. This packet is then forwarded until it reaches an ITR (Ingress Tunnel Router). The ITR checks its local cache to retrieve the corresponding RLOC associated with the destination IP address. If no record is found, ITR contacts the mapping system to retrieve the appropriate RLOC. Once received,

ITR encapsulates the original IP packet into a new packet having RLOC as destination address. The encapsulated packet is then forwarded, relying on legacy routing and forwarding means, until delivery to the appropriate ETR (Egress Tunnel Router). The later de-capsulates the packet and forwards the enclosed IP packet to the next hop. Legacy forwarding capabilities are invoked in the terminating network until delivering the packet to its ultimate destination. This procedure will succeed if and only if the mapping system has been fed with the appropriate entry corresponding to "D."

The set of destinations which are not connected to stub networks adhering to a CES scheme can be reached using dedicated nodes called PTR (Proxy Tunnel Routers). Early CES-enabled networks may place a set of PTRs so as to benefit from the advantages of CES without waiting for a global deployment of the solution.

To meet the scalability requirement imposed by the global inter-domain routing, two critical technical points need to be addressed:

1. Build an efficient mapping distribution system (e.g., see preliminary discussion in (Sriram et al., 2010)).

Table 3. Core edge elimination vs. core edge separation

Technical Argument	Core Edge Elimination	Core Edge Separation
Modifications to hosts and APIs are needed	Yes	No
"Pure" Locator/ Identifier Separation	Yes	No
PI are injected in the DFZ	Yes, until the architecture is globally deployed	No
A mapping system is required	Yes (to maintain Identifier/Locator mapping)	Yes (to maintain mappings between endpoints addresses and RLOCs)

2. Find an optimal location of ITR/ETR to better reduce the size of the inter-domain routing table (e.g., see early empirical analysis in (Wang, Bi, & Wu, 2010)).

BRIEF SOLUTIONS ANALYSIS

CEE provides a solution to restore some of the basic Internet principles introduced in [IEN1, IEN19] but, because of the misalignment between the cost and the benefits, there are barriers that slow down the development of CEE architecture at large. Unlike CES solutions, CEE requires "Hosts" to be modified and stub-networks to adhere while technical concerns are located in the core networks (see Table 1). A quick comparison between CEE and CES solutions is depicted in Table 3.

Note CEE and CES can co-exist.

LISP and Ivip share fundamental design properties (LISP and Ivip do not require changes to hosts and core routers but mandate an evolution of edge nodes to support Map&Encap functions). They slightly differ (e.g., Ivip uses a simple IP-in-IP encapsulation without any specific header, Ivip requires loose interaction between ITR/ETR, etc.). Compared to LISP, Ivip offers some interesting features such as prefix rewriting but unfortunately there is no available Ivip implementation. LISP is the only CES solution which may be tested and validated using vendor-specific implementations.

Other solutions can be considered, but some of these solutions suffer from several drawbacks:

- IRON is underspecified (Templin, 2011). IRON allows for assigning PI and introduces a new Business Actor called Virtual Prefix Service Provider (VP SP). PI addresses are assigned by a VP SP. The routing path is not optimized since it depends on the location of the VP SP nodes. IRON suffers from a lack of incentives to adopt its business model:

  ○ IRON proposes a new business role which denotes an entity which is able to assign PI prefixes.
  ○ It is not trivial to justify why a customer has to pay a VP SP and also a physical Service Provider.
  ○ Dealing with two VP SPs complicates administrative and contractual management for the Customers.

Several questions remain unanswered (e.g., if there is a network outage or a service degradation, which NOC (Network Operations Center) to contact?, How the SLA (Service Level Agreement) will be built? etc.).

- hIPv4 is an IPv4-only proposal (Frejborg, 2011).
- TIDR does not solve the increase of routing tables since core routers should still maintain a full table even if routing entries are dispatched between a "normal" RIB and new table called TIB (Tunnel Information Base) (Adan, 2006).

REFERENCES

Abley, J., Lindqvist, K., Davies, E., Black, B., & Gill, V. (2005, July). IPv4 multihoming practices and limitations.

Adan, J. (2006, December). Tunneled inter-domain routing (TIDR).

Atkinson, R. (2011, February). *ILNP Concept of Operations*.

Bonaventure, O. (2011, November). Recent Internet research results.

Bradner, S., & Mankin, A. (1995, January). The recommendation for the IP next generation protocol.

Bush, R., & Mayer, D. (2002, December). Some internet architectural guidelines and philosophy.

Carpenter, B. (1996, June). Architectural principles of the Internet.

Carpenter, B., Atkinson, R., & Flinck, H. (2010, May). Renumbering still needs work.

Carpenter, B., Boucadair, M., Halpern, J., Jiang, S., & Moore, K. (2011, October). A generic referral object for Internet entities.

Castineyra, I., Chiappa, N., & Steenstrup, M. (1996, August). The Nimrod routing architecture.

Chiappa, N. (1991). *A new IP routing and addressing architecture*. Retrieved from http://ana-3.lcs.mit.edu/~jnc/nimrod/overview.txt

Clark, D. et al. (1991, Decmber). *Towards the future internet architecture.*

Cuda, D., et al. (2011). *Getting routers out of the core: Building an optical wide area network with multi-paths*. Retrieved from http://arxiv.org/PS_cache/arxiv/pdf/1110/1110.1245v1.pdf

Deering, S. (1996, March). The map & encap scheme for scalable IPv4 routing with portable site prefixes. Retrieved from http://irl.cs.ucla.edu/references/Deering-encap.pdf

Farinacci, D., Fuller, V., Meyer, D., & Lewis, D. (2010, October). Locator/ID Separation Protocol (LISP).

Feamster, N., Balakrishnan, H., Rexford, J., Shaikh, A., & Van Der Merwe, J. (2004). The case for separating routing from routers. In *ACM SIGCOMM Workshop on Future Directions in Network Architecture.*

Floyd, S. (2002, November). General architectural and policy considerations.

Fonseca, R., Porter, R., Katz, R., Shenker, S., & Stoica, I. (2005). *IP options are not an option*. Retrieved from http://www.eecs.berkeley.edu/Pubs/TechRpts/2005/EECS-2005-24.html

Ford, M., Boucadair, M., Durand, A., Levis, P., & Roberts, P. (2011, June). Issues with IP address sharing.

Frejborg, P. (2011, July). Hierarchical IPv4 Framework.

Fuller, V., & Li, T. (2006, August). Classless inter-domain routing (CIDR): The internet address assignment and aggregation plan.

Gross, P., & Almquist, P. (1992, November). IESG deliberations on routing and addressing.

Handley, M. (2006, July). Why the Internet only just works. *BT Technology Journal, 24*(3). doi:10.1007/s10550-006-0084-z.

Heiner, H. (2010, September). Topology aggregating routing architecture.

Honda, M., Nishida, Y., Raiciu, C., Greenhalgh, A., Handley, M., & Tokuda, H. (2011, November). Is it still possible to extend TCP? In *Internet Measurement Conference.*

Huston, G. (2001, December). Commentary on inter-domain routing in the Internet.

Huston, G. (2011, November). *The BGP world is flat*. Retrieved from http://www.potaroo.net/ispcol/2011-12/flat.pdf

Huston, G. (2011, November). *BGP growth revisited*. Retrieved from http://www.potaroo.net/ispcol/2011-11/bgp2011.pdf

Instability Report, B. G. P. (n.d.). *Website*. Retrieved from http://bgpupdates.potaroo.net/instability/bgpupd.html

Internet Architecture Board (IAB). (1992, July). IP Version 7.

Jen, D., Zhang, L., Lan, L., & Zhang, B. (2008, September). *Towards a future Internet architecture: Arguments for separating edges from transit core*. Retrieved from http://conferences.sigcomm.org/hotnets/2008/papers/18.pdf

Khare, V. et al. (2009, October). Evolution towards global routing scalability. *IEEE Journal on Selected Areas in Communications, 28*(8).

Kohler, E., Handley, M., & Floyd, S. (2006, March). Datagram congestion control protocol (DCCP).

Li, T. (Ed.). (2011, February). Recommendation for a routing architecture.

Li, T. (2011, May). Design goals for scalable internet routing.

Meyer, D., Zhang, L., & Fall, K. (2007, September). Report from the IAB workshop on routing and addressing.

Moore, K. (2002). On the use of HTTP as a substrate.

Narten, T. (2010, February). On the scalability of Internet routing.

O'Dell, M. (1997, February). GSE: An alternate addressing architecture for IPv6.

Pelsser, C., Maennel, O., Mohapatra, P., Bush, R., & Patel, K. (2011, March). *Route flap damping made usable*. Passive and Active Measurement (PAM).

Re: (RRG, n.d.) Arguments in favour of Core-Edge Elimination vs. Separation? (n.d.). *Website*. Retrieved from http://www.ietf.org/mail-archive/web/rrg/current/msg05801.html

Rekhter, Y., Li, T., & Hares, S. (2006, January). A border gateway protocol 4 (BGP- 4).

RIPE. (2006). *RIPE routing working group recommendations on route-flap damping*. Retrieved from http://www.ripe.net/ripe/docs/ripe-378

RRG. (n.d.). *IRTF Routing Research Group Home Page*. Retrieved from http://tools.ietf.org/group/irtf/trac/wiki/RoutingResearchGroup

Shoch, J. (1978, January). *A note on inter-network naming, addressing, and routing. Internet Experiment Note 19*. Retrieved from http://www.rfc-editor.org/ien/ien19.txt

Sriram, K., Gleichmann, P., Young-Tak, K., & Montgomery, D. (2010, August). Enhanced efficiency of mapping distribution protocols in scalable routing and addressing architectures. In *Computer Communications and Networks (ICCCN), 2010 Proceedings of 19th International Conference*.

Stewart, R. (2007, September). Stream control transmission protocol.

Templin, F. (2010, February). Routing and addressing in networks with global enterprise recursion (RANGER).

Templin, F. (2011, March). The internet routing overlay network (IRON).

Thaler, D. (2011, May). Evolution of the IP model.

Ullmann, R. (1993, June). TP/IX: The Next Internet.

Villamizar, C., Chandra, R., & Govindan, R. (1998, November). BGP route flap damping.

Vogt, C. (2008). Six/one router: A scalable and backwards-compatible solution for provider-independent addressing. In ACM SIGCOMM MobiArch Workshop.

Vogt, C. (2009, December). *Simplifying Internet applications development with a name-based sockets interface*. Retrieved from http://www.sics.se/nbs-project

Vohra, Q., & Chen, E. (2007, May). BGP support for four-octet AS number space.

Wang, Y., Bi, J., & Wu, J. (2010). Empirical analysis of core-edge separation by decomposing Internet topology graph. In *Proceedings of GLOBECOM*, 1-5.

Wang, Z. (1992, November). EIP: The extended internet protocol.

Wang, Z., & Crowcroft, J. (1992, May). A two-tier address structure for the internet.

Wasserman, M., & Baker, F. (2011, June). IPv6-to-IPv6 network prefix translation.

Whittle, R. (2010, March). Ivip (Internet vastly improved plumbing) architecture.

Xu, X. (2010, August). Routing architecture for the next generation internet (RANGI).

Yoo, S. (n.d.). Energy efficiency in the future internet: The role of optical packet switching and optical-label switching.

Section 2
Scalable Routing and Forwarding Architectures

Chapter 2
Inter–Domain Traffic Engineering Using the Origin Preference Attribute

Rolf Winter
University of Applied Sciences Augsburg[1], Germany

Iljitsch van Beijnum
Institute IMDEA Networks, Spain & Universidad Carlos III de Madrid, Spain

ABSTRACT

Inter-domain Traffic Engineering (TE) is an important aspect of network operation both technically and economically. Outbound Traffic Engineering is less problematic as routers under the control of the network operator are responsible for the way traffic leaves the network. The inbound direction is considerably harder as the way traffic enters a network is based on routing decisions in other networks. There are very few mechanisms available today that facilitate inter-domain inbound traffic engineering, such as prefix deaggregation (i.e., advertise more specific prefixes), AS path prepending and systems based on BGP communities. These mechanisms have severe drawbacks such as exacerbating the increase of the size of global routing table or providing only coarse-grained control. In this chapter, an alternative mechanism is described and evaluated. The proposed solution does not increase the size of the global routing table, is easy to configure through a simple numeric value and provides a finer-grained control compared to currently used mechanisms that also do not add additional prefixes to the global routing table.

INTRODUCTION

During the evolution of the Internet, Autonomous Systems (ASes) have become increasingly interconnected. Both at the edge and in the core of the Internet, ASes have continuously increased the number of other ASes they are directly connected to (see e.g. Dhamdhere & Dovrolis, 2008). This trend is mainly driven by the need to increase both capacity and reliability of the connection to the global Internet. Given more than a single attachment point, an Internet Service Provider (ISP) can

DOI: 10.4018/978-1-4666-4305-5.ch002

actually engineer its traffic, i.e., it can influence the way traffic leaves and enters its network.

To do that, ASes need to rely on the Border Gateway Protocol (BGP) (Rekhter, Li, & Hares, 2006), which is used to exchange IP reachability information. BGP however is very limited when it comes to Traffic Engineering (TE). This is especially true for the inbound direction as the flow of traffic depends on the forwarding decision made at other routers in other ASes. In other words, in order to engineer the way traffic enters a network, the route selection process at other routers in other ASes has to be influenced remotely. Unfortunately, BGP has no obvious means built in that allows the origin of an advertisement to express a preference which could be used by other routers in the route selection process.

BGP selects a single best route towards a given destination, whereby a destination is represented by an IP prefix. If more than a single route towards a given prefix is known to a BGP router, it follows an ordered sequence of steps to select the best amongst these routes. This sequence of steps is called the BGP decision process (Rekhter, Li, & Hares, 2006) (see Figure 1). Each step in the process removes routes from the set of candidate routes until a single best route remains, which is subsequently used for packet forwarding.

The first step in the BGP decision process is to compare an operator set preference value called local preference. The local AS has therefore absolute control over the path selection process. A criterion for such preference could be the business relationship with the neighboring AS, such as customer-provider or peer-to-peer (Gao & Rexford, 2001). In the case that multiple routes are equally preferable as perceived by the local AS, other tie breaking rules are applied. The first one is based on the AS path length. Obviously shorter paths are preferred over longer ones as the AS path length seems a reasonable estimate of quality in the absence of other quality metrics. The decision process continues with comparing the origin attribute, the multi-exit discriminator, preferring routes learnt from external BGP peers (E-BGP routes) over routes learnt from internal BGP peers (I-BGP routes) and comparing the interior cost towards the E-BGP exit router. Finally, tie breakers are employed that have no other significance than having different I-BGP routers consistently choose a single "best" route. In other words, these tie breakers could be replaced by any other deterministic rule which results in a single route being chosen.

The above described process has no mechanism directly built in that facilitates inbound Traffic Engineering (TE). Quoting Internet Engineering Task Force (IETF) Request for Comments (RFC) 3221 (Houston, 2001): "At this stage the only tool being used for inter-provider traffic engineering is

Figure 1. Pseudo-code for the BGP decision process

```
if candidate_paths > 1 then
  remove all paths not having the highest LOCAL_PREF
  if candidate_paths > 1 then
    remove all paths not having the shortest AS_PATH
    if candidate_paths > 1 then
      remove all paths not having the lowest ORIGIN:
      if candidate_paths > 1 then
        from each subset of paths learned from the same neighboring AS,
          remove all paths not having the lowest MULT_EXIT_DISC
        if candidate_paths > 1 and at least one path is learned over E-BGP then
          remove all paths learned over I-BGP
          if candidate_paths > 1 then
            remove all paths not having the lowest interior cost towards their NEXT_HOP
            if candidate_paths > 1 then
              remove all paths not learned from the neighbor with the lowest BGP identifier
              if candidate_paths > 1 then
                remove all paths not learned from the neighbor with the lowest IP address
```

that of the BGP routing table"–this has not really changed. In the absence of an explicit mechanism, ISPs have devised means to achieve their goal in three main ways (Van Beijnum, 2002). The first is to make the AS path longer by "prepending" their AS number one or more additional times. The second is making IP prefixes more specific and announcing them selectively. Third, BGP community attributes can be used to perform a limited form of TE. Community attributes (Chandra, Traina, & Li, 1997) are not part of the decision process itself but can trigger certain actions to be applied to an advertisement such as the manipulation of path attributes or filtering.

Note that the first and third mechanisms are rarely used for anything other than TE, but the second mechanism is sometimes cited as a crude security mechanism, and also seems to exist without an obvious explanation in a number of cases. Deaggregating IP prefixes into /24s makes sure someone else cannot steal traffic towards the addresses in question by announcing more specific prefixes. However, it's still possible to do so by announcing the same prefix but with an equal or shorter AS path, so deaggregation is not very useful as a security mechanism.

All of the above mentioned current practices today have certain shortcomings such as an increase in the global routing table or others. Next these shortcomings are reviewed in more detail. The overall goal of this chapter is to explore the general inbound traffic engineering design space and then present a new method that plays out differently regarding the involved engineering tradeoffs.

BACKGROUND

Deaggregating an IP prefix into longer, more specific, prefixes accomplishes traffic engineering due to the fact that BGP speakers perform longest prefix matching and compare only routes towards the exact same prefix. This practice is fairly precise as all traffic will follow the more specific advertisement. However, it results in larger routing tables as more paths than necessary for reachability alone are injected into the global routing system. To put it differently, for the benefit of a single AS, all other ASes are burdened with additional routing table entries and the respective churn. Additionally, the loss of more specific prefixes, which are only announced over a subset of the available neighboring ASes, will lead to disruptions in the packet flow due to path hunting, which is the exploration of longer and longer paths, similar to the count to infinity problem encountered in distance vector protocols. Only when the longest possible paths are explored will the more specific prefix disappear so a less specific prefix covering the same address space is used to deliver packets.

AS path length manipulations on the other hand do not have the same issue. However, path prepending is a very coarse tool where a single AS prepend operation can result in dramatic traffic shifts (Quoitin, Pelsser, Bonaventure, & Uhlig, 2005). This usually is too imprecise except for making one of the paths generally unattractive to select, e.g. a backup path.

An analysis was conducted similar to the one found in Cittadini, Muehlbauer, Uhlig, Bush, Francois, & Maennel, 2010 where prefixes were classified into:

- **Lonely:** A prefix that is not overlapped in any way
- **Top:** A prefix that covers more specific prefixes is however not covered itself
- **Deaggregated:** A prefix that is covered by a less specific prefix both announced by the same AS
- **Delegated:** A prefix that is covered by a less specific prefix announced by a different AS

The RouteViews data for the Level 3 AS (AS3356) was used and the analysis was extended until January 2011. In addition Figure 2 depicts the amount of visible AS path prepending in that routing table. As can be seen from the figure, both AS path prepending and prefix deaggregation are on the increase, which indicates that traffic engineering is increasingly important. Deaggregated prefixes currently constitute about one third of all prefixes found in the global routing table and that fraction is increasing at about 1.5% a year. Additionally, around 15% of all prefixes are AS path prepended. Prefix deaggregation can have reasons other than traffic engineering, however Cittadini, Muehlbauer, Uhlig, Bush, Francois, & Maennel, 2010 show that there is a strong correlation between TE and prefix deaggregation. Also, the path prepending numbers are rather a lower bound as prepended paths are less likely to find their way into the Forwarding Information Base (FIB), which is what is really shown in the figure. Therefore, many prepended paths are in fact not visible from the data.

Finally, community attributes are being widely used to give direct customers more control over the way their routes are distributed or handled by an upstream provider. For instance, communities could be used to control policy that is being applied to a route advertisement (e.g. setting the local preference in a certain, pre-defined range) or to filter route advertisements so that they do not leave the upstream network provider. Another typical application of communities is to perform a finer grained type of AS path prepending where an AS could define into which region (e.g. Europe) an advertisement should be prepended and how many times or even to which AS such an announcement should be propagated. A problem with communities is that only a handful are standardized (the well-known communities), so the vast majority are used in non-standardized ways, i.e. based on configurations local to an AS. That means they cannot be globally interpreted and require configuration and planning.

Given the importance of traffic engineering, it is not surprising that this field of work has received quite some attention in the past. Quoitin, Pelsser, Swinnen, Bonaventure, and Uhlig (2003) is a good survey of traffic engineering techniques using BGP. But more than just research has attempted to improve this important aspect of network operations. Already early in the history of BGP4, attempts in standardization have been made to allow origin networks to have a larger degree of

Figure 2. Prefix and path prepending distribution

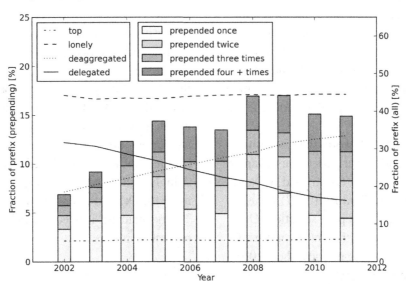

control over the way traffic enters their network (eg Chen & Bates (1996) and Antonov (1995). These proposals either suffered from a high degree of complexity or were severely underspecified, but show that the need for such mechanisms is neither purely academic nor new. Unfortunately, it also shows that accommodating origin preference in BGP is not an easy task to accomplish. Other, more recent trends in IETF show also that the current BGP decision process is too restrictive and operators would like to extend it, at least within their own domain (Retana & White, 2011). While the initial version of this particular document is already from 2002 and no RFC exists to date, discussions have been restarted nearly 10 years after the first publication on the mailing list of the IETF inter-domain routing (IDR) workgroup and implementations of this mechanism do already exist. Also interesting to note is that such a mechanism has similar deployment hurdles as will be discussed later in this chapter. Other efforts in this direction within the IETF have attempted to use for example well-known communities for the purpose traffic engineering (Bonaventure, De Cnodder, Haas, Quoitin, & White, 2003).

There is also a large body of work from the research community. For example, Winick, Jamin, and Rexford (2002) suggest relying on the existing configuration means available but letting operators cooperate when changing configurations. Probably the most closely related piece of work is Gao, Dovrolis, and Zegura (2005), which attempts to optimize AS path prepending. An algorithm is proposed that attempts to determine the optimal amount of prepending for a given prefix advertisement.

There is also lot of work that is complementary to the work described in this chapter. Dhamdhere and Dovrolis (2006) and Teixeira, Griffin, Resende, and Rexford (2007) focus on different aspects of egress path selection. Other work is more concerned with intra-domain traffic engineering such as Applegate and Cohen (2003), which presents an offline TE tool. More elaborate online TE tools have also been proposed such

as the one described in Kandula, Katabi, Davie, and Charny (2005) and yet other work considers mostly the outbound direction and general advice (e.g. Feamster, Borkenhagen, & Rexford, (2003)).

Given all the above, it would be operationally beneficial to work with simple numerical values for preference that can simply be compared by routers in a standardized manner. In the following sections of this chapter, such a mechanism is described which hits the "sweet spot" between the precision of IP prefix deaggregation and the coarse control of AS path prepending, but without the configuration burden of communities and without increasing the global routing table size.

EXPRESSING ORIGIN PREFERENCE

With no appropriate means to perform traffic engineering currently available, BGP needs to be extended to allow an origin AS to express its relative preference for a given prefix advertisement. Signaling origin preference is done through a new optional transitive path attribute, which is called the Origin Preference Attribute (OPA) (Winter & Van Beijnum, 2012). This attribute indicates an origin's relative preference for a given prefix announcement as seen through a particular AS path route. The OPA is a 16-bit signed integer value, which is set by the origin AS and is not changed by any intermediate AS. The BGP protocol specification encourages implementations to propagate unrecognized optional transitive path attributes to their neighbors. As such, we expect that in most cases, the OPA attribute will be propagated in updates by unmodified BGP implementations, and there is no need to negotiate the capability to handle OPA during BGP session establishment. A higher OPA indicates a higher preference. To make the Origin Preference Attribute an effective TE mechanism, it needs to influence the route selection process.

The Place of the Origin Preference in the BGP Decision Process

Before going into the details of how the OPA is influencing the decision process, this section first explains where in the decision process the origin preference comparison should be placed. Generally speaking, the earlier in the decision process the origin preference is considered the more powerful this TE tool becomes and the more likely it will be used by origin ASes instead of prefix deaggregation. On the other hand, the earlier the OPA influences path selection, the less likely it is that other ASes will want to implement it as it might interfere with their own local optimization goals. Given this intrinsic conflict, it is not easy to find the "right" place in the decision process.

A good starting point for these deliberations are the two current practices that work on an Internet-wide scale to achieve inbound traffic engineering–AS path prepending and prefix deaggregation. Path prepending clearly influences the BGP decision process at the AS path length comparison step. Its ineffectiveness however is not due to the place in the decision process but its overly simplistic nature. This limitation is depicted in Figure 3, where on the left side, in the absence of inbound TE attempts, ASes 100, 200 and 300 send their traffic to AS1 through AS10. Only AS400 sends its traffic through AS20. When AS1 prepends its prefix once towards AS10, the ASes that previously used AS10, now switch over to AS20, so AS1 receives 100% of its traffic through AS20. In this example—and, typically, in current operational networks —there is no prepending configuration that balances the incoming traffic roughly equally. The simple numerical comparison and the dense AS level topology is what makes path prepending such a crude tool.

Prefix deaggregation is a very different mechanism and superficially, it seems that the decision process is not affected in the same manner as by AS path prepending, as the same decision process is being executed, just on smaller chunks of the same prefix. What effectively happens however is what RFC 3221 (Houston, 2001) calls "punching a connectivity policy 'hole'" which is shown in Figure 4. In the figure, AS100 has a higher preference for AS10 as a next hop than for AS20. Consequently, in the left side of the figure, AS100 chooses AS10 to forward traffic towards prefix P. On the right side the effect of prefix deaggregation is shown. AS100 now also sends traffic towards the more specific prefix P2 towards AS20, effectively circumventing the local preference of AS100 for parts of the traffic towards P.

Given the above, one can conclude that today's inbound TE mechanisms already influence the decision process fairly early. The authors do believe that the AS path length comparison is important and they do not want to make path prepending ineffective as it is widely used. Therefore, the OPA comparison is placed after the AS path length comparison in the decision process. However, the OPA comparison is not quite a simple numeric comparison of the OPA value as explained next.

Figure 3. Toy topology showing the effect of path prepending

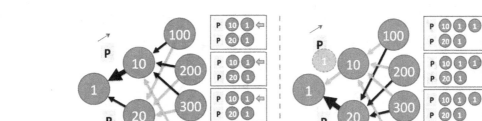

a) No inbound TE   b) Path prepending

Figure 4. Toy topology showing the effect of prefix deaggregation

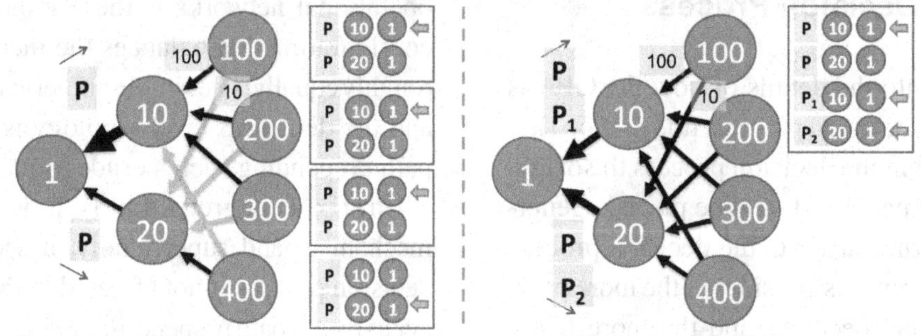

a) No inbound TE

b) Prefix deaggregation

The OPA Decision Process

Using a simple numerical comparison of the OPA value will result in drastic traffic shifts, similar to AS path prepending. In order to have a mechanism that works more fine-grained, the OPA value is used in combination with another value that has properties somewhat comparable to a random number. More precisely, the OPA is added to this other value, which will be referred to as random component R in the remainder of this chapter. R is calculated as follows. For each prefix advertisement received over E-BGP, the origin AS number, the next hop AS number and the local AS number are all XORed to result in a 16-bit unsigned integer. For 32-bit AS numbers, the higher order and lower order 16 bits are simply XORed together. Take AS100 in Figure 5 as an example, where the origin AS (1) is XORed with the next hop AS number (e.g. 10) and the local AS number (100) to result in an R of 111 for the advertisement of P through AS10 and 113 for the advertisement of P through AS20.

Each of the AS numbers that is included in the R value calculation fulfills an important role. The local AS number together with the next hop AS number create an R value that is (with some probability) different for every E-BGP session. This will result in a different R value for the same prefix received from different next hop ASes. Important however is that the difference in these R values at one AS is different at other ASes at

Figure 5. Toy topology showing the effect of the OPA comparison

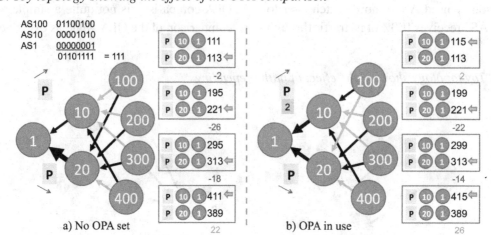

a) No OPA set

b) OPA in use

equal distance from the origin AS. To explain this, consider Figure 5 again. If the R values at AS200 were 211 and 213 (instead of 195 and 221) then the difference between these R values and the R values of AS100 were the same and the same OPA value would influence the path selection process equally. As can be seen in Figure 5, the R value differences are all different, which is what enables a more fine-grained control using the OPA mechanism.

Including the origin AS number as part of R has a completely different reason. Imagine a situation where a number of stub AS all have the same set of upstream providers, e.g. an AS2 that also has AS10 and AS20 as upstream ASes. The result would be that (assuming they do not perform inbound TE using the OPA) the traffic would all flow the same way through the upstream providers, i.e. much more through AS20 than through AS10. Including the origin AS number will, with a certain probability, spread traffic more evenly as default behavior.

A final modification to the operation of the OPA needs to be applied. R is a number between 0 and 65535. As the OPA itself is a singed 16 bit integer, there will be cases where the OPA is not sufficiently large to influence the path selection. Therefore the OPA is multiplied by two, which results in an OPA range between -65536 and 65534. To cater for the corner case that the difference between R values is 65535 the maximum R value is capped to be 65533 so that the OPA can always influence the path selection process.

To follow the example in Figure 5 through. Assuming AS1 wanted to shift traffic from its link to AS20 onto the link between itself and AS10, it needs to add a positive origin preference value on its advertisement for P towards AS10 (or alternatively a negative value towards AS20). In Figure 5 b), AS1 adds a value of 2 to the advertisement towards AS10 which only results in AS100 changing its path selection. All other ASes keep the path they previously selected. Alternatively,

adding 10 in the example would have changed AS300's path selection in addition, and so forth.

There is one important additional constraint on the selection process. The OPA comparison only takes place when prefix advertisements for a given prefix are received that have different OPA values. In case all advertisements have the same OPA value attached (or no OPA set), the set of candidate routes is not changed and the next decision process step takes place. This rule is important, as the OPA decision process step employs a pseudo-random component which will nearly always result in a single best route. However, in case the origin has no discernible preference, the subsequent decision process tie breaking rules should be performed, as they are important for the local AS, such as considering interior cost.

EXPERIMENTAL RESULTS

The OPA comparison was implemented in C-BGP (Quoitin & Uhlig, 2005), a BGP decision process solver, and simulated with it Internet-scale AS-level topologies based on data provided by UCLA (Oliveira, Pei, Willinger, Zhang, & Zhang, 2010). The overall topology consists of over 30,000 ASes and from the same data set the inferred business relationships to set local preference values at the simulated routers were used. The main goal was to evaluate the efficiency of the OPA-based inbound traffic engineering method on a reasonably realistic view of the current Internet.

First, scenarios are shown where the OPA comparison is globally deployed, i.e. every router includes the OPA comparison in the BGP decision process. This really is the ultimate goal. However, later scenarios are evaluated in which only certain ASes implement the OPA comparison.

Behavior of Individual Prefixes-Dual-Homed Case

In order to observe the effect that the OPA has, simulations of a small set of stub ASes, i.e. ASes that do not provide a transit service for other ASes were the starting point. At first, ASes were chosen that were multi-homed to two different network providers, which constitutes the largest fraction of multi-homed ASes on the Internet. Towards one of the upstream network providers a prefix with no OPA set was advertised, to the other network provider the same prefix but with varying OPA values was advertised. The former will be referred to as the non-OPA path/prefix, the latter will be referred to as OPA path/prefix.

In Figure 6, five prefixes are shown exemplary in the top part of the figure. The x-axis shows the OPA value on the OPA prefix and the y-axis shows the fraction of all ASes in the topology that pick the OPA path. Before starting the interpretation of the figure, an ideal mechanism would result in a figure that would be all straight lines, from the lower left side to the top right side. Practically,

this will of course not happen as the OPA comparison is not the first step in the decision process, R is not perfectly random, not all ASes actually receive both prefix advertisements, the decision at one AS can have a direct effect on the decision at other ASes and other reasons.

Those five prefixes were picked because they nicely show that there is a certain range of potential outcomes (mainly depending on where in the topology the origin AS resides) when using the OPA and not because they are a good representation of the average case. There are a large number of prefixes for which the OPA mechanism works quite well. For example, one prefix in Figure 6 can move from about 10% of the ASes that pick the OPA path for the smallest possible OPA value to about 90% for the largest possible OPA value. In other words, when changing the OPA value from the most negative to the most positive value 80% of all ASes in the topology change their selected path to the OPA path. What the figure also shows is that for some ASes, the OPA does not really work: for example, one path is quite "unpopular" (around 30% of the ASes chose

Figure 6. OPA comparison and AS path prepending compared

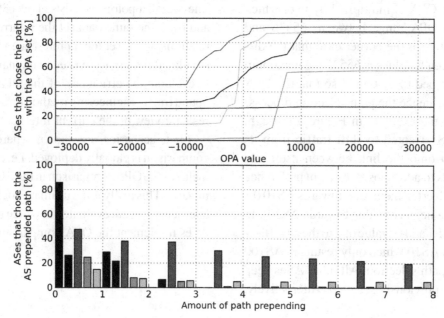

that path) although the OPA value is the largest possible. A smaller OPA value only minimally changes this over the whole range of OPA values. The same applies for paths on the other end of the spectrum (not shown), i.e. they are "popular" even with low OPA value.

The bottom half of the picture shows the same five prefixes for which AS path prepending was used to perform traffic engineering instead. The figure illustrates the rather coarse control of path prepending. When looking at the very left bar in the bar chart, a single path prepend results in well over 50% of all ASes to change their previously selected path. A second AS prepend results in virtually all ASes picking the shorter AS path. Using the OPA mechanism however, there is a much wider range of steps in-between.

The figure also shows that with AS path prepending there are various possible outcomes. In other words, AS path prepending already exhibit some of the behavior one sees at the OPA decision process. Therefore, policy and the position within the topology, which determines how the prefix advertisements are propagated, are the likely factors that lead to this behavior.

Aggregate Behavior- Dual-Homed Case

As a second step, 1000 dual-homed stub ASes were simulated to evaluate the behavior of a larger set of prefixes. Again, these ASes announced their prefixes to one network provider without any OPA set, while varying OPA values were advertised towards the second provider.

Figure 7 shows the results of those experiments. In order to understand how often the OPA decision step is actually executed the figure shows in the upper left corner of the graph the average distribution of where in the decision process a router selects the route to install into the forwarding information base. About 48% only see a single route, mostly because they are single-homed or in addition peer with other ASes that do not advertise the prefix

in question to them. This is an important factor for the OPA mechanism because once a network provider changes its decision because of the OPA decision process, all single-homed customers will also change at the same time. Additionally, a large number of routers pick a single best route at the path length comparison step and only about 7% on average stop at the OPA decision process. The number of routers that stop at the OPA decision process varies based on the OPA used. For small and large OPA values, the fraction of routers that stop at the OPA decision process is smaller than for small numerical values of the OPA (both positive and negative). The deviation from the 7% however (measured at an OPA of 1000) is only slightly above one percent. For such a small average number, the effect can be quite pronounced, as shown before. Finally, still about 15 percent of the routers continue after the OPA decision process. This implies that these routers receive more than one route advertisement for a given prefix, however the OPA value that they observe does not differ.

Both the top and bottom part of Figure 7 show essentially what the top part of Figure 6 has shown, i.e. the OPA value on the x-axis and the percentage of ASes that chose the OPA path on the y-axis. Here, the top part only shows the ASes that break at the OPA decision process, which illustrates the general behavior of the OPA mechanism. The bottom part in contrast shows the full aggregate view of the 1000 prefixes that were simulated.

In the graphs, the 5th/95th percentile, the 1st/3rd quartile and the median and average were plotted. In the top graph, all these lines hardly deviate from each other, which shows that the decision process itself has a nice, even and predictable behavior. Also–as designed–when the OPA is low, none of these ASes pick the route with the low OPA, whereas when the OPA is high, all ASes pick the OPA path. For very large negative and very large positive OPA values there is hardly a change in the route selection process. Only starting

Figure 7. Aggregate behavior (dual-homed stub ASes)

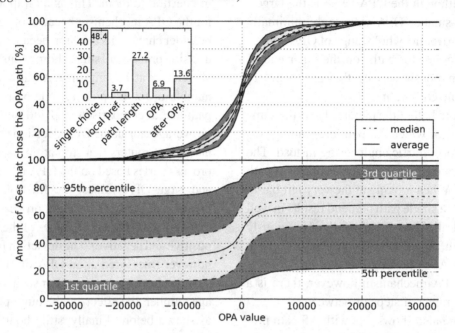

at about -20000 and ending at about +20000 there is a noticeable effect on the decision process with the strongest effect (incline of the graph) when the OPA is a small positive or negative value. In this range of OPA values, there is also a small but noticeable increase in the amount of ASes that pick a route at the OPA decision process step as mentioned before.

The effect on all ASes, i.e. including the ones that do not pick the best route based on the OPA, is shown in the bottom part of the figure. As can be expected based on the behavior individual prefixes have shown before, the effect is not as pronounced and even. On average however, there is a significant number of ASes that change their path selection based on the OPA mechanism. For the minimal OPA value, for 50% of all prefixes 25% or less of the ASes select the OPA path. At the other end of the spectrum around 75% or more pick the one with the OPA set. Given that only around 7% of all ASes pick a route at the OPA decision step; this is a very good outcome.

Figure 8 shows a slightly different view of what happens. The figure shows the distribution of the percentage of ASes that pick the OPA path for the case where the OPA has the lowest and highest possible value. In addition, it shows what the authors termed the OPA range. With OPA range the amount of ASes (in percent) that actually change their path selection when going from the minimal OPA value to the maximum OPA value, i.e the amount of ASes that can be influenced (directly and indirectly) using the OPA mechanism is meant.

Each individual prefix is represented by a dot in the three lines ordered by the percentage of ASes that picked the OPA path. The top line shows the distribution for the minimum OPA value (lower bound). It illustrates how effective the OPA is to make a prefix announcement "unattractive". Over 80% of the prefixes can be pushed below 50% of all ASes to pick OPA path. The bottom line shows the same for the maximum OPA value (upper bound). Here about 80% of the prefixes can be pushed above 50% of the ASes to pick the

Figure 8. OPA range, upper and lower bound

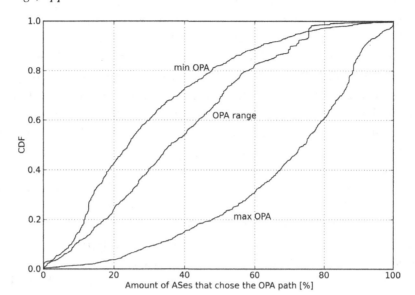

OPA path. An ideal mechanism would of course result in a line that already reaches 1.0 at an x-value of 0 for the minimum OPA case and a line that will stay 0.0 until an x-value of 100 is reached for the maximum OPA value. The next section shows how one can get much closer to this ideal.

The most interesting finding in the figure is however represented by the center line that shows the OPA range, i.e. the fraction of ASes that change their path selection based on the OPA from a minimum OPA value to the maximum OPA value. The graph shows e.g. that for 50% of the prefixes the fraction of ASes that can be influenced by the OPA is above 35%. The top 25% of the prefixes even have an OPA range of 55% and above.

Again, the outcome employing the OPA mechanism is not perfect, but given the constraints, this represents a significant improvement over existing mechanisms.

Combining the OPA and AS Path Prepending

The OPA decision step was deliberately placed after the AS path length comparison. This ef-

fectively restricts the OPA to be only applied in case there are at least two paths of equal length available that have different OPA values attached. This limitation has shown in the results before. The question is, can AS path prepending be used in combination with the OPA to have a bigger impact?

Using AS path prepending, one can change the set of candidate paths that make it to the OPA decision process. Combining both, path prepending and the OPA can therefore result in an overall wider OPA range. It is important however on which path the AS path prepending is performed. Consider the example of routers that receive both a prefix advertisement with and without OPA (or two with different OPA values) that select a path at the OPA decision process. When path prepending the non-OPA path, at all these routers the OPA path will be chosen because now the decision process will break at the AS path length comparison. However, at other routers that have received both advertisements but have chosen the non-OPA path before (because it was shorter) might now be able to pick a path based on the OPA. The resulting effect is that the minimum amount of ASes that pick the OPA path in this AS path prepended scenario is the amount of ASes that picked the OPA path with a maximum OPA value without path prepending. This means one can only increase the number of ASes that pick the OPA path when prepending on the non-OPA prefix advertisement. However, the likely effect is that there is a nice continuous increase in the OPA effectiveness (i.e. there is no big gap between the non-prepended case with maximum OPA and the prepended case with minimum OPA).

The previous 1000 prefixes were simulated again. This time, the non-OPA prefix advertisements were prepended so that the path is one hop longer. The same was done for the OPA prefix. In order to see how much one can actually extend the effectiveness of the OPA mechanism by combining it with path prepending the same analysis as in the previous section was performed. First, let us look at the actual range, i.e. at how much larger the fraction of ASes is that now change the path selection based on the OPA. For this, the ranges of all three scenarios, i.e. prepending once on the OPA path, no prepending and prepending once

on the non-OPA path were combined. The result is depicted in Figure 9.

The figure clearly shows a significant improvement; the unprepended case from Figure 8 is depicted in dotted lines for comparison. The lines are now much closer to the "ideal" as defined in the penultimate paragraph of the previous section. When using the OPA mechanism in combination with path prepending, the effective range is now much larger. For 50% of the prefixes, the range is now about 75% or above. Only around 10% of the prefixes can now only influence 40% of the ASes or less. This makes the OPA mechanism a very effective traffic engineering tool. Additional path prepends can still slightly improve these results but to a much smaller degree.

The best way to think about the combination of AS path prepending and the OPA mechanism is that AS path prepending allows coarse steps and the OPA mechanism is a means to do the fine-tuning within those steps. This is nicely reflected in Figure 10 where the top part shows how the OPA mechanism is affected when the path length of the OPA path is increased by one and in the bottom part where the non-OPA path is prepended once.

Figure 9. OPA range, upper and lower bound (incl. path prepending)

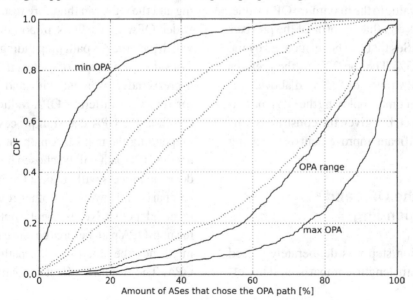

One can see that most paths can now be pushed into regions that have not been reached before by using the OPA mechanism alone. As explained before, when prepending on the non-OPA path, many ASes will now chose the OPA path not based on the OPA value but based on the fact that the OPA path is now in fact shorter. Other ASes will now reach the OPA decision process as both the OPA and non-OPA path are of equal length for them. These can now be influence by the OPA process as shown in the bottom figure. The effect of the OPA is now less pronounced but as already seen in Figure 9, the OPA range can be extended for most paths significantly. The same argument applies in the other direction of course as seen in the top part of Figure 11.

Larger Degrees of Multi-Homing

Although the by far largest number of multi-homed stub ASes in the Internet topology is dual-homed, a significant number of stub ASes in the Internet has more than two providers. Therefore also the behavior of the OPA mechanism in cases where there are more than two providers was analyzed.

Again 1000 ASes were picked that have three upstream providers and 372 (all) stub ASes that have four providers. And again, one of the prefix advertisements was used to add an OPA value to it.

Intuitively, the more advertisements an AS injects into the global routing system, the higher the likelihood that an AS that receives multiple of those will stop earlier in the decision process because it will prefer one prefix based on local preference or one by chance has a shorter AS path than the others. This of course has a spillover effect on later steps in the decision process where ultimately less routers will end up. This effect is depicted in Figure 11, where in the top part the results from the experiments of quad-homed stub ASes is shown and in the bottom part the results for the triple-homed ASes.

As can be seen in the figure, the effect of the OPA becomes a little less pronounced with an increased degree of multi-homing for the reasons mentioned before. On average, the dual-homed case resulted in an OPA range of about 38%. For every provider added, the range decreases by a moderate 4%. However, as seen before, one can

Figure 10. Aggregate behavior (in combination with prepending)

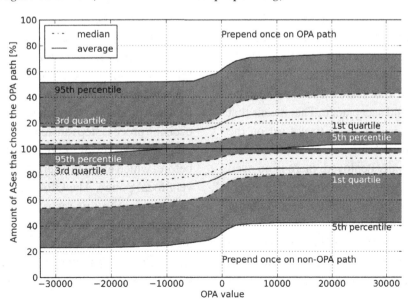

Figure 11. Aggregate behavior (triple-homed and quad-homed stub ASes)

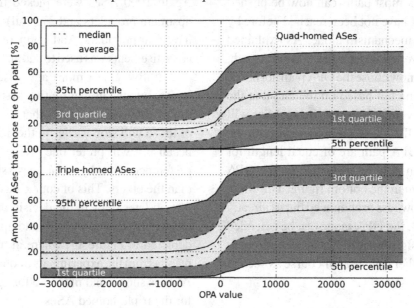

also significantly extend the OPA range here by additionally using path prepending.

Partial Deployment

Partial deployment is an interesting case for various reasons.

For one, it allows to evaluate whether there would be a significant gain when only a subset of the ASes in the Internet employ the OPA mechanism. Also, it is interesting to evaluate which ASes need to implement the OPA decision process in order to have the largest benefit. Finally, the OPA was chosen to be an optional transitive path attribute (Rekhter, Li, & Hares, 2006) for reasons of deployability and acceptance. That means that a network provider can chose to not act on the OPA. Even if the OPA became an IETF Internet standard and globally deployed, there is no need to actually allow it in one's network. The question is, which networks would have reasons to not enable the OPA comparison?

Generally speaking, the decision process preceding the OPA decision step make sure that the network's local preference is adhered to and

that reasonably good (short) paths are chosen. A reason to not include the OPA decision step in the overall decision process must therefore lie beyond the OPA decision process. For example, a network provider may value the utility of a later decision process step, such as the comparison of interior cost. The two steps which indeed might be interesting to operators are the comparison of interior cost and preferring E-BGP-learnt routes over I-BGP-learnt ones. These make sure that packets are either not carried over the internal network or at least take a short path through it. Clearly, it is in an operator's interest to perform this kind of hot potato routing. On the other hand, AS path prepending already aims at forcing the decision process to select a path before these later decision process steps are reached and prefix deaggregation can result in policy holes as explained before, which even, in a certain sense can circumvent local policy. The OPA does not introduce a new problem in this respect, vice versa, in case operators achieve their traffic engineering goals using the OPA mechanism and therefore do not resort to prefix deaggregation, the AS that enables the OPA in their network benefit.

Although OPA is most useful for origin ASes, intermediate ASes also benefit from OPA, because OPA randomizes traffic distribution, rather than depending on the final BGP decision steps as a tie breaker. In current practice, it is not uncommon to see a rather large amount of traffic flow towards the neighbor with the lowest IP address because the final tie breaker prefers the lowest router ID value, which is derived from one of a router's IP addresses.

Nevertheless, a scenario was evaluated where not all ASes in the Internet employ the OPA step as part of their routers' decision process. In particular, ASes were chosen that have a large degree, and therefore might have a reasonably sized internal network where the latter decision steps are of interest. Rather arbitrarily a degree of 50 and above was defined to be the threshold for this, i.e. ASes with less than 50 neighbors do enable the OPA mechanism whereas ASes with a degree of 50 or more do not. 1000 dual-homed stubs were chosen again to have a good basis for comparison. ASes that do not enable OPA were assumed to still propagate the attribute to neighboring ASes.

Figure 12 shows the results from this partial deployment scenario. As can be seen, the OPA now has a minuscule effect (bottom part of the figure) although the ASes that stop at the OPA process still exhibit the previously observed behavior (top part of the figure). This shows that indeed the ASes in the topology with a large degree play a central role in the effectiveness of the OPA mechanism. This comes at no surprise as these ASes in turn propagate their selected path to a large number of other ASes. By making them unresponsive the OPA attached to prefix advertisements, other ASes might not be able to the even reach the OPA decision process. As an example, imagine an AS that is multi-homed to two large ASes which do not react on the OPA. If both those ASes select the non-OPA path then the other AS will never even see the OPA prefix and consequently never execute the OPA decision step. These kinds of effects show in Figure 12. But, as argued before, large ASes actually have an incentive to allow the OPA.

Figure 12. Partial deployment

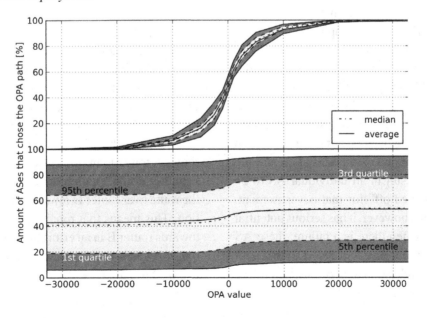

FUTURE RESEARCH DIRECTIONS

The OPA mechanism as outlined in the previous sections has a number of interesting properties. This sections adds a few discussion items, however, to make the reader aware of some of the properties that are inherent to the mechanism but not necessarily obvious at first and a few other, more general observations. This general discussion hints at future research directions.

First of all, the simulations are inherently limited. On the one hand, the data that was used can only be incomplete as it relies on a limited number of vantage points that in particular miss details at the edge of the network (Oliveira, Pei, Willinger, Zhang, & Zhang, 2010). Also the inferred business relationships are subject to errors. It was decided to use an AS-level topology in order to being able to simulate an Internet-scale topology and because there is even less precise data available for router-level topologies. Since the OPA value and the respective decision process is an "AS-wide" metric, restricting the simulations to the AS level however seems to be an appropriate limitation for a first level analysis.

The comparison was also restricted to two widely used inbound TE means–AS path prepending and prefix deaggregation. For completeness sake, there are indeed other means to perform traffic engineering. For example, an origin AS could use the origin attribute as this is part of the decision process but suffers from similar limitations as AS path prepending. Also, an origin AS could in principle include other ASes' AS number in order to make them discard that prefix advertisement since the loop detection algorithm will not allow that prefix to be installed into the RIB. This will result in an individual AS to be basically "switched off" for that advertisement. This can be done, however, it has serious potential consequences: when there is a failure, these AS will in case of failure e.g. not resort to that path advertisement and the origin AS will therefore risk longer convergence times.

Another interesting practice when it comes to inbound TE is scoped advertisements, i.e. prefixes are only advertised to a subset of the providers in order to balance incoming traffic across them. Scoped advertisements are widely observable and therefore an important TE tool (Cittadini, Muehlbauer, Uhlig, Bush, Francois, & Maennel, 2010). However, with the advent of IPv6, the ASes that resort to this mechanism today will not be able to use it in an IPv6 world as they will simply not have more than a single (albeit extremely large) prefix. So they might resort to prefix deaggregation and in the end the scaling trend of the IPv6 routing table might quickly match the IPv4 scaling trend. The OPA mechanism therefore seems to be a good addition to the decision process for IPv6. This is in particular true because deploying new functions in IPv6 will have no impact on the IPv4 world which is still dominant in terms of traffic volume and business relevance. While it is by no means trivial to add it for IPv6 alone, chance are that by restricting it to IPv6 at first results in better chances of actual deployment. Adding it soon would be good, because traffic levels are not sufficiently large at this point that operators need to invest much thought to traffic engineering. Once they do, they will resort to means that are well known and applied in IPv4 – including prefix deaggregation.

Deployment of the OPA mechanism will face one particular deployment hurdle, which is mixed deployment within a single AS. Having a mix of routers in an AS that react to the OPA and do not react to the OPA can potentially result in routing loops. For instance, in Figure 13 routers A and C implement the OPA and prefer the route over router A towards an external destination. Routers B and D do not implement the OPA and prefer the route over router D towards the same destination. This means that router C will send packets towards router B in an effort to get them to A, and router B sends packets towards router C in order to exit through D.

Figure 13. Potential loop problem in intra-AS partial deployment

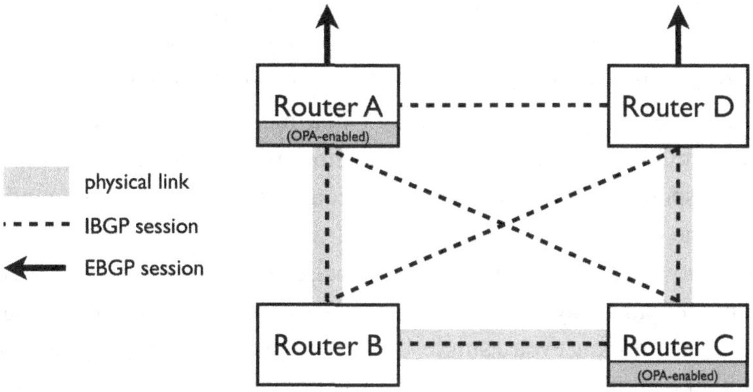

There are two potential answers to the problem. One is to restrict the OPA comparison to routes only learnt via E-BGP. This could result in a significantly reduced utility of the overall mechanism. Another potential road to deployment is to not switch the OPA on until all routers actually are OPA-capable. One could utilize tools that extract the RIBs of routers and topology information to pre-compute whether routing loops will occur, in which order routers need to be OPA-enabled to avoid loops and so forth. Since routing tables constantly change, there will be a remaining risk of transient loops. If routing table feeds were available, this would indeed be an interesting part for future work.

To conclude this discussion let us look at the very nature and some consequences of the OPA mechanism. First of all, the amount of ASes that pick the OPA path, which was used as a measure of the effectiveness of the OPA mechanism, has no 1:1 correlation with the amount of traffic that enters an origin AS through the OPA path. This is the same basic limitation that e.g. AS path prepending has. In an extreme case, if all traffic originates in a single AS, then the OPA mechanism will result in a rather binary operation, i.e. once this single AS changes its path selection, all traffic will shift from the non-OPA path to the OPA path. On the flip side, this also means although for some ASes the OPA mechanism results in a

small OPA range, this might be enough for effective traffic engineering.

Additionally, the OPA mechanism will result to some degree in a trial and error type of operation as it will be unlikely that an origin AS will always chose a good OPA value with the first try. This means that there will be a certain amount of churn in the network due to the OPA mechanism. However, the assumption is that churn is only produced rarely for a given prefix as once a proper OPA value is found it will remain stable for extended periods of time. When first using the OPA for a given prefix it is also worth noting that there is a potential for significant traffic shift even with very small OPA values. This is due to the fact that once an AS receives two or more prefix advertisements with an OPA set, the OPA decision process will take place, whereas before it was simply skipped. Since the OPA decision process employs the random component R, a number of ASes will likely change their path selection mostly based on R alone. This needs to be kept in mind.

Throughout this chapter, it was assumed that if an origin AS was successful in moving the preferred incoming path from a remote AS, it achieves its traffic engineering goals. As a first approximation this is a reasonable assumption, but one has to be careful to avoid the suggestion that if a certain fraction of ASes adjust their path, a matching fraction of incoming traffic moves to a different incoming physical link, as this would assume that all ASes send an equal amount of traffic. This is not the case, as shown by Uhlig (2004, p. 57) for AS/traffic distributions for two locations. In one location, the top 10 ASes are responsible for more than 20% of all traffic and the top 100 ASes are responsible for just under 60% of all traffic. For the other location this is 30% and 72%. As such, moving a large number of low-traffic ASes to another path may have negligible impact on traffic while moving even a single high traffic AS to another path may move several percent of total traffic to another physical link.

These considerations should have little impact on the usefulness of the OPA mechanism, unless the high traffic ASes are consistently part of the subset of ASes that fail to move their preferred path even in the presence of extreme OPA values.

CONCLUSION

Inter-domain traffic engineering is an important aspect of network operations today since a constantly increasing fraction of the networks that constitute the Internet is becoming multi-homed. Not just technical reasons such as an increased reliability of the connection to the global Internet or an increase in capacity is driving the need to control the way traffic flows but also commercial reasons make a finer control over the traffic flow desirable. Certain contractual agreements are subject to traffic ratios which need to be controlled. Another trend that might need a tool different from prefix deaggregation is the recent depletion of the IANA IPv4 address pool and then the APNIC and RIPE NCC IPv4 pools. This might result into smaller prefixes appearing in the global routing table over time as smaller allocations are made to customers. With for example only a /24 available, prefix deaggregation today will not work as many operators de facto filter on this boundary, i.e. a /25 or larger will likely not be globally routed. What this means is that such an AS is left with

very little means to do efficient inbound traffic engineering.

The OPA mechanism presented in this chapter is a proposal to fill this perceived gap in BGP. OPA is a mechanism that can perform finer-grained inbound traffic engineering compared to the coarse control of path prepending but without the drawbacks of prefix deaggregation. The authors believe, based on the simulation results, they have succeeded as the OPA mechanism, especially in combination with path prepending, has proven to be quite effective for a large fraction of multi-homed stub ASes. It cannot be claimed that the OPA mechanism is the perfect inbound TE tool, but given the constraints of BGP and the nature of inter-domain routing, the OPA mechanism can significantly improve and nicely complement today's inbound TE tool set. Ultimately, the hope is to alleviate the need for deaggregation for a large fraction the prefixes observable in today's routing table which constitutes one third of the global routing table today–trend increasing. Furthermore, for small prefixes deaggregation is not an option.

The real-world challenge is that introducing changes to BGP is difficult and standardization of BGP modifications (Van Beijnum & Winter, 2009) can be time consuming. In addition, after a standard has been defined and implemented, it will take many years to deploy modified BGP speakers on the Internet and so the prospects of the OPA mechanism to find its way into the Internet are–realistically speaking–low. The best one can hope for is that this work will spark interest in the operator and vendor community and that some mechanism along the lines of the OPA will find its way into standards. The IETF IDR working group that deals with BGP has recently re-chartered and has embraced scalability improvements as part of their chartered work. Whether this means that the chances have increased that scalable inbound traffic engineering proposals will be worked on remains to be seen.

REFERENCES

Antonov, V. (1995). BGP AS path metrics.

Applegate, D., & Cohen, E. (2003). Making intra-domain routing robust to changing and uncertain traffic demands: Understanding fundamental tradeoffs. *Conference on Applications, technologies, architectures, and protocols for computer communications* (pp. 313-324). doi: 10.1145/863955.863991

Bonaventure, O., De Cnodder, S., Haas, J., Quoitin, B., & White, R. (2003). Controlling the redistribution of BGP routes.

Chandra, R., Traina, P., & Li, T. (1997). BGP Communities Attribute. ISSN 2070-1721

Chen, E., & Bates, T. (1996). Destination Preference Attribute for BGP.

Cittadini, L., Muehlbauer, W., Uhlig, S., Bush, R., Francois, P., & Maennel, O. (2010). Evolution of Internet address space deaggregation: Myths and reality. *IEEE Journal on Selected Areas in Communications, 28*(8), 1238–1249. doi:10.1109/JSAC.2010.101002.

Dhamdhere, A., & Dovrolis, C. (2006). ISP and egress path selection for multihomed networks. *25th IEEE International Conference on Computer Communications* (pp. 1-12). doi: 10.1109/INFOCOM.2006.280

Dhamdhere, A., & Dovrolis, C. (2008). Ten years in the evolution of the internet ecosystem. *8th ACM SIGCOMM conference on Internet measurement* (pp. 183-196). doi: 10.1145/1452520.1452543

Feamster, N., Borkenhagen, J., & Rexford, J. (2003). Guidelines for interdomain traffic engineering. *ACM SIGCOMM Computer Communications Review, 33*(5), 19–30. doi:10.1145/963985.963988.

Gao, L., & Rexford, J. (2001). Stable internet routing without global coordination. *IEEE/ACM Transactions on Networking, 9*(6), 681–692. doi:10.1109/90.974523.

Gao, R., Dovrolis, C., & Zegura, E. W. (2005). *Interdomain ingress traffic engineering through optimized AS-path prepending. 4th IFIP-TC6 international conference on Networking Technologies, Services, and Protocols; Performance of Computer and Communication Networks* (pp. 647–658). Mobile and Wireless Communication Systems.

Houston, G. (2001). Commentary on inter-domain routing in the Internet. ISSN 2070-1721.

Kandula, S., Katabi, D., Davie, B., & Charny, A. (2005). Walking the tightrope: Responsive yet stable traffic engineering. *Conference on Applications, technologies, architectures, and protocols for computer communications* (pp. 253-264). doi: 10.1145/1080091.1080122

Oliveira, R., Pei, D., Willinger, W., Zhang, B., & Zhang, L. (2010). The (in) completeness of the observed internet AS-level structure. *IEEE/ACM Transactions on Networking, 18*(1), 109–122. doi:10.1109/TNET.2009.2020798.

Quoitin, B., Pelsser, C., Bonaventure, O., & Uhlig, S. (2005). A performance evaluation of BGP-based traffic engineering. *International Journal of Network Management, 15*(3), 177–191. doi:10.1002/nem.559.

Quoitin, B., Pelsser, C., Swinnen, L., Bonaventure, O., & Uhlig, S. (2003). Interdomain traffic engineering with BGP. *IEEE Communications Magazine, 41*(5), 122–128. doi:10.1109/MCOM.2003.1200112.

Quoitin, B., & Uhlig, S. (2005). Modeling the routing of an autonomous system with C-BGP. *IEEE Network, 19*(6), 12–19. doi:10.1109/MNET.2005.1541716.

Rekhter, Y., Li, T., & Hares, S. (2006). A border gateway protocol 4 (BGP-4). ISSN 2070-1721.

Retana, A., & White, R. (2011). BGP custom decision process.

Teixeira, R., Griffin, G., Resende, M., & Rexford, J. (2007). TIE breaking: Tunable interdomain egress selection. *IEEE/ACM Transactions on Networking*, *15*(4), 761–774. doi:10.1109/ TNET.2007.893877.

Uhlig, S. (2004). *Implications of the traffic characteristics on interdomain traffic engineering*. (Doctoral thesis). Université catholique de Louvain.

Van Beijnum, I. (2002). BGP: Building reliable networks with the border gateway protocol. *O'Reilly*. Retrieved from http://oreilly.com/catalog/bgp/chapter/ch06.html

Van Beijnum, I., & Winter, R. (2009). A BGP Inter-AS Cost Attribute.

Winick, J., Jamin, S., & Rexford, J. (2002). *Traffic engineering between neighboring domains*. Retrieved August 31, 2012, from http://www. cs.princeton.edu/~jrex/papers/interAS.pdf

Winter, R., & Van Beijnum, I. (2012). Explicitly accommodating origin preference for inter-domain traffic engineering. *27th Annual ACM Symposium on Applied Computing*. doi: 10.1145/2245276.2245389

ENDNOTES

1. The largest part of this work was carried out while the author's main employer was NEC Labs Europe.

Chapter 3
On the Aggregatability of Router Forwarding Tables

Yaoqing Liu
University of Memphis, USA

Lan Wang
University of Memphis, USA

Xin Zhao
Google, USA

Beichuan Zhang
University of Arizona, USA

ABSTRACT

In this book chapter, the authors first present Optimal Routing Table Constructor (ORTC), an optimal one-time FIB aggregation algorithm that preserves strong forwarding correctness. The authors then present four-level FIB aggregation algorithm(s) that can handle dynamic routing updates while maintaining forwarding correctness. Afterwards, the authors evaluate our algorithms using routing tables from RouteViews, and compare the algorithms with ORTC using routing tables from a Tier-1 ISP. The authors found that ORTC's aggregation ratio is better than the Level 1, Level 2 and Level 3 algorithms, but the Level 4 algorithm has better aggregation ratio than ORTC as they relax the requirement of forwarding correctness. Finally, the authors evaluate the potential impact of introducing extra routable space in the Level 4 algorithm and discuss how to limit such negative impact.

INTRODUCTION

Despite growth constraints such as strict address allocation policies (Meyer, Zhang, & Fall, 2007), the routing tables in the default free zone (DFZ) have been growing at an alarming rate in recent years. Currently, a DFZ router stores hundreds of thousands of routes or even a million in tier-1 ISPs. This is in part due to the sheer growth of the Internet, and in part due to the lack of aggregation.

When a customer network multi-homes to multiple network providers to ensure resilient Internet connectivity, the customer's address prefix(es) must be visible in the global routing table in order to be reachable through any of its network providers, thus breaking down provider-based aggregation (Bu, Gao, & Towsley, 2004). Traffic engineering is another contributing factor. For example, a network may try to influence the paths of specific incoming traffic flows by splitting its prefix into

DOI: 10.4018/978-1-4666-4305-5.ch003

several longer ones and injecting them at different network attachment points. Splitting prefixes is also used as a defense mechanism against IP prefix hijacking.

Growing number of globally advertised address prefixes leads to increasing FIB tables, RIB tables, and routing churns. Among these problems, ISPs and vendors are more concerned about the FIB size than RIB size, because it is more difficult to scale up the memory in line cards than in route processors (Fuller, 2006). FIB size can be reduced by FIB aggregation, a purely local solution that can be quickly implemented and deployed in the ISPs. FIB aggregation combines multiple entries in the routing table to one entry in the forwarding table without changing the next hop for data traffic. A simple example of FIB aggregation is the following: if all the longer prefixes, say under 1.0.0.0/8, share the same next hop with the covering prefix 1.0.0.0/8, then only 1.0.0.0/8 needs to be installed in the FIB and all the longer prefixes under 1.0.0.0/8 can be removed from the FIB.

The effectiveness of FIB aggregation depends on how prefixes are distributed over next-hop routers. Generally speaking, the fewer neighbors a router has, the better aggregation it may achieve. In the extreme case that all prefixes share the same single next-hop, aggregation is maximized. According to Li, Alderson, Willinger, and Doyle (2004), although some routers have high degrees up to a couple of hundreds, most connections are with their end-customers, which represent only a small percentage of the address space. The routers still use a small number of transit networks to reach most prefixes.

Besides sharing the same next-hop, prefixes also need to be numerically aggregatable. This is possible due to two factors. First, in IP address allocation, large blocks of Internet addresses are first allocated to Regional Internet Registries (RIRs) and then they further allocate the addresses to networks within the same region. Thus prefixes announced out of the same regions tend to be nu-

merically aggregatable. Second, for prefixes split for traffic engineering or other purposes, a router near the origin network is likely to take different next-hops, but a router further away from the origin network is more likely to have the same next-hop towards these numerically aggregatable prefixes.

Therefore, although FIB aggregation is opportunistic and the aggregation degree varies from router to router, there are inherent properties of the Internet that can make FIB aggregation effective. If FIB aggregation is indeed effective in reducing table size, its most appealing feature is that the impact is limited within a router's data plane. It does not change any routing protocols, or any router's routing decisions. Data traffic still flows on the same router paths. Therefore, it can co-exist with almost any new routing protocols, including those architectural solutions to the routing scalability problem in the long run.

This chapter conducts a systematic analysis and evaluation of FIB aggregation to understand its gains and costs. We recognize that there can be different levels of aggregation, each representing different tradeoffs between table size reduction and computation complexity. We design and implement five algorithms (Level 1, 2, 3, 4A, and 4B) at different aggregation levels, and evaluate them using publicly available routing tables from tens of networks. The results show that the lowest-level aggregation can reduce table size by 30%-50%, making the table the same size as that two and half years ago, while the highest-level aggregation can reduce the table size by 70%, making the table the same size as that eight years ago. The computation time of one aggregation run ranges from tens of milliseconds to a few hundred milliseconds on a commodity Linux machine. Although these numbers may not reflect the computation time on a router, they reflect the relative speed of different levels of aggregation. To handle routing changes, we design and implement algorithms to incrementally update the aggregated FIB upon a change. The full aggregation algorithm is only invoked when the router Central Processing Unit (CPU) load is low or the FIB size becomes above a threshold, thus its computation time is amortized over time. Our evaluation using one month (Dec. 2008) of BGP routing updates shows that compared with unaggregated FIB, the computation overhead of maintaining aggregated FIB over time is small.

In addition to our own algorithms, we present ORTC (Draves, King, Venkatachar, & Zill, 1999), an optimal one-time FIB aggregation algorithm that preserves strong forwarding correctness. Using routing tables from a tier-1 ISP, we found that ORTC's aggregation ratio is better than the Level 1, Level 2 and Level 3 algorithms, but our Level 4 algorithms have better aggregation ratio than ORTC as they relax the requirement of forwarding correctness. Finally, we evaluate the potential impact of introducing extra routable space in our Level 4 algorithm and discuss how to limit such negative impact.

BACKGROUND

There are two types of tables used by routers: Routing Information Base (RIB) for routing and Forwarding Information Base (FIB) for forwarding. RIB is stored in the main memory of a route processor. The route processor receives and processes routing update messages and runs routing protocols, e.g., OSPF (Moy, 1998) and BGP (Rekhter, Li, & Hares, 2006), to compute the RIB. Each RIB entry contains the destination IP prefix and associated route information. For example, BGP maintains the full AS path and many other attributes for each prefix in the RIB. The FIB is derived from the RIB and router configurations. It is stored in line cards, whose job is to forward data packets. Therefore, the FIB usually uses high performance memory, which is more expensive and more difficult to scale. For each destination IP prefix, the FIB has an entry to store the next-hop IP, next-hop MAC address and outgoing interface for fast data forwarding. Figure 1 illustrates these different components in a router.

The conventional way of reducing routing table size is to aggregate the RIB, which will also reduce the FIB size. However, RIB aggregation has very limited adoption in the Internet. At a prefix's origin network, there is little incentive to aggregate the prefix, because the gain of aggregating a small number of self-originated prefixes does not make much difference to the table size. At the same time, the origin network actually has incentives, such as multi-homing and traffic engineering, to split the prefix. At a remote site,

Figure 1. RIB and FIB

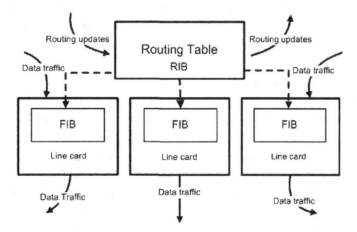

aggregation opportunity is limited since two prefixes must have the same path attributes in order to be aggregated in RIB. Otherwise their path information will be lost and protocol functions may be affected. Forcing aggregation of prefixes that have different paths would also defeat multi-homing and traffic engineering intended by the prefix origin networks.

The introduction of CIDR (Fuller, Li, Yu, & Varadhan, 1993) enabled better aggregation of IP prefixes and slowed down the growth of routing table size considerably for a period of time. However, the increasingly pervasive practice of multi-homing and traffic engineering has again led to the routing scalability problem. In response to this problem, the IRTF Routing Research Group (RRG) (IRTF Routing Research Group, n.d.) was formed in search for a long-term solution. Many proposals are being discussed on the RRG mailing list and at RRG meetings (Li, 2009). In previous work (Jen et al., 2008b), we classified the proposed solutions into two categories, separation and elimination. One of the separation approaches is Map&Encap (Deering, 1996; Hinden, 1996). Several proposed schemes, e.g., LISP (Farinacci, Fuller, Meyer, & Lewis, 2012), APT (Jen et al., 2008a), Ivip (Whittle, 2010), TRRP (Herrin, n.d.), are realizations of the Map&Encap concept. These long-term solutions aim to reduce the routing table size, which inevitably involves changes to the routing architecture and protocols. However, these changes generally take a long time to become a reality. Moreover, they usually change the traffic paths, and may incur extra packet processing overhead.

One proposed approach to reducing FIB size is Virtual Aggregation (VA) (Francis et al., 2009; Ballani, Francis, Tuan, & Wang, 2009). VA designates a small set of routers Aggregated Prefix Routers (APRs) to announce virtual prefixes, so that other routers do not need to install more specific prefixes under those virtual prefixes in their FIB – they simply forward packets to the APRs responsible for the corresponding virtual prefixes.

It can be independently deployed by one ISP, and does not require changes to the routing architecture or protocols. It also allows operators to control FIB size more explicitly by APR configuration. However, VA requires changes to network-wide router configurations and specialized routers to announce virtual prefixes. Moreover, it could introduce extra delays (stretch) in packet delivery. VA allows operators to control FIB size more explicitly by APR configuration.

Simple Virtual Aggregation (S-VA) (Raszuk, Heitz, Lo, Zhang, & Xu, 2012) allows some edge routers not to store some routes in the FIB and does not have the extra stretch issue. For example, if an operator inserts a 12.0.0.0/8 virtual prefix into the forwarding table with next-hop 2, then any prefix that is covered by this prefix and shares the same next-hop 2 will not be installed in the forwarding table. Otherwise, if the descendant prefix has a different next-hop, then the prefix and all the subtree prefixes will remain in the forwarding table. Our evaluation results in this chapter show that S-VA cannot reduce FIB size as much as the FIB aggregation schemes we have proposed.

Similar to S-VA, FIB aggregation is a purely local solution (Richardson, 1996; Draves et al., 1999; Cain, 2002; Zhao, Liu, Wang, & Zhang, 2010). It combines multiple entries in the forwarding table without changing the next hops for data forwarding. This approach is particularly appealing because it can be done by a software upgrade at a router and its impact is limited within the router. It does not require changes to routing protocols or router hardware, nor does it affect multi-homing, traffic engineering, or other network-wide operations.

FIB aggregation may be more effective than RIB aggregation since it only requires prefixes to have the same next-hop in order to be aggregated. For example, considering that a Los Angeles router connects to a Tokyo router, which in turn connects to a Beijing router and a Shanghai router. The Los Angeles router may reach prefixes announced by China Telecom via different paths, some via

Beijing and some via Shanghai. However, in its FIB, most these prefixes take the Tokyo router as the next-hop, making them aggregatable.

It is important to note that FIB aggregation is not a replacement for the long-term architectural solutions because it does not address the root causes of the routing scalability problem. Instead, FIB aggregation is a local solution that can be quickly implemented and deployed in the short-term, and in the long run, it can co-exist and complement architectural solutions.

FIB AGGREGATION

Issues and Problems

The idea of FIB aggregation is rather intuitive, but to our best knowledge, no study has systematically evaluated its potential benefits and costs. FIB aggregation is an opportunistic technique – its effectiveness depends on what prefixes are present in the table, how many of them can be numerically represented by a single prefix, and how many of them share the same next-hop. The benefits of FIB aggregation come with certain costs, such as extra CPU cycles. The costs also depend on the actual aggregation algorithms, and how routing changes are handled to update the aggregated forwarding table. A thorough understanding of FIB aggregation is needed in order to decide whether it is a viable solution.

Most importantly, FIB aggregation should ensure packet delivery and not change the paths that packets take, which we call forwarding correctness. We define two types of forwarding correctness as follows.

1. **Strong Forwarding Correctness:** The longest-prefix lookup of any destination address that appears in the original FIB should return the same next-hop before and after the aggregation. Moreover, any destination

address that does not appear in the original FIB should not appear in the aggregated FIB.

2. **Weak Forwarding Correctness:** For destination addresses that appear in the original FIB, the longest-prefix lookup should return the same next-hop after the aggregation. Weak forwarding correctness allows previously non-routable addresses to become routable.

As we will show in the next section, ORTC, Level 1 and Level 2 algorithms satisfy strong forwarding correctness, while Level 3 and Level 4 algorithms satisfy weak forwarding correctness. The difference between weak and strong forwarding correctness is that the former introduces new prefixes that cover previously non-routable space; therefore, some previously non-routable traffic will be forwarded. This does not violate the correctness requirement since all previously routable traffic is still routable and will follow the same path. On the other hand, allowing extra routable space improves aggregation. For example, ORTC aggregates FIB to the furthest extent under strong forwarding correctness, but Level 4 aggregation can aggregate the FIB more than ORTC. In the next section, we will evaluate the positive and negative impact of allowing extra routable space in FIB aggregation.

Solutions and Recommendations

1. Solutions

In this section, we present ORTC and our Level 1 – Level 4 algorithms.

A. ORTC

Draves et al. (1999) proposed the Optimal Routing Table Constructor (ORTC) algorithm. It traverses the routing table tree structure three times to produce the aggregated FIB. The first pass is a depth-first traversal in pre-order to normalize the tree, so that all the nodes have zero or two children. The expanded nodes have the same next hops as their nearest ancestors that are real nodes. The second pass is a depth-first traversal in post-order to merge next hops, in which two children merge their next-hop sets to form their parent's next-hop set. If the two children have one or more common next hops, the merging uses an intersection operation; otherwise, it uses a union operation. The third pass is a depth-first traversal in pre-order to select each node's next hop and form the aggregated FIB. More specifically, the root can have a next hop randomly selected from its next-hop. From then on, if a node's selected next hop h appears in its child's next-hop set, then the child should have h as its selected next hop, and the child will not be loaded into the FIB. Otherwise, the child will have a next hop randomly selected from its next-hop set, and the child will be loaded into the FIB.

Note that, unlike our Level 1 to Level 4 algorithms, the ORTC algorithm does not include any incremental update mechanism, i.e., whenever there are any changes to the FIB, the aggregated FIB table needs to be recreated from scratch. Therefore, it is infeasible to deploy ORTC in a real network. However, we will still evaluate its aggregation ratio for one-time aggregation, as a way to gauge how well our algorithms perform in terms of aggregation ratio.

B. Level 1 to Level 4 FIB Aggregation

We designed and implemented four algorithms at different FIB aggregation levels. Level 1 aggregation removes prefix p if it shares the same next-hop with its immediate covering prefix p', which is the longest prefix that is less specific than the prefix p. Level 2 aggregation combines sibling prefixes that share the same next-hop into a parent prefix if the parent prefix is nonexistent in the routing table. Sibling prefixes are of the same length, numerically consecutive and numerically aggregatable. Level 3 aggregation combines a set of non-sibling prefixes that share the same next-hop into a super prefix if the super prefix is nonexistent in the routing table. Level 3 aggregation introduces non-routable space between the non-sibling prefixes. Level 4 aggregation combines a set of non-sibling prefixes with the same next hops into a super prefix even if other prefixes in-between exist with different next-hops. Level 4 aggregation may also introduce extra non-routable space underneath the super-prefix.

1. **Level 1 Aggregation:** This technique is illustrated in Figure 2(a). The simplest form of aggregation is to remove prefixes that share the same next-hop with their immediate ancestor prefixes, in which case we say that the "covered prefix" has the same next-hop as the "covering prefix" and can be removed from FIB. Addresses that previously match the covered prefix now will match the covering prefix and still get the same next-hop. Previously non-routable packets, whose table lookup ends up with NULL next-hop, will still be non- routable. This aggregation does not introduce any new prefix or extra routable space into the table.

The algorithm implementing this technique simply traverses the tree recursively from the root node in post-order. When it arrives at a node with a prefix, it compares this prefix's next-hop with its immediate ancestor prefix's next-hop. If they have the same next-hop, it labels the current node NON-FIB, otherwise labels it IN-FIB. The immediate ancestor prefix's next-hop is updated and remembered during the tree traversal. Eventually every prefix node is labeled as either NON-FIB or IN-FIB, and all IN-FIB prefixes comprise the aggregated FIB. The aggregation is done recursively throughout the entire table. The computation time is $O(n)$, where n is the total number of nodes in the tree.

2. **Level 2 Aggregation:** This technique is illustrated in Figure 2(b). In addition to

performing Level 1 aggregation, Level 2 combines sibling prefixes that share the same next-hop into a parent prefix. If the parent node already has a prefix with a different next-hop, then the aggregation cannot be done. Or if the parent node already has a prefix with the same next-hop, then it is part of Level 1 aggregation. Therefore, Level 2 is done when the parent node has no prefix. The net result is to introduce a new prefix to cover two sibling prefixes, but there is no extra routable space introduced, i.e., the aggregated FIB covers the exact address space as the unaggregated FIB.

The algorithm implementing Level 2 aggregation traverses the tree recursively from the root node in post-order. Besides doing Level 1 aggregation, when it arrives at a node without a prefix, it compares this node's two children. If both children have prefixes and use the same next-hop, then both children are labeled NON-FIB, and this current node is assigned the parent prefix and labeled IN-FIB. The aggregation is done recursively throughout the entire table. The computation time is O(n), where n is the total number of nodes in the tree.

3. **Level 3 Aggregation:** This technique is illustrated in Figure 2(c). In addition to performing the Level 1 and 2 aggregations, Level 3 aggregates a set of non-sibling prefixes that have the same next-hop into a super prefix. Between these non-sibling prefixes, non-routable space is allowed. For example, in Figure 2(c), at the bottom level of the tree, there are two nodes with address prefixes (real nodes) sharing the same next hop. However, these two nodes are separated in the tree by two nodes without address prefixes. The prefixes of the two real nodes can be aggregated into a grandparent prefix. A side effect is that this newly inserted prefix covers previously non-routable space; therefore, some previously non-routable traffic (which would have been dropped by this router) will be forwarded along the next-hop of the aggregate prefix. All previ-

Figure 2. *Different levels of FIB aggregation. The binary tree represents part of the IP address space. Nodes labeled with letters are prefixes in the routing table, and the letter represents the next-hop for the prefix. Nodes without labels do not have their corresponding prefixes in the routing table. Filled nodes are extra routable space introduced by the aggregation.*

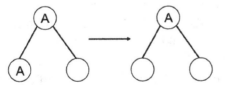

(a) Level 1: Removing covered prefixes

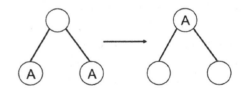

(b) Level 2: Combining sibling prefixes

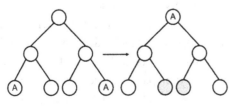

(c) Level 3: Allowing extra routable space

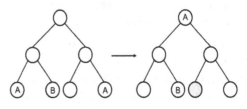

(d) Level 4: Allowing holes in the aggregate

ously routable traffic is still routed along the same path as before. This behavior satisfies weak forwarding correctness but not strong forwarding correctness.

Level 3 aggregation must be implemented with care to ensure its forwarding correctness. For example, in Figure 2(c), two grandchildren prefixes are aggregated into one grandparent prefix. This would be incorrect if there is already a great-grandparent prefix (not shown in the figure) covering the subtree with a different next-hop B, because that means the two middle nodes at the bottom level are not non-routable space and their next-hops would change from B to A after the aggregation. In order to handle this case without introducing much computation overhead, we decide that in our implementation we only apply this type of aggregation to prefixes that do not have any existing ancestor prefixes. In a typical DFZ routing table, about half of all the prefixes have no ancestors and the other half have ancestors, as we verified in our BGP data set from 36 RouteViews' peers. The prefixes that have ancestors can be aggregated by Level 1 and Level 2, therefore our choice does not lose too much aggregation capability.

The algorithm implementing Level 3 aggregation traverses the tree recursively in postorder. Besides doing Level 1 and Level 2 aggregation for all nodes, when it arrives at a prefix that does not have any ancestor, it checks whether this prefix has a sibling node that does not have a prefix. If yes, it returns a pointer of this prefix node to its parent node, which will further pass this pointer up along the tree. When an upper level node has two such pointers, one from a left descendant and another from a right descendant, and these two descendants have the same next-hop, then a new prefix is created at this upper level node and labeled IN-FIB, while the two descendant nodes are labeled NON-FIB. If the two descendants have different next-hops, then aggregation cannot be done and they remain IN-

FIB. The computation complexity is O(n), where n is the number of nodes in the tree.

4. **Level 4 Aggregation:** This technique is illustrated in Figure 2(d). In addition to performing Level 1, 2 and 3 aggregations, Level 4 aggregates a set of non-sibling prefixes with the same next-hop. The difference from Level 3 aggregation is that, in Level 4, between the non-sibling aggregated prefixes, other prefixes with different next-hops are allowed, while Level 3 only allows non-routable space. For example, in Figure 2(d), a node with next-hop B is allowed to be between the prefixes being aggregated, punching a "hole" in the aggregate prefix. This type of aggregation maintains forwarding correctness and may also introduce extra routable space as Level 3 does. For the same reason as in Level 3, our algorithm only applies this type of aggregation to prefixes that do not have ancestor prefixes.

The seemingly trivial difference between Level 4 and Level 3 actually has significant implication to algorithm design. It allows the maximum flexibility for aggregation. However, taking full advantage of it may also require significant computation time. For example, given a set of non-sibling prefixes with different next-hops, which super-prefix should be inserted? Which next-hop should the super-prefix take? Finally, how should the decision be made without too much computational complexity? In this paper, we present and evaluate two different Level 4 algorithms described as follows.

The Level 4A algorithm traverses the tree recursively once in post-order. Besides doing Level 1, 2 and 3 aggregations, when it arrives at a prefix that does not have any ancestor, it returns a pointer of this prefix node to its parent, which will further pass this pointer up along the tree. An upper level node will receive two lists of its descendants, one from its left child and the other from its right child. This node combines the two lists to get all its descendants and their next-hops, picks the most popular next-hop as its own next-hop and inserts a prefix at this node. All the descendants that use the most popular next-hop will be labeled NON-FIB, and other descendants are labeled IN-FIB. If multiple next-hops tie for the most popular, then one of them is randomly selected. The computation time is O(n), where n is the number of nodes in the tree.

The Level 4B algorithm is based on Herrin's proposal (2008). It traverses the tree twice. The first step traverses the tree recursively in post-order, which is like sweeping all tree nodes from bottom up. During this process, the algorithm calculates the most popular next-hop among all descendant prefixes of a node and records this next-hop with the node unless this node already has a prefix with a different next-hop. The second step traverses the tree recursively in preorder, which is like going through all tree nodes from top down. During this process, the algorithm tries to insert new prefixes with the most popular next-hop from all descendants (not just immediate descendants as in Level 4A), as calculated in the previous postorder tree traversal, and label descendant prefixes NON-FIB or IN-FIB accordingly. When there are multiple equally popular next-hops, we randomly select one. Under certain conditions a newly inserted prefix at a higher level of the tree may be redundant and will be removed. The computation time is O(n), where n is the number of nodes in the tree. It tries to do a more thorough aggregation than Level 4A, but will take longer time since it traverses the tree twice.

C. Incremental Update Algorithms

Internet routes change over time, thus the obvious question is how to update the aggregated FIB when there is a change. Re-run the full FIB aggregation will maintain the best aggregation all the time, but it will also incur significant computation overhead. We use the combination of three mechanisms to make sure that the computation cost of updating aggregated FIBs is under the control of operators. First, operators can choose the level of full FIB aggregation that suits their routers the best. Routers with faster CPU and fewer routing updates can use higher level FIB aggregation, otherwise they can use lower level FIB aggregation. Second, we design an algorithm that updates the aggregated FIB incrementally. The algorithm tries to minimize the number of tree nodes that have to be accessed and changed to maintain forwarding correctness after the routing change. It does not attempt to keep table size small. Third, the full FIB aggregation is only invoked when needed, e.g., the table size has crossed a threshold after being incrementally updated for a while, or when the router has free CPU cycles to spare, i.e., the router load is under a threshold.

Processing a routing update includes two steps: updating the RIB and updating the FIB. The second step is straight-forward as we just need to apply RIB changes to FIB. Thus we will focus on describing how the RIB is incrementally updated. In general, when a prefix gets a new nexthop, its nearest descendants need to be re-aggregated, and when a prefix is withdrawn, its nearest descendants need to be de-aggregated. The details differ depending on the level of aggregation. We first define a few basic operations, and then use them to describe the incremental update algorithm for each level.

- **Update-node(p):** When an announcement of prefix p is received, insert the corresponding node if it does not exist in RIB, otherwise update its next-hop information if necessary. If p was previously generated by the aggregation process, label it as a real prefix. Let A be p's nearest ancestor, if nexthop(A) == nexthop(p), label p as NON-FIB, otherwise IN-FIB.
- **Re-aggregate(p):** For each D of p's nearest descendants, if nexthop(D) != nexthop(p), label D IN-FIB. Optionally, if nexthop(D)

== nexthop(p), label D NON-FIB, which does not affect forwarding correctness but reduces the FIB size at the expense of updating more nodes.

- **De-aggregate(p):** Let A be p's nearest ancestor. For each D of p's nearest descendants, if nexthop(D) != nexthop(A), label D IN-FIB. Optionally, if nexthop(D) == nexthop(A), label D NON-FIB, which does not affect forwarding correctness but reduces the FIB size at the expense of updating more nodes. When A does not exist, its next-hop is considered to be NULL and the aforementioned actions still hold.

Using the above basic operations, we describe the incremental update algorithm for each level of aggregation as follows.

Level 1: Upon receiving an announcement of prefix p, update-node(p) and re-aggregate(p). Upon receiving a withdrawal of prefix p, de-aggregate(p) and remove p from the RIB.

Level 2: Upon receiving an announcement of prefix p, update-node(p) and re-aggregate(p). Upon receiving withdrawal of prefix p, de-aggregate(p) and remove p. However, if p's nearest ancestor, A, is a generated prefix, we also need to de-aggregate(A) and remove A to prevent extra routable space.

Level 3: Upon receiving an announcement of prefix p, update-node(p) and re-aggregate(p). During the re-aggregation, if any D is a generated prefix and nexthop(D) != nexthop(p), de-aggregate(D) and remove D. This is needed since in Level 3 aggregation, a generated prefix is not supposed to appear as a descendant of any real prefix, otherwise the forwarding correctness may not hold. The processing of withdrawals is the same as in Level 2.

Level 4: The processing of withdrawals is the same as in Level 2. The processing of announcements is mostly the same as in Level 3, except that the de-aggregation will take place even if a node changes from a generated prefix to a real prefix with the same next-hop. In Level 4 aggregation, it is possible that a generated prefix covers another generated prefix. Therefore when a prefix becomes real, its descendants need to be de-aggregated to make sure that there are no generated prefixes underneath. While in Level 3 aggregation, a generated prefix does not cover another generated prefix.

2. Evaluation Using Public Routing Data

We use publicly available routing tables from tens of networks to evaluate the various FIB aggregation algorithms for their table size reduction, computing times, and extra routable space. We also use BGP routing updates to evaluate our incremental update algorithm.

A. Methodology

The publicly available BGP routing tables are taken from route servers (BGP4.net, n.d.) and the route-views.oregon-ix.net monitor of the RouteViews project (Advanced Network Technology Center at University of Oregon, n.d.). Although these routing tables contain valid next AS hops, they either do not have next-hop router information or do not reflect the diversity of next-hops that an operational router typically has, since the route monitors are not operational routers. Therefore we need to generate realistic next-hops based on known information. Our guideline of this process is trying to overestimate the number of next-hops so that the table reduction results reflect the worst-case scenario, and real routers are likely to have better aggregation ratio.

Routing tables downloaded from route servers contain the i-BGP neighbor address for each prefix. Assuming intra-domain routing uses a single best path, prefixes that share the same i-BGP neighbor will share the same next-hop. Thus, we use the i-BGP neighbor as the next-hop in evaluations (see Figure 3 for the relationship between next-hop, i-BGP neighbor and next-AS-hop). This reflects the worst case scenario since prefixes using different i-BGP neighbors may actually use the same next-hop router in reality, which will improve aggregation.

Routing tables downloaded from RouteViews do not even contain i-BGP neighbor addresses – they contain only the AS path for each prefix. In this case, we use the next-AS-hop for each prefix to approximate the next-hop router based on the assumption that prefixes sharing the same next-AS-hop are likely to share the same i-BGP neighbor and thus the same next-hop router. We use tables from route servers to validate this assumption. For each next-AS-hop, if there is only one i-BGP neighbor, then all the prefixes using this next-AS-hop share the i-BGP neighbor. If there are multiple i-BGP neighbors, the one that carries the most prefixes is called "popular," and we expect that most of the prefixes use the popular i-BGP neighbors. In our experiments, more than 90% of the prefixes indeed use the most popular next i-BGP neighbor in all the valid route server tables. Note that approximating next-hop router using next-AS-hop tends to underestimate the effectiveness of aggregation schemes, since large networks have hundreds to thousands of neighbor ASes, but the number of real next-hops should be much smaller. For example, Router A in Figure 3 has two next i-BGP nexthops, but it only has one real next IP hop through which real traffic needs to go. In this case, if we use i-BGP

neighbors as the next hop, then we underestimate the aggregation capability.

We verify the forwarding correctness of each aggregated FIB by looking up every original RIB prefix and its sub prefixes in the FIB, which should give the same next-hop as that in the RIB. All the results from our FIB aggregation algorithms and incremental update algorithms have been verified to satisfy forwarding correctness.

The evaluation has been done on a Linux machine with an Intel Core 2 Quad 2.83GHz CPU. The implementation uses a single thread and the thread is bound to a single core at runtime. The algorithms are implemented in C and no performance optimization techniques have been attempted. The Patricia trie implementation is taken from the C source code of Perl's Net::Patricia module (Net-Patricia Perl Module, n.d.), which in turn was adapted from MRTD's (MRTD, n.d.) source code.

We use the public BGP routing tables to do the evaluation because these tables come from a diverse set of networks, from tier-1 ISPs to small networks. However, in operational networks, there are other types of routes, such as VPN routes, which can be of a large number too. The FIB aggregation algorithms can be applied to these other types of routes as well, even though this paper does not evaluate the effectiveness of doing so. We also obtained forwarding tables from operational routers and validated our results.

Figure 3. Next-hop, i-BGP neighbor, and next-AS-hop

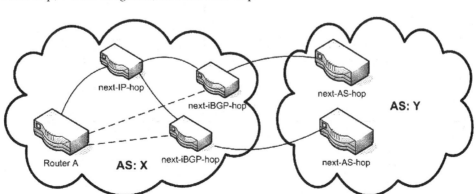

B. Table Size Reduction and Overhead

We apply the four levels of aggregation to 36 routing tables archived at RouteViews on Dec. 31, 2008.

Figure 4(a) shows FIB aggregation ratio, i.e., the ratio of the aggregated FIB size over the original FIB size. The routers are ordered based on aggregation ratio. One can make the following observations:

1. Each level of aggregation can reduce the FIB size more than the previous level, which is expected;
2. Even with the simple Level 1 aggregation, the FIB size can be reduced by 30% to 50%;
3. Level 4 aggregation can reduce the FIB size by 60% to over 90% with the median around 66% – some of the tables have almost all the prefixes sharing the same next-hop, leading to very small aggregated table; and
4. Level 4A is slightly better than Level 4B, although the difference is almost negligible. The results for the tables from the route servers are similar.

To evaluate the effectiveness of FIB aggregation over a longer period of time, we apply it to RouteViews routing tables from 2001 to 2008. For each year, we use all the tables available on Dec. 31, and plot median aggregation ratio in Figure 4(b). The result shows an overall slightly decreasing trend, suggesting that the FIB has become more amenable to aggregation over the years. One possible explanation is that the increasing practice of prefix splitting due to multi-homing and traffic engineering has made a larger percentage of FIB entries aggregatable. We plan to further investigate this phenomenon in our future work.

To understand the significance of the table size reduction results, we plot the size of the routing table from 1994 to 2009 (Figure 5) to translate the size reduction into how many years the clock is turned back for a router. The data is obtained from bgp.potaroo.net, a site that tracks the growth of the BGP table size. This figure shows that the FIB size in Nov. 2000 is around 34% of the FIB size on Dec. 31, 2008, which means that if an ISP uses the Level 4 aggregation algorithm, it will still be able to use routers that were deployed in late 2000, assuming table size is the limiting factor.

Figure 6 shows the computing time for each of the 36 routing tables. The Level 1 to 3 algorithms typically take tens of milliseconds, while the Level 4 algorithms take at most a few hundreds milliseconds. However, an operational router has a different CPU from our commodity Linux ma-

Figure 4. Ratio between aggregated FIB size and routing table size

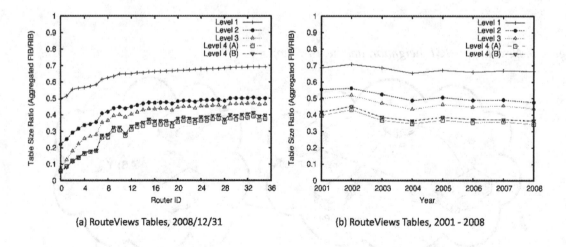

(a) RouteViews Tables, 2008/12/31   (b) RouteViews Tables, 2001 - 2008

chine, and also specialized hardware and software. Thus it is hard to infer a router's computing time from what we report here. Nevertheless, the simplicity of the algorithms and the very short computing time suggest that the computational overhead in an operational router may be small. Moreover, the results can be used to compare the relative speed between different aggregation algorithms. For example, we can observe that Level 4B algorithm is more computationally intensive than the Level 4A algorithm since it traverses the tree one more time.

Note that the full FIB aggregation occurs only when a router initializes its FIB and when the FIB size reaches a given threshold. For subsequent FIB changes, we use *incremental* FIB aggregation, which takes microseconds of CPU time per update (see the following subsection). In addition, FIB aggregation does not affect the routing plane, which exchanges routing messages as normal to propagate routing changes. In summary, FIB aggregation has little impact on routing convergence.

Figure 7 shows the amount of extra routable space measured by the number of equivalent/8

prefixes. Since Level 1 and 2 algorithms do not introduce any extra routable space, they are not included in the figure. To avoid introducing a large amount of extra routable space, we do not aggregate short prefixes. The exact threshold on the prefix length is a tradeoff between aggregation ratio and extra routable space size. We find that the prefix length/15 represents a good trade-off, i.e., aggregating prefixes shorter than/15 will only reduce the table size marginally but will introduce a lot of extra routable space. The result presented in Figure 7 caps the aggregation at/15. Level 3 algorithm introduces less extra routable space than Level 4 algorithms, while Level 4B algorithm has more extra routable space than the Level 4A algorithm. This is mainly because the 4B algorithm aggregates prefixes from top to bottom, which introduces much shorter prefixes than the 4A algorithm.

C. Routing Update Handling

To evaluate the incremental update algorithm, we use one month (December 2008) of BGP updates collected by Route-Views from a peer router at

Figure 5. Historical RIB size

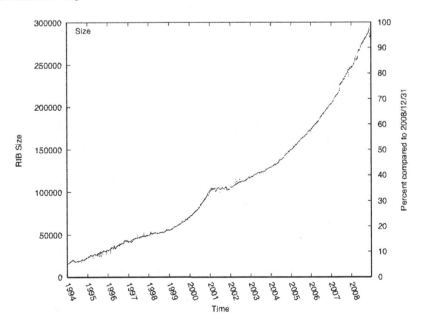

a large ISP (Level 3 Communications). There are totally 7,254,478 routing updates during this month, and we make sure there is no BGP session reset or table transfer in that month.

The processing time is obtained for RIB update and FIB update separately. The results are summarized in Table 1. We make the following observations: (a) the RIB processing time per routing update increases from 0.6µs without aggregation to 0.62µs for Level 1 aggregation (3.3% increase) and 0.64µs for Level 4A aggregation (6.7% increase). The increase is due to the need to update more than one node in the RIB tree, but the small increase suggests that the extra overhead for updating the RIB is minimal; (b) the total FIB processing time (5th column) decreases by 5% (Level 1) to 7% (Level 4A), despite a slight increase in the total number of affected prefix nodes (7th column). This is because each prefix takes less time to update in an aggregated FIB, leading to a lower total FIB processing time. The lower FIB update time per prefix is likely due to the small FIB size after aggregation, which means faster prefix lookup. In summary, FIB aggregation can reduce both the FIB size and FIB update time, with minimal extra RIB processing time.

Among all the updates, 2,914,020 of them cause changes to unaggregated FIB, i.e., an inser-

tion, removal, or a change to the next-hop of a FIB entry. Note that there can be fewer routing updates that cause changes to an aggregated FIB than the unaggregated FIB (see the 4th column of Table 1). For example, the aggregated FIB from Level 4A algorithm has 16,636 fewer updates than the unaggregated FIB. This is due to two reasons. First, some of the route withdrawals are for prefixes already removed from the FIB by the aggregation. Second, the update algorithm minimizes the number of FIB updates at the cost of slightly increased FIB size.

Since the update handling algorithm trades off the FIB size for fewer changes, the FIB needs to be re-aggregated when its size reaches a certain threshold. To estimate how frequently the re-aggregation will be triggered, we measure the growth of the FIB size as our algorithm handles the BGP updates during the month of Dec. 2008 (see Figure 8). The Level 4A aggregated FIB has 104,691 entries on Dec. 1, 2008 (39.2% of the full table size). If the threshold for re-aggregation is set to 150,000 entries (about 55% of the full routing table size), the FIB would be re-aggregated four days later on Dec. 6, 2008. Considering that each full aggregation takes at most a few hundred milliseconds on our commodity PC (perhaps a little longer on a router), incurring this overhead

Figure 6. Computing time (routeviews tables)

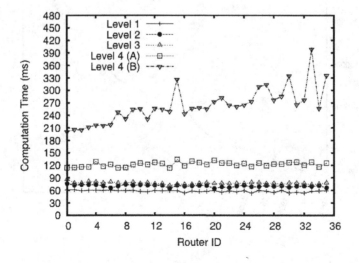

Figure 7. Extra routable address space (routeviews tables)

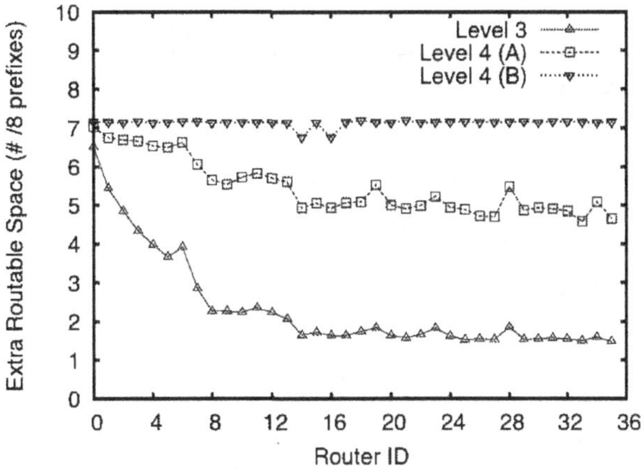

every few days or so should not be a concern for an ISP. Figure 9 confirms that with 150,000 as the threshold re-aggregation indeed happens every few days, for a total number of seven times within this month.

3. Validation Using Tier-1 ISP Data

We obtained three real routing tables located in Washington DC, San Jose, and London from a Tier-1 ISP. Each entry of the tables contains prefix, IP next hop and i-BGP next hop information. In practice, FIB aggregation would be performed using the IP next hop. Our earlier evaluation used the next AS hop, which leads to the same aggregation result as the i-BGP next hop in most cases (except when one i-BGP router connects to multiple ASes, in which case our previous method underestimates the real aggregation ratio). We extracted the FIB interface, IP next hop and i-BGP next hop for each prefix and applied Level 1 to Level 4, and ORTC aggregation to them. We found that ORTC's aggregation ratio is better than the Level 1, Level 2 and Level 3 algorithms, but the Level 4 algorithms are better than ORTC as they relax the requirement of forwarding correctness

Table 1. Processing routing updates in December 2008

Algorithms	Total RIB Proc. Time(s)	Avg. RIB Proc. Time(μs)	Total FIB Updates	Total FIB Proc. Time(s)	Avg. FIB Proc. Time(μs)	Total Affected Prefixes in FIB	No. Prefixes Affected per FIB Update
Un-aggregated FIB	4.37	0.60	2914020	2.58	0.89	2914020	1.000
Level 1 Aggregation	4.47	0.62	2904623	2.45	0.84	2921339	1.006
Level 2 Aggregation	4.51	0.62	2901197	2.44	0.84	2933968	1.011
Level 3 Aggregation	4.64	0.64	2900302	2.42	0.83	2940223	1.014
Level 4A Aggregation	4.67	0.64	2897384	2.40	0.82	2941992	1.015
Level 4B Aggregation	6.41	0.88	2913988	2.61	0.77	3388764	1.162

Figure 8. FIB size after applying Level 4A aggregation algorithm initially and incremental update handling algorithm subsequently

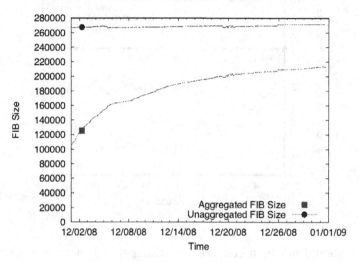

Figure 9. FIB size with periodic re-aggregation

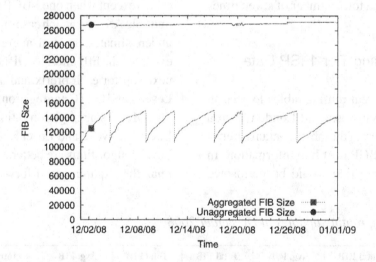

(they maintain weak forwarding correctness while ORTC maintain strong forwarding correctness). We also observed that using the i-BGP next-hop gives us very similar results as using the IP next-hop. In other words, our previous evaluation methodology approximates the real results as shown in Table 2.

We also configured simple virtual aggregation (S-VA) in the forwarding table and obtained the aggregation ratios for i-BGP Next Hops. The aggregation ratios of DC, London and San Jose for S-VA are 78%, 78% and 79%, respectively. We found that it would have better aggregation ratios if we combine S-VA with our Level 1 and Level 2 aggregation algorithms. The aggregation ratios for S-VA combined with Level 1 are 59%, 59% and 60%, better than individual S-VA or Level 1 shown in Table 2. The aggregation ratios for S-VA combined with Level 2 are 44%, 45% and 45%, better than the individual S-VA or Level 2 shown in Table 2.

4. Extra Routable Space: Potential Impact and Control

The difference between weak and strong forwarding correctness is that the former (e.g., Level 3 and 4 aggregations) introduces new prefixes that cover previously non-routable space, therefore some previously non-routable traffic (which would have been dropped by this router) will be forwarded. The impact of extra routable space introduced by weak forwarding correctness depends on how much traffic is destined to that address space. In normal operational conditions, the volume of such traffic should be negligible. However, malicious traffic such as port scanning can have non-routable destinations and in certain cases it may become noticeable. Eventually these packets will be dropped, either because they arrive at a router that does not have a route for these packets, or because the packets' time-to-live expires, but they will consume bandwidth during transit. We have conducted simulation to evaluate these potential problems. More specifically, we evaluate how far a packet with a non-routable destination address can travel if all non-stub ASes deploy Level 4 aggregation and how often loops

form for these data packets. Our evaluation shows that, if deployed with our recommended settings, the Level 4 algorithm results in only a limited number of loops.

We evaluated the Extra Routable Space impact for the Internet traffic in the following steps:

1. **Obtain AS topology map:** In the simulation, we used real AS topology downloaded from UCLA CS website on 01/01/2010 and there are 38,675 ASes in which 6,250 are non-stub ASes.

2. **Compute all shortest paths:** Based on the ASes and their BGP relationships (customer-to-provider, provider-to-customer, peer-to-peer), we calculated the shortest path between any two ASes using the BGP policy. For example, routes from customers will be preferred, the next are from peers and the last are from providers, because sending traffic to customers can generate revenue for the ISP, sending traffic to peers is usually free of cost as long as the traffic type and volume conform to the peering agreement, and sending traffic to providers usually costs money.

3. **Extract AS-level routing tables:** We obtain the AS-level routing tables for all ASes. For example, suppose A B C is a shortest path from A to C via B. Then one entry in the

Table 2. Different aggregation ratios

i-BGP Next Hop	Level 1	Level 2	Level 3	Level 4A	Level 4B	ORTC
DC	0.719228	0.519882	0.476118	0.374610	0.401953	0.433
London	0.721911	0.523878	0.486066	0.402052	0.425912	0.438
San Jose	0.718275	0.520853	0.478093	0.379982	0.407395	0.436
IP Next Hop						
DC	0.686776	0.483562	0.437743	0.328502	0.369141	0.3933
London	0.643844	0.432734	0.379517	0.265814	0.306588	0.3438
San Jose	0.696720	0.494847	0.453795	0.350122	0.390677	0.4073

routing table of A is (C, B), where C is the destination AS and B is the next hop AS for A. This way, we can build the AS-level routing table for A. We apply the same rule to other ASes and obtain all AS-level routing tables.

4. **Obtain prefix-level routing tables:** We also collected the prefixes for each AS according to the origin information in BGP messages on the same day. In other words, one AS can originate multiple prefixes. Then an AS-level routing table can be converted to a prefix-level routing table. For example, suppose AS C originates prefix P1 and P2, then AS A's AS-level routing table entry (C, B) can be converted to two prefix-level routing table entries: (P1, B) and (P2, B), which means any IP addresses falling in prefix range P1 and P2 will use AS B as the next hop. We apply the same rule to other ASes and obtain all prefix-level routing tables.

5. **Apply FIB aggregation algorithms:** We ran Level 2 aggregation on the stub ASes because most of them only have one or two outgoing next hops and thus can be highly aggregated. This Level 2 aggregation will not generate any extra routable space. Then we ran Level 4 aggregation on those non-stub networks.

6. **Find all extra routable space (ERS) prefixes:** After applying Level 4 aggregation on the non-stub networks, the aggregation will generate extra routable space. Through the comparison between an original routing table and an aggregated routing table in a binary tree, we can find out the prefixes that represent extra routable space. We call these prefixes ERS prefixes.

7. **Compute the Next Hop Table for all ERS prefixes after aggregation:** The ERS prefixes may result in extra routable space for multiple aggregated routing tables, so for each ERS prefix, we compute the next hop AS on all ASes based on their aggregated routing tables. We apply the same rule for all ERS prefixes, and obtain a matrix table. The column fields are ERS prefixes and the row fields are next hop ASes. From this table, one prefix can easily start from one AS to find the next hop AS, and then jump to the corresponding next hop AS and find out the next AS. The process will end up with either a destination AS (the next hop AS is itself) or a loop.

8. **Compute the Hop Count Table:** As the previous step described, one prefix can obtain its hop count from a starting AS to a destination AS. If there a loop, then the loop count is infinity and the destination AS is the last visited AS in the loop.

9. **Find out all loops:** We can traverse the Hop Count Table to find out all the prefix-AS pairs that end up in a loop.

From all the aggregated routing tables, we found a total of 260,120 ERS prefixes, of which 24,024 introduce loops among 38,675 ASes. The total number of loops for all the prefixes and ASes in the experiment is 136,641,340. Given there are 10,060,141,000 combinations of ASes and prefixes, our results indicate that only 1.36% of them will have loops due the Level 4 aggregation with weak forwarding correctness. Here, we are assuming that all the non-stub ASes apply Level 4 aggregation technique, the actual percentage of loops will be much less than 1.36% if not all non-stub networks do Level 4 aggregation. Moreover, we are assuming that all the ERS prefixes have traffic destined to them, which should be rare under normal network conditions.

Note that it is possible to limit the size of extra routable space. For example, one can disallow aggregation for prefixes whose lengths are shorter than a threshold. We found that the best tradeoff between table size reduction and extra routable space size is achieved when the aggregation stops at the prefix length of 15. Furthermore, null-routed prefixes can be inserted to remove the extra routable space. In general, network operators can choose the level of aggregation that is the best fit to their networks based on the tradeoff among table size reduction, computation time and extra routable space.

FUTURE RESEARCH DIRECTIONS

We plan to continue our research on FIB aggregation in the following areas. First of all, we plan to apply our aggregation algorithms on more global routing tables and obtain their aggregation ratios. Currently, we use routing tables and updates mainly from the RouteViews project and they are only e-BGP data. We plan to collect real and diverse data including both i-BGP and e-BGP data from ISPs to verify our results. Secondly, we are going to investigate the concerns from router venders about the integration of FIB aggregation to existing router operating systems. For example, most router operating systems recursively resolve next hops of prefixes in the routing tables or forwarding tables; some routing tables (and forwarding tables) utilize multiple paths to forward traffic. Based on these concerns, we need to improve our algorithms to make them more feasible for practical use. Thirdly, we are going to implement them on a software-based router and finally work with router vendors to implement them on real hardware routers to evaluate the memory savings and computational overhead.

CONCLUSION

We have presented an in-depth analysis of FIB aggregation and the results suggest that it is a viable short-term solution to the problem of growing FIB table size. Our aggregation algorithms reduces the FIB size by as much as 70% and requires no hardware changes or network-wide software/configuration changes, thus reducing the need for ISP router upgrades in the short term. During this time, the research community and the industry can design and deploy long-term solutions to reduce

both the routing table and the FIB table. Moreover, FIB aggregation can co-exist with any long-term solution to further reduce ISPs' operational costs.

REFERENCES

Advanced Network Technology Center at University of Oregon. (n.d.). *The routeviews project.* Retrieved from http://www.routeviews.org

Ballani, H., Francis, P., Tuan, C., & Wang, J. (2009). Making routers last longer with ViAggre. In *Proceedings of NSDI.*

BGP4.net. (n.d.). *IPv4 route servers.* Retrieved from http://www.bgp4.net/rs

BGP. (n.d.). *Border gateway protocol.* Retrieved from http://tools.ietf.org/html/rfc4271

Bu, T., Gao, L., & Towsley, D. (2004). On characterizing BGP routing table growth. *Computer Networks*, *45*(1), 45–54. doi:10.1016/j.comnet.2004.02.003.

Cain, B. (2002). *Auto aggregation method for IP prefix/length pairs.* Retrieved from http://www.freepatentsonline.com/6401130.html

Deering, S. (1996). *The map & encap scheme for scalable IPv4 routing with portable site prefixes.* Retrieved from http://arneill-py.sacramento.ca.us/ipv6mh/map-n-encap.pdf

Draves, R., King, C., Venkatachary, S., & Zill, B. D. (1999). Constructing optimal IP routing tables. In Proceedings of IEEE INFOCOM..

Farinacci, D., Fuller, V., Meyer, D., & Lewis, D. (2012). *Locator/ID separation protocol (LISP).* Internet draft. Retrieved from http://tools.ietf.org/html/draft-ietf-lisp-23

Francis, P., Xu, X., Ballani, H., Jen, D., Raszuk, R., & Zhang, L. (2012). *FIB Suppression with virtual aggregation.* Internet Draft. Retrieved from http://tools.ietf.org/html/draft-ietf-grow-va-06

Fuller, V. (2006). Scaling issues with routing+multihoming. In *Proceedings of the Sixty Seventh Internet Engineering Task Force*. Retrieved from http://www.ietf.org/proceedings/67/slides/v6ops-13.pdf

Fuller, V., Li, T., Yu, J., & Varadhan, K. (1993). *Classless inter-domain routing (CIDR): an address assignment and aggregation strategy*. Retrieved from http://www.ietf.org/rfc/rfc1519.txt

Herrin, W. (2008). *Opportunistic topological aggregation in the RIB-FIB calculation?* Retrieved from http://psg.com/lists/rrg/2008/msg01880.html

Herrin, W. (n.d.). *Tunneling route reduction protocol (TRRP)*. Retrieved from http://bill.herrin.us/network/trrp.html

Hinden, R. (1996). New Scheme for Internet Routing and Addressing (ENCAPS) for IPNG. *RFC 1955*. Retrieved from http://www.ietf.org/rfc/rfc1955.txt

IRTF Routing Research Group. (n.d.). *Website*. Retrieved from http://www.irtf.org/charter?gtype=rg&group=rrg

Jen, D., Meisel, M., Massey, D., Wang, L., Zhang, B., & Zhang, L. (2008a). *APT: A practical tunneling architecture for routing scalability*. Technical Report No. 080004. UCLA. Retrieved from http://www.cs.ucla.edu/~meisel/apt-tech.pdf

Jen, D., Meisel, M., Yan, H., Massey, D., Wang, L., Zhang, B., & Zhang, L. (2008b). Towards a future internet routing architecture: Arguments for separating edges from transit core. In *Proceedings of ACM workshop on Hot Topics in Networks*.

Li, L., Alderson, D., Willinger, W., & Doyle, J. (2004). A first-principles approach to understanding the Internet's router-level topology. In *Proceedings of ACM SIGCOMM*.

Li, T. (2009). *Preliminary recommendation for a routing architecture*. Retrieved from http://tools.ietf.org/html/draft-irtf-rrg-recommendation-02

Meyer, D., Zhang, L., & Fall, K. (2007). Report from the IAB workshop on routing and addressing. *RFC 4984*. Retrieved from http://www.ietf.org/rfc/rfc4984.txt

Moy, J. (1998). *OSPF version 2*. Retrieved from http://www.ietf.org/rfc/rfc2328.txt

MRTD. The multi-threaded routing toolkit. (n.d.). *Website*. Retrieved from http://mrt.sourceforge.net/

Net-Patricia Perl Module. (n.d.). *Website*. Retrieved from http://search.cpan.org/dist/Net-Patricia/

Raszuk, R., Heitz, J., Lo, A., Zhang, L., & Xu, X. (2012). *Simple virtual aggregation (S-VA)*. Retrieved from http://tools.ietf.org/html/draft-ietf-grow-simple-va-12

Rekhter, Y., Li, T., & Hares, S. (2006). A border gateway protocol (BGP-4).

Richardson, S. J. (1996). *Vertical aggregation: A strategy for FIB reduction*. Retrieved from http://tools.ietf.org/html/draft-richardson-fib-reduction-00

Whittle, R. (2010). *Ivip (Internet vastly improved plumbing) architecture*. Retrieved from http://tools.ietf.org/html/draft-whittle-ivip-arch-04

Zhao, X., Liu, Y., Wang, L., & Zhang, B. (2010). On the aggregatability of router forwarding tables. In *Proceedings of IEEE INFOCOM* (pp. 848–856). Piscataway, NJ, USA: IEEE Press. doi:10.1109/INFCOM.2010.5462137.

ADDITIONAL READING

Chang, D.-F., Govindan, R., & Heidemann, J. (2002). An empirical study of router response to large BGP routing table load. In *Proceedings of the 2nd ACM SIGCOMM workshop on Internet Measurment* (pp. 203–208). New York, NY, USA: ACM.

Degermark, M., Brodnik, A., Carlsson, S., & Pink, S. (1997). Small forwarding tables for fast routing lookups. In ACM SIGCOMM (pp. 3–14).

Griffin, T., Li, T., Massey, D., Vogt, C., Wang, J., & Zhang, L. (2010). *Scaling the internet routing system: An interim report (Guest Editorial).* IEEE JSAC special issue on network routing scalability. IETF Global Routing Operations (GROW) Working Group. (nd). *Website.* Retrieved from http://datatracker.ietf.org/wg/grow/charter/

Khare, V., Jen, D., Zhao, X., Liu, Y., Massey, D., & Wang, L. et al. (2010). Evolution towards global routing scalability. *IEEE JSAC, 28*(8), 1363–1375.

Li, Q., Wang, D., Xu, M., & Yang, J. (2011). On the scalability of router forwarding tables: Nexthop-selectable FIB aggregation. In Proceedings of IEEE INFOCOM.

Liu, Y., Zhao, X., Nam, K., Wang, L., & Zhang, B. (2010). Incremental forwarding table aggregation. In *Proceedings of IEEE GLOBECOM.*

Meng, X., Xu, Z., Zhang, B., Huston, G., Lu, S., & Zhang, L. (2005). IPv4 Address Allocation and BGP Routing Table Evolution. In ACM SIGCOMM CCR..

Tariq, A., Jawad, S., & Uzmi, Z. A. (2011). TaCo: Semantic equivalence of IP prefix tables. In *Proceedings of ICCCN.*

Uzmi, Z. A., Nebel, M., Tariq, A., Jawad, S., Chen, R., Shaikh, A., et al. (2011). SMALTA: Practical and near-optimal fib aggregation. In *Proceedings of the seventh Conference on Emerging Networking Experiments and Technologies* (pp. 29:1–29:12). New York, NY, USA: ACM.

Vogt, C. (2008). Six/one router: A scalable and backwards compatible solution for provider-independent addressing. In *Proceedings of the 3rd International Workshop on Mobility in the Evolving Internet Architecture* (pp. 13–18). New York, NY, USA: ACM.

Xu, Z., Meng, X., Lu, S., & Zhang, L. (2003). Impact of IPv4 address allocation practice on BGP routing table growth. *IEEE Computer Communication Workshop.*

Zhang, L. (2006). *An overview of multihoming and open issues in GSE.* IETF Journal.

Zhao, X., Pacella, D. J., & Schiller, J. (2010). Routing scalability: An operator's view. *IEEE JSAC, 28*(8), 1262–1270.

KEY TERMS AND DEFINITIONS

Extra Routable Space: The non-routable space introduced by weak forwarding.

FIB: Forwarding Information Base.

FIB Aggregation: Merge multiple FIB entries into one.

FIB Update Handling: Handle updates on the aggregated FIB.

RIB: Routing Information Base.

Strong Forwarding Correctness: The longest-match lookup of any destination address should end up with the same next-hop before and after the aggregation.

Weak Forwarding Correctness: For destination addresses that have non-NULL next-hops before the aggregation, longest-match lookup should end up with the same next-hop after the aggregation.

Chapter 4

APT:
A Practical Tunneling Architecture for Routing Scalability

Dan Jen
Center for Naval Analyses, USA

Michael Meisel
ThousandEyes, USA

Daniel Massey
Colorado State University, USA

Lan Wang
The University of Memphis, USA

Beichuan Zhang
The University of Arizona, USA

Lixia Zhang
University of California, USA

ABSTRACT

The global routing system has seen a rapid increase in table size and routing changes in recent years, mostly driven by the growth of edge networks. This growth reflects two major limitations in the current architecture: (a) the conflict between provider-based addressing and edge networks' need for multihoming, and (b) flat routing's inability to provide isolation from edge dynamics. In order to address these limitations, we propose A Practical Tunneling Architecture (APT), a routing architecture that enables the Internet routing system to scale independently from edge growth. APT partitions the Internet address space in two, one for the transit core and one for edge networks, allowing edge addresses to be removed from the routing table in the transit core. Packets between edge networks are tunneled through the transit core. In order to automatically tunnel the packets, APT provides a mapping service between edge addresses and the addresses of their transit-core attachment points. We conducted an extensive performance evaluation of APT using trace data collected from routers at two major service providers. Our results show that APT can tunnel packets through the transit core by incurring extra delay on up to 0.8% of all packets at the cost of introducing only one or a few new or repurposed devices per AS.

DOI: 10.4018/978-1-4666-4305-5.ch004

INTRODUCTION

The Internet routing scalability problem reflects a fundamental limitation of the current Internet routing architecture: the use of a single, inter-domain routing space for both transit provider networks and edge sites. A natural solution is to separate these two fundamentally different types of networks into different routing spaces. As estimated by Massey et al. (2007), removing edge-site prefixes from the inter-domain routing system could reduce the global routing table size and update frequency by about one order of magnitude.

In addition to improve scalability, this separation can provide other benefits. End hosts will not be able to directly target nodes within the routing infrastructure, and this topology hiding feature will increase the difficulty of DoS (Denial of Service) and other attacks against the Internet core. Edge networks will enjoy benefits such as better traffic engineering and the ability to change providers without renumbering. The idea of separating end customer sites out of inter-domain routing first appeared in Deering (1996) and Hinden (1996), in which the scheme was named "Map & Encap": the source maps the destination address to a provider that serves the destination site, encapsulates the packet, and tunnels it to that provider. This idea started to attract attention from vendors and operators after the recent IAB report (Meyer et al., 2007) and has been actively discussed at the IRTF Routing Research Group (IRTF RRG Working Group, n.d.; Li, 2011). However, the original proposal was only an outline. It did not solve a number of important issues such as how to distribute the mapping information, how to handle failures, how to ensure security, and how to incrementally deploy the system.

In this chapter, we present *APT (A Practical Tunneling architecture)*, a design for a concrete realization of the Map & Encap scheme that addresses all of these above issues. APT uses a hybrid push-pull model to distribute mapping information, a data-driven notification mechanism to handle physical failures between edge sites and their providers, and a lightweight public-key distribution mechanism for cryptographic protection of control messages. APT can be incrementally deployed with little to no new hardware, and incurs extra delay on no more than 0.8% of all packets, according to our trace-driven evaluation.

Note that separating core and edge networks only redefines the scope of inter-domain routing; it does not change any routing protocols. Therefore, other efforts of designing scalable routing protocols, e.g., compact routing (Krioukov et al., 2007) and ROFL (Caesar et al., 2006), are orthogonal and are not affected by the change in architecture.

BACKGROUND

Since APT is a realization of the Map & Encap scheme, we begin with an explanation of how Map & Encap works.

There are two types of networks in the Internet: *transit networks* whose business role is to provide packet transport services for other networks, and *edge networks* that only function as originators or sinks of IP packets. As a rule of thumb, if the network's AS number appears in the middle of any AS path in a BGP (Rekhter et al., 2006) route today, it is considered as a transit network; otherwise it is considered as an edge network. Usually Internet Service Providers (ISPs) are transit networks and end-user sites are edge networks (e.g., corporate networks and university campus networks). The IP addresses used by transit networks are called *transit addresses* and the IP addresses used by edge networks are called *edge addresses*. The corresponding IP prefixes are called *transit prefixes* and *edge prefixes*.

Map & Encap does not change any underlying routing protocols. It changes the *scope* of routing announcing only transit prefixes into the global routing system. In other words, the inter-domain routing protocol for transit networks maintains reachability information only to transit prefixes, resulting in smaller routing tables and fewer routing updates. To deliver packets from one edge network to another, border routers between the edge networks and the core network need to tunnel the packets across the transit core, as illustrated in Figure 1. When a host in *Site1* sends a packet to a host in *Site2*, the packet first reaches *Site1*'s provider, *ISP1*. However, routers in *ISP1* cannot forward the packet directly to *Site2* since their routing tables do not have entries for any edge prefixes. Instead, *ISP1*'s border router, *BR1*, maps the destination address to *BR2*, a border router in *ISP2* that can reach *Site2*. Then the packet is encapsulated by *BR1*, tunneled through the transit core, decapsulated by *BR2* and delivered to *Site2*.

We call a border router that performs encapsulation when tunneling packets an *Ingress Tunnel Router (ITR)*, and one that performs decapsulation an *Egress Tunnel Router (ETR)*. A border router connecting a transit network to an edge network usually serves as both ITR and ETR, and can be referred to as a *Tunnel Router (TR)* in general. Internal ISP routers or routers connecting two ISPs do not need to understand the tunneling mechanism; they function the same way as they do today, only with a smaller routing table.

Related Work

There have been a number of efforts to address the scalability problem of global routing system (Li, 2011). We briefly describe these designs and highlight APT's differences in comparison.

Subramanian et al. proposed HLP (2005) to address the routing scalability problem. HLP divides the Internet routing infrastructure into many trees, each with tier-1 providers as the root. The design goal is to confine local routing instability and faults to each tree. However, as noted by the HLP designers, Internet AS connectivity does not match well to a model of non-overlapping trees. In fact, multihoming practices have been increasing rapidly over time, which stands in direct opposition to HLP's attempt to divide the routing infrastructure into separable trees. In contrast, as demonstrated in the next section (*The APT Protocol*), APT separates the transit core of the routing infrastructure from the edge networks, greatly facilitating edge multihoming.

Figure 1. Separating transit and edge networks

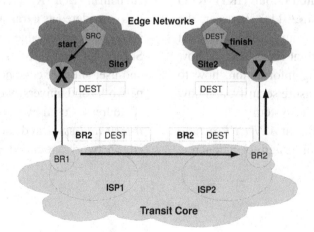

CRIO (Zhang et al., 2006) represents another effort to address routing scalability. In order to reduce the global routing table size, CRIO proposes to aggregate otherwise non-aggregatable edge prefixes into "virtual prefixes." The routers that advertise these virtual prefixes become the proxy tunnel ends for traffic going to the prefixes they aggregate. Thus, some traffic may take a longer path.

On the operational Internet, the inherent conflict between provider-based addressing and site multihoming has long been recognized (Meyer et al., 2007). Two solutions to the problem, Map & Encap and GSE (O'Dell, 1997) were proposed more than ten years ago. Both proposals separate edge networks from the transit core in the routing system. GSE uses the low-order bytes of IPv6 addresses to represent the address space inside edge networks, and the high-order bytes for routing in the transit core. Like Map & Encap, GSE needs a mapping service to bind the two address spaces. They propose storing the mapping information in DNS. This approach avoids the need for a mapping system such as APT, but brings up a number of other issues. Zhang (2006) provides an overview of open issues with GSE, some of which are shared by any routing separation design, e.g., handling border link failures and edge-network traffic engineering, which are addressed in APT.

Since 2007, the IRTF Routing Research Group has been actively exploring the design space for a scalable Internet routing architecture and the working group has recently produced a recommendation (Li, 2011). Among the proposed solutions, a notable one is LISP (Farinacci et al., 2012). LISP defines a service interface between ITR/ETR and mapping resolvers and mapping servers, so that different mapping systems can be implemented without impacting ITR/ETR operations. The mapping system that is under active development is called LISP Alternative Topology (ALT) (Farinacci et al., 2011). Collectively LISP and ALT represent another realization of the Map & Encap scheme, which differs in a number of significant ways from APT. One difference is in mapping information distribution. APT distributes a full mapping table to every transit AS, allowing each AS to decide how many mapping servers to deploy to balance the tradeoff of cost versus performance. ALT keeps the mapping information at the originating edge networks, and builds a global hierarchy of servers to forward mapping requests and replies. Another major difference is the location of TRs: APT prefers provider-edge routers to align cost with benefit as well as facilitate incremental deployment, while LISP prefers TR deployment at customer-edge routers.

Iannone and Bonaventure (2007) reported the results of an evaluation of ITR caching performance in LISP using traffic traces collected between a university campus and its ISP. It demonstrated the effects of cache size, lifetime, and cache miss rate, and the impact on traffic. We also evaluated APT performance using data traces collected from operational networks. While Iannone and Bonaventure (2007) use data from one edge network (which is appropriate for LISP), our evaluation is based on data traces from provider-edge routers that typically serve multiple edge-network customers.

Another approach to reduce routing table size is to use compact routing, i.e., trade longer paths for less routing state. However, a recent study determined that this type of routing cannot handle routing dynamics very well (Krioukov et al., 2007).

THE APT PROTOCOL

Challenges to Realization

There are a number of significant challenges that we must face when designing a practical realization of the Map & Encap scheme. These challenges define a number of tradeoffs that must be kept in careful balance when developing a concrete design.

TR Placement: In order to ensure all traffic is properly tunneled, a TR must be on the path between an edge network and its provider. Thus, we should pick the router at one end of the link connecting an edge network to its provider in the transit core. But the question is which of these two routers is more suitable for becoming a TR. From a technical standpoint, a provider-side router will generally serve many edge-side routers. As a result, there are fewer provider-side routers, but each one handles a greater quantity of traffic. From an economic standpoint, someone has to pay for the new infrastructure, but edge networks and transit networks have different incentives to do so.

Making Mapping Information Available at TRs: Mapping information describes a relationship between a transit network and an edge network, which is not necessarily known by other parties on the Internet. In order to avoid service quality degradation, it is important to minimize potential data loss and delay introduced by the extra step of retrieving this mapping information. Ideally speaking, if all mapping information were to be pushed to all ITRs, delay and loss would be minimal. However, the mapping table size would start with approximately the size of the current default-free zone (DFZ) routing table, and potentially grow quickly by one or two orders of magnitude. On the other hand, not equipping ITRs with the full mapping table would require pulling mapping information from a remote location. This implies a lookup delay, during which packets will incur additional latency and/or loss.

Scalability: Since the main goal of Map & Encap is to solve the routing scalability problem, any realization of the Map & Encap scheme must itself be scalable. Due to the high cost of deployment, any change to the Internet architecture must be designed not to merely postpone the problem, but to counteract it as best we can.

Maintaining Reliability: Today, the Internet often relies on the inter-domain routing protocol to discover failures in connectivity to edge networks. Once edge networks are removed from the transit core's routing tables, this method of discovering edge network failures will no longer be possible. Thus, a Map & Encap scheme must provide a new way to discover these failures if we intend to maintain the reliability of the current network.

Security: Mapping solution can provide new opportunities to improve network security, but can also provide new opportunities for attackers to hijack or redirect traffic. A good design should exploit the former, and provide lightweight methods to prevent the latter.

Incremental Deployment: On the Internet, one simply cannot set a flag day when all sites will switch to a new design, no matter how great an advantage the design offers. As a result, any design must explicitly assume incremental deployment. We must offer backwards compatibility for sites that are slow to adopt APT and also offer incentives for sites to adopt it.

Design Principles

We intend for APT to be a practical, deployable design for the real-world Internet. To ensure that our design meets this goal, we adhere to the following design principles.

- *Do no harm* to Internet services or service quality. Improve scalability while causing as little disruption as possible to current Internet services.
- *Align cost with benefit* by ensuring that no one is paying so that someone else can profit. We must acknowledge that the Internet infrastructure is owned and managed by a number of independent entities that operate on a for-profit model.
- *Allow flexibility* for operators to make tradeoffs between performance and resources. Different administrative domains that make up the Internet will want to make such tradeoffs in different ways, and will only deploy a new system if it is flexible enough to allow this.

How APT Works

APT places TRs at the provider-side of the link between edge networks and their providers (see Figure 2). There are two main reasons for this, derived from our design principles. First, since Map & Encap is intended to solve the routing scalability problem and release the pressure on ISP routers, it is natural that ISPs should pay the cost. This is one way in which APT aligns cost with benefit. Second, a tunnel has two ends, the ITR and the ETR. A solution should allow, but not require, both ends to be placed in the same administrative domain, such as within the network of a single ISP. This allows unilateral deployment of APT by a single ISP. Had we chosen to place TRs at the customer-side, no single edge network would be able to benefit from unilateral deployment.

To distribute mapping information, APT uses a hybrid push-pull model. All mapping information is pushed to all transit networks. However, within each transit network, only a small number of new devices called *default mappers (DMs)* store the full mapping table. ITRs store only a small cache of recently used mappings. When an ITR receives a data packet, it looks for an appropriate mapping in its cache. If such a mapping is present, it can encapsulate the packet and forward it directly to an appropriate ETR. Otherwise, it forwards the packet to a DM (the xTR is configured with the anycast address of the local DMs). The DM treats the packet as an implicit request for mapping information. In response, it sends an appropriate mapping to the requesting ITR, which stores the mapping in its cache. Meanwhile, the DM encapsulates and forwards the packet on behalf of the ITR. This process is illustrated in Figure 2.

Default mappers and tunnel routers have very different functionality. DMs are designed to manage the large mapping table, but only need to forward a relatively small amount of data traffic. This is because tunnel routers cache recent mapping results and DMs only need to handle cache misses. TRs have small routing tables, but need to forward very large volumes of traffic. This distinction will become even more prominent in the future as the Internet grows larger to include more edge networks and the traffic volume continues to increase. Since DMs and TRs are likely to be implemented in separate devices, both their

Figure 2. Example topology for data forwarding

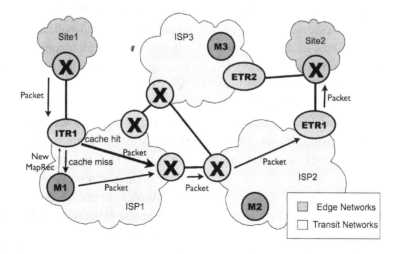

hardware and software can be engineered for their specific purposes and both can scale appropriately for their specific tasks.

The association between an edge and a transit network may change due to either provider changes or border link failures. Provider changes occur when an edge network switches providers – an event that occurs in human time scale, likely measured in weeks or months. Physical failures of the links between transit and edge networks, however, can occur more frequently. In APT, only infrequent provider changes will trigger updates to the mapping table and be propagated to all transit networks. APT does not update the mapping table due to physical failures. Rather, APT takes a data-driven approach to edge-network unreachability notification. APT only informs certain senders of the failure, i.e., only those senders that are attempting to communicate with an unreachable edge network will receive the failure notification. This greatly reduces the scale of the physical failure's impacts.

Thanks for not storing the entire mapping table at every ITR, APT requires drastically less storage than a pure push model. By using data-driven local queries, APT mitigates the delay and prevents the loss associated with a pure pull model. By propagating the mapping table to all transit networks, APT allows individual networks the flexibility to manage their own mapping systems. A transit network can install more DMs to increase robustness and decrease latency, or fewer DMs to decrease the cost of deployment. By using data-driven failure notifications, APT notifies senders of edge-network unreachability while still eliminating the traffic caused by current edge-network routing updates. All of these design decisions honor our principles of doing no harm, aligning cost with benefit, and allowing for flexibility.

Default Mappers

In APT, a default mapper, or DM, performs the following functions:

- Maintaining the full mapping table. More specifically, it authenticates new mapping entries before accepting them, and removes entries that have exceeded their Lifetime value (see "Mapping Distribution Protocol").
- Propagating mapping information to other DMs in neighboring ASes. DMs in different networks peer to form a DM overlay network via which mapping information is propagated throughout the entire transit core.
- Providing local ITRs with mapping information as needed. DMs provide a central management point for local traffic engineering policies. When an ITR requests mapping information, a DM can direct traffic by deciding which ETR address to provide in response.
- Forwarding packets in the event of an ITR cache miss.
- Handling transient failures without updating the mapping table. When long-term changes such as provider changes happen, mapping table entries are updated by the originating network's operator. Routing churns, on the other hand, will not cause changes in the mapping table.

Although APT can work with just one DM in each transit AS, an AS may install multiple DMs for high robustness and load balancing, with each DM maintaining the full mapping table. To efficiently manage and communicate with multiple DMs, an AS configures an internal multicast group, *DMall*, and an internal anycast group, *DMany*. Packets sent to *DMall* will be forwarded to all of the DMs in the same AS, and any router in the AS can reach the nearest DM by sending packets to *DMany*. Thus, adding or removing DMs is transparent to other routers in the same AS.

Note that *DMany* (*DMall*) is an anycast (multicast) group local to a single AS. To prevent potential abuse, *DMany* and *DMall* are configured for internal use only. Any packet coming from outside of the AS destined to *DMany* or *DMall* will be dropped at the AS border. In the case that anycast is useful for external communication, a separate address, *DMany_ext* is set up for external use. There is no multicast group for external use. If some external information needs to reach all DMs in an AS, it is always sent to one specific DM or to *DMany_ext* for authentication and verification before being sent to *DMall*.

Mapping Information

The mapping information in APT associates each edge prefix with one or more transit addresses, each belonging to an ETR in an ISP that serves the particular edge network. The ETR must have a direct connection to the edge network owning the prefix. For example, if a university owns the address prefix a.b/16 and has two Internet service providers ISP1 and ISP2, then a.b/16 will be mapped to the ETRs in ISP1 and ISP2 that directly connect to the university network.

To support traffic engineering, APT associates two values with each ETR address: a priority and a weight. When an ITR looks up the mapping information for an edge prefix, the ETR with the highest priority is picked. When multiple addresses have the same priority, they will be used in proportion to their weight. If an edge network wants to have one provider as a primary entry point for its incoming traffic and another as a backup, it can simply assign a lower priority to the address(es) of the ETR(s) at its backup provider. If the network wants to load balance its incoming traffic between multiple providers, it can assign the same priority to multiple ETRs and use appropriate weights to split the traffic.

Mapping information for an edge prefix is generated in the following way. First, the edge network owning the prefix sends priorities and weights to each of its providers. Next, a default mapper in each provider announces a *MapSet* containing the edge prefix, its own ETR addresses for that prefix, and the edge network's priorities and weights.

Formally speaking, for an edge prefix p and its provider network N, MapSet$(p, N) = \{(d,w) \mid$ d is an ETR address in N and d is directly connected to p, and w is the priority and weight information for d $\}$. Note that one edge prefix may be mapped to multiple ETRs in the same provider network. If p is multihomed to m providers to m providers $N_1, N_2, ..., N_m$, MapSet$(p) = \cup_{i=1}^{m}$ MapSet(p, N_i). To distinguish MapSet(p,N) from MapSet(p), we call the former a *Provider-Specific MapSet* and the latter a *Complete MapSet*, or simply a *MapSet*. Furthermore, we use the term *MapRec* to refer to the mapping from an edge prefix to any *single* ETR address.

Data Forwarding

Recall that an edge prefix's MapSet can contain many ETR addresses. When tunneling a packet to such a prefix, one of these ETR addresses must be selected as the tunnel egress. In order to keep TRs as simple as possible, we place all ETR selection logic in default mappers, including enforcement of the MapSet's priorities and weights. This allows ITRs to avoid any decision-making when forwarding high volumes of data and allows centralization of policy decisions.

To enable this, APT ITR caches contain only MapRecs. MapRecs contain mappings from an edge prefix to a *single* ETR address. When an ITR receives a packet from an edge network, it first tries to find a MapRec matching the destination address in its cache[1]. If the lookup is successful, the packet is tunneled from the ITR to the ETR address contained in the MapRec, just like in Figure 1. When the ITR has a cache miss, it tunnels the packet to *DMany*, the anycast address of the local DMs.

ITRs also maintain a *cache idle timer (CIT)* for each MapRec in their cache. The CIT for a MapRec is reset whenever the MapRec is accessed. Once a MapRec has been idle for an amount of time greater than the CIT value, the MapRec is flushed from the ITR's cache. The CIT is important for the performance of APT under edge-network reachability failures (see "Failure Detection and Recovery").

Upon receiving a tunneled packet from a local ITR, a DM first performs a longest-prefix match in its mapping table to find the MapSet for the destination address. It then selects one ETR address from the MapSet based on the priority, the weight value, and local policy. The DM then creates a MapRec and sends it to the ITR who sent the data packet. Other than the edge prefix and selected ETR address, the MapRec contains a CIT value assigned by the DM. Finally, the DM tunnels the packet to the selected ETR address, with the tunnel source address set to the original ITR.

Until the ITR receives the DM's response, it will continue to forward packets with the same destination prefix to the DM. The DM will continue to forward these packets, but will suppress duplicate control messages to the ITR using a *Deaf Timer* for the (ITR, edge prefix) pair. It will retransmit the MapRec only when the timer expires.

To illustrate the above process, Figure 2 shows a simple topology, where *Site1* and *Site2* are two edge networks, each owning edge prefix P_1 and P_2, respectively. *ISP1*, *ISP2* and *ISP3* are transit networks. A node in *Site1* sends a packet to a node in *Site2*. When this packet arrives at *ITR1*, it looks up the destination address d in its MapRec cache. There is no matching prefix, so *ITR1* sends the packet to a default mapper (*M1* in this case) by encapsulating the packet with *DMany (ISP1)* as the destination address. When this packet arrives at *M1*, it decapsulates the packet and performs a longest-prefix match in its mapping table using the destination address d. Since d matches the prefix P_2, it will find the MapSet for P_2 containing *ETR1* and *ETR2*. *M1* selects *ETR1* based on the priority value, responds to *ITR1* with a MapRec that maps P_2 to *ETR1*, and then encapsulates the packet with *ETR1* as the destination address and sends it out.

Failure Detection and Recovery

In today's Internet, edge networks achieve higher reliability through multihoming. When connectivity to one provider fails, packets can be routed through other providers. Today, when such a connectivity failure occurs, this information is pushed into the global routing table via BGP. In APT, edge network connectivity is reflected in a mapping table that does not adjust to physical failures. Thus, an ITR may attempt to tunnel packets to an ETR that has failed or has lost connectivity to the edge network. APT must be able to detect such failures and route the affected traffic through an alternate ETR. Generally speaking, there are three types of failures that APT must handle:

1. The transit prefix that contains the ETR has become unreachable.
2. The ETR itself has become unreachable.
3. The ETR cannot deliver packets to the edge network. This can be due to a failure of the link to its neighboring device in the edge network, or a failure of the neighboring device itself.

Handling Transit Prefix Failures: An ITR will not necessarily be able to route traffic to all transit prefixes at all times. If an ITR attempts to tunnel a packet to an ETR in a transit prefix that it cannot currently reach, it treats this situation much like a cache miss and forwards the packet to a local default mapper. In Figure 3, *ITR1* has no route to *ETR1*, so it will forward the packet to its default mapper, *M1*. In its forwarding table, *M1* will also see that it has no route to *ETR1*, and thus select the next-most-preferred ETR for *Site2*, *ETR2*. Then *M1* tunnels the packet to *ETR2* and replies to *ITR1* with the corresponding MapRec. *M1* can assign a relatively short CIT to the MapRec in its response. Once this CIT expires, *ITR1* will forward the next packet destined for *Site2* to a default mapper, which will respond with the most-preferred

MapRec that is routable at that time. This allows *ITR1* to quickly revert to using *ETR1* once *ETR1* becomes reachable again.

Handling ETR Failures: When an ETR fails, packets heading to that ETR are redirected to a local DM in the ETR's transit network. This redirection is achieved through the intra-domain routing protocol (IGP); each DM in a transit network announces a high-cost link to all of the ETRs it serves. When an ETR fails, the normal IGP path to the ETR will no longer be valid, causing packets addressed to the ETR to be forwarded to a DM. The DM will attempt to find an alternate ETR for the destination prefix using its mapping table and tunnel the packet to that ETR.[2] The DM also sends an *ETR Unreachable Message* to the ITR's DM, informing the ITR's DM that the failed ETR is temporarily unusable. How the ETR's DM determines the ITR's DM address will be discussed in the following section.

To avoid sending the address of an unreachable ETR to any subsequently requesting ITRs, default mappers also store a *Time Before Retry (TBR)* timer for each ETR address in a MapSet. Normally, the TBR timer for each ETR is set to zero, indicating that it is usable. When an ETR becomes unreachable due to a failure, its TBR timer is set to a non-zero value. The DM will not send this ETR address to any ITR until the TBR timer expires. We will refer to the action of setting a MapRec's TBR to a non-zero value as "invalidating a MapRec."

In Figure 4, traffic entering *ISP2* destined for *ETR1* should be directed to *M2*, the default mapper in *ISP2*, according to *ISP2*'s IGP. When *M2* receives such a data packet, *M2* will tunnel the packet to *ETR2*, and notify *M1*, the default mapper in *ISP1*, of *ETR1*'s failure by sending an ETR Unreachable Message to *DMany_ext(Site1)*, the external anycast address for *ISP1*'s DMs (obtained via the Mapping Distribution Protocol). M1 can then send a new MapRec containing ETR2 to ITR1. Similar to the previous case, the CIT for this MapRec will be relatively short.

Handling Edge Network Reachability Failures: The final case involves a failure of the link connecting an ETR to its neighbor in an edge network or the failure of the neighbor itself. This case is handled similarly to the previous case, except that the message sent to the ITR's default mapper will be of a different type, *Edge Network Unreachable*. In Figure 5, when *ETR1* discovers it cannot reach *Site2*, it will send packets destined for *Site2* to its DM, *M2*, setting the *Redirect Flag* when encap-

Figure 3. An example of a transit prefix failure

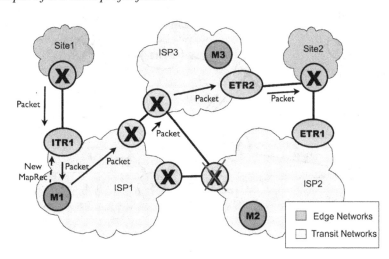

Figure 4. An example of a single ETR failure

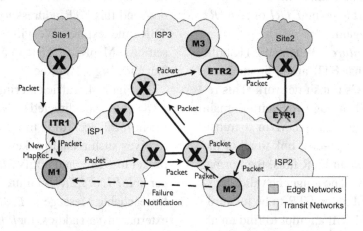

sulating the packet. The Redirect Flag signals to *M2* that the packet could not be delivered and should be re-routed. *M2* will redirect the packet to *ETR2* and then send an Edge Network Unreachable Message to *M1*.

Mapping Distribution Protocol

Making mapping information available to ITRs is one of the most important challenges in realizing a Map & Encap scheme. APT adopts a hybrid push-pull approach: it pushes the mapping information to DMs in all transit networks, but lets ITRs pull the mapping information from DMs.

DM Mesh: In APT, mapping information is distributed via a mesh of overlay connections between DMs. These overlay connections are configured manually based on contractual agreement, just as how links are set up in BGP. Two neighboring APT ASes should establish at least one DM-DM connection between them. They can also choose to have multiple DM-DM connections for reli-

Figure 5. An example of a failure of the link connecting an ETR to its edge network

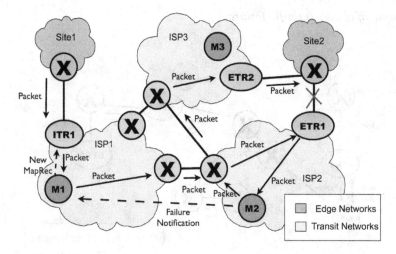

ability. An AS can configure one or multiple DMs to connect to external DMs, but it is not required that all of its DMs have external connections. The DMs that have external connections will forward incoming mapping information to their local *DMall* group, from which DMs without external connections will learn the mapping information.

Having the DM Mesh congruent to the AS topology facilitates incremental deployment and aligns maintenance and setup cost with benefit. Mapping information is just a small amount of additional data transmitted between two neighboring ASes that already have a contractual agreement for exchanging traffic. Since mapping exchange is bi-directional, it should benefit both parties equally. This means that both parties have incentives to maintain the connection well and fix any problems quickly.

The Dissemination Protocol: DMs exchange MDP messages using an OSPF-style flooding protocol, without the topology and path computation parts of OSPF. An MDP message has a header and a payload. Different payload types are supported. For mapping dissemination, the payload is provider-specific MapSets and the provider's *DMany_ext* address. For security purposes, MDP is also used to propagate public keys and prefix lists for provider networks, which will be discussed below.

A DM originates MDP messages to push its own provider-specific MapSets to other provider networks. For instance, a customer network with prefix p is dual-homed through providers X and Y. Provider X's DM(s) would generate an MDP message containing *MapSet(p,X)* and *DMany_ext(X)* and send this message to its neighboring DMs. After this message propagates throughout the transit core, DMs in other networks will know the addresses of the ETRs in X's network via which prefix p can be reached. In case they need to send feedback information to X, they will use the address *DMany_ext(X)* to reach X's DMs. Similarly,

provider Y will announce *MapSet(p,Y)* and its own *DMany_ext(Y)*. After receiving the provider-specific MapSets *MapSet(p,X)* and *MapSet(p,Y)*, DMs combine them to get the complete MapSet for prefix p, including ETRs from both networks X and Y. Putting all MapSets together, a DM gets the complete mapping table to reach all edge prefixes.

The header of an MDP message contains control information necessary for efficient data dissemination. It includes (1) the AS number of the originator of the message, (2) a sequence number, and (3) a Lifetime. The combination of the AS number and the sequence number uniquely identifies a message. It is used by a receiver to determine whether an incoming message is new. The Lifetime is used to make sure an outdated message will expire at certain time.

When a DM receives an MDP message from a neighboring DM, it will check whether this is a new message and make sure that the message has a Lifetime greater than one. Outdated, expired, or duplicate messages will be dropped. Accepted messages will be forwarded to all neighboring DMs except the one from which the message was received. Message transmission is acknowledged at every hop. The sending DM will retransmit the message if there is no acknowledgment from the receiving DM within certain time. The Lifetime of a received Mapset is decremented as time goes by. Eventually, a MapSet will expire. It is the originating DM's responsibility to periodically re-generate its MDP messages to refresh other DMs. A DM can also explicitly withdraw its previous announcements by sending out a withdrawal message onto the DM mesh.

Since customer-provider relationships are usually stable for at least a month due to contractual obligations, the message Lifetime and the refresh frequency can be set to the scale of days or weeks, which mean the volume of MDP traffic should be easily manageable. Other techniques in OSPF are also incorporated to help efficient dissemination.

For instance, every time a DM reboots, it will synchronize its mapping table with its neighbor DMs to learn the most recent MapSets and sequence numbers.

Cryptographic Protection

While our design makes the global routing system more scalable and more flexible, we also need to make sure its security is not compromised. In answering this challenge, we intend to make APT as secure as the current Internet at least, making improving where practical.

APT adds new control messages that attackers could forge to manipulate packet forwarding. This constitutes a major security threat. For instance, a forged failover notification message could prevent ITRs from using certain ETRs, and a forged MapRec or MapSet could divert large quantities of traffic to arbitrary ETRs.

In APT, we add cryptographic protection to all control messages. We assume that every transit network has its own public-private key pair and signs all APT control messages that it generates. Receivers verify the signature before accepting a message. As in many other large scale systems, the main challenge in enabling cryptographic protection is how to distribute public keys in the first place. APT does not rely on a Public Key Infrastructure (PKI) for key distribution, since a PKI would require a significant amount of effort and coordination among all transit networks. The slow progress or lack of progress in deploying PKI-based solutions in the Internet (e.g., DNS-SEC (Arends et al., 2005) and SBGP (Kent et al., 2000)) suggests the need for an alternative that does not require a rigid delegation infrastructure.

Key Distribution: APT employs the DM Mesh to propagate every transit network's public key to all other networks in the transit core. To prevent attackers from forging someone else's public key, we require that every network have its neighbors verify and sign its key. For instance, if *X* has two neighbors, *Y* and *Z*, then *X* should have both neighbors verify *X*'s public key and sign it. *X* will announce its key together with *Y* and *Z*'s signatures through the DM Mesh. Similarly, *X* will also vouch for *Y* and *Z*'s public keys.

Once every network announces its own key together with its neighbors' signatures, this information forms a web of trust, which a receiver can use to determine whether to trust a public key. For instance, assume *X* already trusts the public keys of networks *Z* and *R*. If *X* receives a message carrying *W*'s public key and signatures from *Z* and *R*, then *X* can verify these signatures. If the two signatures indeed belong to *Z* and *R*, respectively, *X* will trust this message, record *W*'s public key, and forward the message to its peers. Each network can configure its threshold for trusting a key, as long as this threshold is greater than one. Later, *X* can also use *W*'s signature to verify other messages. If an attacker announces a false public key for *W*, he will not be able to forge the signatures of *Z* and *R*. In this case, *X* will discard the attacker's forged key.

Neighbor signatures are done when two neighbor ASes configure their DM connections. They verify the keys and signatures offline. Keys have a finite time-to-live after which they will expire. Keys can be replaced or revoked via a Rollover message or a Withdrawal message, respectively. These messages are signed by the old keys as well as the new keys if there are any. ASes should periodically rollover their keys, obtaining signatures from their neighbors for the new keys.

Attack Detection: Recall that APT adds cryptographic protection to all control messages. If private keys are compromised or networks misbehave, they can pose security threats that signatures cannot prevent. For instance, a misbehaving network, due to either operational errors or malicious acts, may inject mapping information for prefixes belonging to other networks, effectively hijacking other's traffic. This problem exists in the current Internet. In APT, we take advantage of the DM mesh and the flooding protocol to quickly detect such incidents, which is a significant improvement over the current Internet.

In APT, edge networks do not participate in the mapping dissemination process. However, they can still check the correctness of their mapping information by setting up an MDP monitoring session with their providers.[3] MDP ensures that a message will reach every provider network without changes. If there is an announcement of a false mapping for some edge prefix, the transit network(s) legitimately associated with that edge prefix will receive the message. Yet, since each provider only announces its own provider-specific MapSet, it cannot know whether another provider-specific MapSet for the same edge prefix is legitimate. A rogue network announcing a forged provider-specific MapSet for the same edge prefix would go undetected. Thus, the burden of detecting false announcements falls on edge networks. If the edge network is monitoring MDP messages, it can quickly detect the false announcement and take action. If the edge network is not monitoring MDP messages, the situation is no worse than it is today. In the current Internet, edge prefixes are announced in BGP. BGP is a path-vector routing protocol, which does not propagate every announcement everywhere. If a prefix is hijacked, the real owner of the prefix may not receive the false announcement, and the attack will go undetected.

A serious attack that a rogue network can launch is to map a large number of edge prefixes to a single ETR. This would redirect a large amount of traffic to that ETR, effectively constituting a distributed denial-of-service (DDoS) attack. To prevent this, DMs sign and announce the list of their own transit prefixes in MDP, propagating the message to every transit network. Receivers can verify the signature and record the list of transit prefixes. To understand how this prevents the aforementioned type of DDoS attack, assume X announces the transit prefix containing ETR e, which is verified and accepted by all other transit networks. If rogue AS Z attempts to map edge prefixes $a/8$ and $b/8$ to e, other transit networks can detect that Z does not own the transit prefix containing e, and will reject the false mapping information.

If Z tries to defeat this scheme by signing and announcing one of X's prefixes in MDP, it will be quickly detected by X. Other networks will detect this conflict as well. They can use past history to help decide which announcement to trust before the problem is resolved. If a network has trusted X's announcement for a long time in the past, it can continue to trust X until the conflict is resolved, likely due to actions X will take.

Evaluation

In this section, we present an evaluation of APT's feasibility using real traffic traces. Whether APT is feasible depends on its data delivery performance and hardware requirements, which in turn are affected by traffic characteristics, since APT uses a data-driven approach to pull mapping information from DMs. We therefore used data-driven simulation to evaluate the packet delay introduced by caching at ITRs, the cache size at ITRs, and the amount of data traffic redirected to DMs. Below, we first describe our simulator and data sources, and then present our results.

The TR Cache Simulator: The cache hit rate at ITRs is critical to overall APT performance. A high hit rate will ensure that few packets will experience redirection delay and each default mapper can serve multiple TRs without being overburdened. To evaluate the TR cache hit rate, and therefore the load placed on default mappers, we simulated TR caching using traces from real provider-edge (PE) routers. We used a number of different cache and network parameters to determine their effect on the cache hit rate.

Our cache simulator examines destination address d of each packet in a traffic trace and attempts to perform a longest-prefix-match lookup of *d* in its prefix cache, *C*. If a match is found, this is counted as a cache hit. If no match is found, this is counted as a cache miss and a new cache entry is added for *d* after a certain delay. The delay is a configurable parameter used to emulate the round-trip time between the ITR and a DM. The prefix used for the new cache entry is determined by a real BGP routing table. This is feasible only when the address *d* is not anonymized. Otherwise, the simulator uses *d*/24 as the prefix. Note that we are underestimating our cache performance in the latter case, as most prefixes in the BGP routing table are shorter than/24. In reality, we could use a smaller cache and have a lower miss rate.

A maximum cache size *m* can also be specified. If there is a cache miss when *C* already contains *m* entries, the least-recently used prefix is removed from *C* before the new cache entry is added. Prefixes can optionally be removed from *C* once they have remained inactive for a specified interval of time, or cache inactivity timeout (CIT).

Data Sources: We ran the simulator on packet-level traces from two real PE routers.

FRG: This trace was collected at the FrontRange Gigapop in Colorado. It consists of all traffic outbound to a tier-1 ISP during the period 09:00 to 21:00, Mountain Standard Time, on November 7, 2007. In our analysis, we used a list of actual prefixes retrieved from the RIBs at RouteViews Oregon, also on November 7, 2007. When using a limited-size cache with this data set, the maximum size was 4,096 entries, less

than ten percent of the total number of prefixes seen in the trace (52,502).

CERNET: This trace was collected at Tsinghua University in Beijing, China. It consists of all traffic outbound from the university through a particular PE router into the CERNET backbone from 09:00 to 21:00, China Standard Time, on January 23, 2008. This data was anonymized using a prefix-preserving method before analysis, so, though addresses remain in the same prefix after anonymization, they cannot be mapped to a real BGP prefix list. Instead, every prefix is assumed to be a/24. This provides us with a worst-case estimate, assuming/24 continues to be the longest prefix length allowed in the network. Since this results in a significantly larger number of total prefixes in the trace (985,757), we used a larger maximum when simulating a limited cache size: 65,536.

Results: In our simulations, we used four different combinations of cache size and CIT value. The cache size was either unlimited or an order of magnitude smaller than the total number of prefixes seen in the trace. The CIT value was either infinity or 30 minutes. During each run, the simulator emulated four different latencies for retrieving mapping information from a default mapper: zero (an instantaneous cache add), 10ms, 30ms, and 50ms. We selected 50ms as our worst-case delay based on (AT&T) and (Keynote Systems), which show that a single, carefully placed default mapper in the network of most tier-1 ISPs in the United

Table 1. Cumulative cache miss rates for both data sets with three different cache types and best- and worst-case default-mapper latencies.

Data Source	% Miss Rate					
FRG	0.001	0.002	0.004	0.005	0.537	0.687
CERNET	0.054	0.059	0.198	0.207	0.756	0.810
Delay (ms)	0	50	0	50	0	50
Type	Optimal		With CIT		With Limit	

States would be reachable from any hypothetical TR in that network within approximately 50ms.

Table 1 shows cumulative cache miss rates. "Optimal" refers to a cache with unlimited size and an infinite CIT. "With CIT" refers to a cache with unlimited size and a CIT of 30 minutes. "With Limit" refers to a cache with limited size and a CIT of infinity or 30 minutes – the results are the same regardless of the CIT value. This suggests that entries are replaced before their CIT timer expires. Only the best and worst case delays (zero and 50 ms) are shown.

We can make the following two observations. First, the miss rate is well below 1% in all cases. In other words, less than 1% of the traffic was redirected to the local DM. The worst case miss rate is 0.810% for the CERNET data set with a fixed cache-size limit and 50ms delay to receive new mappings. As stated above, we predicted this data set to be a worst case based on our use of /24 prefixes for all addresses.

Second, a 50 ms delay in adding new cache entries had a mostly negligible effect on the miss rate, compared with no delay. One explanation is that the inter-packet delay for initial packets to the same destination prefix is longer than 50 ms most of the time. This is plausible considering that initial packets are usually for TCP connection setup or DNS lookup, which takes one round-trip time before the next packet is sent.

These results suggests that moving the mapping table from the ITRs to a local DM has negligible impact on overall performance, providing strong support for our design decisions.

Figure 6 shows cache sizes in number of entries and Figure 7 shows the number of packets that would be forwarded to a default mapper per minute, both for the FRG data set. We omit the figures for CERNET, as they are similar to those for FRG.

Two things are apparent from these results. First of all, latency between TR and default mapper has a minimal or, in most cases, undetectable effect on the default mapper load. This is consistent with our earlier results on cache miss rate.

Second of all, the packet-forwarding burden placed on default mappers is quite manageable. Even a TR at a high-traffic, provider-edge router would place a load on the default mapper of less than 1,000 packets per minute in the normal case with a cache size above 30,000 entries. In a more extreme case where such a TR had only a 4,096-entry capacity, the load placed on the default mapper would still be under 50,000 packets per

Figure 6. ITR cache size (FRG). The first data point was sampled two minutes into the trace.

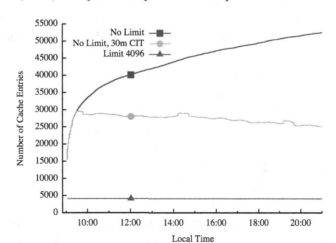

Figure 7. Default mapper load (FRG). The first data point was sampled two minutes into the trace.

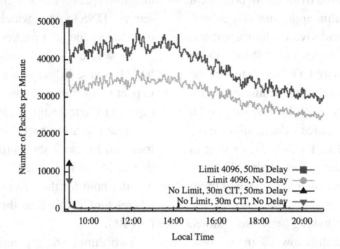

minute. Using this data, we can make a conservative estimate of the number of TRs that a single default mapper can support. Assuming the worst case from our simulations of 50,000 redirected packets per minute per TR, even a default mapper running on commodity 2001 PC hardware would have enough forwarding capability to support hundreds of TRs (Morris et al., 1999).

Incremental Deployment

On the Internet, one simply cannot set a flag day when all sites will switch to a new design, no matter how great an advantage the design offers. As a result, APT explicitly assumes incremental deployment. Our design offers incentives for sites that adopt APT. An APT-capable ISP will be able to reduce the routing table size in its internal routers. Moreover, our design allows backwards compatibility for sites that are slow to adopt APT by converting mapping information in APT networks to BGP routes that can be used by legacy networks.

Before we delve into the details, we define the following terms. If a transit AS has adopted APT, it is called an *APT AS*. Otherwise, it is called a *non-APT AS*. A topologically connected set of APT ASes form an *APT island*. Note that

our design allows individual ISPs to deploy APT unilaterally, without any coordination with other ASes. Such an ISP would simply form a new APT island. Unconnected APT islands do not exchange mapping information with each other.

Edge Networks: APT offers various incentives for edge networks to use APT providers. The Map N Encap solution allows all edge networks to use provider-independent addressing, which eliminates forced renumbering due to provider change, and also eases multihoming. In addition, APT mappings are a powerful tool for traffic engineering. Currently, an edge network may use AS-path padding or address de-aggregation for load balancing. However, these techniques provide only rudimentary control over which route is selected by a traffic source. In APT, an edge network can clearly specify traffic preferences among all of its APT providers. This explicit approach to managing inbound traffic greatly simplifies existing practices and achieves more effective results.

These benefits come at minimal to no cost for edge networks. Because the APT design focuses on placing new functionality in transit networks, all changes go virtually unnoticed by edge networks. The only new task for an edge network is to provide traffic preference information to its providers. If necessary, a transit provider can generate this traffic engineering information on behalf of its edge-network customers, and APT can be incrementally deployed *without any changes* to edge networks.

Transit Networks: All transit ASes will continue to use BGP to reach transit prefixes, even if all of them adopt APT. Edge prefixes are handled differently. APT islands configure their border routers as TRs so that their customers' data packets will be encapsulated and decapsulated as they enter and exit the AS. An APT island can then remove all customer edge prefixes from their BGP routing tables.

APT ASes must still allow their customers to interact with the rest of the existing system. To explain how this is done, we must answer three questions:

What information do APT ASes use to reach their customer edge prefixes? Inside an APT island, the APT ASes exchange mapping information with each other (see "Mapping Distribution Protocol"). This allows their default mappers to maintain a mapping information table for the entire island. We will call this the *island mapping table*.

How can an APT AS reach edge prefixes served by non-APT ASes? All transit ASes will continue to use BGP to reach those edge prefixes connected to non-APT ASes. Note the following differences from the current Internet: (a) APT ASes do not run BGP sessions with their customer networks in edge address space, and (b) the BGP routing tables maintained by routers in APT ASes do not contain those edge prefixes that are already in the island mapping table (unless a prefix is connected to both an APT AS and a non-APT AS.

How can an edge network connected to a non-APT AS reach an edge prefix connected to an APT AS? APT ASes at the border of an APT island must advertise the edge prefixes in their island mapping table to their non-APT neighbors via BGP.

An APT island grows larger by connecting one of its DMs to a DM in another APT island. When two APT islands merge, their island mapping tables merge into a single, larger island mapping table. As a result, each router in the merged island can remove the island mapping table prefixes from their BGP tables, offsetting the increase in mapping table size. Furthermore, the increase in mapping table size will affect only a small set of devices (default mappers), while essentially all routers can benefit from the reduction in BGP table size. As the APT island grows, the BGP tables of the island routers will continue to shrink, providing incentive for non-APT ASes to join the island (and for APT islands to merge). APT providers can also offer their customers all of the benefits mentioned above.

Interoperation Under Partial Deployment: We now describe how to enable communication between APT and non-APT networks, or between two different islands, using the topology in Figure 8. Suppose edge network *Site1* is a customer of *ISP1*, and thus is a part of *APT Island 1*. *Site3* and *Site4* are customers of *ISP3* and *ISP4* respectively. They are part of *APT Island 2*. *Site2* is a customer of *ISP2*, which is a non-APT network. *Site3* is also a customer of *ISP2*.

How can a non-APT site like *Site2* reach an APT site, such as *Site1*? Recall that *Site1*'s prefixes are not in the BGP tables of any router in *APT Island 1*, but they *are* in the *APT Island 1* mapping table. Thus, ISPs at the border of Island 1 need to convert the mapping information for *Site1* into a BGP route and inject it into non-APT networks. Since default mappers maintain a complete island mapping table, they can do the conversion – the converted BGP route will contain only the announcing DM's own AS number (the AS where traffic will enter the island) and *ISP1* (the AS where traffic will exit the island towards *Site1*). In addition, if *Site1* has an AS number, its AS number will appear at the end of the BGP path in order to be consistent with current BGP path semantics. The details of the path taken within the APT island are not relevant to the BGP routers in the legacy system. DMs will advertise these routes to their networks' non-APT neighbors in accordance with routing policies. Eventually, *Site2* will receive the BGP route to *Site1*. These APT BGP announcements will include a unique community tag X so that other BGP speakers in *APT Island 1* can ignore them.

The above works fine for sites whose providers are all from the same APT island, but what about sites that multihome with ISPs both inside and outside of the island? To support this type of multihoming, we require that all APT routers check their BGP tables *before* attempting to encapsulate a packet. Otherwise, packets would always route through APT providers to the destination site, never using the non-APT provider. Furthermore, the DMs at island border ISPs will still announce these sites' prefixes into BGP, but will tag these announcements with a unique community tag Y(different from X) telling other BGP speakers in the island that the destination sites are multihomed to ASes inside and outside the island. Note that Y must differ from X. BGP announcements with community tag X can be ignored by non-DM routers in the APT Island. However, announcements with community tag Y cannot be ignored by island nodes.[4]

To see how these requirements support the above multihoming, we will go through an ex-

Figure 8. Example topology for incremental deployment

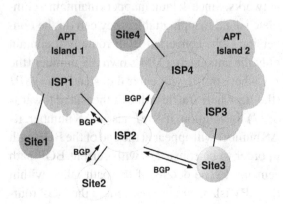

ample. In Figure 8, *Site3* multihomes with an APT AS(*ISP3*) as well as a non-APT AS(*ISP2*). Thus *Site3* will have 2 types of routes announced into BGP – a traditional BGP route announced by *ISP2*, and an injected BGP route announced by APT ISPs at the border of *APT Island 2*. The injected BGP route will include a unique community tag Y telling other BGP speakers in *APT Island 2* that *Site3* is multihomed to ASes inside and outside *APT Island 2*. Receivers of the announcements will choose one route to store in their loc-RIB, using standard BGP route selection. When a border router in *APT Island 2* receives packets destined to *Site3*, it first checks its BGP table *before* looking in its cache. It will find one of the 2 BGP routes in its loc-RIB. It then checks the route community attribute value. If the value is Y, then it knows the route is an injected route, and it attempts to encapsulate the packet via standard APT practices. If the value is anything other than Y, the router does not encapsulate the packet and routes the packet via standard BGP.

We now explain how an APT site can communicate with an non-APT site. For example, how can *Site1* reach *Site2*? When an ITR in *ISP1* receives a packet from *Site1*, it first looks for the prefix in its BGP routing table (as mentioned in the previous example). Since the prefixes of non-APT ASes are stored in a TR's BGP routing table, the ITR will find a match, check the route's community attribute, and discover that the prefix belongs to a non-APT AS. The packet is then forwarded toward the destination using the forwarding table generated by BGP.

How do two unconnected APT islands communicate with each other? In our figure, *Site4* is a customer of *ISP4*, an APT network, but *ISP4* is not in the same island as *Site1*'s provider, *ISP1* (i.e. there are some non-APT networks in between). Unconnected APT islands do not exchange mapping information with each other, so *Site4*'s prefixes will not be in *APT Island 1*'s mapping table, and *Site1*'s prefixes will not be in

APT Island 2's mapping table. However, the two islands will still receive each other's BGP routes injected using the method described previously. As a result, *Site1* will communicate with *Site4* just as it would with the customer of a non-APT network using BGP routing information, and vice versa.

Routing Policy and Mapping

As previously noted, the inter-domain routing protocol is outside the scope of the APT design. If APT were deployed on the current Internet, BGP would continue to serve this purpose. In other words, BGP will still be used to find paths between ITRs and ETRs that are in different ASes.

However, an ETR is a necessary hop in any APT routing path, but multihomed destinations have more than one ETR to choose from. Therefore, APT ETR selection can have an effect on routing paths. In this section, we intend to clarify how APT can affect BGP routing paths, and what kinds of policies are both possible and necessary to support in APT to maintain the flexibility of current routing policy.

One might believe that there are three situations in which policy can be applied to mapping information in APT: (1) When a provider-specific MapSet is created, (2) when a default mapper selects an ETR from a MapSet, and (3) when propagating MapSets to other transit networks. However, APT chooses to make policy applied in situation 1 take first priority and use situation 2 only to break ties. We believe that source-specific mappings are too expensive to support; they would defeat our hybrid push-pull approach. Therefore, APT negates the usefulness of situation 3.

To understand why, consider the following. Since the path taken by a BGP update determines the path of data flow, the path of each BGP update must be carefully managed through policy. This is not the case for MapSet announcements. MapSets do not change based on the path by which they are propagated. In fact, APT guarantees this – any

modification made to a MapSet during propagation will cause signature verification to fail and propagation to end. Furthermore, it is in the interest of the party owning an ITR, or sending party, to have access to *all* MapSets in the network. This will allow the sending party to provide the most robust service to their customers.

The result is that applying policy along the path via which a MapSet is propagated will not have any desirable effect. For example, assume, for the sake of argument, we used a policy-rich protocol, such as BGP, for MapSet update propagation. Accordingly, some transit network X withholds an update for some MapSet m from their peer Y. Y wants to receive all updates for all MapSets, so Y simply peers with Z, who *is* willing to send updates for m. The MapSet updates for m that Y receives from Z are *identical* to the updates that it would have received from X, were X willing to forward them. Therefore, all that X has accomplished by withholding MapSet updates from Y is to force Y to find an additional peer. More importantly, X's application of policy does not have any effect on the routing paths between X and Y. This is due to the fact that the method by which Y selects an ETR for any given destination edge address is entirely unrelated to the method by which it received the corresponding MapSet.

Table 2.

Mapping Distribution	Push from origin network to all ASes, pull from ITRs from local DMs.
Mapping Security	Sign each mapping entry; distribute keys over the DM mesh.
Failure Handling	Redirect packets to DMs to find alternative ETRs to use.
Deployment	Incrementally deployable and can interoperate with legacy networks.

CONCLUSION

In this chapter, we have presented a practical design for a new tunneling architecture to solve the routing scalability problem. APT deploys default mappers in transit networks to maintain the full table of mappings from edge prefixes to the addresses of their transit providers, so that data packets can be tunneled over the transit core. The DMs form a mesh congruent to the underlying network topology and use the mesh to flood mapping information. To secure mapping data distribution and all control messages, DMs cryptographically sign messages and use a novel scheme based on neighbor signatures to distribute public keys. To minimize control overhead, data delay, and data loss, APT adopts a data-driven approach to handle cache misses at ITRs as well as temporary unreachability of ETRs; data packets are used both to signal DMs to provide mapping information to ITRs and to allow DMs to forward these data packets in the meantime.

Looking at the bigger picture, APT necessarily brings additional complexity into the Internet architecture. Thus, a question naturally arises: why is it necessary to change the existing routing architecture?

We believe the answer lies in the fact that the Internet has grown by orders of magnitude. In an article by J. B. S. Haldane, "Being the right size" (Haldane, 1928), the author illustrated the relationship between the size and complexity of biological entities using a vivid example. As stated in the article, "a typical small animal, say a microscopic worm or rotifer, has a smooth skin through which all the oxygen it requires can soak in." However, "increase its dimensions tenfold in every direction, and its weight is increased a thousand times, so ... it will need a thousand times as much food and oxygen per day. Now if its shape is unaltered its surface will be increased only a hundredfold, and ten times as much oxygen must enter per minute through each square millimeter of skin." This is why every large animal has a lung, an organ specialized for soaking up oxygen. The author concludes that, "for every type of animal there is a most convenient size, and a large change in size inevitably carries with it a change of form." It would be unimaginable for small insects to have lungs. On the other hand, it is also impossible for big animals to live without lungs.

In the case of the Internet, the existing architecture, where all autonomous systems live in the same routing space, was designed more than a decade ago when the Internet was very small in size. Today, not only has the Internet grown beyond its designers' wildest imaginations, but the goals of individual networks have diverged. Edge networks are multihomed for enhanced reliability and performance, while ISPs are specialized for high-performance, yet economical, packet delivery service. The different goals of different parties have brought different and conflicting requirements to the shared address and routing space. Thus, the original architecture can no longer meet the functional requirements of today's grown-up Internet. A new routing architecture is needed to accommodate the growth of the Internet and the differentiation of individual networks, and APT is exactly such an attempt.

REFERENCES

Arends, R., Austein, R., Larson, M., Massey, D., & Rose, S. (2005). Internet engineering task force. *DNS Security Introduction and Requirements.*

AT&T. (n.d.). *U.S. network latency.* Retrieved from http://ipnetwork.bgtmo.ip.att.net/pws/network_delay.html

Brim, S., Chiappa, N., Farinacci, D., Fuller, V., Lewis, D., & Meyer, D. (2008). *LISP-CONS: A content distribution overlay network service for LISP.* Retrieved from http://tools.ietf.org/html/draft-fuller-lisp-cons-04

Caesar, M., Condie, T., Kannan, J., Lakshminarayanan, K., Stoica, I., & Shenker, S. (2006). ROFL: Routing on Flat Labels. In *Proc. of the ACM SIGCOMM*.

Deering, S. (1996, March). *The map & encap scheme for scalable IPv4 routing with portable site prefixes*. Presented at Xerox PARC.

Farinacci, D., Fuller, V., & Meyer, D. (2011). *LISP alternative topology (LISP-ALT)*. Retrieved from http://tools.ietf.org/html/draft-fuller-lisp-alt-10

Farinacci, D., Fuller, V., Oran, D., & Meyer, D. (2012). *Locator/ID separation protocol (LISP)*. Retrieved from http://tools.ietf.org/html/draft-farinacci-lisp-23

Fuller, V., & Farinacci, D. (2012). *LISP map server interface*. Retrieved from http://tools.ietf.org/html/draft-ietf-lisp-ms-16

Haldane, J. B. S. (1928). *Being the right size*. Retrieved on May 12, 2008, from http://irl.cs.ucla.edu/papers/right-size.html

Hinden, R. (1996). *RFC 1955: New scheme for internet routing and addressing (ENCAPS) for IPNG*. Retrieved from http://tools.ietf.org/html/rfc1955

Iannone, L., & Bonaventure, O. (2007). On the cost of caching locator/ID mappings. In *Proceedings of the CoNext Conference*.

IRTF RRG Working Group. (n.d.). *Website*. Retrieved from http://www.irtf.org/charter?gtype=rg&group=rrg

Kent, S., Lynn, C., & Seo, K. (2000). Secure border gateway protocol. *IEEE Journal on Selected Areas in Communications*, *18*(4). doi:10.1109/49.839934.

Keynote Systems. (n.d.). *Internet health report*. Retrieved from http://www.internethealthreport.com/

Krioukov, D., Claffy, K. C., Fall, K., & Brady, A. (2007, July). On compact routing for the Internet. *ACM SIGCOMM CCR*, *37*(3), 43–52. doi:10.1145/1273445.1273450.

Li, T. (2011). Internet research task force. *RFC 6115: Recommendation for a Routing Architecture*.

Massey, D., Wang, L., Zhang, B., & Zhang, L. (2007, August). A scalable routing system design for future Internet. In *Proceedings of the ACM SIGCOMM Workshop on IPv6 and the Future of the Internet*.

Meyer, D., Zhang, L., & Fall, K. (2007). Internet engineering task force. *RFC 4984: Report from the IAB Workshop on Routing and Addressing*.

Morris, R., Kohler, E., Jannotti, J., & Kaashoek, M. F. (1999). The click modular router. *SIGOPS Operating Systems Review*, *33*(5), 217–231. doi:10.1145/319344.319166.

O'Dell, M. (1997). *GSE - An alternate addressing architecture for IPv6*. Retrieved from http://tools.ietf.org/html/draft-ietf-ipngwg-gseaddr-00

Rekhter, Y., Li, T., & Hares, S. (2006). Internet engineering task force. *RFC 4271: A Border Gateway Protocol*.

Subramanian, L., Caesar, M., & Ee, C. T., Handley, M., Mao, Z. M., Shenker, S., & Stoica, I. (2005). HLP: A next generation inter-domain routing protocol. In ACM SIGCOMM.

Zhang, L. (2006). An overview of multihoming and open issues in GSE. *IETF Journal*, 2.

Zhang, X., Francis, P., Wang, J., & Yoshida, K. (2006). Scaling IP routing with the core router-integrated overlay. In *Proceedings of ICNP*.

ADDITIONAL READING

Bu, T., Gao, L., & Towsley, D. (2004, May). On characterizing BGP routing table growth. *Computer Networks, 45*(1), 45–54. doi:10.1016/j. comnet.2004.02.003.

Feamster, N., Gao, L., & Rexford, J. (2007). How to lease the Internet in your spare time. *ACM SIGCOMM CCR, 37*(1), 61–64. doi:10.1145/1198255.1198265.

Huston, G. (2001). Analyzing the Internet BGP routing table. *Internet Protocol Journal, 4*(1).

Li, J., Guidero, M., Wu, Z., Purpus, E., & Ehren-kranz, T. (2007, April). BGP routing dynamics revisited. *ACM SIGCOMM CCR, 37*(2), 7–16. doi:10.1145/1232919.1232921.

Meng, X., Xu, Z., Zhang, B., Huston, G., Lu, S., & Zhang, L. (2005, January). IPv4 address allocation and BGP routing table evolution. In ACM SIGCOMM CCR.

Oliveira, R., Izhak-Ratzin, R., Zhang, B., & Zhang, L. (2005). Measurement of highly active prefixes in BGP. In IEEE GLOBECOM.

Xu, W., & Rexford, J. (2006). MIRO: Multi-path inter-domain routing. In ACM SIGCOMM.

Yang, X., Clark, D., & Berger, A. (2007, August). NIRA: A new routing architecture. *IEEE/ACM Transactions on Networking, 15*(4). doi:10.1109/ TNET.2007.893888.

ENDNOTES

1. In practice, the ITR would maintain a small BGP table and check this before the cache. This is done for backwards compatibility.
2. If the alternate ETR is in a different network, whether to forward packets in this situation is determined by the contractual agreement between the edge network and its providers.
3. Note that the monitor does not make any announcements, it simply passively examines all incoming MDP messages.
4. More specifically, the announcements cannot be ignored by ITRs and island border routers that peer with non-island neighbors. Other island routers can still ignore the announcements.

Chapter 5
Routing Architecture of Next-Generation Internet (RANGI)

Xiaohu Xu
Huawei Technology, China

Meilian Lu
Beijing University of Posts and Telecom, China

ABSTRACT

This chapter describes a new Identifier/Locator split architecture, referred to as Routing Architecture for the Next Generation Internet (RANGI), which aims to deal with the routing scalability issues. Similar to the Host Identity Protocol (HIP) architecture, RANGI also introduces a host identifier (ID) layer between the IPv6 network layer and the transport layer and hence the transport-layer associations (e.g., TCP connections) are no longer bound to IP addresses, but to the host IDs. The major difference from the HIP architecture is that RANGI adopts hierarchical and cryptographic host IDs which have delegation-oriented structure. The corresponding ID to locator mapping system in RANGI is designed to preserve a "reasonable" business model and clear trust boundaries. In addition, RANGI uses special IPv4-embeded IPv6 addresses as locators and hence site-controllable traffic-engineering and simplified renumbering can be easily achieved while the deployment cost of such new architecture is reduced greatly.

INTRODUCTION

It has been widely recognized that the underlying reason for the so-called routing scalability issue (Meyer, Zhang, & Fall, 2007) is the overlapping semantics of IP address which is used as both locator and identifier in current Internet architecture. This overload of the IP address role makes it impossible to renumber the addresses in a topologically aggregate way in case of host or network site mobility or re-homing. An approach for solving the routing scalability issue is to separate the identifier role from the locator role of the IP address.

Host Identity Protocol (HIP) (Moskowitz & Nikander, 2006) is a well-known Identifier/Locator separation architecture which is developed by IETF (Internet Engineering Task Force) and IRTF

DOI: 10.4018/978-1-4666-4305-5.ch005

(Internet Research Task Force). The major goal of HIP is to support host mobility, host multi-homing and enhance communication security. However, since HIP uses flat labels (i.e., hash values of the public keys) as host identifiers, there is no any hierarchy in the host identifier namespace and therefore it is impossible to introduce any hierarchy into the corresponding mapping system. As a result, it is impossible for multiple operators over the world to manage and operate such mapping resolution infrastructure in a cooperative way just as what they did in their 2G or 3G mobile communication systems.

This chapter describes a new ID/Locator split architecture, referred to as Routing Architecture for the Next Generation Internet (RANGI). Similar to the Host Identity Protocol (HIP) architecture, RANGI also introduces a host identifier (ID) layer between the IPv6 network layer and the transport layer and hence the transport-layer associations (e.g., TCP connections) are no longer bound to IP addresses, but to the host IDs. The major difference from the HIP architecture is that RANGI adopts hierarchical and cryptographic host IDs which have delegation-oriented structure. Therefore, the corresponding ID to locator mapping system in RANGI has a reasonable business model and clear trust boundaries. In addition, RANGI uses special IPv4-embedded IPv6 addresses as locators and hence site-controllable traffic-engineering and simplified renumbering can be easily achieved while the deployment cost of such new architecture is reduced greatly.

SOLUTION DESCRIPTION

The RANGI architecture is described in details in the following sub-sections.

Host Identifiers

In RANGI, host IDs are hierarchical and 128-bit long. As depicted in Figure 1, a host ID consists of two parts:

1. The leftmost n-64 bits part is the Administrative Domain Identifier (AD ID) which has embedded organizational affiliation and global uniqueness, and
2. The remaining part is the Local Host ID which is generated by computing a cryptographic one-way hash function from a public key of the ID owner and auxiliary parameters, e.g., the ID owner's AD ID.

The binding between the public key and the host ID can be verified by re-computing the hash value and by comparing the hash with the host ID. As these identifiers are expected to be used along with IPv6 addresses at both applications and APIs (Application Programmable Interfaces), especially in the RANGI transition mechanisms defined in (Xu, 2009), it is desired to explicitly distinguish host IDs from IPv6 addresses (i.e., locators) and vice versa. Hence, a separate prefix for identifiers should be allocated by the IANA. As

Figure 1. Host identifier structure

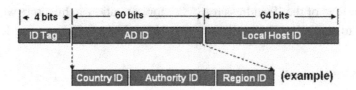

a result, leftmost 4 bits in the AD ID field should be reserved to fill this dedicated prefix.

The approach of generating hierarchical RANGI host IDs is similar to that for Cryptographically Generated Addresses (CGA) (Aura, 2005). The major difference is that the prefix of the RANGI host ID is AD ID, rather than ordinary IPv6 address prefix. In CGA, the process of generating a new address takes three input values: a 64-bit subnet prefix, the public key of the address owner as a DER-encoded ASN.1 structure of the type "SubjectPublicKeyInfo" and the security parameter "Sec," which is an unsigned three-bit integer. In contrast, the process of generating a hierarchical host ID in RANGI also takes three input values: the AD ID, the public key of the host ID owner and the security parameter Sec. Therefore, the process of generating RANGI host IDs can be compatible with that for CGA.

The benefits of using hierarchical host IDs in RANGI include but not limited to:

1. Manage the global identifier namespace in a scalable way.
2. Hold a reasonable economic model and clear trust boundaries in the corresponding ID/Locator mapping system because the whole namespace can now be assigned in a hierarchical manner to multiple authorities according to the AD ID structure contained in the host identifier.
3. Ease the transition from the current Internet to RANGI because the legacy hosts could use this hierarchical host IDs as legacy IPv6 addresses and therefore the packets containing such host IDs in the IP address fields could be forwarded normally by routers.

In RANGI, the global uniqueness of host IDs is guaranteed through a registration mechanism. Since the AD IDs are globally unique and owned by the corresponding host ID registration and administrative authorities of different countries respectively, the local host IDs are only required to be unique within the corresponding AD scope.

Since the ID/Locator mapping entries for hierarchical host IDs can be stored in the corresponding authoritative servers according to the organizational structures in the host IDs, just like what Domain Name System (DNS) does, the resolution infrastructure for hierarchical host IDs in RANGI can be operated by multiple entities in a cooperative way.

Host Locators

RANGI uses special IPv4-Embeded IPv6 addresses (Bao et al.1, 2010), which is comprise two parts 96 bits LD (Location Domain) ID and 32 bits Local Locator, as shown in Figure 2.

LD ID is an address prefix assigned by ISP (Internet Service Provider), which is used for routing between domains, and Local Locator is unique in each domain. This IPv4-embedded IPv6 structure is convenient for IPv4/IPv6 transition.

ID/Locator Mapping Resolution

ID/Locator split implies a need for storing and distributing the mappings from host IDs to locators.

In RANGI, the mappings from Fully Qualified Domain Names (FQDNs) to host IDs are stored in the DNS system, while the mappings from host IDs to locators are stored in a distributed ID/Locator

Figure 2. RANGI locator structure

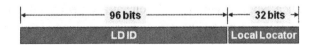

Mapping System (ILMS) which can be built on the current DNS infrastructure.

A detailed mapping lookup example is given as follows:

1. A host ID will be transformed into a FQDN format string. Firstly, a host ID is expressed as "country-code.authority-code.region-code. local-host-ID" by inserting dots between adjacent fields, then by reversing the fields and attaching with the suffix "rangiid.arpa." It is transformed into a FQDN-format string as "local-host-ID.region-code.authority-code. country-code.rangiid.arpa."

2. The FQDN-format string is used as a key to locate the authoritative DNS server which maintains the desired resource records.

In order to facilitate such a lookup process, a new sub-domain "rangiid.arpa." needs to be inserted into the current domain name hierarchy. This sub-domain can delegate its own sub-domains according to the hierarchy of the FQDN-format string of the host ID. A new Resource Record (RR) named RANGI is also defined for the ID/Locator mappings, in which the NAME field is filled with the FQDN-format string of a host ID, while the RDATA field is filled with the corresponding locator information, including but not limited to an IPv6 address (i.e., locator) and its preference, and so on.

To prevent the Man-in-the-Middle attacks during mapping lookups, the DNS Security Extensions (DNSSEC) (Arends et al., 2005) is strongly recommended for the origin authentication and integrity assurance of the DNS data.

To prevent DNS recursive servers caching antique ID/Locator mapping information, the TTL (Time to Live) of a RANGI RR for a mobile host should be set to 0 or a very small value. However, if a host (i.e., Correspondence Node) wants to cache the RR of the communicating host (i.e., Mobile Node), it can reset the TTL of that RR to a reasonable value internally.

The secure DNS dynamic update mechanism defined in (Wellington, 2000) is directly used for dynamically updating the ID/Locator mapping entries in the ID/Locator mapping system in a secure way.

Basic Communication Procedure

Application layer of RANGI source host resolves FQDN of destination host to ID through the DNS. Transport layer uses ID instead of IP address to establish connection with corresponding host. ID layer resolves ID to locator through interaction with ILMS, and is responsible for handling RANGI protocols. ID layer replaces ID in data packet from upper layer to corresponding locator, and in reverse, replaces locator in data packet from lower layer to corresponding ID. Network layer is responsible for sending/receiving data packet according locator, and setup IPSec (Kent & Seo, 2005) secure association.

Before communication, two RANGI hosts need to establish an IPSec secure association firstly, then send data packets using ESP (Encapsulating Security Payload) (Kent, 2005) transport mode. During communication, IPSec association is identified with <DST, SPI>. During the procedure of establishing an IPSec association, host will bind SPI (Security Parameters Index) with ID and establish a mapping table of SPI/ID. After receiving a data packet, host can easily find the corresponding ID, and then find the RANGI secure association.

Host Mobility and Multi-Homing

To some extent, host multi-homing is similar to host mobility since their effects on the network and on correspondents are identical.

In RANGI, when a host physically moves from one attachment point of network to another in the event of mobility or re-homing, it should inform its current correspondents of its new locator as soon as possible. Furthermore, it needs to update its locator information on the ID/Locator mapping authoritative server timely. In the case of simultaneous mobility, at least one of the communicating entities should resolve the correspondence node's new locator from the ID/Locator mapping system so as to continue their communication.

RANGI ARCHITECTURE: IMPLEMENTATION DETAILS

This section describes the following implementation aspects of RANGI architecture.

- Implementation of ID/Locator Mapping System infrastructure
- Implementation of host protocol stack based on the open source code (HIPL, n.d.)
- Host Mobility, Multi-homing and traffic engineering

ID/Location Mapping System

Architecture of RANGI Mapping System

RANGI Mapping System consists of two components (see Figure 3): IDMS (ID Management System) and ILMS (ID/Locator Mapping System). IDMS is responsible for ID management, including host ID registration, cancellation and conflict detection; ILMS is responsible for the management of the ID/Locator mapping information, including the process of registration/update/ query of mappings.

Hierarchical Structure of IDMS

IDMS has a hierarchical structure as shown in Figure 4. Each IDMS is responsible for the management of IDs which belong to its AD domain. IDMS also provides with ILMS TSIG (Transaction SIGnature) (Vixie et al., 2000) shared secrets, so as to secure the dynamic updating process of mappings on ILMS.

Hierarchical Structure of DNS-Based ILMS

In order to support ID/Locator Mapping, DNS-based ILMS will specify a new resource record, and authorize a new domain in current domain name space to manage these mapping records. ILMS organizes hierarchical structure in accordance with the identity of RANGI, as shown in

Figure 3. Functional architecture of RANGI mapping system

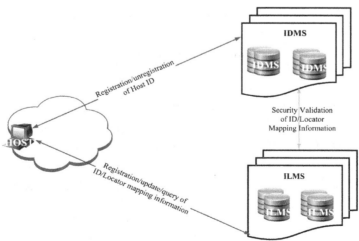

Figure 4. Hierarchical structure of IDMS

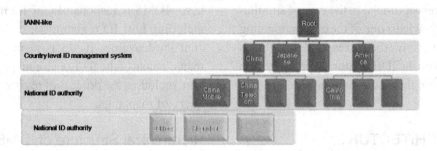

Figure 5. This hierarchical structure brings trust boundaries into the mapping system. RANGI will register a new sub-domain referred to as "rangiid" which is attached to "arpa."

Domain rangiid is organized according to AD ID layered structure: domain country is located at tier 1, domain authority is located at tier 2, and domain region is located at tier 3.

1.   RANGI RR (Resource Record)

RANGI RR stored in ILMS consists of three types: NS, AAAA and RANGI.

NS RR is used to specify the name of DNS, which will be used to specify the server name of local domain, sub-domain and other domain in ILMS. ILMS looks up the name of authorized DNS using NS RR. AAAA RR is used to specify the corresponding IPv6 address of the specific domain name, which will be used to obtain the DNS address of local domain, sub-domain and other domain in ILMS.

RANGI is a new defined RR type, which is mainly used to implement the ID/Locator mapping. RANGI RR is organized as following:

```
name type class ttl Rdata
```

Where:

• *name* maintains the host ID resource record (RR), the index of RANGI RR. This

Figure 5. Hierarchical structure of DNS-based ILMS

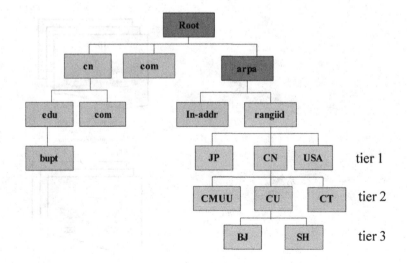

index is the diverse of host ID with a suffix "rangid.arpa."

- *Rdata* stores locators mapping to host ID.
- *type* is a 16 bits field, which specifies the type of RR. For RANGI RR, the value of this field is 52.
- *class* is a 16 bits field, which is usually set as IN.
- *ttl* is a 32 bits field, which identifies the time to live of a RR.

2.   System model of ILMS

ILMS servers are deployed according to the structure of DNS, which are divided into local ILMS servers and foreign authority ILMS servers. RANGI hosts send Query/Update requests by resolver to access the RR maintained in ILMS servers. ILMS servers and resolvers in RANGI hosts constitute the ILMS system model as in Figure 6.

The detailed data flow is shown in Figure 7.

When ILMS receives the Mapping Query message from RANGI-Client, ILMS will handle the message as following:

- Check if it is authorized to maintain this mapping record;
- If TRUE, then lookup the record from local Database; otherwise lookup the record from mapping cache or upper ILMS server recursively;
- Return the response message which contains ID/Locator mapppings.

When ILMS receives the Mapping Update message from RANGI-Client, ILMS will handle the message as following:

- Compare the updating ID/Locator mappings with the corresponding records in local database;
- Modify the lifecycle of existing mapping records or add new mappings;
- Return the update result to RANGI-Client.

DataManager is a program running in ILMS, which is responsible for checking periodically the lifecycle of each RANGI records. When the value of lifecycle is zero, DataManager will send a Mapping Delete message to ILMS to delete the corresponding mapping record.

Figure 6. System model of DNS-based ILMS

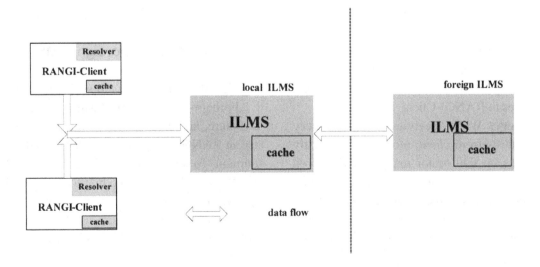

Figure 7. Data flow of DNS based ILMS

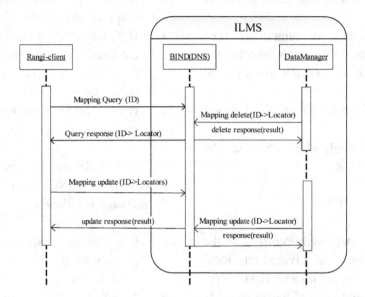

Implementation of Local ILMS

Local ILMS is located in RANGI LD (Location Domain), which is implemented based on open source (isc.org, n.d.). In order to support the new ID/Locator function of ILMS, during the implementation of local ILMS, we mainly enhance four modules of BIND: client, query, clinet_error and cache.

The new functions of these modules are described below:

- **Client:** Receives mapping query requests from RANGI-Client, parses the requests and sends the query requests to module *query*. When receiving the handling results from *query*, it constructs the response messages to RANGI-Client.
- **Query:** When receiving mapping query requests from *client*, module *query* firstly looks up ID/Locator mapping RRs stored in local cache. If no requested RR is found, *query* will send the mapping query request to Foreign-ILMS and receive the corresponding result, then construct responding data packet and send to *client*.

- **Client-error:** When receiving wrong mapping query requests, *client* will send the requests to module *client-error*. *Client-error* will analyse the reason of error, and return the results to *client*.
- **Cache:** When successfully querying a mapping record from foreign-ILMS, local-ILMS will cache the mapping result in local *cache*, so that improving the efficiency of following queries.

Figure 8 describes the data flows that local-ILMS receiving correct mapping query request.

Implementation of Foreign-ILMS

Foreign-ILMS is also developed based on BIND.

Foreign-ILMS servers form a converse tree structure, and each ILMS server maintains different RANGI mapping resources from different domain. To support the new functions of foreign-ILMS, we enhance six modules of BIND: client, query, update, register, client_error and DataBase.

The enhanced functions of these modules are the process of RANGI RRs and the map-

Figure 8. Data flow when local-ILMS receiving correct query

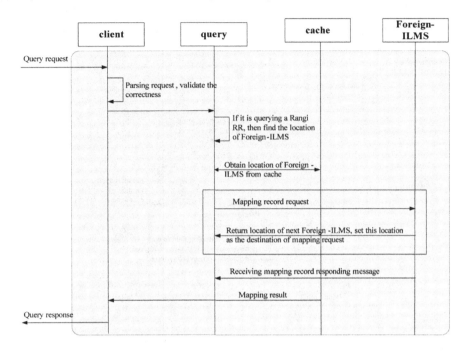

ping request/update requests and corresponding responses.

As an example, Figure 9 describes the data flows that foreign-ILMS receiving correct query request and update request.

ILMS Supporting Host Multi-Homing and Mobility

In case of host multi-homing, ILMS should maintain multiple ID/Locator mapping information for host. In addition, host multi-homing may cause the unusable of registered address before, so ILMS should support deleting the expired addresses. For above requirements, design the RANGI mapping record as shown in Figure 10, at least including four fields: ID, Preference, Aging and Locator. Aging field is set by ILMS server, the other three fields are set by host.

When host moves, mobile host should update its locators in ILMS. In order to support host mobility, local ILMS with cache should not cache the RANGI mapping record so as to avoid the inconsistent of mapping information maintained by local cache and foreign authority ILMS server.

RANGI Host

Message Flows of RANGI Host in the Initiating Phase

Figure 11 describes the message flows of RANGI host in the initiating phase, mainly including the handling of host side.

1. When RANGI host is initiated, it will generate host ID using CGA with AD ID, public key and the related security parameters.
2. Host sends ID register request to IDMS using IDMS_LOC obtained before. Host ID and the related security parameters are included in the register request. If failed register, then repeat the register procedure for three times; if register successfully, IDMS will send back

Figure 9. Data flow when foreign-ILMS receiving correct query

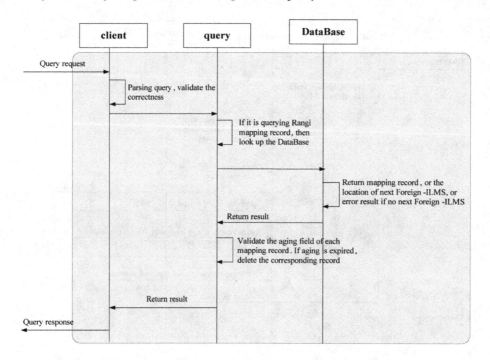

register success message with ILMS_LOC and signing information.

3. Host send a DNS update request to ILMS to update ID_TO_LOC mapping information, ILMS send back the updating result.

4. When host A want to initiate communication with host B, host A will send a query request to local DNS to query the mapping information of host domain name to ID of host B.

5. Host A converses the ID of host B to the form of domain name.

6. Host A send a DNS query request to ILMS using the conversed ID to get ID_TO_LOC

mapping information, then ILMS send back the locator of host B.

7. Host A and host B setup a secure association, and the following data is transmitted in the protection of IPSec ESP.

Generation and Register of Host ID

Host ID consists of AD ID and local host ID. AD ID can be applied from organization like ICANN (The Internet Corporation for Assigned Names and Numbers). Local host ID is generated by CGA. Finally, AD ID and local host ID compose a 128 bits host ID. Local host ID is unique within an

Figure 10. Format of mapping information supporting host multi-homing

ID	Preference	Aging	Locator

Figure 11. Message flows of RANGI host in initiating phase

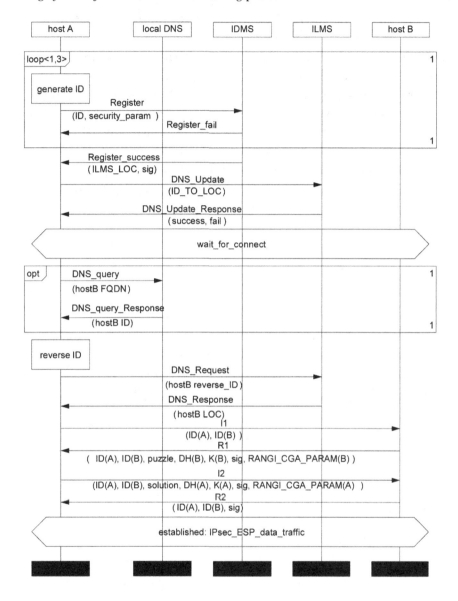

AD, and host ID is globally unique. The register function of host ID is implemented as part of IDMS client, which is usually located in the RANGI host. IDMS client is responsible for sending ID register request and receiving register result from IDMS. Its main functions include: read the locator, certificate, RSA public key and private key of IDMS belong to a specific ID management domain from configuration file; initiate the ID register procedure, and send ID register request

to IDMS, in which the identify of user is carried for authentication; receive the register response and authenticate the IDMS; record the locator of ILMS returned by IDMS.

Update and Query of Mapping Information

After host is initiated or host locator is changed, RANGI host needs to update the ID_TO_LOC mapping. RANGI host will select the globally routable locators, and update the ID_TO_LOC mapping information in ILMS. ILMS client is located in RANGI host, the query and update procedure is provided through ILMS client communicating with ILMS servers. In cases of host multi-homing or mobility, ILMS may return multiple locators for a specific host ID, the ILMS client must provide all the locators to host, then host will select a locator for communicate.

Basic Communication between RANGI Hosts

The basic communication scenario of RANGI is shown in Figure 12.

Application layer of RANGI host resolves FQDN of destination host to ID through the DNS. Transport layer uses ID instead of IP address to establish connection with corresponding host, so the effect caused by IP address is screened. ID layer resolves ID to locator through interaction

Figure 12. Basic communication scenario of RANGI

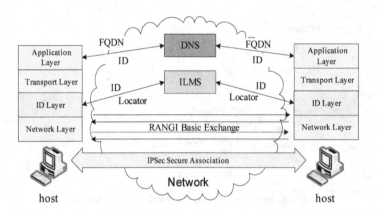

Figure 13. Basic handshake procedure in RANGI

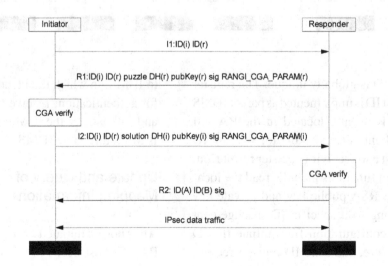

with ILMS, and is responsible for handling RANGI protocols. ID layer replaces ID in data packet from upper layer to corresponding locator, and in reverse, replaces locator in data packet from lower layer to corresponding ID. Network layer is responsible for sending/receiving data packet according locator, and setup IPSec secure association.

Before communication, two RANGI hosts need to establish an IPSec secure association firstly, then send data packets using ESP transport mode. During communication, IPSec association is identified with <DST, SPI>. During the procedure of establishing an IPSec association, host will bind SPI with ID and establish a mapping table of SPI/ID. After receiving a data packet, host can

Figure 14. Sending procedure of RANGI data packets

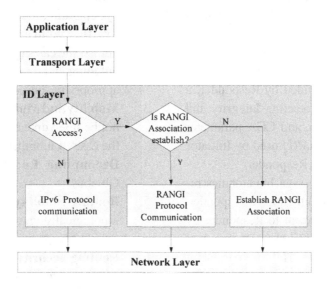

Figure 15. Receiving procedure of RANGI data packets

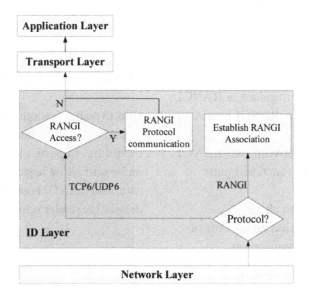

easily find the corresponding ID, and then find the RANGI secure association.

All RANGI hosts must perform RANGI basic exchange to establish a secure association before communication with other hosts. RANGI basic exchange is similar with that of HIP, consisting of four messages (see Figure 13).

1. Initiator send I1 message to Responder, in which including IDs of Initiator and Responder, *ID(i)* and *ID(r)*. If Initiator doesn't know the ID of Responder, then set *ID(r)* as null.
2. Responder responds I1 using R1, in which including a puzzle, Diffie-Hellman parameters *DH(r)* provided by Responder, a sign *sig* used for protecting integrity and initial authentication, and CGA parameter *RANGI_CGA_PARAM(r)* used by Initiator to authentication the Responder.
3. After receiving R1 message, Initiator must resolve the puzzle and authenticate Responder, then send back the result to Responder by message I2. Message I2 includes the result of puzzle, *solution*, Diffie-Hellman parameter *DH(i)* provided by Initiator, *sig* which is the sign of I2 by Initiator using its private key, and CGA parameter *RANGI_CGA_PARAM(i)* used for Responder authenticating the Initiator.
4. Responder authenticates Initiator, and send back message R2.

After the handshaking procedure, a RANGI association is setup, and two RANGI hosts can transmit data.

Basic communication between two RANGI hosts mainly includes three functional parts:

- RANGI communication check
- RANGI IPSec association establishment
- RANGI protocol communication

The detail handling of sending/receiving a data packet is shown in Figure 14 and Figure 15.

CONCLUSION

RANGI achieves almost all of goals (Li, 2007) set by IRTF RRG (Routing Research Group), which are listed below:

1. **Routing Scalability:** Scalability is achieved by separating identifiers from locators.
2. **Traffic Engineering:** Hosts inside a multi-homed site can suggest the upstream ISP for outgoing and returned packets by using the appropriate source locator.
3. **Mobility and Multi-homing:** Sessions will not be interrupted due to locator change in the case of mobility or re-homing.
4. **Decoupling Location and Identifier:** Obvious.
5. **Routing Stability:** Since the locators are topologically aggregatable, routing stability could be improved greatly.
6. **Routing Security:** RANGI reuses existing routing system and does not introduce any new security risk into the routing system.
7. **Incremental Deployability:** RANGI proxy allows RANGI-aware hosts to communicate to legacy IPv6 hosts, and vice-versa.

FUTURE RESEARCH DIRECTIONS

How to realize smooth transition from legacy IPv6 to RANGI architecture will be studied further in the future. In particular, further work will focus on how to allow legacy IPv6 hosts to communicate with RANGI hosts, and vice versa. For more details, the reader is invited to refer to (Xu, 2009).

REFERENCES

Arends, R., Austein, R., Larson, M., Massey, D., & Rose, S. (2005, March). Protocol modifications for the DNS security extensions (RFC 4035). Retrieved from http://www.ietf.org

Aura, T. (2005, March). Cryptographically generated addresses (CGA) (RFC3972). Retrieved from http://www.ietf.org

Balakrishnan, H., Lakshminarayanan, K., Ratnasamy, S., Shenker, S., Stoica, I., & Walfish, M. (2004, September). A layered naming architecture for the internet. In *Proc. ACM SIGCOMM*.

Bao, C., Huitema, C., Bagnulo, M., Boucadair, M., & Li, X. (2010, October). IPv6 addressing of IPv4/IPv6 translators (RFC6052). Retrieved from http://www.ietf.org

HIPL. (n.d.). *Website*. Retrieved from http://hipl.hiit.fi/hipl/release/

isc.org. (n.d.). *Website*. Retrieved from https://www.isc.org

Kent, S., & Seo, K. (2005, December). Security architecture for the internet protocol (RFC4301). Retrieved from http://www.ietf.org

(Kent, 2005) Kent, S. (2005, December). IP Encapsulating Security Payload (RFC4303). Retrieved from http://www.ietf.org

Li, T. (2007, July). Design goals for scalable internet routing (RFC6227). Retrieved from http://www.ietf.org

Meyer, D., Zhang, L., & Fall, K. (2007, September). Report from the IAB Workshop on Routing and Addressing (RFC4984). Retrieved from http://www.ietf.org

Moskowitz, R., & Nikander, P. (2006, May). *Host Identity Protocol (HIP) Architecture* (RFC 4423). Retrieved from http://www.ietf.org

Vixie, P., Gudmundsson, O., Eastlake, D., & Wellington, B. (2000, May). Secret key transaction authentication for DNS (TSIG).

Wellington. (2000, November). Secure domain name system (DNS) dynamic update (RFC3007). Retrieved from http://www.ietf.org

Xu, X. (2009, July). Transition mechanisms for routing architecture for the next generation internet (RANGI).

Chapter 6
Topology Aggregating Routing Architecture (TARA):
A Concept for Scalable and Efficient Routing

Heiner Hummel
Hummel Research, Germany

ABSTRACT

TARA (Topology Aggregating Routing Architecture) is a novel architecture which allows to generate a map of the Internet. TARA allows to maintain and compute a precise topology of the near surrounding and lesser zoomed topologies the more remote they are. In the context of TARA, nodes are identified with "locators" which are derived from longitude/latitude degrees/minutes/seconds. TARA is designed to satisfy advanced traffic engineering such as computing QoS-inferred paths or non congested paths. TARA achieves these goals without requiring an increase of RIBs and FIBs. TARA solves also the issues of dynamic update churn as currently experienced in BGP-based Internet. TARA is also designed with mobility requirements in mind. Indeed, Mobility is supported without requiring dependency on home agents or care-of-address servers. Note, the Time-To-Live mechanism is neither needed nor used in TARA-forwarding. TARA supports various multicast, broadcast, MP2P (multipoint-to-point), anycast and MP2MP (multipoint-to-multipoint) communication schemes. In particular a stateless concept for multicast is outlined; this concept may serve as a pattern for anycast and MP2MP applications. TARA is fully prepared to cope with the IPv4-unicast address depletion issue.

INTRODUCTION

TARA is a completely different architecture compared to the current state of the art. It adopts a novel approach to solve the issues encountered by current Internet routing architectures.

TARA proposes a new concept which is based on new enhancements of existing protocols (e.g., BGP, OSPF, IS-IS) such that any TARA router from a particular well-determined geographical region will get to know all TARA links that interconnect any two TARA routers from that region,

DOI: 10.4018/978-1-4666-4305-5.ch006

no matter to which customer or service provider networks they belong to. All TARA links from a given region will form a topology for which a well-skimmed representative topology "of lesser zoom" will be computed (consisting of a subset of its nodes and respective path links which interconnect them) and combined with alike skimmed topologies for neighboring regions. The combined topology will serve as a basis for computing an even lesser zoomed topology, representing the respectively enlarged area. Altogether and by four recursive cycles, five maps of less and lesser zoom for the entire Internet will be created. As a result, a TARA router would maintain a TARA map with itself fairly in the middle, surrounded by the complete and precise topology of its region, which is surrounded by less and lesser zoomed topologies the more remote the Internet routers are located. Towards each node of the TARA map a shortest, as well as QoS-inferred and current traffic load sensitive, routes will be computed and their respective first hops stored in a new type of FIB (Forwarding Information Base). In case a next hop shall be retrieved for a packet whose destination node won't be in the TARA map, the geographically closest node from the TARA map will be selected and the respective next hop looked up.

TARA would use BGP and OSPF/IS-IS for installing a TARA-Overlay network (similar to RFC2457/4364-MPLS-VPNs), however not for building multiple private networks. If TARA is widely deployed, this would eliminate completely the scalability issue encountered by current Internet architecture. This is achievable because TARA routers won't originate reachability prefixes for locally attached hosts nor forward received reachability prefixes from stub areas. For that aim, TARA can be deployed incrementally without requiring all BGP speaker to be TARA-aware.

TARA is a true location/Identifier separation solution. TARA locators indicate the location information. More precisely; there are 64800

spherical rectangles, resp. triangles at the poles, limited by consecutive longitude and latitude degrees, herein called geopatches. Their numbering and further intersection due to minutes and seconds will form the Unicast TARA Locator.

The unicast TARA Locator of a particular (destination) host shall be retrievable by DNS look-up queries. IP packets destined to a remote host are then forwarded to the identified egress router without ensuring whether the destination is reachable from there or not. If not, and if the destination is a mobile host, a well-scoped broadcast search will be preceded.

The aforementioned capabilities (i.e., computing less zoomed maps and doing well-scoped broadcast) are two from many more examples which are based on All Links Spanning Tree (ALST) computations. As it will be shown below, an ALST[d] is built by converting all network links to arcs which are, loop-free, bound to destination/root node d. A sub-tree thereof is the Dijkstra tree, herein called All Nodes Spanning Tree ANST[d].

While, by starting from any arbitrary node, Dijkstra (i.e., the ANST[d]) yields just one path towards d. The ALST[d] yields multiple shortest and multiple detouring paths (i.e., arc sequences). With some applied caution, i.e. by bestowing the forwarded packet with proper detour process description, additional paths are enabled where arcs are even passed in tail-ward direction. Altogether, any router can properly judge how each of its adjacent links would serve packet forwarding to some given destination node, from being a "best hop" to being a "no-go." Even more, any individual router can do so with respect to all other network nodes' adjacent links as well, which enables a 100% routing orientation such that there is no reason for worrying about loops anymore. In this context, the need for a TTL-based mechanism might be subject to re-consideration. The rationale adopted by TARA is endless loops can be prevented rather than reported.

Subsets of ALST[d] arcs may not only form paths, but also well-confined regions with well-determined remote nodes which enable well-scoped broadcast. Any node X may originate broadcast messages and send them towards the tail nodes of the adjacent arcs according to ANST[X] (resp. ALST[X]) which are to be transitively forwarded in the same way. Any passed node needs to know X, an indication whether using ANST or ALST, and an indication which defines the limit of the scope.

As an illustration, the following are application examples: Advertisement (alternative to flooding), traffic load notification, search for the roaming mobile host with X being its previous point of attachment, maintenance checks for surrounding links, and – important! – the seizure/release of subnetwork (i.e., geopatch-) wide shared resources like multicast addresses as will be shown.

Each broadcast application needs an adequate indication about its scope. It could be geopatch-wide, geopatch cluster-wide or limited by a given number of hops away from X. An important usage example is traffic load balancing or congestion handling by congested node X (see below for more details).

TARA enables MP2P forwarding, typically in response to broadcast. Upon receiving a broadcast message a timer-supervised object may be instantiated which waits with respect to each forwarded broadcast message a response and combines the received response messages as to forward just one single sample to where it has received the broadcast message before. An application usage of MP2P forwarding is: response messages for acknowledging the release of a multicast address.

Furthermore, it will be shown how to compute Steiner Trees[1] and how to take advantage thereof.

TARA also enables Constraints-Based Routing (CBR). Whatever is state-of-art in intra-domain routing as to mark individual links and nodes with QoS class attributes and to compute CBR-inferred paths based on a respectively selected topology, can be done with TARA links and nodes as well, no matter whether these TARA-links are intra- or inter-domain links. In addition, the CBR-inferred path may be computed such that it preferably uses the intra-domain network rather than the external network – and vice versa.

Geographical constraints might be considered: E.g., as to compute routes which meander between nodes of "danger" as to bypass geographical regions, or routes à la Columbus who sailed to the West in order to get to the far East.

TARA allows for Mobile IP without the need for home-agent or care-of–address. The design adopted by TARA allows potentially all hosts be mobile nodes without having impact on the size of routing tables. In addition, TARA provides stateless multicast where both the sender as well as the receivers may be roaming eventually.

Finally, TARA supports a solution to re-use the same IPv4 address in several locations. This design allows coping with the IPv4 address depletion issue.

BACKGROUND

The following gives some background related to two big concerns: (1) the lack of an intelligent network layer and (2) the scalability problem of the Internet routing system.

IETF and ITU-T competed for many years, with IETF's TCP/IP winning over ITU-T's ISDN and B-ISDN. The kernel of the concern was as follows:

With IP forwarding each IP packet is "connection-less" and forwarded individually whereas according to ISDN/B-ISDN a signaling connection is established and also terminated, which in return establishes/controls/terminates a host-data connection. Hereby it reserves the required bandwidth and channels, takes all actions for enabling a host data transmission that complies with the indicated QoS requests.

This ITU-T approach influenced the IETF's IntServ school of thought with Resource Reservation Protocol (RSVP) and Multi Protocol Label Switching (MPLS) as visible outcomes. However the promoters for the connection-less forwarding fought back and created Differentiated Services (DiffServ). The basic idea of DiffServ is: A router has no knowledge about the traffic load in the surrounding neighborhood; all it knows is the actual length of the waiting queue of incoming packets. By introducing several such queues prioritized IP flow handling was accomplished which should match IntServ's capability for handling different services. TARA does not try to turn the wheel in favor of IntServ, instead it accepts the DiffServ-based approach and yet enables an intelligent network layer for the "connection-less" IP forwarding by reducing the so-called routing update churn to fairly zero. This is achieved by disseminating traffic load update information all over a well-scoped geographical neighborhood of a congested node or node cluster and by providing routing algorithms which are beyond what can be achieved by the current IETF state of the art.

In July 2002, at the London IETF meeting it was spoken out: "We definitely need a new routing architecture; however, there is no need for any rush. We will have ten years time for its implementation." In the years after the loc-id-split idea was born and it seems that the IETF would learn from the postal service which expects envelopes to contain a) the name of the receiver (identifier) and b) the address (locator) of the receiver. However there is more to learn and adopt from the postal network's behavior: Indeed, an ingress post office never requests to be informed about all moves of all people in the world such that it knows the accurate egress post office for each eventually letter to be sent out. Instead the postal service takes the risk and forwards a letter eventually to the wrong destination postal office, from where it will be returned to the sender in case the receiver had moved to some different location. This extra effort, however, is a little payment compared with the immense costs for the reachability updates. Hence, although all postal addresses form a hundred thousand times bigger network than the Internet, the postal service

neither has nor will ever have a problem similar to the IETF's scalability problem.

DFZ (Default Free Zone) routers have to maintain Routing Information Bases (RIBs) with millions of routes and Forwarding Information Bases (FIBs) with about 400,000 entries. Caching technology is needed for better performance. And yet, multiples of these millions of routes are hereby prevented for good: As a matter of fact, the employed distance vector algorithm conceives the earth being a disk rather than a ball, its logic does not envision that hopping to more remote routers may get you to some point from where on the route to the destination becomes shorter than from the current position. Hence routes à la Columbus are disabled, e.g.- as to prefer long distance routes across continents at night-time rather than in busy hours. Also, distance vector provides just the downstream part, not the upstream part, i.e. no (transit) router can ever see the upstream part of the routes for which it is transit.

SOLUTION AND RECOMMENDATION

TARA Architecture Overview

All TARA routers contribute to build Internet topology maps of five different zooms (denoted as TARA levels). A TARA router will see the precise Internet topology of that geo-patch it belongs to as well as more and more skimmed topologies of bigger and bigger surrounding geo-patch clusters. A geo-patch is a spherical rectangle/triangle limited by consecutive longitudes and latitudes.

Each TARA router forms a TARA map by combining excerpts of the five maps such that the more zoomed excerpt replaces the less-zoomed one. It is like the combination of city map, county-, state- and world map, with the more detailed map replacing its part in the less detailed map.

The TARA router computes a best unicast next hop with respect to each TARA map node. The weight value is still the number of hops: a link from the most zoomed map gets value "1," a path of some less zoomed map gets a value equal to the sum of the weight values of links that this path consists of.

Unicast packet forwarding is achieved based on the destination TARA Locator taken from a pre-pended TARA header. TARA Locator is a unique information derived from the egress TARA router's longitude/latitude degrees/minutes/seconds. Although egress TARA router may not be contained in the TARA map, the best next hop with respect to the right/closest proxy node from the TARA map will be executed, either by means of one or three single-offset table lookups. In either case an additional table-offset is required in case there are multiple constraint-based routes to the looked-up destination node.

There are two major pillars TARA is built upon:

1. The All-Links-Spanning-Tree (ALST) and respective follow-up algorithms.
2. The use of the geographical coordinates.

TARA Pillar 1: All Links Spanning Tree and Related Algorithms

In intra-domain routing there is at least Dijkstra's spanning tree the state of art which however is only an All Nodes Spanning Tree (ANST). Much more efficient is an All Links Spanning Tree (ALST) per potential destination node "d" (short name: ALST[d]), where all network links are converted to arcs, directed towards this destination node d, and such that no single loop of arcs were generated. As a result, with respect to any destination node, a router is enabled to properly esteem each network link of the entire visible network topology, with respect to passing them in either of the two directions.

In particular a transit router would, with respect to some particular destination node, recognize two groups of adjacent links:

1. Links which become arcs heading-off this router, and
2. Links which become arcs heading-to this router.

Figure 1. All-links-spanning-tree ALST[Dest]

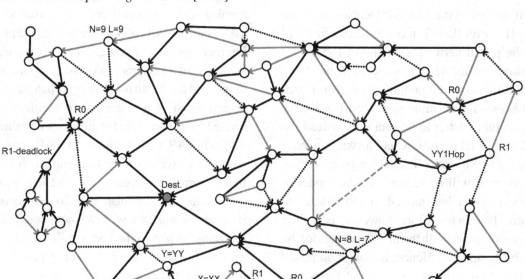

Also, a transit router would recognize even more:

1. A downstream sub-network being the sum of all arc sequences which start at this transit router and end at the destination node,
2. An upstream sub-network being the sum of all arc sequences which start at whichever well-recognizable upper rim and would definitely pass the current transit router.

Note that all network routers will hereby have a consistent view.

Figure 1 shows an ALST[Dest] rooted at the node named "Dest".

- **Solid black arc:** Best as by regular Dijkstra
- **Dotted arc:** Equally best
- **Dashed arc:** Not best however head node is closer to the destination than the tail node
- **Solid grey arc:** Head and tail node have the same distance to the destination node.
- The single dashed arc/link has weight value "3", all others weight value "1"

Constructing ALST[d]: Build the Dijkstra ANST (i.e., all solid black arcs) and, hereby during the iteration, store the sequence by which the network nodes are finally assigned their single off-going best (solid black) arc. Let us call this node sequence "NS". After Dijkstra visit node after node of this sequence NS and convert all so far not yet converted links, which are adjacent to the currently visited node, into dotted/dashed/solid grey arcs heading to the currently visited node. Obviously, no single loop of arcs will occur.

Forwarding along solid grey arcs: Due to the method how the ALST is computed, no loop can occur by forwarding towards the head node only. However this is not sufficient because forwarding towards the tails of solid grey arcs isn't any worse. Therefore by means of some simple recursive algorithm each node with at least one adjacent

solid grey arc may compute the number of links and the number of nodes of that solid grey cluster it belongs to. If the number L of links is smaller than the number N of nodes of that cluster then the cluster is mesh-free and forwarding can disregard the directions of the solid grey arcs, provided that forwarding is not done to that node from which the packet is received.

Otherwise the cluster contains meshes. In this case end-less loops inside the solid grey cluster can be prevented by limiting the number of solid grey hops to the total number of solid grey arcs of the cluster. See further below also how this kind of detour is guided by Detour Indication and Remaining Hops Counter attributes.

The Remaining Hops Counter works like the Time-To-Live counter: i.e. it enforces the dropping of the packet in case it has reached the value zero. In other words, if no hop to some node which is closer to the destination couldn't be made in time.

Figure 1 shows that node which is captured "N=8 L=7". It belongs to a mesh free cluster of solid grey arcs which comprises 8 nodes and 7 links. See also the node captured "N=9 L=9". It belongs to a mesh-containing cluster of solid grey arcs which comprises 9 nodes and 9 links.

Forwarding via more remote nodes: With respect to any more remote neighbour node a current router can algorithmically determine whether:

1. There is a 3-hops detour via this neighbour node such that the first hop is done towards the tail node of a solid black or dotted arc followed by two best next hops (toward the heads of solid black or dotted arcs) as to reach a router which is closer to the destination than the current router.
2. There exists a longer detour via this neighbour node consisting of a pair of tunnels, i.e. a first shortest tailward bound tunnel followed by a second shortest headward bound tunnel towards some other node at which one further dashed/dotted/solid black hop must

be done. This is achieved by determining the end nodes of all these tunnels.

3. There exists a longer detour via this neighbour node whereby multiple pairs of shortest upstream/downstream tunnels are needed to reach some node at which one further dashed/dotted/solid black hop must be done. This is achieved by determining the end nodes of all these tunnels.

4. A hop to that neighbour node would enter a deadlock sub-network.

3-hops-detour:

R0→ R1→YY1Hop→any closer node

Figure 1 (to the right) shows a 3-hops-detour: How must router R0 prepare itself for the situation that it has to forward packets, destined for node Dest, to tail node router R1 of a solid black or dotted arc?

R0 realizes that a 3-hops-detour can be done. By proper detour instruction it enforces R1 to do a best next hop (but not back to R0), here to node YY1Hop. That node (YY1Hop) shall forward the packet to the head of an adjacent dashed/dotted/

solid black arc and clear the detour instruction. If R1 or YY1Hop can not comply with the detour instruction the packet must be dropped.

Long detour via more remote nodes: If forwarding via the tail node of an adjacent arc cannot be done by a 3-hops-detour, it either requires a long detour or the packet must be dropped if there is no long detour available or if the detour required too much effort, i.e. too many tunnel pairs.

Figure 1 (at the bottom) shows how router R0 shall prepare itself for the case it has to forward the packet (being destined for node Dest) via neighbour node R1.

Two different algorithms compute (in this particular case) the same results: Take tunnel from R0 (via R1) to more remote node XX (resp. X, determined by the other algorithm), then tunnel to node YY (resp. Y) which is as close to the destination as is R0 itself. Node YY (resp. Y) must forward the packet to the head of a dashed/dotted/solid black arc and clear the conveyed detour instruction.

Figure 2 shows an excessive detour comprising four (4) pairs of tunnels.

Z indicates the destination node.

Figure 2. Extremely long detour

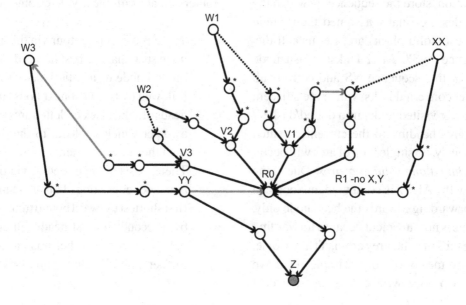

One of the two algorithm doesn't find a detour in case packets were to be forwarded from R0 to R1: that is why "R1 - no X,Y."

The second and obviously better algorithm yields a detour like this:

From R0 (via R1) tailward to XX, then headward to V1, then tailward to W1, then headward to V2, then tailward to W2, then headward to V3, then tailward to W3 then headward to YY, followed by one more hop to the head node of some adjacent dashed/dotted/solid black arc and the detour is completed. The transited nodes of these tunnels are captured with stars in Figure 2.

Entering a no-go area – see Figure 1 to the left: Packet forwarding from R0 to R1 is a "no-go." It would enter a dead-end area. Therefore if at R0 all adjacent links were blocked except the link to R1, then the packet has to be dropped nevertheless.

Guiding Procedures in Case of Detours

(See "TARA forwarding information" Section) Below the procedure to follow:

Step 1:

- Packet shall be forwarded to the head node of a solid black or dotted or dashed arc: No guiding required (Detour Indication = 0).

Step 2:

- Packet shall be forwarded via a solid grey arc which belongs to a solid grey cluster of links which does not contain any meshes: No guiding required (Detour Indication = 0).

Step 3:

- Packet shall be forwarded via a first solid grey arc which belongs to a mesh containing solid grey area:

  - The Detour Indication of received packet is = 0.
  - Set Detour Indication to 1. Set Remaining Hops Counter to the number of arcs of this solid grey cluster.

- Packet shall be forwarded via some additional solid grey arc which belongs to a mesh containing solid grey area: The Detour Indication of received packet is equal to 1, decrement Remaining Hops Counter.

- If it becomes zero a hop to some node which is closer to the destination is necessary, otherwise the packet must be dropped.

- Whenever Detour Indication is set to 1 and a hop to some node which is closer to the destination is about to be done, then set Detour Indication to zero (i.e., the detour is completed).

Step 4:

- Packet shall be forwarded to the tail node of a dashed/dotted/solid black arc. The Detour Indication of received packet is = 0.

- Determine whether (a) the packet will hereby enter a dead end area, or (b) can from there get to some node which is closer to the destination by passing two other dotted or solid black arcs (= 3-hops-detour), or c) will require a longer detour.

- If (a) applies, don't forward the packet.

- If (b) applies, set Detour Indication to "2" ("3-hops-detour") and Remaining Hops Counter to "2".

  - The receiving tail-node will forward the packet to the head node of a dotted or solid black arc (no solid grey and no dashed arcs) but not to where the packet comes from. It will recognize this case because the received packet has the Detour Indication set to "2" while the Remaining Hops Counter is set to "2". The packet will decrement the Remaining Hops Counter (i.e., set to "1").

○ The next node will undertake the same operation. In other words, it will forward the packet to the head node of only some dotted or solid black adjacent arc. Because the Remaining Hops Counter is equal to "0", it will also set Detour Indication flag to "0" before it forwards the packet to some node which is closer to the destination than the node that started the detour.

- If (c) applies, determine the needed pairs of shortest tunnels/loose hops which form the detour-path. Each pair starts with a loose hop (i.e., tunnel) tailward to some more remote nodes, followed by a loose hop headward to some node which is closer to the destination. The end node of the last tunnel must do one more best hop and the detour is completed. Then, setup the TARA forwarding information accordingly.

- When the packet arrives at that node whose TARA Locator matches the received first upstream TARA Locator this upstream TARA Locator is cleared and forwarding continues towards the node which matches the first downstream TARA Locator. When that node has been reached, the first pair is deleted and the number of pairs decremented. Any transit node in-between will perform TARA forwarding towards the first appearing TARA Locator.

Conclusion

Detouring a detour is not allowed. If such a situation were encountered the packet has to be dropped. One might argue ECMP is sufficient; however there are cases where no single ECMP next hop is available and, eventually, a long detour is the only available route.

Altogether a "100% routing orientation" is accomplished which eliminates the fear about loops and makes the Time to Live (TTL) mechanism superfluous. TARA enables this "100% routing orientation" for the combined intra-and inter-domain routing and as such it does not require "micro-loops" or "not-via"-forwarding mechanisms defined within IETF.

The ALST[d] (and its sub-tree ANST[d]) provides also a view towards the upstream.

This view enables well-scoped broadcast for disseminating traffic congestion notification to the surrounding area of a congested node. Combined with the geographical location information the surrounding nodes may be induced to divert the flows as to bypass the congested node partially via South, partially via North, North-East, North-West, etc. This is also meant by achieving "100% routing orientation" which is certainly different from the DiffServ's approach.

All-Links-Spanning-Tree Rooted at Multiple Nodes $d_1, d_2, \ldots, d_n$

By minor modifications of ALST[d] we can build an All Links Spanning Tree rooted at multiple nodes $d_1, d_2, \ldots, d_n$; its short name be ALST[$d_1, d_2, \ldots, d_n$].

Constructing ALST[$d_1, d_2, \ldots, d_n$]: Introduce an artificial root node d with links of equal weight value =0 to $d_1, d_2, \ldots, d_n$. The rest is like computing an ALST[d] rooted at one particular destination node. Additionally, during the Dijkstra iteration, whenever a node X is assigned its final predecessor node Y, do also assign the respective d_i -node it is bound to.

```
(d.predecessor:= d; d.bound_to:= d;//
init
….. //iteration
X.predecessor= Y;
if X.predecessor equal d then
```

```
X.bound_to:= X; else X.bound_to:=
Y.bound_to)
```

ALST[$d_1,d_2,\ldots,d_n$] intersects the entire topology in sub-networks of nodes and links, i.e.- with nodes which are closest to one of the "n" d_i - nodes and links which have become arcs directed towards the respective d_i -node (a tie-break rule may apply in case of equal distance). See Voronoi diagram[2].

Imagine an Operation and Management (OAM) server d_i which either wants to communicate with all its surrounding client nodes or which wants to assess the status of all its surrounding client links. In the first case this OAM d_i node broadcasts OAM messages towards the neighbouring tail nodes (of all adjacent solid dark arcs) which will be forwarded upstream along only solid black arcs as to reach all surrounding client nodes. In the second case this OAM d_i node as well as all surrounding nodes forward the message towards the tail nodes of all adjacent arcs as to pass all surrounding client links. No overlapping will occur when node d_i communicates with its surrounding

nodes/links and node d_k does the same with its surrounding nodes/links as well.

Furthermore, the ALST[$d_1,d_2,\ldots,d_n$] will be the key for building less zoomed maps: Indeed so-called watershed nodes can be identified, i.e.- nodes where Dijkstra best-hop arc sequences start out as to end at different root nodes d_i. A pair of such two sequences yields a path-link between these two root nodes. The sum of such path will form the skimmed topology in a next less zoomed map.

The resulting less zoomed map will mainly consist of triangular meshes (see also Delaunay-Triangulation[3]), though in principle its shape may be arbitrary.

Last but not least, a very good Steiner Tree ST[$d_1,d_2,\ldots,d_n$] can be formed, based on ALST[$d_1,d_2,\ldots,d_n$], as follows:

- Start with "n" Steiner Trees each of which just consists of node d_i.
- Visit node after node of node sequence NS, detect hereby watershed nodes (of "lowest

Figure 3. Screenshot, displaying algorithmically determined ALST[d1, d2,....,d14]

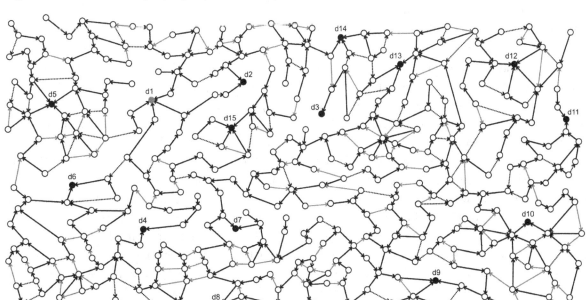

level") and combine eventually different Steiner Trees by the path-halves between that watershed node and the different d_i nodes. Hereby there are two alternatives:

○ Eventually only fractions of the two path-halves will be added, i.e. the parts between the watershed node and the first node where a path-half hits the respective Steiner Tree. Consequently, the resulting Steiner Tree can branch at any participating node.

○ Both path-halves will be added entirely. Consequently, the resulting Steiner Tree can branch only at d_i – nodes.

By having combined all Steiner Trees, we have built a single Steiner Tree $ST[d_1,d_2,...,d_n]$ which interconnects $d_1,d_2,...,d_n$.

TARA Pillar 2: Use of Geographical Coordinates

The globe may be conceived as 180 rings of spherical triangles/rectangles, starting at the South pole with a ring of 360 spherical triangles, each of which is limited by two longitudes and latitude 89° South from the Equator. Towards North there follow 178 rings of 360 spherical rectangles, each of which is limited by two consecutive longitudes and latitudes. Finally there is a last ring of 360 spherical triangles around the North pole. Any of these spherical triangles/rectangles is called geo-patch or (1,1)-geo-patch.

Each geo-patch is assigned a geo-patch number from 1 to 64800, starting at the South Pole with that (1,1)-geo-patch which is limited by the two longitude degrees 0 and 1 East, the South Pole and latitude 89 South, winding from there in eastbound direction, while forming a full circle such that number 360 is assigned to that (1,1)-geo-patch, which is limited by the two longitude degrees 1 West and 0, while number 361 is assigned to that (1,1,)-geo-patch, which is limited by the longitude

degrees 0 and 1 East and the latitudes 89 South and 88 South. While winding in eastbound direction and while winding towards the North Pole, the last number 64800 is assigned to that (1,1)-geo-patch which is limited by the longitudes 1 West and 0, the latitude 89 North and the North Pole. With respect to any spherical triangle and rectangle, its limiting lines to the West and to the South will belong to it.

The geo-patch number (geopatch#) is also called square degree#.

We also introduce (m, n)-geo-patch-clusters consisting of m rows of n (1, 1)-geo-patches, arranged from 'South to North in the same way and get altogether:

- 180 rows/rings each containing 360 (1, 1)-geopatches for the most zoom-1 map
- 60 rows/rings each containing 120 (3, 3)-geopatch-clusters for the zoom-2 map
- 30 rows/rings each containing 60 (6, 6)-geopatch-clusters for the zoom-3 map
- 15 rows/rings each containing 30 (12, 12)-geopatch-clusters for the zoom-4 map
- 5 rows/rings each containing 10 (36, 36)-geopatch-clusters for the least zoom-5 map

From given geographical coordinates (longitude lo, latitude la) we derive the (1, 1)-geopatch-row#, (1, 1)-geopatch-column#, and the(1, 1)-geopatch# as follows:

Deriving the (1, 1)-geo-patch-# from the geographical coordinates (longitude lo, latitude la):

If lo is 0 (Greenwich) or some degree East of Greenwich then (1, 1)-geopatch-column# = lo +1.

If lo is some degree West of Greenwich then (1, 1)-geopatch-column# = 360-lo.

If la is 0 (Equator) or some degree North of the Equator then (1, 1)-geopatch-row# = 90 + la +1

If la is some degree South of the Equator then (1, 1)-geopatch-row# = 90-la (1, 1)-geopatch# = ((1,1)-geopatch-row# - 1) • 360 + (1, 1)-geopatch-column#

Note that inversely:

```
(1, 1)-geopatch-row# = Integer ((1,
1)-geopatch# +359)/360);
(1, 1)-geopatch-column# = 1 + ((1,
1)-geopatch# modulo 360);
```

A (1, 1)-geopatch,

```
is part of a (3, 3)-geopatch cluster
identified by
(3, 3)-geopatch-cluster-row# =  In-
teger((1, 1)-geopatch-row# -1)/3) +1
;
(3, 3)-geopatch-cluster-column# = In-
teger((1, 1)-geopatch-column# -1)/3)
+1 ;
(3, 3)-geopatch-cluster# =
((3, 3)-geopatch-cluster-row#
```

```
-1)·120+(3, 3)-geopatch-cluster-col-
umn#
is part of a (6, 6)-geopatch cluster
identified by
(6, 6)-geopatch-cluster-row# =   In-
teger((1, 1)-geopatch-row# -1)/6) +1
;
(6, 6)-geopatch-cluster-column# = In-
teger((1, 1)-geopatch-column# -1)/6)
+1 ;
(6, 6)-geopatch-cluster# =
((6, 6)-geopatch-cluster-row# -1)·60
+ (6, 6)-geopatch-cluster-column#
is part of a (12, 12)-geopatch clus-
ter identified by
(12, 12)-geopatch-cluster-row# =  In-
teger((1, 1)-geopatch-row# -1)/12) +1
;
(12, 12)-geopatch-cluster-column#
```

Figure 4. Forming the unicast-TARA locator

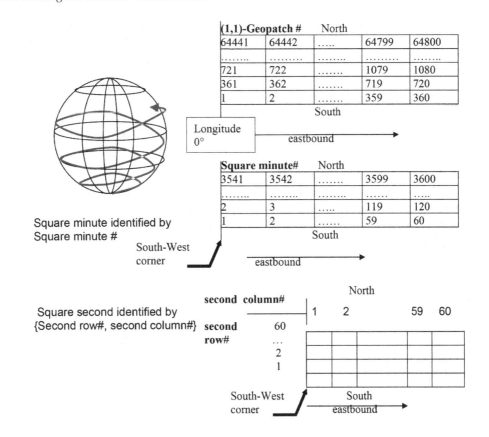

```
= Integer((1, 1)-geopatch-column#
-1)/12) +1 ;
(12, 12)-geopatch-cluster# =
(12,12)-geopatch-cluster-row# -1)·30
+ (12, 12)-geopatch-cluster-column#
is part of a (36, 36)-geopatch clus-
ter identified by
(36, 36)-geopatch-cluster-row# =  In-
teger((1, 1)-geopatch-row# -1)/36) +1
;
(36, 36)-geopatch-cluster-column#
= Integer((1, 1)-geopatch-column#
-1)/36) +1 ;
(36, 36)-geopatch-cluster# =
(36, 36)-geopatch-cluster-row# -1)·30
+ (36, 36)-geopatch-cluster-column#
```

The (1, 1)-geopatch# may also be called square-degree#.

A (3, 3)-geopatch-cluster consists of 3 rows and 3 columns of (1, 1)-geopatches.

A (6, 6)-geopatch-cluster consists of 2 rows and 2 columns of (3, 3)-geopatch-clusters.

A (12, 12)-geopatch-cluster consists of 2 rows and 2 columns of (6, 6)-geopatch-clusters.

A (36, 36)-geopatch-cluster consists of 3 rows and 3 columns of (12, 12)-geopatch-clusters.

Square Minutes

A (1, 1)-geopatch shall be intersected into 60 rows and 60 columns which reflect geographical minutes with respect to longitudes and latitudes, i.e. it contains 3600 square minutes each of which is assigned a square minute# as follows.

```
Square minute# derived from given
longitude minute x and latitude min-
ute y.
if (1, 1)-geopatch-row# < 91 (i.e.
South of the Equator)
then minute row# = 60 -y else minute
```

```
row# = y+1
else minute row# = y+1.
if (1, 1)-geopatch-column# > 180
(i.e. West of Greenwich)
then minute column# = 60- x
else minute column# = x+1.
square minute# = (minute row# -1)
times 60 + minute column#
```

A square-minute encompasses its rim to its West and to its South.

Square Seconds

A Square minute shall be intersected into 60 rows and 60 columns which reflect geographical seconds with respect to longitudes and latitudes, i.e. it contains 3600 square seconds each of which is assigned a second row# and a second column# as follows (In order to avoid waste of router's memory we do not allocate for each of 3600 square minutes a 3600-elements-sized square-second-table, where most of them are expected to be completely empty, hence we will use second row# and second column# but no square second#).

```
Second row# and second column# de-
rived from given longitude second x
and latitude second y.
if (1, 1)-geopatch-row# < 91 (i.e.,
South of the Equator)
then second row# = 60 -y else
else second row# = y+1.
if (1, 1)-geopatch-column# > 180
(i.e., West of Greenwich)
then second column# = 60- x
else second column# = x+1.
```

A square-second encompasses its rim to its West and to its South.

Any TARA router will have and will advertise, in compliance with its geographical location, a Unicast TARA Locator like this one:

```
Unicast TARA Locator = {
    square degree #, // Range 1 to
64800   16 bits
    square minute #, // Range 1 to
3600   12 bits
    second row#,     // Range 1 to 60
6 bits
    second column# // Range 1 to 60
6 bits
```

Notes:

1. Inverse mapping from TARA Locator to the geographical coordinates is no big deal.
2. It is not necessary that square minute #, second row #, second column# match precisely the physical location of a TARA router. It is only necessary that different TARA routers with the same square-degree # have unique {square minute #, second row #, second column# } triples.

We may anticipate finer granularity to identify fractions of square seconds. But there is no urgent need for it.

IPv4 Address Depletion Issue

How to preserve global uniqueness given that IPv4 unicast addresses are depleting? This is an extremely severe problem.

To solve this issue, TARA adopts the approach which consists in combining

the host's IPv4 unicast address with its TARA Unicast Locator. An IPv4 address which has already been assigned to some host attached to any legacy IP router can be conceived as {geopatch# =0; IPv4 address}. This IPv4 address can be re-

used for another host which is attached to some TARA router, however in such a way that the pair {geopatch# from that router's TARA Locator; IPv4 address} is unique.

With respect to multicast (and also to anycast and MP2MP) TARA proposes the instance identification based on (geopatch# of the sender; 2 octets sized instance number) and shows how to handle the respective seizing and releasing. Global well-known multicast respectively anycast services shall be identified by {geopatch# = 648001 respectively =64802; standardized number}.

For this to work, it is required that an FQDN (e.g., www.mycompany@com.) is mapped to {unicast IPv4 address;unicast TARA Locator}. Hence the query must be done by the source host and it must be directed to DNS and not to any alternative resolution service.

In case the ingress router is a TARA router then the source host has to prepend a TARA header. Otherwise, it has to prepend, in addition, a GRE Header with destination IPv4 address = 0.0.0.0 or the one of a near TARA router. Note, this means that in future any additional TARA router must get a unique IPv4 address to speak {geopatch # = 0; IPv4 address } space..

Building the TARA Map

Similar to Google-Map several (e.g., five) Internet topologies of different zooming levels shall be constructed by the concerted effort of all TARA routers. The closest zoom topology will be the precise topology of the entire Internet. By some algorithm the closer zoomed map will be skimmed for generating the less zoomed map - recursively four times as per the above example. All TARA routers all over the Earth will see the whole least zoomed map, whereas TARA routers of a confined geographical area will be the only ones, that can see the respective excerpt from the closest zoomed map.

Any TARA router of (1, 1)-geopatch with number X1 shall get to know all internal links as well as all (outgoing) border-to-border links and collect them in its collect TARA map.

The border nodes of X1 compute their representative contribution for the (3, 3)- geopatch cluster of number X2 and export them to the other parts thereof, including the outgoing border-to-border links. Likewise there will be imports. All imported links will be disseminated all over X1 and will be added to the TARA map of any TARA router inside X1.

In case some border-to-border link shows up twice in the TARA map (due to "export/outgoing" and "import/incoming") one instance of appearance can be deleted.

The border nodes of X2 compute their representative contribution for the (6, 6)- geopatch cluster of number X3 and export them to the other parts thereof, including the outgoing border-to-border links. Likewise there will be imports. All imported links will be disseminated all over X2 and will be added to the TARA map of any TARA router inside X2.

In case some border-to-border link shows up twice in the TARA map (due to "export/outgoing" and "import/incoming") one instance of appearance can be deleted.

The border nodes of X3 compute their representative contribution for the (12, 12)- geopatch cluster of number X4 and export them to the other parts thereof, including the outgoing border-to-border links. Likewise there will be imports. All imported links will be disseminated all over X3 and will be added to the TARA map of any TARA router inside X3.

In case some border-to-border link shows up twice in the TARA map (due to "export/outgoing" and "import/incoming") one instance of appearance can be deleted.

The border nodes of X4 compute their representative contribution for the (36, 36)- geopatch cluster of number X5 and export them to the other parts thereof, including the outgoing border-to-

border links. Likewise there will be imports. All imported links will be disseminated all over X4 and will be added to the TARA map of any TARA router inside X4.

In case some border-to-border link shows up twice in the TARA map (due to "export/outgoing" and "import/incoming") one instance of appearance can be deleted.

As a result any TARA router will have a single map which contains the more and more skimmed topologies of its own hierarchy of geopatch clusters. It is advisable to store the content of the TARA map in such a way, that each part for some particular zooming level can be accessed as a whole.

Scrolling

There are locations such that the next neighbour node not only belongs to a different (1, 1)-geopatch, but also to a different (3, 3)-, (6, 6)-, (12, 12)-, and possibly even to a different (36, 36)-geopatch-cluster. We should avoid the Istanbul effect!

Istanbul effect means: It would be bad if a city map of Istanbul contained the European part with all the details, but for the Asian part just what you get about Istanbul from a road map for whole Asia.

A TARA router must be enabled to ask such a neighbour node to be given the topologies of its hierarchy of geopatch or geopatch clusters (at most up to level 4, at least up to level 2) and to disseminate this information all over its own (m, n) geopatch or geopatch-clusters of the own hierarchy - up to at most level 4, up to at least level 2.

FORMING THE TARA NETWORK OF ZOOMING LEVEL 1 (CLOSEST ZOOM)

Especially in the early deployment phase a contiguous TARA network is to be formed by interconnecting clusters of TARA-links/TARA-nodes by means of intra-geopatch GRE tunnels and inter-geopatch GRE tunnels. Any such GRE tunnel shall be originated by that endpoint TARA router whose TARA Locator is the smaller one, i.e. which is more southern and, as a tie breaker, more western eventually.

At first, a TARA router will advertise its existence by advertising its IPv4 address together with its TARA Locator by means of inter-domain wide BGP UPDATE messages; respectively intra-domain wide OSPF LSA packets.

Thereafter, any two adjacent TARA routers shall recognize that they are connected by a strict TARA link and will flood this information via such strict TARA links and limited to their common geopatch that all TARA routers of a particular cluster of a particular geopatch get to know the topology thereof. This topology will include strict TARA-links learnt by OSPF/IS-IS as well as by BGP but exclude what is outside the particular geopatch. Note, the smallest cluster ever is of course a single TARA router with no single adjacent strict TARA link.

Separated clusters of the same geopatch shall be interconnected by means of GRE tunnels as follows: TARA router R_A being cluster A's most northern router will initiate a GRE tunnel to TARA router R_B being mini-cluster B's most southern router. In case there are multiple R_A's and/or R_B's being suitable candidates, those R_A, R_B shall be elected which are most western. Across this GRE tunnel the two clusters will exchange their topology information and flooded onwards so that each TARA router of the combined cluster will know the combined topology.

Note that such clusters may be homed by multiple geopatches due to strict TARA-links crossing the respective geopatch borders. The exchange of the topological information, however, shall hereby not cross the geopatch limits.

This phase is completed as soon as all clusters inside a particular geopatch are combined.

In a next phase the resulting clusters have to be interconnected by inter-geopatch GRE tunnels – for reasons of simplicity while ignoring whether or not they are already interconnected by strict TARA links- as follows:

The most northern/western TARA router R_A from geopatch A initiates a GRE tunnel to the most southern/western TARA router R_B from geopatch B with B being A's northern neighbour geopatch.

The most northern/eastern TARA router R_A from geopatch A initiates a GRE tunnel to the most northern/western TARA router R_B from geopatch B with B being A's eastern neighbour geopatch.

Eventually and analogously further GRE tunnels might be built which are nearest to the 30 minute longitude resp. latitude line.

Should hereby any neighbour geopatch be empty then a GRE tunnel to the over next northern resp. over next eastern neighbour geopatch shall be built.

As a result a world-wide TARA topology of zooming level 1 is established whereby each TARA router knows the topology of the own geopatch.

The BGP UPDATE message of a TARA router for propagating all adjacent TARA-links shall contain

```
 - purpose of propagation:
  (0 = building mini-clusters
   1 = building arbitrary clusters,
   10 = building less zoomed,
   11 = for scrolling)
per adjacent TARA-link
 - the zooming level (1 to 5) with 1=
closest and 5= least zoomed map
 - the respective geo-patch (cluster)
#
 - the remote endpoint TARA router B,
with its IPv4 address and its TARA
Locator
 - link type (strict, loose, "GRE
tunnel" crossing some non-TARA net-
work part)
 - the weight of this TARA-link (= 1
if strict link, =number of its hops
if loose link,
approximated value if GRE tunnel-
```

link)
 - a distinction whether it is a in-
tra- or inter-domain link
 - QoS constraints as known
 - more (like additional info for
scrolling, or optionally: an explicit
list of geo-patch
   numbers and/or geo-patch cluster
numbers the two link-adjacent TARA
routers
   would represent -ffs)

A TARA link shall be advertised by that end node only which has the smaller TARA Locator.

A TARA link is of type "strict" if both ends of the physical link are TARA routers. A TARA-link is of type "GRE tunnel" if a GRE Tunnel is needed to connect its endpoint TARA routers across classical Internet routers. Hereby a to be standardized rule is required for assigning an adequate weight value (e.g., based on the spherical geo-distance). A TARA link is of type "loose" if it is rather a path which consists of multiple concatenated TARA links, each of which is of any of the three link types.

FORMING THE TARA TOPOLOGY OF ZOOMING LEVELS 2, 3, 4 AND 5

Having learnt the topology of TARA links inside its own geopatch or geopatch-cluster, each TARA router is algorithmically enabled to compute a well-skimmed topology thereof which shall represent this geopatch or geopatch cluster at the next less zoomed level.

(Step 1) In a first step the set of all representative nodes shall be determined: Hereby all border nodes (i.e. nodes with links to other geopatches or geopatch-clusters) will be part of this set. Standardized rules shall help to determine the number of additional representative nodes: In a less populated area the entire more zoomed topology may reappear in the next less zoomed topology. In a dense populated area a well determined quota and/or an upper bound number of representative nodes may be applied. Let us assume "n" further representative nodes have to be determined, in addition to "N" border nodes. It shall be done as follows as to accomplish some kind of equal distribution:

Figure 5. Computing a less zoomed map: step 1

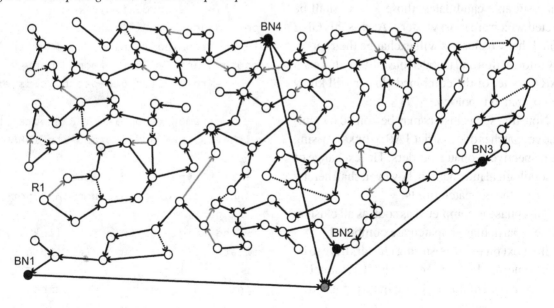

- We compute the ALST rooted at the "N" border nodes and determine the last network node R_1 for which a shortest path is hereby determined.
- It will be the one which is furthest away from the "N" border nodes. It is the last node in node sequence NS.
- We compute again the ALST but this time rooted at the "N" border nodes and R_1 as to determine R_2 being furthest away from the "N" border nodes and from R_1. We repeat this iteratively until we compute the ALST rooted at the "N" border nodes and $R_1, \ldots R_{n-1}$ for getting R_n.

Figure 5 shows the ALST[BN1, BN2, BN3, BN4] for an example network with four border nodes BN1, BN2, BN3 and BN4. See the artificial root node d and its artificial links to BN1, BN2, BN3 and BN4.

The last node of Node Sequence NS of ALST[BN1, BN2,BN3,BN4] shall be node R1.

BN2, BN3 and BN4; R1 shall be the only nodes to reappear in the less zoomed map.

(Step 2) In a second step we determine the set of representative (path-)links which connect these five representative nodes: We compute the ALST [BN1, BN2, BN3, BN4, R_1], identify the

resulting watershed nodes and consequently the wanted path-links as well as their weight values.

Watershed nodes W12a and W12b are in the middle of the shortest path between BN1 and BN2. The same applies for WR14a and WR14b between R1 and BN4, W23a and W23b between BN2 and BN3, and finally W34 between BN3 and BN4.

The weight value for BN1–BN2 path is "13" (equal to the number of the respective hops). The weight value for BN3–BN4 path is "18."

Marginal note: Watershed nodes XR14a and XR14b are in the middle of a path between R1 and BN4 however that path is not the shortest between R1 and BN4!

Note, where necessary, by employing some tie-break rules, the determination of the representative topology can be made such that any network node would automatically get the identical result.

Simpler alternative for building a less zoomed map: Build ALST[all N border nodes]. Start from these N border nodes, move tailward and select every k-th node to re-appear in the less zoomed map again. The value k may be a standardized function depending on the number of Border nodes and the number of all nodes of the more zoomed map.

Figure 6. Computing a less zoomed map: step 2

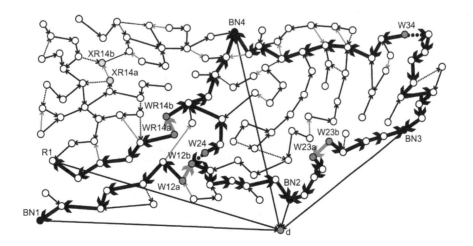

Filling and Using TARA Unicast Forwarding Tables

Based on its TARA map a TARA router computes the entries of its TARA-forwarding tables as described by the following. There will be tables t1, t2, t3, t4 which form the TARA unicast FIB. Based on the destination TARA Locator as of some received IP packet's prepended TARA-header a TARA router retrieves the next hop information from its Unicast TARA forwarding tables as described by the following.

Unicast-Destination is outside from the current router's (1,1)-geo-patch: For the sake of forwarding to another (1, 1)-geo-patch the current router shall maintain a table t1 with 64800 next-hop entries. By means of one Dijkstra it computes the next-hop to all nodes of the TARA map. At first let's consider those nodes which have a different geopatch number than the current router itself. Among them, we select the one which is nearest according to their Dijkstra path lengths and enter with proper geopatch# offset the respective best next hop into table t1.

There will be many t1-offsets which would probable index some ocean or desert area where there is no single TARA router. These t1-offset elements will be some default value but should never be used. There may be others for which

the TARA map doesn't have any node. Here, we should look for the relative closest TARA router which happens to be in the TARA map, and enter its respective best next hop here as well.

Unicast-Destination is inside of the current router's (1,1)-geo-patch: We cannot afford a 3600 times 3600=12,960,000 entries sized table, i.e. a matrix for each square second. Hence, for the sake of forwarding to any TARA router x from the current router's (1,1)-geo-patch we employ tables t2, t3, t4. Table t2, indexed by TARA router X's square-minute number, will refer to some table t3.

Table t3, indexed by TARA router X's second row#, will refer to some table t4. Table t4, indexed by TARA router X's second column#, will contain the next hop towards X. or an indication that the current router is already the egress. In this case forwarding shall take place classically.

There will be just one single table t1 with 64800 entries. There will be just one single (sparsely filled) table t2 with 3600 entries (a minority of these entries refer to some particular t3-tables). There will be multiple tables t3 with 60 entries each. There will be multiple table t4 with 60 entries each.

When an IP packet with a prepended TARA-header is received the next hop for unicast forwarding is determined as follows:

Figure 7. TARA unicast FIB, part 1

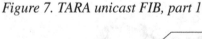
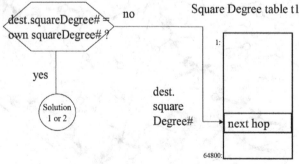

(square degree# and geopatch# are synomyms)

Figure 8. TARA unicast FIB, part 2

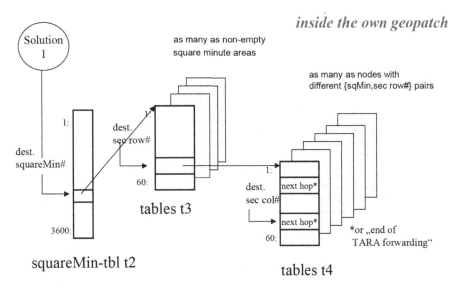

Take the received destination TARA Locator. Is its square-degree# equal to the current router's square-degree#?

If not, index table t1 with the received square degree# and retrieve next hop info.

Else, take the received square minute# to offset table t2 for retrieving a particular table t3.

Then index table t3 with the received second row# for retrieving a particular table t4.

Index table t4 with the received second column# and retrieve the *next hop information.*

(Less favored) Unicast alternative with respect to very populated geopatches: The retrieved *next hop information* may, with respect to constraint-based-routing and in case of unicast forwarding, consists of even a list of next hops to be indexed by the CBR index from the TARA header. The indexed list element, just like other next hop information for non unicast forwarding, shall provide:

- The physical link to be used,
- If applicable, GRE encapsulation information/instruction,
- If applicable, detour start information/instruction (starting a 3-hops detour,
- Detour/entering a meshy subnetwork of equal distance to the destination),
- Reference to alternative next hop in case forwarding via this link doesn't work.

Or, it indicates that the current router is the endpoint of TARA forwarding and references the respective procedure.

As a result, next hop lookup becomes very fast, no matter whether we can serve with best hops or, temporarily, e.g. due to traffic congestion with alternative hops. No caching is required in any case! Moore's law becomes applicable!

Endpoints of TARA Forwarding

Which entity will prepend (respectively remove) the TARA header?

In case IPv4 addresses aren't globally unique anymore and that uniqueness is established by combining it with any Locator (be that as of TARA or as of LISP) the respective header with the locator information must be pre-pended by the

Figure 9. TARA unicast FIB (alternative for dense populated areas)

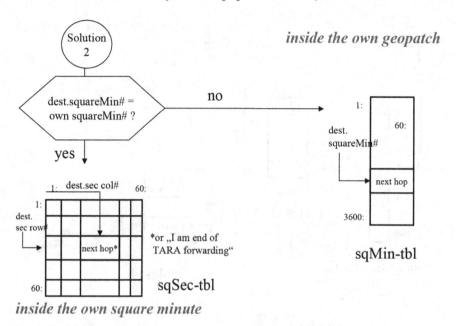

inside the own square minute

source host (you can't either post a letter to Mr. Li and let the ingress post office add the address – in case of Mr. Li one among millions)

The TARA router X does not advertise reachability information with respect to its locally attached hosts, nor does it forward reachability information received from any stub network. Instead X makes sure that the hereby referred hosts will retrieve DNS entries which not only contain their IPv4 addresses but also the geographical coordinates of TARA router X (see RFC1712) – or even better the TARA Locator of X itself.

However the TARA router does advertise the default mapper prefix of length zero.

By doing so a TARA router which is nearest to the source host can attract packets for being TARA forwarded to destination hosts that are attached to some TARA router and whose reachability is not propagated world-wide.

With respect to non-local and non-stub addresses a TARA router behaves like a normal BGP (resp. OSPF/IS-IS) router.

Start of TARA Forwarding

The source host gets to know the destination's TARA Locater (e.g. by DNS query request) and prepends the TARA header.

The ingress TARA router may act as a proxy (i.e. intercepts the DNS response or even initiates a DNS query request by itself to retrieve and store the destination's locator). The ingress TARA router will prepend TARA headers to packets destined to that destination appropriately and indicate its own TARA Locator as source TARA Locator. Another alternative is the packets are attracted to the nearest TARA router (as that a downstream router has propagated prefix reachability of length 0) and that one acts just like the ingress TARA router as described. Note these two alternatives afford world-wide IPv4 address uniqueness.

TARA-Forwarding Information

The TARA forwarding information put inside the prepended TARA header (alternative syntax is also possible, see below) encompasses the following:

Forwarding Type (3 bits):

- 000 = Unicast,
- 001= Multicast,
- 010 = MP2MP,
- 011= Broadcast to all nodes,
- 100 = Broadcast via all links,
- 101 = MP2P from all nodes,
- 110 = MP2P via all links,
- 111 = anycast).

If Forwarding Type = Unicast:

```
actual TARA Locator of the destina-
tion (5 octets)
home geopatch# of destination (2 oc-
tets)
TARA Locator of source (5 octets)
home geopatch# of source (2 octets)
CBR-Index (6 bits)
```

Detour Indication (2 bits)

- 00 = no detour
- 01 = passing mesh containing area of solid grey arcs
- 10 = 3-hops-detour
- 11 = long detour

Remaining Hops Counter (5 or 6 bits), used while forwarding within mesh containing area of solid grey arcs, or for guiding a 3-hops-detour

Number of tunnel pairs for long detour minus ONE (2 bits)

00 = 1 pair of tunnels,.... ; 11= 4 pairs of tunnels

List of tunnel pairs. Each list-element consists of

```
upstream TARA Locator (5 octets)
downstream TARA Locator (5 octets)
```

If Forwarding Type = Broadcast to all nodes or Broadcast via all links

```
Source TARA Locator of root node X of
ANST[X] resp. ALST[X]
```

Broadcast Rim (2 bits):

- 0 = geopatch boundary
- 1 = ingress traffic rim
- 2= zeroed Remaining Hops Counter

Broacast Scope (3 bits), applicable if Broadcast Rim =geopatch boundary:

- 0= Square minute wide,
- 1= area of destination's geopatch-number
- 2 = area of destination's geopatch-number plus of all first degree neighbor
- (1,1)-geopatches
- 3 = area of destination's geopatch-number plus of all up to second degree
- neighbor (1,1)-geopatches
- 4 = area of destination's geopatch-number plus of all up to third degree
- neighbor (1,1)-geopatches

If Forwarding Type = MP2P from all nodes or MP2P via all links

Destination TARA Locator of root node X of ANST[X] resp. ALST[X]

If Forwarding Type = Multicast:

Destination TARA Locator {home-geopatch# of sender;

2-octets-sized multicast instance#, H'00}

Unicast source TARA Locator of the sender of this packet or message

End of TARA Forwarding

The packet has arrived at that TARA router X that is identified by the destination TARA Locator. X will remove the TARA header. There are three possible scenarios:

1. The destination host is locally attached. The current TARA router will deliver the packet to the destination host.

2. Reachability information, originated by some other non-TARA router and collected by the current TARA router X, indicates how to forward the packet classically.

3. The destination host, being mobile, is roaming and has just moved away from TARA router X to TARA router Y, i.e. the DNS query to resolve TARA Locator isn't up to date anymore. In this case the current TARA router X instantiates an FSM-object which originates a well-scoped broadcast search to all nodes of X'es geopatch. By Eventually TARA a router Y response to this broadcast search and tells the FSM-object inside X that the wanted destination host is currently attached to it. The FSM-object takes care that further packets are now forwarded to Y. It also sends a notification message to the ingress TARA router and instructs that one to send further packets to the new egress TARA router Y. The ingress TARA router confirms the receipt of the notification to the FSM-object inside X where upon that would terminate/delete itself.

Stateless Multicast

Beside the above described unicast TARA-forwarding a model for multicast TARA-forwarding is outlined by the following.

This model is stateless as, in general, most participating nodes do only employ a single TARA multicast FIB entry. Special knowledge and intelligence however has to be allocated at the sender's TARA router S, at the receivers' TARA routers R_i and at proxy-sender nodes PS_j each of which is a delivery tree node where the delivery tree enters a particular geopatch.

At first, a sender needs to get a globally information for identifying its particular multicast instance. It will consist of its home geopatch# and

a 2-octet-sized multicast instance # whose seizure/release is commonly managed by all TARA routers of that geopatch: By means of "broadcast to all nodes" followed by a respective "MP2P from all nodes" a common understanding about the current busy or idle state of any such multicast instance # can be achieved. The TARA router with the smallest locator (being most South and secondly most West) may originate such a communication for synchronizing all nodes, e.g.- by broadcasting a 256 octets sized bitmap table which shows the current status (busy=1/idle=0) of all multicast instance numbers. Being triggered by the sender, a sender's TARA router S may seize a particular idle number and inform, by broadcast, all the other nodes which either agree (ACK) or disagree (NACK) and communicate this by MP2P forwarding to S.

A single NACK will overrule all other ACKs. For releasing an instance number a simple broadcast without responses will be sufficient. (Note that a similar mechanism could be applied in order to hand out blocks of IPv4 addresses of geopatch-local uniqueness!) As soon as the multicast instance number is seized S instantiates a respective sender's multicast entity (SME).

Potential receivers and their TARA routers (which may be spread all over the globe) may learn about a particular TARA multicast locator by means outside of this scope however.

The SME will maintain an image of that delivery tree part which is inside the own geopatch, enhanced by the links to the immediately adjacent proxy sender nodes.

The same applies to any PS_j which of course will also know its immediate upstream neighbour. The SME also maintains a list of all PS_j.

The delivery tree consists of "next-hop-stars" allocated inside the participating nodes. A next-hop-star comprises:

1. The multicast TARA Locator which is {geopatch# of S; multicast instance #},

2. The TARA Locator of the current node incl. indication whether it is sender node, proxy sender node, receiver node or any other (pure transit) node,

3. The TARA Locator of the upstream neighbour (uplink),

4. The variably-sized list of downstream neighbors' TARA Locators.

At node S the uplink however indicates a reference to the sending host and at nodes R_i certain downlinks will indicate references to receiving hosts. These references will point to instructions and data for communicating with that sender resp. receivers (e.g. by stripping off the TARA header and mapping the 4 octets sized multicast TARA Locator to a respectively unique LAN-Multicast-address (note: Eventually, R_i is leaf node and inner node concurrently).

Such next-hop stars must be retrievable

- For downstream forwarding the sender's IP flow,
- For up and downstream forwarding of certain messages of this model (rather than using unicast forwarding).

For this purpose they should be queue elements. A table with 64800 queue header elements is to be indexed by the geopatch# of the multicast TARA Locator and the elements of the hereby selected queue should be queued in ascending order with respect to their multicast instance numbers. Either linear or binary search may be applied for retrieving the right next-hop-star queue element. They may be considered being the "multicast-FIB."

Initial Delivery Tree

Before the multicast transmission starts multiple receivers may have sent JOIN messages to the sender and which are brought to the attention of the SME. The following describes a special treatment of the hereby collected JOINs from receivers R_1, R_2, ...R_n from inside the same geopatch.

The JOIN messages, being unicast-forwarding packets with pre-pended TARA-headers, convey the sender S's and the receiver R_i's IPv4-addresses as well as TARA Locators and must also convey {sender's geopatch#; multicast instance#}.for identifying the right SME.

The SME computes and stores a Steiner Tree (as explained above) which interconnects S and R_1, R_2, ...R_n, recognizes its own position thereof and allocates its "next-hop-star" in accordance with this Steiner Tree.

A BUILD-message shall be forwarded via each downlink of this next-hop-star which conveys the set of TARA Locators {S, R1, R_2, ...R_n}. Based on this set each receiving node will compute the same identical Steiner Tree, identify its own position inside of it and determine and store again its own "next-hop star." This process is transitively repeated – and an initial delivery tree built.

Adding Another Receiver

Thereafter the SME adds branches to it by handling (the collected) JOINs of receivers from outside this geopatch one by one, i.e. by the same process by which such a JOIN is received later on while the transmission is performed.

JOIN Handling of Receiver R_k: JOIN message of receiver R_k is brought to the attention of the SME. The SME determines whether this request shall be handled by itself or by some particular PS_j.

This node C (in charge) will be S if R_k and S are from the same geopatch, it will be some PS_j if R_k and PS_j are from the same geopatch, otherwise it will be S or some PS_j whose geopatch ever is closest to R_k's geopatch.

C computes ALST[all delivery tree nodes seen by C] and gets graft node G.

It also gets the path between G and R_k if R_k is from the same geopatch. Otherwise we get a path between G and a new proxy-sender node PS_{j*}.

C sends a GRAFT-message to G (using unicast forwarding). G enhances its next-hop-star with another downlink in direction towards R_k and sends also an ADD_BRANCH message to R_k. This message will allocate a new next-hop-star at each passed node. In case it gets to PS_{j*} that node will instantiate a proxy-sender multicast entity PSME which will send a NEW_PROXY_SENDER message to S indicating its TARA Locator. It will compute its path either down to R_k or down to another PS_j, store this path as its initial delivery tree part, and forward the ADD_BRANCH towards R_k.

Quitting the Multicast Transmission

R_k may quit by sending a QUIT-message towards sender node S while hopping along the uplinks of the next-hop-stars. Hereby any passed next-hop-star with only one downlink is removed. Where it hits a node Q which has more than one downlink, it removes that downlink by which it reaches Q. From here on the message is only forwarded along the uplinks of the passed next-hop-stars without doing any changes to the delivery tree, however while conveying the information about the removed downlink at Q. This information instructs the next upper proxy-sender node (resp. the sender node) to delete the branch of its stored delivery tree part which starts with the conveyed downlink at Q and ends either with a receiver's node or a proxy-sender node.

Mobility of the Receivers

A roaming receiver is –essentially- a receiver who quits and re-joins.

Mobility of the Sender

A roaming sender requires a change of the delivery tree. Eventually some branch needs to be deleted and/or some other branch to be added. The upstream/downstream direction may partially or totally be changed. Associated, from two border-to-border neighbor nodes one node will loose, the other one gain the proxy-sender functionality. The previous sender node S will loose and the new sender nodes S_{new} will gain the sender node functionality.

The sending host is the only entity which initially knows both TARA routers S and Snew and requests Snew to organize a re-direction of the delivery tree by the following three steps: 1) add shortest branch between delivery tree and S_{new} 2) delete branch between S and the (enhanced) delivery tree, 3) twist upstream/downstream direction and swap proxy-sender nodes accordingly 4) bestow new sender node as well as new proxy-sender-nodes with adequate knowledge.

S_{new} behaves like a new receiver node and sends a JOIN to S, which is handled as above.

Thereafter it unicasts a Remove_Sender message to S.

If at S the next-hop-star contains more than one downlink, its uplink is deleted as well as the SME (S) and a Remove_Sender_Conf message is returned to S_{new}. Otherwise the entire next-hop-star is deleted as well as the SME (S) and a Remove_Sender_Branch (which also conveys the TARA Locator of S_{new}) is sent to that single downstream neighbour node. This message is forwarded in the same way while deleting the hereby used next-hop-star until it gets to some node whose next-hop-star contains more than one downlink. There the next-hop-star's uplink is deleted and a REMOVE_SENDER_CONF message is unicasted to S_{new}.

Next, at S_{new} the next-hop-star is "redirected." The downlink which so far conceives the sending host as being a receiver becomes the uplink, and the so far uplink becomes a downlink. A TWIST_DIRECTION is then sent to all downlink neighbors.

It conveys two addressees where to report a) any link of the delivery tree b) any proxy-sender node. Initially both addressees are set to S_{new}.

There it is processed by modifying the next-hop-star as follows:

If the link L1 by which the message is received is not the uplink because a different link L2 is the uplink, then L1 becomes uplink, L2 becomes downlink and the message is forwarded via all old or new downlinks.

When ever the message is to be forwarded across a geopatch-border, the first node will lose its proxy-sender; the second will gain the proxy-sender status. Each one will notify Snew by an appropriate Proxy_Sender_Status message.

Whenever the Twist_Direction message encounters a new or old proxy-sender node PS_j that node will replace the previous addressee which is to be notified about any a passed new or old uplink by some DELIVERY_TREE_LINK message.

Anycast

The above described stateless multicast might be a pattern how to implement anycast service, inclusively the seizing and releasing of geopatch-wide unique anycast instance numbers and the structuring of the anycast-FIB.

- Well-scoped anycast: There are many usefull anycast services like getting to the nearest hotel, nearest gas station, nearest parking slot, etc. which exploit the WHERE-property and for which a limited scope of dissemination appears to be appropriate. Each network node within such scope would have to compute an ALST[all anycast destinations], find thereof its own position and therefore its best next hop with all the detour capabilities as for unicast forwarding.
- Generalized anycast: An example is the discovery of a DNS server might be such a service.

From the 2 octets number range there are 2^{16} − 64800=736 spare values which are not used by ordinary geopatch numbers, hence the value 64801 might represent a "well-known" geopatch # and the standardized anycast TARA Locator could be {64801;1 }. By computing ALST[d_1,... d_n] with DNS nodes d_i each node can easily form

a respective anycast entry in the FIB which is {{64801;1}; next hop}.

Below are losted some proposal for TARA Locators to be standarized:

- anycast-TARA Locator = {64801; s } with s standardized number
- multicast-TARA Locator = {64802; s } with s standardized number
- MP2MP-TARA Locator = {64803; s } with s standardized number

Traffic Load Balancing and Congestion Handling

Traffic load balancing resp. Congestion handling is a genuine task of the network and not of the hosts! All existing IETF-activities (conex, shim) however shift this task to the host: Traffic notifications are sent to the host's TCP-session. TCP shall reduce the transmission speed instead that the network diverts the flows around the node/area of congestion. Multi-homing: Experiencing poor transmission via Service Provider A, induces switching to Service Provider B, hoping (without knowing) for the better.

TARA provides the tools and the concept for balancing the traffic load respectively solving congestions by well-scoped communication between any (transit) node T and those upstream nodes which forward particular flows such that they will pass T.

A node T may observe its traffic load and may differentiate whether it is due to flows to a) one particular destination-TARA Locator, b) to multiple destination-TARA Locators which however would enter/leave node T by one particular adjacent link or by some particular group of adjacent links or by all its adjacent links:

1. By computing ALST[d], with d being a destination-TARA Locator, a (transit-) router T will see its respective upstream sub-network (herein called upstream sector) i.e. recognize all nodes which would forward

packets, which are destined for d, such that they will pass this current transit router T.

2. The upstream sectors with respect to d_i of the hereby confined flows can be compared and that one which encompasses the others relates to d_{I*} is selected.

3. T may broadcast Traffic Notification messages to the nodes of d_{I*} 's upstream sector, asking for appropriate actions not only for flows to d_{I*} but for all flows which would pass T.

4. T broadcasts Traffic Notification messages to the nodes of its own upstream sector which convey a maximal hop counter which is decremented by each hop.

The goal cannot be to relocate the point of congestion. By evaluating the three TARA Locators of the own (A), the destination node (B) and the congested (C) a direction for the by-pass detour can be determined: If the direction A-to-C is left from direction A-to-B then compute a detour to the right. If the direction A-to-C is right from direction A-to-B then compute a detour to the left. This is to divide the traffic load rather than to relocate it. The detour computation would be just a slight modification of the "long detour via more remote nodes" from above. The conveyed long-detour information in the TARA-header is exactly the same.

TECHNICAL SIDE ISSUES

Drop out of Nodes of Less Zoomed Topologies

Assume, a node drops out, which appears in zooming level 5. What sudden update churn will hereby be generated all over the world? The answer: None! This node reappears at all lower zooming levels 4, 3, 2 and 1. Let's consider all nodes at zooming level 1 which are closer to this (failing) node than

to any other representative node at zooming level 2. They will be the failing node and may decide whether or not to world-wide communicate the failing node.

Partitioning

A (m, n) geopatch/geopatch cluster may eventually be partitioned. But the nodes of each partition would realize it by learning about certain incoming links which they do not know as being outgoing links. Appropriate actions might be taken as to deal with this situation.

Hiding Intra-Domain Topology

There is the repeatedly raised argument that ISPs won't like to disclose their own topologies to their competitors. Although it is a basic principle of TARA that all TARA-links of a particular region (geopatch), intra- and inter-domain links alike, shall form the closest zoomed part of the TARA map, which of course means sharing that information also with the competitors, the mentioned argument can be fulfilled:

It would be sufficient if each ISP border node would advertise to the outside a faked topology pretending that each ISP border node had a strict link or a path link (of correct path length) to each internal TARA router from the same geopatch.

Besides that it may be beneficial for an intra-domain network which spans multiple geopatches and which e.g. consist of only TARA routers, if each of them knows precisely the entire topology of the own network, i.e. topological parts which are not shared with other networks.

FUTURE RESEARCH DIRECTIONS

Diverse new routing capabilities and services have already been mentioned which are only possible because TARA is able to deal with the WHERE-property.

There will be more of them:

Safest routing, i.e. to get sufficiently far away from the current place, no matter where that might be, while keeping away as far as possible from surrounding nodes of danger.

Evacuation routing (remember hurricane Kathrina in New Orleans), i.e. computing $ALST[d_1, \ldots d_n]$ with d_i being nodes where the city is exited, which converts all links (streets) into arcs (one way streets) such that the throughput is doubled.

CONCLUSION

TARA ambitions to create an intelligent network layer where better routing is enabled. For that aim, TARA provides better tools than simple mapping.

The scalability problem is eliminated. Even unexpected high growth rates due to new applications (e.g., massive deployment of sensors) won't cause trouble: IPv4 addresses do not have to be globally unique, additional zooming levels can easily be added to the TARA-topology, as well as "host-nodes," e.g. for certain types of hosts where privacy is not an issue, to the closest zoomed map.

REFERENCES

Delauney-Triangulation. (n.d.). In *Wikipedia*. Retrieved from http://en.wikipedia.org/wiki/Delaunay_triangulation

Tree, S. (n.d.). In *Wikipedia*. Retrieved from http://en.wikipedia.org/wiki/Steiner_tree_problem

Voronoi diagram. (n.d.). In *Wikipedia*. Retrieved from http://en.wikipedia.org/wiki/Voronoi_diagram

KEY TERMS AND DEFINITIONS

ALST[d]: All links spanning tree rooted at node d.

ALST[$d_1,d_2,\ldots,d_n$]: All links spanning tree rooted at nodes $d_1,d_2,\ldots,d_n$.

Anycast TARA Locator: {geopatch number, anycast instance number} with per geopatch unique anycast instance number, or {64801; standardized/well-known instance number}.

Geopatch: A spheric rectangle limited by two consecutive longitudes and two consecutive latitudes, respectively the North resp. the South pole, two consecutive Longitude and the nearest latitude.

(m, n)-Geopatch Cluster: M consecutive rows each of which consists of n consecutive geopatches.

Multicast TARA Locator: {geopatch number, multicast instance number} with per geopatch unique multicast instance number, or {64802; standardized/well-known instance number}.

Next-Hop-Star: A multicast FIB element which comprises an uplink and several downlinks.

Second Column Number: A value between 1 and 60.

Second Row Number: A value between 1 and 60.

Square Degree Number: Synonym of geopatch-number, a value between 1 and 180x360= 64800.

Square Minute Number: A value between 1 and 60x60 = 3600.

ST[$d_1,d_2,\ldots,d_n$]: Steiner Tree interconnecting the nodes $d_1,d_2,\ldots,d_n$.

TARA Map: The combined topology of the geopatch and geopatch clusters the TARA router belongs to, enhanced by the intra-domain topology of TARA nodes and links.

Unicast TARA Locator: 4-Tupel {geopatch number, square minute number, second row number, second column number}.

Section 3
Advanced Features

Chapter 7
Routing Optimization for Inter–Domain Traffic Engineering under Identifier Network

Hongke Zhang
Beijing Jiaotong University, China & Beijing University of Posts and Telecommunications, China

Wei Su
Beijing Jiaotong University, China

Changqiao Xu
Beijing University of Posts and Telecommunications, China

Hongbin Luo
Beijing Jiaotong University, China

ABSTRACT

The routing architecture of today's Internet is facing scalability problems. Multi-homing, traffic engineering, suboptimal address allocations are making the Forwarding Information Base (FIB) of the Default Free Zone (DFZ) growing at a nonlinear rate. Such scalability problems are mainly caused by the overloading of the IP address semantics. That is, an IP address represents not only the location but also the identity of a host. To address the scalability problem, Identifier Network, as a novel proposed network architecture, separates the identifier and locator roles of IP addresses into two evolving spaces: Accessing Identifier (AID) and Routing Identifier (RID) by Identifier/Locator separation mechanism. Such separation provides opportunities to reconsider routing optimization for inter-domain Traffic Engineering, as which is a main contribution to the Border Gateway Protocol (BGP) routing table growth.

Based on Identifier Network, we propose a solution for traffic engineering, which can be divided into two distinct parts: End-to-End traffic engineering and Neighbor-to-Neighbor traffic engineering. For each scenario, we develop a routing decision method for both routers and other network entities, such as IDMS (Identifier Mapping Server in Identifier Network). To analyze the feasibility of the solution, we collect Routeviews data set and the results show that the scheme proposed could reduce the burden of the core routing table.

DOI: 10.4018/978-1-4666-4305-5.ch007

INTRODUCTION

With the rapid development of Internet, today's Internet has become the center of the global information, resource, application and service. However, the Internet is facing serious scaling problems (Xiaoliang, 2010; Meyer, 2007). In 2007, there were about 200,000 IP address prefixes in the routing tables of the core Internet Routers (Huston, 2012). Until 2012, the routing entries have exceeded 400,000 prefixes for IPv4 and almost 11,000 prefixes for IPv6, and the global routing table size has experienced an increase in a nonlinear rate (Huston, 2012; Elmokashfi, 2010). Regarding the working report of Internet Assigned Numbers Authority (IANA) (Meyer, 2007), the reasons contributing to the fast explosion of the global routing table mainly include the following: multi-homing, inbound Traffic Engineering (TE), non-aggregated address allocations (a big portion of which is inherited from historical allocations), and business events such as mergers and acquisitions.

To address this routing scalability problem, many organizations including IETF (Internet Engineering Task Force) LISP (Locator/ID Separation Protocol) Working Group (LISP, 2012) and IRTF (Internet Research Task Force) RRG (Routing Research Group) (RRG, 2012) have discussed the idea of separating the node's identity from its topological location. Identifier Network, as a novel ID/Loc (Identifier/Locator) separation architecture, separates the identifier and locator roles of IP addresses into two evolving spaces: Accessing Identifier (AID) and Routing Identifier (RID).

The AID indicates a host's identity and is applied in the transport and application layers, whereas the RID indicates the current topological location of a host and is used in the network layer. In addition, Access Router (AR) deploys on the edge of the core network and provides the mapping functionalities between the AID and RID.

The ID/Loc separation solution not only can reduce the routing table size in the Default Free Zone (DFZ) (Quoitin, 2007) and natively support mobility (Zhang, 2009; Luo, 2011), but also provides promising opportunities to reconsider routing optimization for inter-domain (inbound) traffic engineering.

In this chapter, we propose a solution for implementing Traffic Engineering in Identifier Network. The method contains two distinct parts: End-to-End traffic engineering and Neighbor-to-Neighbor traffic engineering. For each scenario, we develop a routing decision scheme for both routers and other network entities, such as IDMS (Identifier Mapping Server in Identifier Network) (Luo, 2011). The aim of both the above proposed solutions is to reduce the burden of the core routing tables.

In Identifier Network, the routers in the core network do not need to maintain the AID information, which reduces the burden of the routing in the core network. In addition, the RID would be allocated in a manner strictly conforming to the topology of the core network in the proposed TE solution of Identifier Network, and the allocation result would be stored in the mapping system, so any arbitrary deaggregation of the RID space is not allowed. Using Routeviews data set, we analyze the burden of the core routing table.

The rest of the chapter is organized as follows: we first review the related works. Then, we give an overview of Identifier Network including the architecture, the design principles, work procedures, current deployment and its benefits. Next, we introduce the design of traffic engineering under separation and mapping mechanism and describe the details of protocol design regarding relative situation. After that, we analyze the feasibility of the solution and provide the results in term of reducing the burden of the core routing table. Finally, we discuss the trends of Identifier Network in the future. The last section concludes this chapter.

BACKGROUND

Identifier/Locator Separation Routing Architecture

During the last 30 years, the Internet grew at a rapid rate. As of this writing, there are more than 2,606,620,052 hosts (Huston, 2012) and about 70,000 different Autonomous Systems (ASes) in the Internet today. The ever-increasing user population, as well as multiple other factors including multi-homing, traffic engineering, and policy routing (Meyer, 2007), have been driving the growth of the global routing table at a nonlinear rate. As of May 2012, the core routing table has in excess of 410,000 entries (Houston, 2012). Furthermore, the inter-domain routing protocol Border Gateway Protocol (BGP) (Rekhter, 2006) in the Internet is a flat structure, that is to say, a connectivity flap to any destination network may trigger routing updates to propagate throughout the entire Internet, even when no one is communicating with the unstable destination network at the time. The mass of BGP Update messages occupy a lot of bandwidth and impact the Central Processing Unit (CPU) utilization on the core routers. Besides, the routing table size and the messages process load also have negative impact on the scalability of the inter-domain routing system.

The root cause of the routing scalability problem is the fact that the IP address semantics are overloaded. That is, an IP address represents not only the location but also the identity of a host. Therefore, several recent schemes (Li, 2011) propose to replace the IP namespace in today's Internet with a locator namespace and an identifier namespace. The locators are used to represent the locations of hosts, while the identifiers (ID, also called EID in some cases) are used to represent the identity of the host. Besides, a mapping system that can supply an appropriate locator for any given end-point identifier (EID) is needed. The ID/Loc separation mechanism is considered as a

promising method to solve the routing scalability problem (Chen, 2011).

Though many proposals share the same principles of problem-solving, the ID/Loc separation, they differ in how to achieve this goal. We observe that all the ID/Loc separation proposals fall into one of two categories:

1.   Host-based,
2.   Network-based.

We give a simple introduction of the proposals and comparison between these solutions and our proposed Identifier Network.

Edge networks (could also be interpreted as access networks) growth is directly reflected in the core routing table size, and unstable edge networks can flood the entire Internet with frequent updates. Network-based ID/Loc separation proposals split the edge networks from the transit core in the routing architecture. Thus, the core routing table size only grows with the number of Internet Service Providers (ISPs), which is much smaller and grows slower compared to that of edge networks. More importantly, separation will also greatly reduce routing churn. The separation includes two main approaches: (1) the Map & Encap, which is adopted by APT (Jen, 2008), LISP (Farinacci, 2012), TRRP (Herrin, 2008), and (2) the address rewriting, which is used in Six-One Router (Vogt, 2008) and GSE (O'Dell, 1997). Due to the absence of edge prefixes from the core routing table, a mechanism that maps a destination edge prefix to one or more transit addresses that correspond to that edge network's attachment points to the transit core is required. From an architectural standpoint there are three possible ways in which a mapping system could supply mapping information. It can provide individual answers to specific requests (Pull), or distribute (Push) all the mappings onto listeners, or both (Pull/Push). Proposed Pull-based mapping systems include LISP-DHT (Mathy, 2008) and

LISP-TREE (Jakab, 2010), while LISP-NERD (Lear, 2012) is a Push-based mapping system. LISP+ALT (Farinacci, 2012) and LISP-CONS (Brim, 2008) are hybrid push and pull models. The Identifier Network is a network-based ID/Loc separation proposal, which makes use of the address rewriting at the edge network's attachment points to separate the edge networks and the transit core, and adopts a Distributed Hash Table DHT-based approach (Luo, 2009) to build the mapping system.

By using the host-based ID/Loc separation mechanism, each multihomed edge network will receive from each of its network providers an address block. The multihomed edge network must not inject Provider Independent (PI) prefixes or more specific Provider Aggregatable (PA) prefixes into the routing system. However, each host in a multihomed site is assigned multiple PA addresses. The multihomed host needs to dynamically control the locator selection and detect the paths using. The host-based ID/Loc separation mechanism can separate the identifier and locator roles between the OSI Layer 3 and Layer 4. Layer 3 protocols ensure that whatever the locator used, the identifier appearing at the Layer 4 will remain the same for the life of a given flow. To perform the ID/Loc separation in a host, there also are two categories: introducing new sublayer and dividing the IP address. HIP (Moskowitz, 2008) and Shim6 (Nordmark, 2009) utilize the new sublayer to map between the identifier and the locator, while ILNP (Atkinson, 2012) divides the IP address into high order bits and low order bits which separately perform the locator role and identifier role. Though the host which may use an ID to identify could have multiple locators, it hardly makes use of these locators simultaneously in the current host protocol stack, which have potentially reliability problem. For example, in multipath transfer, a host with one ID will also have only one receiver buff, so it must solve the receiver buff blocking problem firstly. Multipath TCP (MPTCP) (Ford, 2011) and CMT-SCTP (Iyengar, 2006; Xu, 2012) also could be considered

as a kind of ID/Loc separation mechanism, but the ID is a locator set.

Both the network-based and host-based ID/Loc separation can achieve the same goal of scalable routing system with scalable support for multi-homing and inbound TE. However, there are important differences when deploying in practice. Since the routing scalability problem is mainly the ISPs' responsibility, they would have incentive to deploy a solution once it is available. Though the host-based ID/Loc separation does not change the routing architecture, it requires changes of the protocol stack upgrade at end hosts. The reduction of the de-aggregation prefix in the core routing table depends on the number of hosts that implement the new protocol stack. The ISPs can do nothing but wait for a unanimous action by all the end hosts before the routing table begins to scale. The routing system has no control over edge site deployment of new solutions. Thus, the network-based ID/Loc separation is more promising in the deployment. Network-based ID/Loc separation also reduces the impact of edge network on the core network, and the mapping at the edge of the core network could record the data source which makes it easy to trace attack packets back and mitigate the DDOS (Distributed Denial of Service). Moreover, with the help of the mapping service, an edge network can explicitly express its ingress traffic engineering preferences in the mapping information, without injecting more specific prefix to the core routing table.

Traffic Engineering (TE)

With the growing importance of Internet and data networks, Traffic Engineering (TE) is widely used by network operators. On the one hand, TE aims at improving the traffic performances and optimizing the resource usage. On the other hand, TE also can be used to improve the reliability. Since an end-to-end data delivery needs to go through different ASes, TE comprises both intra-domain TE and inter-domain TE.

Intra-domain TE is an optimization problem where the intra-domain routing is used to optimize the way the traffic is forwarded in the network. To reach this goal, the intra-domain routing usually assign the link weight according to the traffic matrix. The best possible traffic matrix estimate could be got by following either an optimization approach or a statistical approach. The optimization approach takes the information from the topology as well as traffic counters in the network, and applies these constraints to compute the traffic matrix (Uhlig, 2006). While the statistical inferences takes information from the topology and traffic counters and determines the distributions that fit with the observations (Medina, 2002). Since the Intra-domain TE is relatively easy to deploy in practice, we put more focus on the interdomain TE in the inbound traffic control.

Inter-domain TE utilizes the BGP to perform the inter-domain traffic management, such as load balancing, redundance. BGP is a path-vector routing protocol where a BGP router at the border of each AS announces to its BGP neighbor routers the prefixes it can reach. Since BGP is a single path routing protocol, it could leverage the path selection to impact the traffic forwarding.

BGP allows ASes to enforce their routing policies by using the attributes, such as Local-Pref, AS path length, MED (Multi-Exit Discriminator) and communities. These attributes are used to manage the traffic. The Local-Pref gives a priority to the routes for a prefix. BGP chooses the route with the highest Local-Pref as the best route. Combining with the community attribute, an AS could set some prefixes advertised in a specific community, while neighbor ASes configure different communities with different Local-Pref values to inbound traffic. The ASes also can add the prefix to other communities, like NO_EXPORT community, to restraint the routing advertisement. AS path length is another technique to control the traffic. If an AS tries to avoid the traffic from its neighbors passing through, it repeats its AS number multiple times in a AS path when the AS announces a prefix

to its neighbors (a.k.a., AS Path prepending), since the longer AS path has lower priority to be selected. If an AS is connected with several routers to its neighboring AS, the MED is used to attract the traffic. The MED allows an AS to signal the peers which point it prefers to import the traffic. BGP mixes the route selection in the control plane with the traffic forwarding in the data plane, which brings complicate and trivial configurations for the operators.

In current Internet, the most used method for adjusting inter-domain traffic is to advertise specific prefixes in more detailed granularity, or prefix de-aggregation. The principle of prefix de-aggregation is to announce more specific prefixes to the preferred neighbors and less specific prefixes to the least preferred neighbors. As routing in the Internet is made on a longest prefix matching basis, a more specific prefix is always preferred to a less specific one. Consider the topology shown in Figure 1, in order to inform the upstreaming AS about the willingness of controlling the inbound traffic from specific access point, prefix 172.16.0.0/16 could probably be split into *p1* 172.16.128.0/17 and *p2* 172.16.0.0/17, each of which cover some parts of the range of 172.16.0.0/16. Furthermore, *p1* and *p2* are advertised from two different interconnection points, denoted as *loc-a* and *loc-b*. The de-aggregation of prefix 172.16.0.0/16 is for the

Figure 1. Topology of TE in current Internet

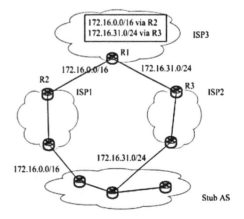

131

sake of instructing traffic destined for prefix *p* in a load-balanced manner, traffic will be directed through access points identified with *loc-a* and *loc-b* into user AS. Unfortunately, as we discuss above, the de-aggregation of prefixes for inter-domain TE results in 20%-25% additional growth of the global routing table size. Therefore, there is a need to optimize the routing for the support of scalable inter-domain TE imminently.

A network-based ID/Loc separation mechanism provides a chance to redesign the inter-domain TE. Leveraging the mapping system, network-based ID/Loc separation migrates the pressure of the growth of global routing table size which is caused partly by the inter-domain TE in the stub network to the mapping system. As a result, not only lots of de-aggregation prefixes will be eliminated, but also the ISPs could control the inbound and outbound traffic accurately by adjusting the mapping entries (Donnet, 2008). However, the de-aggregation prefixes may still exist in the core network, as only BGP could be used there to control the traffic. Therefore, we reconsider the inter-domain TE, at both end-to-end level and neighbor-to-neighbor level, under the architecture of the Identifier Network to optimize the routing.

OVERVIEW OF IDENTIFIER NETWORK

As results of China National 973 program Fundamental Research on the "Architecture of Universal Trustworthy Network and Pervasive Services" (Grant No. 2007CB307100) (973, 2006; Zhang, 2007; Dong, 2007), Identifier Network is a novel network architecture based on the Locator/Identifier separation and mapping scheme, as shown in Figure 2.

As shown in Figure 2, Identifier Network contains two layers: Infrastructure layer and pervasive services layer. In this architecture, there are four identifiers:

1. Routing Identifier (RID),
2. Access Identifier (AID),
3. Connecting Identifier (CID),
4. Service Identifier (SID).

In the Identifier Network, SIDs are used to describe all types of data/service in a unified manner, CIDs are used to uniquely identify connections, AIDs are used to identify elements in the edge network such as hosts and routers and RIDs are used to route data packets in the core network.

Figure 2. The overview of the architecture of identifier network

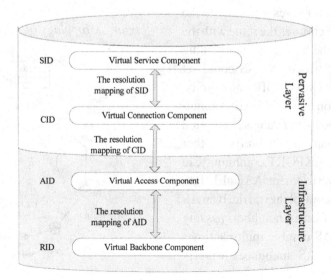

When a service provider wants to publish a service in the Identifier network, he registers both the SID of this service and the AID which could provide this service. And when a user requests a service, he looks up the SID of the service and the AID of its provider corresponding to the service description in the Identifier network. Then, a connection is built to transmit the data of this service, and the CID of this connection is also created based on the SID, the AIDs of provider and requester. During the transmission, for each packet, the source and destination AIDs are mapped to RIDs to be routed in the core network. Till then, all of the mappings are built. Doing this, the user can obtain a service from the Identifier network. Besides, based on these identifiers, there are three mappings connecting different components. Next, we will introduce the architecture briefly.

The main purpose of Infrastructure layer is providing diversified access for network and terminals, assuring the trust and mobility of communication and information exchange to support pervasive service. In Infrastructure layer, we use AID to denote the identity of terminal, RID to denote the location of terminal. AID and RID divide the Infrastructure layer into two components: virtual backbone component (VBC) and virtual access component (VAC). VBC uses RID to solve the problems of routing and management of location, while VAC uses AID to take charge of the access of terminals. Different from the notion of Virtual Prefix [RFC6179] which is based on virtual network, VAC is not about virtual overlay networks, it just uses AID to represent the identity information of user, and when the user is moving, its AID will not change, instead, the change is the mapping relationship between AID and RID.

Different from the Infrastructure layer, pervasive services layer is in charge of the session, control and management for various services, which are provided by carriers or third party value-added service providers. These services carried by pervasive service layer include IPTV, VoIP, Web page browsing and so on. Pervasive services layer creates virtual service component (VSC) and virtual connecting component (VCC). VSC uses SID to describe various services, while VCC uses CID to establish multiple connections for one service. Besides, pervasive services layer uses mapping of SID to connect VSC and VCC, mapping of CID to connect VCC and VAC. The mapping of SID translates the services into multiple service connections, and each service connection will have its own characteristics according to the specified service. For example, the delay requirements of connections will be different for VoIP and file downloading. Therefore, the pervasive services layer can support various kinds of services. The mapping of CID translates the service connection into multiple connections in Infrastructure layer. The mapping reflects the idea of "one service to multiple connections" and guarantees the reliability of services.

Different from the traditional architectures of OSI (Open System Interconnection) 7 layers model, Identifier Network is a novel architecture. The Infrastructure Layer could be interpreted as an integration of the Physical, Data Link, Network and Transport Layer, and the Pervasive Services Layer could be interpreted as an integration of the Session, Presentation and Application Layer. It combines users, services and resources into a whole, realizing the universal access and providing pervasive services for users. Next, we will introduce Infrastructure Layer and Pervasive Services Layer respectively.

Infrastructure Layer

As mentioned above, infrastructure layer consists of VAC, VBC and the mapping between AIDs and RIDs (Figure 2).

VAC achieves the pervasive access by introducing the concept and scheme of AID. Users could communicate with each other at anytime, anywhere and share the most widespread pervasive services. In contrast, VBC realizes the resource configuration and coordination at the core networks by introducing the concept and scheme of RID. The mapping between AIDs and RIDs supports four operation modes: one-to-one, one-to-many, many-to-one and many-to-many. The definition of mapping of AID is in literature (Zhang, 2007).

The idea and design plan of infrastructure layer is shown in Figure 3.

User locates in the VAC, in which the AID represents the identity information of terminal or subnet, being only used in VAC. While the RID in the VBC represents the location information of terminal or subnet, being only used in VBC. The access router realizes the mapping from AID to RID through resolution mapping of AID. By this way, we could implement the separation between indentify information and location information. The communication flows in the Identifier Network are as follows:

1. When $User_1$ with AID_1 wants to establish a connection, it finds the AID of remote user through a global system, such as Domain Name System (DNS). Then User1 sends a packet with AID_1 and AID_2 as the source and destination.

2. The Access Router AR_1 receives the packet, finds the AID-to-RID mapping and maps the source and destination to RID_1 and RID_2. Then AR1 forwards the packet to core network.

3. In the core network, the packet is forwarded to AR_2 according to the RIDs. AR_2 maps the source and destination to AID_1 and AID_2, and forwards the packet to $User_2$.

The infrastructure layer has the following advantages:

1. The one-to-one mapping between AIDs and RIDs resolves the scalability problem (Dong, 2008) caused by the overloading of the IP address semantics. With the help of separation, the network supports mobility more conveniently. When the various access networks change their location, only the RID needs to be changed. However, the AID representing the identity information is maintained. Thus, the communication between two hosts will not be disrupted by adjusting the mapping relationships.

2. Guarantee the security and privacy of users. In Identifier Network, AID represents identity information of users, while RID is only used for forwarding in core networks. By the separation between AID and RID,

Figure 3. The design of infrastructure layer

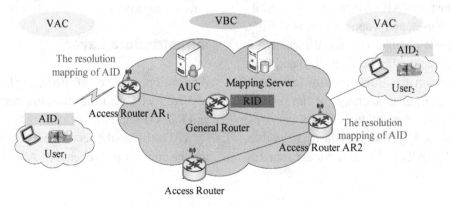

AID containing the identity information will not be transmitted in core networks. Therefore, AID is hard to intercept in the core network, and other users could not intercept the information through identity information to make an attack, providing the security assurance effectively. Besides, the potential attacker could not intercept the information in core networks to analyze the identity of user, providing the privacy assurance.

3. Guarantee the controllability of network. When a terminal or subnet wants to create a new application for AID, the network administrator authenticates the access request through the contract information. Then, the administrator will assign the suitable resources to the requesting user to provide corresponding quality of service guarantees according to the contract information.

4. To adapt different novel internet applications, the mapping from AID to RID supports multiple types: one-to-many, many-to-one and many-to-many. When the one-to-many mapping is implemented at the same location, different RIDs may have different priorities or parameters of traffic engineering. Having multiple RIDs could satisfy different demands of various applications on the same terminal. Additionally, the one-to-many mapping may be implemented at different access locations to support multiple access technologies. Different AIDs of the same terminal could be resolved into the same RID at the same access location. The many-to-one mapping reflects the identity diversity of users. Another many-to-one mapping means multiple AIDs could be mapping into the same multicast RID at different access locations to establish multicast path for multiple nodes. So, the AID and RID could support multicast well. Besides, when multiple AIDs of the same node access the network at different access locations, administrator will assign a unique RID for each AID respectively. This many-to-many

mapping scheme could protect the security of network traffic effectively.

Pervasive Service Layer

As show in Figure 2, pervasive layer consists of VSC, VCC and the mapping between SIDs and CIDs.

VSC is the foundation for realizing the pervasive service. It not only provides the universal description and presentation of various services, but also provides a system to control and manage the services. By introducing SID, various services could be sorted and described in a unified way. The mapping of SID connects the VSC and VCC together and establishes communication for many kinds of services.

VCC introduces the CID as identification of both connection and user. A CID identifies a connection which is used to achieve a service. If the user changes his location due to mobility, the system only updates the mapping between AID and RID, but the CID and AID both remain invariant. And only the users authorized by the CID could use its connection, other users could not use the connection of this CID except passing the authentication of this CID. Therefore, VCC could efficiently support mobility and security. Mapping of CID could implement the mapping from CID to AID. The explicit introduction of the process of mapping is in literature (Zhang, 2007; Dong, 2007).

The detailed design of pervasive service layer is shown in Figure 4.

The mapping of SID may have four types: one-to-one, one-to-many, many-to-one and many-to-many.

1. **One-to-one mapping:** Is the state-of-art standard in the current internet and telecommunication networks. In Internet, only one TCP or UDP connection is used to achieve a service. In telecommunication networks, only one circuit connection is employed to support a service.

Figure 4. The design of pervasive service layer

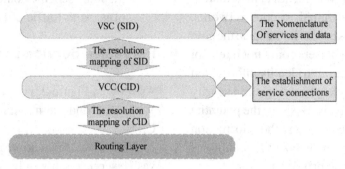

2. **One-to-many mapping:** Classifies the data of one application into different flows. One flow is based on multiple connections to shorten the delivery latency.
3. **Many-to-one mapping:** Means multiple types of flows from one service are transmitted as soon as one connection is established. Users could configure different connection modes depending on the types of flow to improve delivery efficiency.
4. **Many-to-many mapping:** Implements the idea that multiple applications are operated at multiple connections. Multiple applications could be decomposed into many types of traffic flows, which are delivered through multiple connections. The many-to-many mapping could enhance the transmission capability by differential services for different traffic flows.

The mapping of CID connects the VCC and infrastructure together and finishes the mapping from one CID to multiple CID. Thus, we could choose multiple paths to improve the transmission reliability. The mapping of CID may also have four types: one-to-one, one-to-many, many-to-one and many-to-many.

1. **One-to-one mapping:** Is the main operating mode in the current internet.

2. **One-to-many mapping:** Could improve the reliability by switching the formal AID to another AID, when the former one is failure.
3. **Many-to-one mapping:** Could solve the problem of head block and improve the transmission reliability further.
4. **Many-to-many mapping:** Established multiple connections with multiple CID. Traffic flows are transmitted at multiple paths simultaneously. Besides, the multiple paths routing could reduce the delivery latency obviously and attackers could not capture the whole packets by listening only one flow.

Through the analysis of the pervasive service layer above, we could induce its working principle as follows:

Firstly, we should use the SID to name different services. By the SID, we could schedule the service coordinately and provide diverse services based on the framework of Identifier Network. When a user requires a specified service, he or she can find the service through SID query system using the unique SID. And then, the service establishes one or many connections with virtual connection component. Each connection will be mapped into one or many infrastructure layers to choose path. The multiple paths could improve the delivery reliability and load balance. By this way, we could realize the pervasive service in Identifier Network.

Through the design above, pervasive service layer overcomes two defects in traditional Internet and telecommunication networks: lack of unified service identifier and lack of appropriate mapping from SID to service connection. Meanwhile, with the help of SID we can name and manage services uniformly and realize the controllability of services in the whole network. And as the unique identity, CID remains invariant at the whole process of communications to support the mobility.

To show how the pervasive service layer works in Figure 4, we take the service of file downloading as an example. In file downloading, the servicer registers the service in the network firstly; then the client looks up the file in the network, and gets the SID; after that, a connection is built between the servicer and the client based on the SID and their AIDs to achieve the service, and a CID is created to identify this connection; till then, the mapping between SID and CID, and the mapping between CID and AID are both created in the pervasive service layer. And then, in the infrastructure layer AID will be mapped with RID to transmit data in the network. Therefore, the service of file downloading could be achieved by the mappings from SID to CID, CID to AID and AID to RID.

DESIGN TRAFFIC ENGINEERING IN IDENTIFIER NETWORK

In this Section, we begin to present our design for implementing traffic engineering in Identifier Network. In order to elaborate the aspiration and details of our method for implementing inter-domain TE, we provide explanations of the proposed traffic engineering solutions in two specific circumstances, both of which consist of the comparison of the solution proposed in this chapter with traditional methods, also the advantage and deficiency of the proposed solution.

End-to-End Traffic Engineering

To ensure the end-to-end performance such as optimizing one-way delay and loss, the access networks require the network providers to guarantee reliable end-to-end transmission. For this purpose, it has become effective tools for network service providers to establish resilient data tunnels with link bandwidth for specific users. ISPs are always adjusting the routes in their networks to control and reassign the traffic according to current network performance in order to achieve overall optimal utilization of the routing infrastructure.

From an inter-domain perspective, there is a tight relationship between traffic engineering and multi-homing. Multi-homing lays an appropriate located upwards in the path have to maintain several entries. As shown in Figure 1, prefix p, which could be aggregated as one entry, has been artificially cut into subprefixes, and these subprefixes would be send out through BGP Network Layer Reachability Information (NLRI) advertisement with their attribute set unaggregatable, which further exacerbates the routing table explosion problem. Reflected in the global routing table, there will be T entries for border routers in the upstream ISP $(p_1\text{->}loc_1, p_2\text{->}loc_2,...p_T\text{->}loc_T)$, in Figure 4 which p_i denotes the destination field and loc_i denotes nexthops corresponding to specific destination, $i \in 1,2,...,T$.

In Identifier Network, the AID-to-RID mapping maintained by the ARs and IDMSes can determine the best destination locator to use. The selection of the best source RID and the best destination RID are two instances of the same problem. Indeed, the RID decision algorithm is the same for the source and the destination RID at ARs (i.e., an AR chooses the RIDs with the lowest priority values). However, from an operational point of view, these problems are very different. Firstly, the selection of the source locator only depends on local policies as the mappings in the AID-to-RID Database are built locally. Secondly, the selection of the destination locator depends on the AID-to-RID Cache policies in the remote AR. For outgoing TE, the source AR determines the interfaces by selecting the source RID. Priorities and weights can be adapted to help the decision.

Next, we discuss the inbound TE. Assume AID prefix p is assigned to be the TE prefix used for controlling inbound traffic, all the things that border routers in access networks need to do is to maintain one entry in its routing table (p->$orgin$), in which origin denotes the real location where p originates, with p and origin both served as AIDs. The origin field could only be used in the access network. Meanwhile, we reflect the user AS's will of instructing inbound traffic by the AID-to-RID resolution system, or IDMSes. A TE mapping table will be introduced to maintain the corresponding relationship between the AIDs and multiple RIDs after traffic engineering implementation.

Here a detailed explanation of the method will be given and Figure 5 shows the topology of networks. *Src* and *Dest* denote the data sender and receiver located in access networks, respectively. ISP_1 and ISP_2 connect to *Src* in the core network. Assume ISP_1 and ISP_2 have been allocated with RID prefixes p_{ISP1} and p_{ISP2}, and *Src* with the AID prefix p_{Src} to both IDMSes in ISP_1 and ISP_2. The mapping resolution system would create a one-to-many mapping for p_{Src}: $[p_{Src}, p_{ISP1}; p_{ISP2}; \dots p_{ISPT}]$.

The mapping relationship would be propagated to IDMSes located in other domains through the mapping resolution system, and the resolution information is used to instruct the substitution between the packets' source and destination AID and their RIDs. The pseudocode of the protocol is as follows in Figure 6

Neighbor-to-Neighbor Traffic Engineering

The end-to-end traffic engineering has a moderate application constraint, that is, it could only be used on the edge of the core network (more specifically speaking, the juncture of the core and edge networks). It needs the supports from both the sender's and receiver's network, which restraints the scope of the applicability. It needs to step further to explore the traffic engineering circumstances in the core network, as much more TE implementations also exist there. In this chapter, we propose a TE method that could be used between the stub networks' service providers (first-hop ISPs) and upstreaming neighbours (providers' provider). It aims to reduce the routing table size of core routers and optimize the routing in the core network.

Under the Identifier Network, the IDMSes are used to store the mapping relationships between the AIDs and RIDs. Since transmission of packets is related only to RIDs in the core networks, we design the new TE method on top of both the routing infrastructure and IDMS resolution system. We develop our implementation method under the following assumptions: there is at least one IDMS located in every ISP in core network. With

Figure 5. End-to-end TE

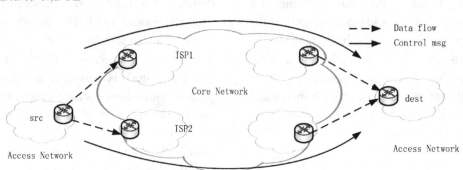

Figure 6. Pseudocode of end-to-end TE

```
Router
1 RID = cache_table_lookup(AID)
2 if RID ==NULL then
3    mapping_request(AID, IDMS)
4    RID=recv_response(IDMS)
6    if (count_RID(RID)>1) then
7       RIDbest = choose(RID)
8 else
9    nexthop=fetch_nexthop(RIDbest)

IDMS
10 recv_mapping_request(AID)
11 RID = dest
12 RID = map_table_lookup(AID, MAP_TABLE)
13 if (RID != NULL) then
14    router_response(RID)
15 else
16    reponse null to router
```

a specific interactive protocol, such as LISP-DHT (Mathy, 2008), LISP-TREE (Jakab, 2010) and LISP+ALT (Farinacci, 2012), the IDMSes could retrieve AID-to-RID relationship and provide the forwarding nexthop. Tracing back to the origin of separation and mapping mechanism, some principles lying behind the aspiration of the method we discussed above turn up to be present:

1. Only RID is used for data transmission in core network under the Identifier Network;
2. The assignment of RIDs strictly follows the topology aggregation policy, which could be expressed using relationship between ASes as follows:
    a. Customer AS gets its RID prefixes from its provider ASes, that is

    if $ISP1=customer(ISP2)$

    then $RID_{ISP1} \in RID_{ISP2}$

    b. Routers in the core network are responsible for storing the aggregated RID prefixes for their customers:

    if $ISP3=provider(ISP1)$ &&
    $ISP3=provider(ISP2)$

    then $RID_{ISP1} \in RID_{ISP3}$ &&
    $RID_{ISP2} \in RID_{ISP3}$

With the discussion above, we step further to detail the method. Considering the topology in Figure 9, we accurately deploy the IDMSes in *ISP1*, *ISP2* and *ISP3* for granted, herein we mean accurate by the following criterions, which strictly conforms to the assumptions discussed earlier: $IDMS_{ISP1}$ and $IDMS_{ISP2}$ are in charge of storing accessed end-hosts' AID prefixes and corresponding provider allocated (*ISP3*) RID prefixes in their AID-RID mapping table; the RID assignment policy is well represented by the structure of IDMSes and using some interactive protocol; IDMSes could retrieve AID-to-RID relationship and forwarding nexthop. Routers in the upstreaming providers should aggregate the RID prefixes as aggressive as possible.

Up to this point, it is necessary to explain what the IDMS is doing in the process of data forwarding and how it works. The organization of the mapping relationship in IDMS is depicted in Figure 7. The mapping table is organized using a bidirectional hashing linked list, facilitating the store, lookup, and delete of specific mapping items. There are two kinds of information stored in IDMS, AID-to-RID mapping relationship and forwarding nexthop records for the specific prefixes, the former indicates the corresponding relationships between the AID and RID prefixes under local administration, the later provides the nexthop lookup for the routers in the same ISPs and splits the traffic. In the AID hash table, each AID is hashed to one hash value. When the mapping information is requested, AR hashes AID and searches the hash table according to its hash value. And the RID hash table works in a similar way. It is needed to exploit proper use of the IDMS database to assist forwarding decision made by AR.

Under the Identifier Network, the border routers maintain just one entry per summarized prefix, attached with multiple nexthops in IDMS which leads traffic to destination learned from other ISPs. Thus, any traffic towards prefix *p* arriving at a border router will trigger a request *r* requiring nexthop information. Upon receiving the request, IDMS would look up its own mapping relationship table to decide which nexthop should be used, depending on the traffic situation and configuration, then send the result back to the border router. Then routing lookup in the border router would inform the router about the right outgoing interface. Pseudocode of this process is as follows:

The edge network is a relative concept. In the core networks there are still edge networks which are the providers for the access of the stub networks. For the sake of reliability, the edge part (ARs) in the core networks also needs multiple network providers, that is, it is multihomed. Though the locators in the core network are assigned following the topology aggregation policy strictly, it still produces de-aggregation prefixes in the control plane of routing system in the core network.

Figure 9 shows a scenario how to utilize the IDMS to impact the traffic forwarding and reduce the size of the global routing table. In Figure 9, despite the R3 advertises 172.16.31.0/24 to R1, the R1 has no exactly this entry in its routing table, as it could aggregate 172.16.31.0/24 with 172.16.0.0/16. When R1 receives packets whose destination is 172.16.0.0 but has a longer subnet mask, R1 follows the algorithm in Figure 6 to select the nexthops. For example, if the destination is 172.16.31.0/24, R1 would get the nexthop from the

response returning from the IDMS, and forwards the traffic to the R3. As a result, the Identifier Network optimizes the routing when performing the neighbor-to-neighbor TE in the core networks. Since many nexthops are maintained in the IDMS, the operator could configure different nexthops manually to split the traffic when necessary.

Using the bidirectional index characteristic of the mapping table to alleviate the over explosion of routing table size is the essence of our method. Packets going through the border routers would experience three lookups and one message interaction. Three lookups respectively is the lookup in the FIB of the border router in core network, the lookup in the TE routing table of the border router and the lookup in the mapping table in IDMS. One message interaction is the request for nexthop r and its reply. The extra lookup will not add too much delay since the method greatly reduces the size of the global routing table.

PERFORMANCE ANALYSES AND DISCUSS

The goal of this work is to minimize the influence to the routing table size growth brought by the TE practice. In order to evaluate the feasibility of our method, we give a data analysis of the current

Figure 7. Structure of AID-to-RID mapping table

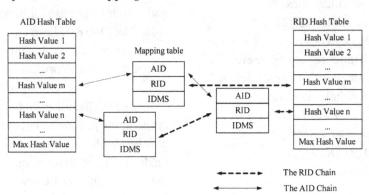

Figure 8. Pseudocode of neighbor-to-neighbor TE

```
Router
1 nexthop = route_cache_lookup(dest)
2 if nexthop ==NULL then
3    nexthop = route_lookup(dest, fib)
4    if count_nexthop(nexthop)>1 then
5       traffic_request(dest, IDMS)
6       nexthop = routnext
7    else
8       nexthop = fetch_nexthop(nexthop)
9 forward_packet(nexthop, packet)
IDMS
10 recv_traffic_request(dest)
11 RID = dest
12 routnext = map_table_lookup(dest, MAP_TABLE)
13 if (routnext != NULL) then
14    router_response(routnext, dest)
15 else
16    reponse null to router
```

routing table information, which is collected from RouteViews (RouteViews, 2012).

Tian Bu and Lixin Gao (Tian, 2002) has given a working report of the global routing table growth, in which the reason of driving the growth has been given: multihoming, failure to aggregate, load balancing and some other economic reasons. Failure to aggregate is attributed by the following practice: to accommodate the continuously scaling of the Internet, allocated prefixes have been further deaggregated to more fine-grained prefix spaces for providing access services for smaller ASes.

In Identifier Network, network has been divided into two independent routing spaces, the core and access network respectively. In the core network, the RID would be allocated in manner strictly conforming to the topology of the core network, and the allocation result would be maintained in the IDMS system, so any arbitrary deaggregation of the RID space is not allowed. We have made data analysis of the Routeviews BGP "show ip bgp" data set collected in the late 2008, and separate the prefix whose prefix and prefix length doesn't conform to the allocation record maintained in CAIDA (CAIDA, 2012). The result is depicted as Figure 10. As shown in the

figure, the deaggregated prefixes have occupied a large amount of the prefixes allocated. Under the TE in the Identifier Network, a majority of these prefixes would no longer pose much burden on the core routers.

Multihoming and Load Balancing (Traffic Engineering) have been more intimately related among the main force driving the FIB increase, as discussed above in this chapter. We adopted similar criterion with (Tian, 2002) to identify the prefixes of multihoming and TE. A multihoming prefix would be advertised by its own AS. Furthermore, by the network providers it connects to in a manner of its prefix contained in another more general prefix. The criterion we used is as follows, and for example, 127.0.0.0/8 contains 127.1.0.0/16.

p1 contains p2, if len(p2)≥len(p1) & addr(p2)/ $2^{32-len(p1)}$ =addr(p1)/$2^{32-len(p1)}$

Next, we extract the prefixes not introduced by TE (potentially be introduced by the failure to aggregate cause) from the multihoming prefixes. We identify the "failure to aggregate" prefixes by

Figure 9. A scenario of neighbor-to-neighbor TE

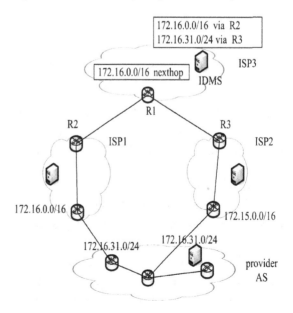

Figure 10. Prefix deaggregation trends

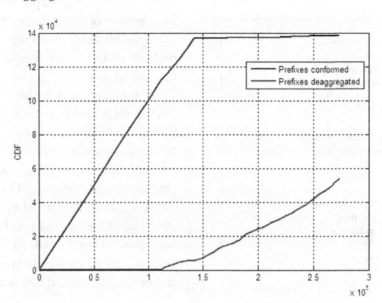

Figure 11. Stub deaggregate prefixes vs. transit prefixes

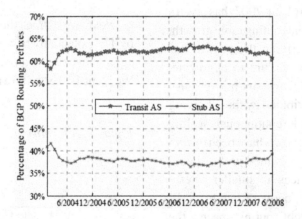

aggregating the prefixes advertised by one AS as aggressive as possible, and the rest of which could not be aggregated is considered to be failure to aggregate.

In Identifier Network, we need to consider the prefixes of core and access network separately. Generally speaking, ASes can be classified into two categories: stub and transit. Stub ASes correspond to edge networks, which do not forward traffic for their neighbors. Transit ASes correspond to custom networks, which provide data delivery service for other ASes (Dong, 2009). Based on the ASes information, we filter the RouteViews RIBs, and distinguish the routing prefixes belonging to either transit ASes or stub ASes. Figure 11 illustrates the percentage of prefixes belonging to transit ASes and stub ASes respectively. The routing prefixes belonging to stub ASes, which account for 35%-40% of total routing prefixes, will be wiped off from the global routing table. These prefixes would not be advertised in a deaggregated manner as that in current Internet, thus help reduce the speed of the global routing table growth.

FUTURE RESEARCH DIRECTIONS

Before concluding the chapter, it is important to outline the next steps related to the work presented in this chapter. Therefore, we present our planned direction of future work in this section. The Identifier Network provides a chance to reconsider the traffic engineering under the ID/Loc separation situation. Future work will look into optimizing the algorithm of lookup in the IDMS, measuring the performance when using policies in the mapping responses and evaluating the impact of the cache in the routers.

In addition, it is planned to extend the test network to gather experience with running and optimizing our solutions in larger network environment. A potentially new direction which combines the ID/Loc separation with MPLS (Multiprotocol Label Switching, [Rosen, 2011]) in the intradomian traffic engineering is at the research plan of the next months.

CONCLUSION

In this chapter, we propose a novel method for implementing traffic engineering including End-to-End traffic engineering and Neighbor-to-Neighbor traffic engineering in Identifier Network. This solution focuses on the routing optimization introduced by traffic engineering requirements. It borrows idea from the strong conformation of RID allocation to topology introduced by the separation between the access and core networks, and the interaction between the IDMSes of RID allocation information. It also requires no additional network entities for the implementation.

To analyze the feasibility of the solution, we collect the latest Routeviews BGP data and the results show that the proposed traffic engineering solution could reduce the burden of the core routing table.

ACKNOWLEDGMENT

This work was supported in part by the National Basic Research Program of China (973 Program) under Grant 2013CB329100 and 2013CB329102, by the National Natural Science Foundation of China (NSFC) under Grant No. 61232017, 61001122 and 61003283, by the National High-Tech Research and Development Program of China (863) under Grant No. 2011AA010701.

REFERENCES

Atkinson, R. J., & Bhatti, S. N. (2012). *ILNP architectural description*. Retrieved from http://www.ietf.org

Brim, S., Chiappa, N., Farinacci, D., Fuller, V., Lewis, D., & Meyer, D. (2008). *LISP-CONS: A content distribution overlay network service for LISP*. Retrieved from http://www.ietf.org

Bu, T., Gao, L., & Towsley, D. (2002). *On routing table growth*. INFOCOM.

CAIDA. (2012). *Website*. Retrieved from http://www.caida.org/home/

Chen, J., Dong, P., Zhang, H., & Zeng, Y. (2011). A routing scalability model for core-edge separation internet with hybrid routing. *IEEE Communications Letters, 10*(15), 1142–1144. doi:10.1109/LCOMM.2011.080811.111285.

Dong, P., Qin, Y., & Zhang, H. (2007). Research on universal network supporting pervasive services [in Chinese]. *Acta Electronica Sinica, 35*(4), 599–606.

Dong, P., Wang, H., Qin, Y., Zhang, H., & Kuo, S.-K. (2009). *Evaluation of scalable routing architecture based on locator/identifier separation*. IEEE Globecom. doi:10.1109/GLOCOMW.2009.5360746.

Donnet, B., Iannone, L., & Bonaventure, O. (2008). Interdomain traffic engineering in a locator/identifier separation context. In *Proc. of Internet Network Management Workshop 2008 (INM)*(pp. 1-6).

Elmokashfi, A., Kvalbein, A., & Dovrolis, C. (2010). On the scalability of BGP: The role of topology growth. *IEEE Journal on Selected Areas in Communications, 28*(8), 1250–1261. doi:10.1109/JSAC.2010.101003.

Farinacci, D. Fuller, Oran, V., D., Meyer, D., & Brim, S. (2012). *Locator/ID Separation Protocol (LISP)*. Retrieved from http://www.ietf.org

Farinacci, D., Fuller, V., Meyer, D., & Lewis, D. (2012). *LISP alternative topology (LISP+ALT)*. Retrieved from http://www.ietf.org

Ford, A., Raiciu, C., Handley, M., Barre, S., & Iyengar, J. R. (2011). Architectural guidelines for multipath TCP development (RFC 6182). Retrieved from http://www.ietf.org

Herrin, W. (2008). *Tunneling route reduction protocol (TRRP)*. Retrieved from http://bill.herrin.us/network/trrp.html

Huston, G. (2012). *Growth of the BGP table - 1994 to present*. Retrieved from http://bgp.potaroo.net/

IETF. (2011). The internet routing overlay network (IRON) (RFC6179). Retrieved from http://tools.ietf.org/html/rfc6179

IETF. (2012a). *IETF locator/ID separation protocol*. Retrieved from http://datatracker.ietf.org/wg/lisp/

IETF. (2012b). *IRTF routing research group*. Retrieved from http://tools.ietf.org/group/irtf/trac/wiki/RoutingResearchGroup

Iyengar, J. R., Amer, P. D., & Stewart, R. (2006). Concurrent multipath transfer using SCTP multihoming over independent end-to-end paths. *IEEE/ACM Transactions on Networking, 14*(5), 951–964. doi:10.1109/TNET.2006.882843.

Jakab, L., Cabellos-Aparicio, A., Coras, F., Saucez, D., & Bonaventure, O. (2010). LISP-TREE: A DNS hierarchy to support the LISP mapping system. *IEEE Journal on Selected Areas in Communications, 28*(8), 1332–1343. doi:10.1109/JSAC.2010.101011.

Jen, D., et al. (2008). APT: A practical tunneling architecture for routing scalability. Technical Report 080004, UCLA.

Lear, E. (2012). *NERD: A not-so-novel EID to RLOC database*. Retrieved from http://www.ietf.org

Li, T. (2011). Recommendation for a routing architecture (RFC 6115). Retrieved from http://www.ietf.org

Luo, H., Zhang, H., & Qiao, C. (2011). Efficient mobility support by indirect mapping innetworks with locator/identifier separation. *IEEE Transactions on Vehicular Technology, 60*(5), 2265–2279. doi:10.1109/TVT.2011.2152867.

Luo, H., Zhang, H., & Zukerman, M. (2011). Decoupling the design of identifier-to-locator mapping services from identifiers. *Computer Networks, 55*(4), 959–974. doi:10.1016/j.comnet.2010.12.009.

Luo, H. B., Qin, Y. J., & Zhang, H. K. (2009). A DHT-based Identifier-to-locator mapping approach for a scalable internet. *IEEE Transactions on Parallel and Distributed Systems, 20*(12), 1790–1802. doi:10.1109/TPDS.2009.30.

Mathy, L., & Iannone, L. (2008). LISP-DHT: Towards a DHT to Map Identifiers onto Locators. *In Proc. of the ACM ReArch Conference.*

Medina, A., Taft, N., Salamatian, K., Bhattacharyya, S., & Diot, C. (2002). Traffic matrix estimation: Existing techniques and new directions. *ACM SIGCOMM Computer Communication Reviews, 32*(4), 161–174. doi:10.1145/964725.633041.

Meyer, D., Zhang, L., & Fall, K. (2007). Report from the IAB Workshop on Routing and Addressing (RFC 4984). Retrieved from http://www.ietf.org

Moskowitz, R., Nikander, P., Jokela, P., & Henderson, T. (2008). Host identity protocol (RFC 5201). Retrieved from http://www.ietf.org

Nordmark, E., & Bagnulo, M. (2009). Shim6: Level 3 multihoming shim protocol for IPv6 (RFC 5533). Retrieved from http://www.ietf.org

O'Dell, M. (1997). *GSE – An alternate addressing architecture for IPv6.* Retrieved from http://www.ietf.org

973. Project. (2006). *Website.* Retrieved from http://www.most.gov.cn/bstd/bstdbsfw/bstdfxzxk/bstdfxz973/bstdfxz973jg/200608/t20060810_35340.htm

Quoitin, B., Lannone, L., Launois, C., & Bonaventure, O. (2007). Evaluating the benefits of the locator/identifier separation. In *Proc. of SIGCOMM MobiArch'07.*

Rekhter, Y., Li, T., & Hares, S. (2006). A border gateway protocol 4 (BGP-4) (RFC 4271). Retrieved from http://www.ietf.org

Rosen, E., Viswanathan, A., & Callon, R. (2001). Multiprotocol label switching architecture (RFC 3031). Retrieved from http://www.ietf.org

RouteViews.org. (2012). RouterViews Project. Retrieved from http://www.routeviews.org/

Uhlig, S., Quoitin, B., Lepropre, J., & Balon, S. (2006). Providing public intradomain traffic matrices to the research community. *ACM SIGCOMM Computer Communication Review, 36*(1), 83–86. doi:10.1145/1111322.1111341.

Vogt, C. (2008). Six/one router: A scalable and backwards-compatible solution for provider-independent addressing. In *Proc. of ACM SIGCOMM MobiArch Workshop* (pp.13-18).

Xiaoliang, Z., Dante, J. P., & Jason, S. (2010). Routing scalability: An operator's view. *IEEE Journal on Selected Areas in Communications, 28*(8), 1262–1270. doi:10.1109/JSAC.2010.101004.

Xu, C., Liu, T., Guan, J., Zhang, H., & Muntean, G.-M. (2012). CMT-QA: Quality-aware adaptive concurrent multipath data transfer in heterogeneous wireless networks. *IEEE Transactions on Mobile Computing,* 99.

Xu, C., Zhao, F., Guan, J., Zhang, H., & Muntean, G.-M. (2012). QoE-driven user-centric VoD services in urban multi-homed P2P-based vehicular networks. *IEEE Transactions on Vehicular Technology,* 99.

Zhang, H., & Su, W. (2007). Fundamental research on the architecture of new network---Universal network and pervasice services [in Chinese]. *Acta Electronica Sinica, 35*(4), 593–598.

Zhang, L., Wakikawa, R., & Zhu, Z. (2009). Support mobility in the global Internet. In *Proceedings of the 1st ACM Workshop on Mobile Internet through Cellular Networks.*

ADDITIONAL READING

Daniel, O., & Awduche, Bijan, J. (2002). Internet traffic engineering using multi-protocol label switching (mpls). *Computer Networks, 40,* 111–129. doi:10.1016/S1389-1286(02)00269-4.

Dino, F., & Vince, F. (2009). LISP Map Server.

Eliot, L. (2008). NERD: A not-so-novel EID to RLOC Database.

Florin, C., Lorand, J., Albert, C., Jordi, D., & Virgil, D. (2009). Coresim: A simulator for evaluating locator/id separation protocol mapping systems. In Trilogy Future Internet Summer School poster session.

Iannone, L. & Bonaventure, O. (2007). On the cost of caching locator/id mappings. *ACM CoNEXT*.

Jianli, P., Raj, J., Subharthi, P., & Chakchai, S. (2010). MILSA: A new evolutionary architecture for scalability, mobility, and multihoming in the future internet. *IEEE Journal on Selected Areas in Communications, 28*(8), 1344–1361. doi:10.1109/JSAC.2010.101012.

Juhoon, K., Luigi, I., & Anja, F. (2011). Deep dive into the lisp cache and what isps should know about it. In *IFIP International Conference on Networking, volume 6640 of Lecture Notes in Computer Science (LNCS)* (pp. 267-278).

Launois, C., Quoitin, B., & Bonaventure, O. (2006). Leveraging networking performance with IPv6 multihoming and multiple provider-dependent aggregatable prefixes. *Computer Networks, 50*(8), 1145–1157. doi:10.1016/j.comnet.2005.09.013.

Pan, J., Paul, S., Jain, R., & Bowman, M. (2008). MILSA: A mobility and multihoming supporting identifier locator split architecture for naming in the next generation Internet. *IEEE GLOBECOM'08*.

Randall, A., Saleem, B., & Stephen, H. (2010). Evolving the Internet architecture through naming. *IEEE Journal on Selected Areas in Communications, 28*(8), 1319–1325. doi:10.1109/JSAC.2010.101009.

Ruomei, G., Constantinos, D., & Ellen, W. (2005). Interdomain ingress traffic engineering through optimized aspath prepending. In *Proceedings of IFIP Networking* (pp. 647-658).

Scott, B., Noel, C., Dino, F., Vince, F., Darrel, L., & David, M. (2011). LISP-CONS: A content distribution. Overlay network service for LISP.

KEY TERMS AND DEFINITIONS

Autonomous System (AS): Is a collection of connected IP nodes under the control of the same administrative entity.

ID/Loc Separation: The IP address semantics are overloaded. More specifically speaking, an IP address represents not only the location but also the identity of a terminal. The ID/Loc separation splits the dual semantic of the IP address, and supplies the mapping relationship between the locators and the end-point identifiers.

Identifier: A stable value that can be used to identify a terminal. Anything could be used as an identifier as long as it is topologically and geographically independent (i.e. remains unchanged when the terminal roams around).

Identifier Network: A new network architecture which adopts the ID/Loc separation mechanism at the infrastructure layer and aims to provide a uniform named service architecture to build a pervasive service layer.

Locator: The IP address that indicates the terminal's current location. It could be the IP address of the terminal itself, or the IP address of the network entity that is currently serving the terminal.

Multi Protocol Label Switching: Multi-protocol Label Switching (MPLS) refers to a mechanism in telecommunication networks which forwards data packets among network nodes using so-called labels. MPLS allows for the creation of "virtual channels" between distant nodes that can carry packets of different protocols such as IP or Ethernet.

Traffic Engineering: Traffic Engineering (TE) deals with network engineering and performance optimization of networks. One of its main objectives is to facilitate reliable and efficient network operations while at the same time considering optimizations of network resource utilization and traffic performance.

Chapter 8
The Map-and-Encap Locator/ Identifier Separation Paradigm:
A Security Analysis

Damien Saucez
Inria Sophia Antipolis, France

Luigi Iannone
Telecom ParisTech, France

Olivier Bonaventure
Université catholique de Louvain, Belgium

ABSTRACT

Internet lacks of strong security mechanisms, opening the way to a plethora of different manners in which integrity and availability can be compromised by malicious activities. Furthermore, the trend shows an increase of security threats, at least in the foreseeable future. Despite such situation, new proposals for Future Internet architectures mostly aiming at solving scalability issues do rather neglect security aspects.

Among candidate Future Internet architectures, the ones based on the Locator/Identifier separation paradigm has been largely explored, but security had no major role in these research activities. We present a security threats analysis of such approach using the Locator/Identifier Separation Protocol (LISP) as a running example.

The chapter does not overview the merits of the Locator/Identifier separation paradigm. Rather, the aim is to provide a thorough analysis of the security aspects, assessing the security level of the architecture and providing recommendations on possible practices to improve it.

DOI: 10.4018/978-1-4666-4305-5.ch008

INTRODUCTION

Since its creation, the Internet has grown at a rapid pace and the protocols, whose principles have been designed more than thirty years ago at the dawn of the Internet, are starting to show their scalability and maintainability limits (Meyer, Zhang, & Fall, 2007; BGP Routing Table Analysis Report).

To give the Internet a second birth, removing (or at least evading) current limitations, allowing continuing its growth, improving its scalability and performance, Future Internet architectures are under consideration, mostly (if not always) based on the Locator/Identifier separation paradigm. It exists a general consensus in the research community, but also among Internet operators and manufacturers, that such a paradigm is the most promising technology that, if correctly engineered, can be incrementally deployed, enhancing Internet's scalability and even providing additional benefits (e.g., scalable support for multi-homing and flexible traffic engineering) (Li, 2011; Quoitin, Iannone, de Launois, & Bonaventure, 2007; Saucez, Donnet, Iannone, & Bonaventure, 2008).

Due to its open nature, in the Internet attacks and security threats are commonplace, and where their number is relentlessly growing (Wood et al., 2012). Therefore, for every proposed Future Internet architecture, its security model and threats analysis becomes of primary importance, and should be carried out with care, preferably even before any commercial deployment (Bos et al., 2009). Unfortunately, reality is different. Current research activities on Future Internet seldom tackle security aspects, very often providing only a very short and high-level analysis.

In the aim of bridging this gap, this chapter presents a security analysis for map-and-encap based Locator/Identifier separation approaches, taking the Locator/Identifier Separation Protocol (LISP) as running example of such kind of architectures in order to provide real and concrete cases.

The Locator/Identifier Separation Protocol (LISP) (Farinacci, Fuller, Meyer, & Lewis, 2012), first proposed by Cisco at the IRTF (Internet Research Task Force) and now under specification at the IETF (Internet Engineering Task Force), is an instantiation of the paradigm separating locators and identifier. Its success is also due to its inherent properties of incremental deployability, which is a very important adoption incentive factor for any new architecture. Indeed, in order to design a viable solution, existing constrains (e.g., current OS protocol stack implementations, inter-domain routing, and prefix allocation policies) have to be taken into account, avoiding disrupting the existing communication infrastructure, whilst providing benefits, hence incentives, for early adopters (Iannone & Levä, 2010).

The present chapter starts by providing some background information, describing the map-and-encap Locator/Identifier separation in its LISP instantiation. Except for the LISP specific header, the main functioning of the protocol is valid for any other solution in the same class (e.g., Menth, Hartman, & Klein, 2010; Frejborg, 2011; Jen, Meisel, Massey, Wang, Zhang, & Zhang, 2007). The reader familiar with LISP or the general Locator/Identifier separation paradigm can safely skip this overview. Then, a brief introduction on the main class of attacks (at network layer) and the way they are carried out is proposed.

It is out of scope to present an exhaustive taxonomy of all possible attacks that can be carried out in the Internet; rather, the focus is limited to threats that are relevant in the Core/Edge separation context. Note, that this does not mean that other attacks are not possible, but only that there is no difference (i.e., they can be carried out in the exact same way) between the new architecture and the current Internet architecture. Furthermore, here we assume a generic IP connectivity/transfer service, without making the difference between using IPv4 or IPv6, since, in the present context and from a security viewpoint, the two versions are equivalent. Afterward, the presented class of attacks is instantiated in the context of LISP, in order to analyze the threats and the available countermeasures available to mitigate as much as possible consequences of such malicious activities. The presented analysis is partially based on work carried out in the IETF and reported in Saucez, Iannone, and Bonaventure (2012). As mentioned before, despite the importance of having a security analysis for any new Internet architecture the literature lacks of extensive works on this topic. The few existing related works are reviewed right before discussing the outcome of the presented security analysis, providing some recommendations and deployment guidelines.

BACKGROUND

Compared to other Locator/Identifier separation proposals, LISP takes a conservative approach, without introducing a brand new namespace, but rather modifying the semantic of the existing IP addressing space depending on the scope, then using such addresses in a map & encap approach (Farinacci et al., 2012; Meyer, 2008).

LISP introduces two categories of addresses, namely the Routing LOCators (RLOCs) and the Endpoint IDentifiers (EIDs), both being usual IP addresses with just a different routing scope. Addresses from the RLOC space are assigned to border routers by the Internet Service Providers, while stub networks end-systems use EIDs

addresses assigned from the EID Space. Stub networks (also called edge networks) are positioned at the edge of the Internet and are only source or destination of IP packets, not offering transit services. This type of Locator/Identifier separation is also called core-edge separation and is represented in Figure 1.

The address semantic change introduced by LISP has the advantage of being non-disruptive, maintaining compatibility with any device using the IP protocol. Furthermore, such a change allows LISP to solve the scalability issues related to the routing table's growth that the current Internet architecture is facing and that is the fundamental motivation of all the hype around Locator/Identifier separation in recent years. In more practical terms, by separating the edge from the core, LISP enables in the latter to only advertise routes towards the RLOCs (by means of the Border Gateway Protocol – BGP, by Rekhter, Li, & Hares, 2006). This is not the case in the current architecture, where all of the addressing spaces, including stub networks, are advertised leading to restless growth of the Routing Information Base (RIB) (Quoitin et al., 2007).

Because of this separation, routers in the core of the Internet are not aware anymore about EIDs assigned to hosts. To maintain end-to-end connectivity, packets are tunneled between edge networks using encapsulation. LISP tunneling

Figure 1. Core-edge separation in the LISP context

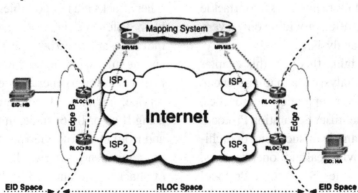

consists in prepending a LISP-specific header to the original packet and then encapsulating everything in an UDP datagram. To uniquely identify LISP-encapsulated packets the destination port is set to the well-known value 4341. Note that the inner (original) packet uses EID addresses, also used for forwarding inside the source and destination stub networks, while the outer IP header uses RLOC addresses, for forwarding in the core Internet. The LISP-specific header contains flags and other information related to traffic engineering and RLOCs' reachability and its format is depicted in Figure 2. Further details about the LISP-specific header content can be found in the original LISP specifications (Farinacci et al., 2012). Border routers performing LISP encapsulation at the packet's source stub network are indicated as Ingress Tunnel Routers (ITRs), while border routers at the packet's destination stub network are called Egress Tunnel Routers (ETRs), all of them are indicated by the general term xTRs.

In order to actually perform tunneling there is the need of a way to bind EIDs with RLOCs, in other words to know the locators (RLOCs) associated to EIDs. In practical terms, the original packet is using EIDs and it is necessary to be able to select the RLOCs that have to be used in the outer header. Such binding is obtained through a map function coupling EID prefixes with a set of RLOCs: these are the so-called mappings.

These mappings are made available to all xTRs through a mapping distribution system, also simply called Mapping System. Differently from any other routing entity in the Internet, based on proactive advertisement of all known routing information, the mapping distribution system works within an on-demand fashion method more similar to the Domain Name System (DNS). This means that in order to obtain mappings used for encapsulation operation, xTRs query the mapping system in order to obtain all mappings related to a certain EID only when necessary (usually, but not exclusively, at the beginning of a new flow transmission).

In the context of LISP several different proposals exist for possible Mapping Systems, like for instance LISP+ALT (Fuller, Farinacci, Meyer, & Lewis, 2010), LISP-DDT (Fuller, Lewis, & Farinacci, 2012), and LISP-TREE (Jakab, Cabellos-Aparicio, Coras, Saucez, & Bonaventure, 2010). These Mapping Systems are queried with a simple Map-Request packet asking for a mapping for a specific EID. The Mapping System replies to this message with a Map-Reply packet carrying the requested mapping. Nevertheless, in order to provide some mapping system agility, i.e., the possibility to easily switch between different mapping systems, LISP defines a uniform front-end (Fuller & Farinacci, 2012). This approach separates the data-plane (i.e., packets' encapsulation and forwarding) from the control-plane (i.e., mapping

Figure 2. LISP-specific packet header format

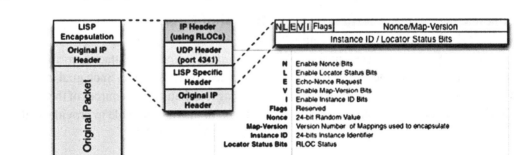

registration and distribution). Two types of servers offering an Application Programming Interface - API independent from the specific mapping system implement the front-end: Map-Servers (MS) and Map-Resolvers (MR). The role of Map-Servers is to announce into the mapping system the existence of mappings. To this end, ETRs register their mappings through a Map-Register message, which is acknowledged by Map-Servers with a Map-Notify message. Conversely, Map-Resolvers are used by ITRs to retrieve mappings from the mapping system through a Map-Request message. The requested mapping is sent back with a Map-Reply message either by the destination ETR or the Map-Resolver, depending on whether or not the latter works in proxy-mode.

All the LISP elements described insofar work together to ensure end-to-end communication between end-systems in the following way. Assuming that, in Figure 1, host HB needs to communicate with HA, HB sends a normal IP packet using EID HB as source address and EID HA as destination address. The packet is forwarded inside Edge B until it reaches one of the ITRs, for instance R1. The latter maintains a LISP-Database where all local mappings, i.e., the mappings for the EIDs of Edge B, are stored. Such database is used to select the source RLOC of the outer header of the LISP encapsulation. Concerning the destination RLOC, the ITR sends a Map-Request message to a Map-Resolver, which will send back a Map-Reply containing the necessary mapping (assuming the MR is working in proxy-mode). From the obtained mapping an RLOC can be selected as destination address of the encapsulated packet, which is then forwarded in the Internet. The mapping is also kept in a temporary LISP-Cache, avoiding querying the mapping system for each and every packet. When the encapsulated packet reaches one of HA's RLOCs, let's say R4, the latter decapsulates the packet and forwards it to the final destination HA.

SECURITY THREATS: A BRIEF ATTACKS TAXONOMY

In order to understand security risks related to attacks, it is important to understand the different classes of security threats (or attack types) and techniques to carry out malicious activities. The present overview is not meant to be exhaustive, providing a complete taxonomy of existing types of attack (Igure & Williams, 2008). Rather, it aims at reviewing the most relevant attacks, which will be explored in the context of the Locator/Identifier separation paradigm.

Intrusion

An *Intrusion attack* consists in an attacker gaining remote access to some resources (e.g., a host, a router, or a network) that are normally denied to him/her. Depending on the victim and the resource that attacker is targeting, such type of attack is carried out either exploiting software bugs or leveraging in design weaknesses. A classic example of such kind of attack is the attacker trying to intrude in a firewall-protected network. The attacker can try to explore possible misconfigurations or holes in the set of rules of the firewall in order to introduce malicious traffic in a network or access restricted servers. The worst scenario is when the attacker is able to take partial/total control of the victim, having access to private information or being able to execute malicious code either to disrupt the normal functioning or to launch other attacks toward other victims.

Denial of Service (DoS)

A *Denial of Service (DoS)* attack aims at disrupting a specific targeted service. Such goal is achieved by trying to exhaust the resources of the victim up to the point that it is not able to provide a reliable service to legit traffic and/or systems. To this end, attackers try to invoke processes and/or services that consume CPU time, memory, bandwidth, or other scarce resources. Processes and services that do not require any kind of authentication in order to identify legitimate service requesters are exposed to such kind of attack. However, since authentication itself is a service, it is as well vulnerable to such kind of attacks. A classic example of such kind of attack is the attacker opening a large number of connections to a server, until connection establishment resources of the servers are exhausted, leading to legitimate clients not able to establish new connections, hence experiencing a service denial due to lack of resources. Furthermore, the attacker can mount parallel attacks, by first compromising other systems through an intrusion attack and then starting the attack contemporaneously from those systems toward the victim. This is usually called a Distributed Denial of Service (DDoS) attack.

Eavesdropping

Eavesdropping consists in collecting the traffic of a target in order to gain any type of restricted and sensitive information such as passwords, session tokens, or any kind of confidential information, through deep packet inspection. Unless the attacker aims at simply disrupting the original communication, this type of attack is usually carried out in a way such that the target does not even notice the attack. In the particular simple case of the attacker positioned on the path of the target traffic, it is called a Man-in-the-Middle attack. However, this is not a requirement to carry out an eavesdropping attack. Indeed the attacker might be able, for instance through an intrusion attack on a weaker system, either to duplicate or even re-direct the traffic, in both cases having access to the raw packets. A classic example of such kind

of attack is packet sniffing in public un-protected Wi-Fi networks. This is the ideal case where, since packets are transmitted without encryption the attacker just needs a simple sniffer software in order to have access to data.

SECURITY THREATS IN LISP

The previous section provided a brief taxonomy of attacks, proposing three main classes (i.e., intrusion, Denial of Service, and Eavesdropping). This section describes how these types of attacks can be carried out in the context of the Locator/Identifier Separation paradigm. For the sake of clarity, and without loss of generality, attacks are described specifically leveraging on LISP. Nevertheless, the proposed scenarios can be easily adapted to any specific protocol relying on the map-and-encap principle. Furthermore, the aim is not to point provide a how-to carry out attacks in practice, but rather to have a fair security assessment compared to the standard level of security of the current Internet.

Intrusion

The risk of intrusion with LISP is relatively limited, except that an attacker willing to introduce in a system can spoof either the source EID or the source RLOC. For example, if an access list denies packets with a particular address (RLOC or EID), the attacker can spoof addresses that are allowed to enter the network. This attack allows the attacker to inject packets in a network but is not able to receive packets resulting from the intrusion, as the source address is not the address of the attacker. Nevertheless, the attacker can combine this attack with cache poisoning (described in Section "Denial of Service"), making possible to receive back packets successfully intruding the network. In this case, the poisoned mapping must associate the source EID (spoofed or not) in the forged packet with the real address of the attacker.

Denial of Service

Denials of Service attacks are achieved in LISP as in today's Internet. The attacker generates packets with spoofed addresses (RLOC and/or EID) and sends them at a rate that leads to the overloading of target links and routers, or creating state that disrupt the service. In the case of spoofed addresses, filtering techniques alone are not sufficient to avoid the attack as the addresses themselves cannot be trusted, making counter measures hard to deploy.

From this viewpoint, the separation between the locator and the identifier roles of addresses is a boon for attackers willing to achieve DoS through spoofing. Indeed, EIDs are assigned independently of the topology, so there is no direct way to legitimate mappings between EIDs and RLOCs. Host-based solutions like HIP (Moskowitz, Nikander, Jokela, & Henderson, 2008) or Shim6 (Nordmark & Bagnulo, 2009) use cryptography to ensure that the locators belong to the legitimate owner of the identifier. Unfortunately, LISP cannot offer this solution as LISP is invisible to hosts and it would be operationally too expensive for routers to perform such verification, because cryptographic computation is hardly performed at line rate, causing an important slow-down of forwarding operation. Therefore, as in the current Internet, when an attacker spoofs the source EID address, the packet's destination site believes that the packet has been sent from the host with the spoofed EID, instead of the real packet's originator. Similarly, when the source RLOC is spoofed, the core Internet considers that the packet comes from the spoofed RLOC instead of the attacker that actually forged the encapsulation. Furthermore, the destination EID site believes that the spoofed RLOC is the locator of an ITR for the source EID, while, in reality, it might not. Obviously, an attacker can use at the same time RLOC and EID spoofing.

Spoofing is also an attack vector used to make DoS attacks against statefull middle-boxes (e.g., Network Address Translator (NAT), Firewall). Indeed, any statefull system has a limited memory, stopping functioning properly when this limit is reached. For instance, assuming a Network Address Translator (NAT) device supports at most N concurrent flows, sending N packets with randomly chosen spoofed addresses (EID or RLOC depending where the box is placed) will create N different states in the NAT device. Thus, new and legitimate flows will be rejected because of the lack of memory to create new state.

EID spoofing can be used indirectly to carry out DoS attacks on the mapping system. To do so, the attacker sends packets with a random source EID. If the destination network is not configured properly with filters or firewalls, then a packet is likely to be sent back to this fake source EID (e.g., ICMP error, TCP SYN + ACK), which might be encapsulated. However, as the EID is random, this will lead to a cache miss at the ITR and then trigger a Map-Request. Such a scenario is depicted in Figure 3. If those Map-Requests are generated at high rate, target's control plane might suffer a denial of service.

Another vector for DoS attacks is the so-called Gleaning mechanism. Gleaning assumes that traffic is bidirectional (which is a very likely); hence xTRs may "glean" mapping information from traffic in one direction to encapsulate traffic in the opposite direction. Normally, a Map-Request is sent for the first packet in the opposite direction and, as long as the mapping is unknown, packets might be dropped. Gleaning information allows xTRs to create temporary mapping and avoid dropping packets. When an xTR receives a packet, source EID and source RLOC are extracted and a temporary mapping is created. The mapping binds the EID to the RLOC so that any further packet sent back to the EID is encapsulated with that mapping. To validate the mapping, the xTR sends a Map-Request for the EID on the mapping system. However, as long as no Map-Reply is retrieved, the gleaned mapping is used.

Figure 3. Mapping system DoS through spoofing. The attacker sends packets to random EID destination using a spoofed EIDs (HV and HR). The reply eventually sent by the destinations triggers cache miss on the xTR of their domain, which will send a Map-Request to the mapping system. This may overload certain Mapping System Servers.

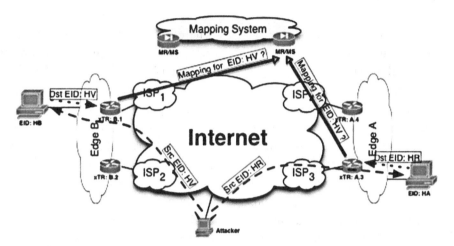

An attacker can use EID spoofing to disrupt or redirect traffic, by forging a LISP-encapsulated packet whose source EID is the address of the destination host under attacks and the source RLOC address is an invalid RLOC. If no mapping was known before for the target EID, then the attack is successful. An attack that alters the content of the EID-to-RLOC Cache of an xTR is also called a Cache Poisoning attack. The gleaning attack can be extended to cause a denial of service attack using xTRs as relays. In this case, instead of putting an invalid RLOC in the forged packet, the attacker puts the RLOC of the target of the relay attack. If the attacker is able to inject the fake mapping in several xTRs, the result is that all the traffic from the relays is diverted to the targeted node, potentially overloading it.

Another form of attack aiming at poisoning, or actually exhausting, the cache is the de-aggregation attack. This attack aims at filling up the EID-to-RLOC Cache. There is no particular rule for ITRs when their EID-to-RLOC Cache is full, however, a solution is to either remove some old mapping entries or to prevent the insertion of new ones, which eventually leads to a DoS on the ITR. The de-aggregation attack simply consists in providing many mappings for an EID site. For example, if the attacker is the legitimate owner of the 10.0.0.0/24 EID prefix, by distributing mappings for every single EID (10.0.0.X/32), ITRs can be forced to up to 2^8 mappings. The risk in IPv4 is relatively limited, but in IPv6, any attacker can easily provide at least 2^{72} mappings (longest prefix allocations in IPv6 is/56, with a 128-bits address, this leaves the remaining 72 bits for network address assignment), which is certainly much more than an EID-to-RLOC Cache can sustain. Playing with the Time-To-Live (TTL) associated to mappings, which in LISP is a 32-bits value expressing (in minutes) how long a mapping can be considered as valid, can increase the impact of cache poisoning attacks. For instance, if the TTL is long (e.g., 1 year), the malicious mappings can remain in the EID-to-RLOC Cache for a long period of time. On the contrary, if the TTL is small the EID-to-RLOC Cache must be updated frequently which might overload the ITR or the mapping system.

Control packets are of prime interest for attackers as they are used to control the system (basically where to send what). To avoid attackers to register fake mappings in the Mapping System, Map-Register messages are protected with an authentication mechanism (Farinacci, Fuller, Meyer, & Lewis, 2012). Map-Register messages are authenticated with a MD5 HMAC (Turner, & Chen, 2011) with the HMAC key being a shared secret between the ITR and its Map Server. However, Map-Requests and Map-Replies have no authentication mechanism. Typical information in a Map-Request is the EID prefix (or address) to get a mapping for, a nonce, and the list of locators of the ITR that sent the Map-Request. Map-Replies carry the mapping that associate the corresponding EID prefix to a list of locators. To determine to which Map-Request a Map-Reply belongs, it includes the request nonce. Unfortunately, the nonce does authenticate neither the ITR that sends the Map-Request, nor the origin or validity of the mapping. An attacker can then mount a relay attack by forging Map-Requests or Map-Replies. For instance, the attacker can forge a high volume of Map-Requests, putting the address of the DoS victim as requester; hence, the Map-Reply is sent to the targeted node instead of the attacker. As a result, the target receives unsolicited messages (that are dropped after processing) on its control plane, which will waste resources, without being able to determine the origin of the attack. This

relay attack can be as well as an amplification attack, since Map-Replies can be larger. Indeed, a Map-Request can be as small as 40 bytes + the IP and UDP headers, while its corresponding Map-Reply has is $12 + (R * (28 + N * 24))$ bytes long, where N is the maximum number of RLOCs in a mapping and R the maximum number of records in a Map-Reply. Since up to 255 RLOCs can be associated to an EID-Prefix and 255 records can be stored in a Map-Reply, the maximum size of a Map-Reply is above 1 MB showing a size factor of up to 39,193 between the message sent by the attacker and the message sent by the ETR. Therefore, the packets that eventually arrive at the target can be much larger than the packets initially sent by the attacker, consuming a large chunk of victim's bandwidth. This scenario is depicted in Figure 4.

The previous attack can be also carried out by sending Map-Requests packets to ETRs. Indeed, when an ITR wants to probe an ETR, for instance to test its reachability, it sends a Map-Request tagged with the P-bit (Section 6.1.2 of Farinacci, Fuller, Meyer, & Lewis, 2012; Probe-bit indicating that a Map-Request has to be treated like a locator reachability probe). Upon reception of

Figure 4. Relay and amplification DoS. The attacker sends map-requests for random EIDs (HV and HR), appending the RLOC of the victim (A.3). The Map-replies, which are larger than the original requests, are all sent back to the victim, wasting bandwidth and processing power.

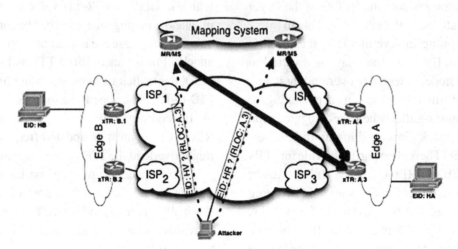

such request, the ETR sends back a Map-Reply, with the P-bit set as well, to the source RLOC of the Map-Request. Therefore, an attacker can use a forged probe to generate a relay/amplification attack as shown previously (but without involving the Mapping System).

The separation between locators and identifiers combined to the map-and-encap concept offers an elegant design with a clear distinction between the control plane (i.e., the mappings) and the data plane (i.e., encapsulation and forwarding), where the data-plane cannot interfere directly on the control-plane. Nevertheless, for performance reasons, LISP authorizes to leak part of the control-plane information into the data-plane, within the LISP header. This header can contain mapping information that have repercussion on the control-plane and can thus be used to carry out attacks.

For instance, mapping can have a version number (Iannone, Saucez, & Bonaventure, 2012) that is used to determine if the EID-to-RLOC Cache of an xTR is up to date. The version number can be leaked in data-plane packets to help faster convergence to the correct mapping (cf., Figure 2). When an ITR encapsulates a packet, the latter is tagged with the version number of the mapping used to select the destination RLOC. The ETR receiving the packet checks the version number on decapsulation. If the version number is different than the version number held by the ETR, the latter notifies the ITR to update the mapping it is using since it is outdated. A malicious user can then use fake version numbers to trigger unnecessary control plane events at the ETR. It can also be used in conjunction with spoofed addresses to perform relay attacks (i.e., the ETR sends a notification of invalid version to the attack target instead of sending it to the attacker). Similarly, the map-version of the mapping used to determine the source RLOC can also be provided in the data-plane packets (cf., Figure 2). In this case xTRs, on decapsulation checks the source map-version number. If the version is not the same as the one it caches in its EID-to-RLOC Cache, it will query

the mapping system to get the latest mapping. Again, an attacker can use this version number to trigger unnecessary load on the control plane.

Other forms of attacks based on data-plane packets can leverage on other LISP header fields. For instance, data-plane packets can also carry reachability information by the mean of the Locator Status Bit (LSB) (cf., Figure 2). The LSB is a vector of bit optionally put in data-plane packets to indicate the reachability of the ETR RLOCs of the source site. The position i-th in the vector tells whether or not the i-th RLOC in the mapping associated to the source EID is reachable. While LSB can be of great help in trustworthy environment without attackers, it is a major security flaw for Internet traffic. Indeed, if an attacker can spoof a source EID, then it is possible to control the usage of the spoofed EID's site ETRs by forging the LSB. For example, if the attacker sends a LSB with all bits set to zeros (meaning RLOC not reachable), then no RLOC can be used and no traffic will be sent to the site resulting in a DoS, potentially with one single packet. A more subtle attack consists in setting only some specific entries in the LSB. The attacker can then redirect all the traffic to one particular ETR, typically to overload it.

Eavesdropping

Cache poisoning attacks are not limited to DoS but can also be used for eavesdropping, by injecting fake state that redirects the traffic.

This attack can be easily carried out in the context of gleaning. To this end it is sufficient for the attacker to use as source RLOC its own IP address, while spoofing the source EID. The result is that all traffic for this EID will go through the attacker.

An attacker can also leverage on control plane packets to eavesdrop traffic. Map-Requests can piggyback mappings; hence they can be used to push mappings to xTRs. An attacker can push a mapping to an ETR by sending a Map-Request with a fake mapping piggybacked to it. More specifically, if the attacker desires to eavesdrop the traffic for an EID prefix, it is sufficient to piggyback a mapping binding the target EID prefix to its IP address (used as RLOC). When an ETR receives such mapping, it installs the mapping in its EID-to-RLOC Cache, resulting in traffic redirected to the attacker.

A harder attack consists in a compromised ETR providing invalid mappings to legitimate Map-Replies, more specifically overclaiming EID prefixes. An overclaiming attack (Maino, Ermagan, Cabellos, Saucez, & Bonaventure, 2012) consists in using an EID prefix in the mapping that is larger than the prefix that is covering the requested EID. For example, if an attacker is attributed the EID prefix 10.0.0.0/24, the mappings cannot provide a larger prefix. Nevertheless, in the lack of specific checks, nothing prevents the attacker to reply with a mapping for a larger prefix, e.g., 10.0.0.0/8. In this case, the EID prefix might cover an EID prefix of another LISP site (e.g., 10.0.1.0/24). With an overclaiming attack, an attacker can thus eavesdrop the traffic of another site or generate denial of service attacks. This attack can be pushed at its paroxysm if the EID prefix in the mapping is the largest possible (e.g., 0.0.0.0/0) as it means that it will cover all the possible EID prefixes. However, as the EID-to-RLOC Cache is based on longest-prefix matching, using large prefixes might not be always fruitful for the attacker. However, the attacker can combine overclaiming and de-aggregation to succeed a cache poisoning attack. For example, if the attacker EID prefix is 10.0.0.0/24, it is not possible to provide a mapping for 10.0.1.0/24. But, since a Map-Reply can contain several mappings, it is possible to finally control this prefix. To this end, the attacker can send a mapping with an EID prefix that covers at the same time the requested EID and the attack target prefix, as well as a mapping for the attack target prefix itself. For instance, if the request is for 10.0.0.1, and the target prefix is 10.0.1.0/24, the Map-Reply can contain the mapping 10.0.0.0/23

and a mapping for 10.0.1.0/24. The reply is perfectly legitimate according to the requested EID, thus the attack is successful.

SOLUTIONS AND RECOMMENDATIONS

Previous sections have shown how an attacker can construct attacks by leveraging LISP, or any map-and-encap Locator/Identifier separation solution. Even though a system in the Internet can never be fully protected against malicious users, we give general recommendations that would mitigate the impact of attacks against map-and-encap approaches.

It is worth noting that with the expected increasing deployment of spoofing prevention techniques such as Baker and Savola (2004) or SAVI (Nordmark et al., 2012); it can be expected that attackers will become less capable of sending packets with a spoofed source address. In general, filtering can be used to at least mitigate attacks. On the one hand, an ITR should always verify that the source EID of a packet that it is encapsulating belongs to one of its EID prefixes, which is not the case in some current implementations of LISP. On the other hand, if an ETR also plays the role of ITR, it might check that the source locator of a packet it receives for decapsulation is in the list of locators for the source EID. To avoid rejecting legitimate packets, the encapsulated packet must contain the map version of the source mapping and this version must correspond to the version in the received EID-to- RLOC Cache. If a higher security level is needed, cryptography techniques like IPSec (Kent & Seo, 2005; Williams & Richardson, 2008) could be used, but the solution does not scale as xTRs can have to process tens thousands of concurrent flows (Iannone & Bonaventure, 2007).

While the gleaning mechanism allows starting encapsulating packets to a certain EID in parallel with the Map-Request to obtain a mapping when a new flow is established, it creates important security risks. A first option would be to strictly limit the number of packets that can be forwarded via a gleaned entry. However, overall the benefits of gleaning, i.e., avoiding the loss of the first packet of a flow, seems very small compared to the associated security risks. Hence, the safest recommendation would be to disable gleaning. Furthermore, packet loss ratio observed in the Internet is probably already orders of magnitude larger than the improvement provided by the gleaning mechanism.

Farinacci et al. (2012) recommend to rate limit the control messages that are sent by xTRs. This limit is important to deal with DoS attacks. However, simple rate limitation techniques, e.g., implemented with a token bucket, on all the Map-Request and Map-Reply messages sent by an xTR are not sufficient (and can actually lead to other forms of DoS). An xTR should distinguish between different types of control plane packets, such as Map-Request messages that it sends to refresh expired mapping information; Map-Request messages that it sends to obtain mapping information because one of the served hosts tried to contact an external EID; Map-Request/Map-Replies messages sent as reachability probes; Map-Request messages sent to support gleaning (if used). These control plane messages are used for different purposes. Indeed, fixing a global rate limit for all control plane messages increases the risk of Denial of Service attacks if a single type of control plane message can exceed the configured limit. This risk could be mitigated by either specifying a rate for each type of control plane messages, or keeping the maximum rate for all control plane messages, but prioritize them according to the list above (with the highest priority for message aiming at refreshing mapping for on-going communications).

As already mentioned, there is no mechanism in LISP that allows an ITR to verify the validity of the Map-Reply messages it receives. Indeed, the nonce only allows an ITR to verify that a Map-Reply responds to a Map-Request previously sent. Solutions that allow verifying the validity and integrity of bindings between EID-Prefixes and their RLOCs (e.g., Saucez et al. (2012) and Maino et al. (2012)) still have to be studied in detail. Nevertheless, having such kind of mechanisms would allow xTRs to ignore non-verified mappings, improving security. The drawback in this case is the fact that such verification often relies on cryptography which might be too costly for low-end routers or too hard to deploy at large scale.

It is worth to notice that, if successful, cache poisoning attacks are the most severe, as they give attacker full control on the traffic. However, there is a difference between cache poisoning attacks using control-plane packets and those using data-plane packets. On the one hand, the former can be avoided easily with cryptography as packets are specifically made to transport control information and the overhead is acceptable. On the other hand, the origin of data-plane packets is hardly authenticated making them more dangerous. For this reason, it is recommended to use information learned from the data-plane packets only after verification through the mapping system (possibly with low priority compared to other operations in the system). The map-version number is an example of this concept. Indeed, map-version does not carry forwarding information but only notification of possible mapping changes. Therefore, when resources are sufficient enough, the ITR can query the mapping system to verify if a new mapping is available and install it if it is the case.

Finally, numerous attacks seen earlier (see Section "Security Threats in LISP") can be avoided if a firewall (or an Access Control List is configured on the xTRs) is used. Indeed, data-plane packets sent by attackers must have a destination EID in the site they are sending the packet to. Therefore, a firewall can check that the inner packet is targeted to a host that is up and running and that the packet is valid for this host (e.g., a TCP SYN packet on port 80 should not be received by the laptop of a user). If the packet is not validated, it should be dropped silently. However, this approach implies firewall to be placed before the ITRs and then the firewalls must be able to extract the inner packet of a LISP-encapsulated packet.

FUTURE RESEARCH DIRECTIONS

In this chapter, we have seen that the Locator/Identifier separation paradigm is subject to various security threats. However, solutions proposed so far are variation of filtering techniques (e.g., access lists, rate limit) and are not extremely robust. For long-term security solutions, cryptography is certainly a necessity. Indeed, one reason why attacks can be mounted today is that the origin of attacks is hard to detect. In addition, it is hard if not impossible to determine whether a packet is legitimate or if an attacker has altered it. To tackle these issues, cryptography could be used. On the one hand, authentication techniques based on cryptography could be used to determine exactly the origin of packets, resulting in better efficiency for filter-based protections. On the other hand, cryptography could be used to validate information contained in packets. Simply signing the mappings would block any attack based on mappings alteration/forging. If more protection is needed, for example to prevent overclaiming attacks, the content of mappings itself could be validated. For instance, when a site receives an identifier prefix, it could receive at the same time a certificate from a third party. If the certificate is attached to the mapping, one can check that the mapping is not the result of an over-claiming attack.

To avoid relay attacks mounted with cache poisoning, locators could also be bound to site by using certificate or any validation technique. Hence, an attacker could only provide locators

that belong to the site the identifier is part of. The main argument against cryptography and certificates today is that it requires, on the one hand, processing power, and, on the other hand, the deployment of a third party infrastructure to manage certificates. These arguments are perfectly right but in the forthcoming future, if attacks continue to grow, the impact of attacks might be such that the price to pay for security would be lower than the cost of undergoing attacks.

CONCLUSION

The Core/Edge separation paradigm is a promising solution to solve the scalability problem of the Internet. The Core/Edge separation paradigm separates the two roles of IP addresses – the locator role of IP that determines the position of hosts on the topology and the identifier role of IP that determines the host for communications. However, while many efforts are spent to ensure the scalability and manageability of the future Internet, very little is done to make it more secure. Unfortunately, the common practice of ignoring security issues is a problematic misjudgment. Indeed, attacks in the current Internet are very common and the frequency and impact of attacks is always growing. In this chapter, we have explored the security threats applicable to the Core/Edge Separation paradigm. For the sake of example, we have described these attacks on the Locator/Identifier Separation Protocol (LISP), due to its popularity and real deployment experience (LISP4). We have seen that malicious systems can use many different techniques to carry out attacks, such as intrusion, denial of service, or eavesdropping. Interestingly, we have shown that most of attacks are the results of flaws in techniques used to optimize the operation of the protocol, e.g., reduce convergence time. This confirms that security issues must be taken in considerations at the early step of the development of protocols.

Based on our observations, we proposed several recommendations to make LISP and the Core/Edge separation paradigm in general more robust. The proposed solutions do not require any architectural change, but can't, unfortunately, offer perfect protection. For long-term solutions, LISP has to be adapted to support strong authentication and validation mechanisms. However, robustness against security threats comes at the cost of complex management and operation. This very last point raises the long-standing question of the tradeoff between the cost of an attack and the risk it really represents.

REFERENCES

Atkinson, R., & Bhatti, S. (2012, July). ILNP Architectural Description.

Atkinson, R., Bhatti, S., & Hailes, S. (2009). ILNP: Mobility, multi-homing, localised addressing and security through naming. *Telecommunication Systems*, *42*(3-4), 273–291. doi:10.1007/s11235-009-9186-5.

Bagnulo, M., García-Martínez, A., & Azcorra, A. (2005, April). Efficient security for ipv6 multihoming. *ACM SIGCOMM Computer Communication Review*, 35.

Baker, F., & Savola, P. (2004, March). Ingress filtering for multihomed networks (RFC 3704). Retrieved from http://www.ietf.org/rfc/rfc3704.txt

BGP. (n.d.). *BGP routing table analysis report*. Retrieved from http://bgp.potaroo.net

Bos, H., Jonsson, E., Djambazova, E., Dimitrov, K., Ioannidis, S., Kirda, E., & Kruegel, C. (2009, March). Anticipating security threats of a future internet (Whitepaper). EU FP7 Project FORWARD.

Farinacci, D., Fuller, V., Meyer, D., & Lewis, D. (2012, February). Locator/ID separation protocol (LISP). IETF.

Frejborg, P. (2011, July). Hierarchical IPv4 framework (RFC 6306). Retrieved from http://www.ietf.org/rfc/rfc6306.txt

Fuller, V., & Farinacci, D. (2012, March). LISP map server. Retrieved from http://www.ietf.org

Fuller, V., Farinacci, D., Meyer, D., & Lewis, D. (2010, October). LISP alternative topology (LISP+ALT). Internet Engineering Task Force.

Fuller, V., Lewis, D., & Farinacci, D. (2012, March). LISP delegated database tree. Retrieved from http://www.ietf.org

García-Martínez, A., Bagnulo, M., & van Beijnum, I. (2010, September). The shim6 architecture for ipv6 multihoming. *IEEE Communications Magazine*. doi:10.1109/MCOM.2010.5560599.

Gurtov, A. (2008). Host identity protocol (HIP) – Towards the secure mobile internet.

Iannone, L., & Bonaventure, O. (2007, December). On the cost of caching locator/id mappings. In *the 3rd ACM Annual CoNEXT Conference (CoNEXT'07)*.

Iannone, L., & Levä, T. (2010, May). Modeling the economics of Loc/ID split for the future internet. In *Towards the Future Internet – Emerging Trends from the European Research*. IOS Press.

Iannone, L., Saucez, D., & Bonaventure, O. (2012, March). Lisp map-versioning. Retrieved from http://www.ietf.org

Igure, V., & Williams, R. (2008, 1st Quarter). Taxonomies of attacks and vulnerabilities in computer systems. *IEEE Communications Surveys & Tutorials, 10*(1).

Jakab, L., Cabellos-Aparicio, A., Coras, F., Saucez, D., & Bonaventure, O. (2010, October). LISP-TREE: A DNS hierarchy to support the LISP mapping system. *IEEE Journal on Selected Areas in Communications*. doi:10.1109/JSAC.2010.101011.

Jen, D., Meisel, M., Massey, D., Wang, L., Zhang, B., & Zhang, L. (2007, November). APT: A practical transit mapping service.

Kent, S., & Seo, K. (2005, December). Security architecture for the internet protocol (RFC 4301). Retrieved from http://www.ietf.org/rfc/rfc4301.txt

Krishnan, S., Thaler, D., & Hoagland, J. (2011, April). Security concerns with IP tunneling (RFC 6169). Retrieved from http://www.ietf.org/rfc/rfc6169.txt

Li, T. (2011, February). Recommendation for a routing architecture (No. 6115) (RFC 6115). Retrieved from http://www.ietf.org/rfc/rfc6115.txt

LISP4. (n.d.). *Website*. Retrieved from http://www.lisp4.net/

Maino, F., Ermagan, V., Cabellos, A., Saucez, D., & Bonaventure, O. (2012, March). LISP-security (LIS-SEC).

Menth, M., Hartmann, M., & Klein, D. (2010, April). Global locator, local locator, and identifier split (GLI-Split). Technical Report No. 470, University of Wuerzburg.

Meyer, D. (2008, March). The locator identifier separation protocol (LISP). *Internet Protocol Journal*, *11*(1), 23–36.

Meyer, D., Zhang, L., & Fall, K. (2007, September). Report from the IAB Workshop on Routing and Addressing (RFC 4984). Retrieved from http://www.ietf.org/rfc/rfc4984.txt

Moskowitz, R., Nikander, P., Jokela, P., & Henderson, T. (2008, April). Host identity protocol (RFC 5201). Retrieved from http://www.ietf.org/rfc/rfc5201.txt

Nordmark, E., & Bagnulo, M. (2009, June). Shim6: Level 3 multihoming shim protocol for IPv6 (No. 5533) (RFC 5533). Retrieved from http://www.ietf.org/rfc/rfc5533.txt

Nordmark, E., Bagnulo, M., & Levy-Abegnoli, E. (2012, May). FCFS SAVI: First-come, first-served source address validation improvement for locally assigned IPv6 addresses (RFC 6620). Retrieved from http://www.ietf.org/rfc/rfc6620.txt

Quoitin, B., Iannone, L., de Launois, C., & Bonaventure, O. (2007, August). Evaluating the benefits of the locator/identifier separation. In the *2nd ACM/IEEE workshop on mobility in the evolving internet architecture* (mobiarch'07).

Rekhter, Y., Li, T., & Hares, S. (2006, January). A border gateway protocol 4 (BGP-4) (RFC 4271). Retrieved from http://www.ietf.org/rfc/rfc4271.txt

Saucez, D., Donnet, B., Iannone, L., & Bonaventure, O. (2008, October). Inter-domain traffic engineering in a locator/identifier separation context. In *Proc. of Internet Network Management Workshop* (INM'08).

Saucez, D., Iannone, L., & Bonaventure, O. (2012, March). LISP threats analysis.

Turner, S., & Chen, L. (2011, March). Updated security considerations for the MD5 message-digest and the HMAC-MD5 algorithms (RFC 6151). Retrieved from http://www.ietf.org/rfc/rfc6151.txt

Williams, N., & Richardson, M. (2008, November). Better-than-nothing security: An unauthenticated mode of IPsec (RFC 5386). Retrieved from http://www.ietf.org/rfc/rfc5386.txt

Wood, P., Nisbet, M., Egan, G., Johnston, N., Haley, K., Krishnappa, B.,..., Watson, A. (2012, April). Internet security threat report – trends (Vol. 17; Tech. Rep.). Symantec Corporation.

ADDITIONAL READING

Arends, R., Austein, R., Larson, M., Massey, D., & Rose, S. (March 2005). DNS security introduction and requirements (RFC 4033). Retrieved from http://www.ietf.org/rfc/rfc4033.txt

Aura, T. (March 2005). Cryptographically generated addresses (CGA) (RFC 3972). Retrieved from http://www.ietf.org/rfc/rfc3972.txt

Avoine, G., Junod, P., & Oechslin, P. (2007). *Computer system security.* Lausanne, Switzerland: EPFL-Press.

Bagnulo, M. (2009, June). Hash-based addresses (HBA) (RFC 5535). Retrieved from http://www.ietf.org/rfc/rfc5535.txt

Choi, N., You, T., Park, J., Kwon, T., & Choi, Y. (2009, February). ID/LOC separation network architecture for mobility support in future internet.

Kim, J., Iannone, L., & Feldmann, A. (2011, May). A deep dive into the LISP cache and what ISPs should know about it. In *the 10th IFIP Internation Conference on Networking (Networking'11).*

LISP4. (n.d.). *Website.* Retrieved from http://www.lisp4.net/

LISPMon. (n.d.). *Website.* Retrieved from http://www.lispmon.net/Locator/ID Separation Protocol

Menth, M., Hartmann, M., & Höfling, M. (2010, October). FIRMS: A future internet mapping system. *IEEE Journal on Selected Areas in Communications.* doi:10.1109/JSAC.2010.101010.

Meyer, D. (2008, March). The locator identifier separation protocol (LISP). *Internet Protocol Journal, 11*(1), 23–36.

Meyer, D., & Lewis, D. (2009, January). Architectural implications of locator/id separation.

Saucez, D., & Iannone, L. (2009, August). How to mitigate the effect of scans on mapping systems. In Trilogy summer school.

Saucez, D., Iannone, L., Bonaventure, O., & Farinacci, D. (2012). Designing a deployable future internet: The locator/identifier separation protocol (LISP) case. *IEEE Internet Computing.* doi:10.1109/MIC.2012.98.

Sriram, K., Gleichmann, P., Kim, Y.-T., & Montgomery, D. (2010, August). Enhanced efficiency of mapping distribution protocols in scalable routing and addressing architectures.

Chapter 9
A Hierarchical Approach to Reduce Power Consumption in Core and Edge Networks:
A Metric–Based Proposal

Shankar Raman
Indian Institute of Technology Madras, India

Balaji Venkat
Indian Institute of Technology Madras, India

Gaurav Raina
Indian Institute of Technology Madras, India

ABSTRACT

The authors present a metric-based hierarchical approach to reduce power consumption in core and edge networks. The proposal considers both unicast and the multicast cases. For unicast, the metric used is consumed-power to available-bandwidth and for multicast the metric is consumed-power to available-replication-capacity.

With unicast, the metric is used to determine a low-power path between sources and destinations. The source and destination entities could be attached to Autonomous Systems (ASes) or to routing areas within the Autonomous System. Determining a low-power path within an Autonomous System provides a unique challenge as the topology of the constituent areas may not be known. To that end, we propose the use of a selective leak technique for disclosing low-power paths. Additionally, the proposed method can also be used to determine disjoint or redundant paths for load-balancing or fault tolerance. With multicast, the metric serves the twin purpose of finding low-power multicast paths as well as multicast replication points. Once low-power paths in either the unicast or the multicast cases are identified, then currently available traffic engineering techniques could be used to route the data packets.

DOI: 10.4018/978-1-4666-4305-5.ch009

INTRODUCTION

IP traffic, in the near future, is expected to increase significantly (Dhamdhere, 2011). To handle the increased volume in traffic, it is natural to expect that devices with higher capabilities as well as capacities have to be used in the Internet. It has been recently suggested that to cater for the anticipated increase in traffic, the Internet would need four times the current number of devices (CiscoPress, 2012). Increase in the number of devices readily translates into higher energy consumption for the Internet which, as of 2007, was one percent of the total generated power (Baliga, 2007). Therefore, it becomes imperative to provide solutions that help to reduce power consumption.

A currently popular method for reducing power consumption is the following (Bianzino, 2012a; Gupta, 2003):

- Combine the traffic of low utilization links, and
- Switch-off the links that are currently not being used.

However, this simple method does not explicitly consider the impact of increased utilization on neighboring routers, the power consumption associated with switching links on and off, and finally the impact of configuration changes on the line-cards.

In contrast, we work with the assumption that links do not operate in isolation which motivates the need for a distributed approach to reduce power consumption. In essence, our proposal involves three stages:

- Discover the topology,
- Compute a low-power path, and
- Use traffic engineering techniques such as Resource Reservation Protocol – Traffic Engineering (RSVP, 2001; 2008) to route the data through a low-power path.

The discovered topology is represented as a connected graph. When considering the interconnection discovery between Autonomous Systems (AS) (defined as inter-AS) we use the Border Gateway Protocol (BGP) (Rekhter & Li, 1995) strand information to discover the topology. For topology discovery within Autonomous Systems, i.e., the intra-AS approach, we propose the *selective leak* technique whereby the identified low-power paths within a routing area are transferred to other routing areas a-priori by the Area Border Router (ABR).

In the graph topology that is discovered, for unicast the metric used is consumed-power to available-bandwidth and for multicast the metric is consumed-power to available-replication-capacity. The metric determines the cost of the link in the topology and we apply the Constrained Shortest Path First (CSPF) algorithm to establish a low-power path between the source-destination pairs. To implement the proposed scheme, we rely on some additional information to be carried by the routing protocols such as Multi-Protocol Label Switching (MPLS) (see Viswanathan, 1998) for its evolution), Border Gateway Protocol (BGP) and Interior Gateway Protocols (IGP) such as Intermediate System to Intermediate System (IS-IS) (Callon, 1990) and Open Shortest Path First (OSPF) (Moy, 1997). Once low-power paths are identified, we apply the Inter-AS TE Label Switched Path based Traffic Engineering (TE) techniques (Le Roux, 2005) to establish a path to forward the data packets. The path is formed by an ordered set of neighboring network elements (typically *AS* in inter-AS scenario, *areas* in an intra-AS scenario and *routers* within an area). In this chapter, we show the applicability of our technique to MPLS-based networks.

We outline some desirable aspects of any new proposal:

1. Easy to integrate with existing protocols.

2. Be decentralized, scalable and independent of technology.
3. Provide a distributed solution, as entities do not operate in isolation.
4. Provide incentives to the Internet Service Providers (ISPs), to deploy low-power and high bandwidth devices.

If a service provider's billing model is based on the consumed bandwidth, then our proposed approach will provide the requisite incentive to device manufacturers to produce low-power and high bandwidth devices.

It is also natural to ask how performance-related objectives like maximizing the link utilization, are affected by current schemes for power reduction. Recent work in IP networks does suggest that current power saving schemes have negligible influence on network performance (Bianzino, 2012). Thus at this stage we do not investigate the impact on performance for our scheme.

We now outline, in some detail, the importance and the different ways in which the power reduction problem has been considered both by the research community and industry.

BACKGROUND

The exponential growth of the Internet has led to increase in the demand for bandwidth in core and edge networks which has lead to an increase in power consumption. Estimates of power consumption for the Internet predict a 300% increase, as access speeds increase from 10 Mbps to 100 Mbps (Baliga, 2007). Various approaches have been proposed to reduce power consumption which range from designing low-power routers and switches to the use of TE methods (Bianzino, 2012).

The key concepts used in most approaches for reducing power consumption are reengineering, dynamic adaptation and sleeping/standby modes of operation. These ideas have been applied at different levels: at the user device, and the access, edge, and core network level. Reengineering

considers energy efficient architectures, dynamic adaptation modulates the capacities based on traffic loads and service level agreements, and sleeping/standby modes are activated to work in low energy states. A detailed review may be found in (Bolla, 2011).

High performance routers and switches form the essence of access, edge and core networks. Since they have power-hungry components like memory, Ternary Content Addressable Memory (TCAM), as well as operations such as booting, reconfiguration etc., there is a need for monitoring the energy consumption in these devices (Adelin, 2010). Most of the proposed strategies include switching off components or redirecting the load to improve utilization. Such strategies can be followed for different types of access, core, wired and wireless networks. For a specific discussion on reducing power consumption in wired networks, along with Quality of Service (QoS) (e.g. Vereecken, 2011; Gelenbe, 2009).

The need for power-aware network design and routing/forwarding in wired networks was proposed in (Chabarek, 2008). This paper concludes that power awareness must be a part of design, configuration and management of networks, as well as the protocols. The work documented in (Chiaraviglio, 2009) considers a real IP backbone along with a real traffic profile to show that more than 23% savings could be achieved in a year by adopting selective powering off of devices in the Internet.

Another opportunity for power reduction is to design routing protocols in a manner that lead to a reduction in the consumed power. For example, BGP updates have negligible effect on router power consumption (Adelin, 2010). Modifications to routing protocols have been proposed to find low-power paths for forwarding data packets in the Internet (Raman, 2012a). There have been major efforts in redesigning and rerouting in core networks (Idzikowski, 2012; Hon-Wai, 2011).

Routed protocols like IP have been used for energy management. The IP-based approach uses OSPF protocol to find low-power paths. The link weights of graph topology are adjusted to reflect the consumed power (Amaldi, 2011). Once the low-power path has been identified, TE methods are used to establish the paths. Energy-aware distributed TE scheme taking into account QoS is proposed in (Atahansiou, 2011). Here too, the links are put to sleep in the network. Rerouting arising out of these schemes is used for load-balancing and fault tolerance.

Multicasting in wireless networks has received much attention as wireless networks consume more power while transmitting data than wired networks. The problem of power reduction in multicast trees has been addressed in the context of ad-hoc wireless networks (Junhai, 2009). Algorithms based on ant colony optimization have been proposed for low cost multicast trees (Zhang, 2011). However, these algorithms work on decreasing processing costs by optimizing network/link capacity and reducing one-way delay. To the best of our knowledge, as of today, no work exists on combining power reduction with multicast replication points in wired networks.

In (Yoo, 2011) the importance on having a metric-based approach for energy efficiency is stressed. The metric they propose is the power-to-performance ratio where the performance could be measured in terms of goodput, capacity and throughput. These metrics are considered only at the device level. In contrast, the metrics we propose in this chapter, for the unicast and the multicast cases, are applicable for inter-AS and intra-AS systems.

In the next section, we elaborate on four important aspects of power reduction that should be addressed by any new proposal.

MAIN FOCUS OF THE CHAPTER

Issues, Controversies, Problems

We now outline four important aspects that any approach for power reduction should be capable of addressing.

Should cater for both unicast and multicast scenarios: Multicast provides an important scenario for the Internet. Today, most proposals consider mainly low-power path routing with unicast traffic. Multicast traffic has received a lot of attention in wireless networks, but not in the wired domain. Any new proposal should be able to address both the unicast and the multicast traffic scenarios. Having different methods for these two scenarios might lead to unnecessary processing burden in the routers, which might hinder its scalability.

Should not rely on just switching off unused links: Most approaches to optimize energy pursue the following approach: measure, monitor and respond to the system energy usage by switching off unused or under-utilized links. Such an approach could be effective for reducing power locally. The effect on the network is not clearly understood. Further, the power usage involved in turning on and rebooting/reconfiguring the device is often not explicitly considered. We note that Service Level Agreement (SLA) requirements may not even permit the links to be switched off. Also services provided by ISPs like Virtual Private Networks (VPNs) can be affected by such re-routing decisions.

Should follow an hierarchical and distributed approach: For scalability, it is important that the algorithms proposed for inter-AS should also be applicable to intra-AS situations. Networks do not work in isolation, so any proposal should be both distributed and hierarchical. The algorithms should be applicable at every level of the hierarchy.

Should provide incentives for ISP for adoption: The engineering proposals should be aligned with commercial incentives for rapid and widespread adoption. Today, the device manufacturers and the ISPs operate independently of each other, and there is no incentive for manufacturers to work towards low-power and high bandwidth devices. An ISP's revenue model is based on the consumed bandwidth, which in turn lead naturally to more power consumption. If the proposed method chooses routers that consume low-power and increase the data flow through them, then this indirectly provides encouragement for ISPs to purchase low-power and high bandwidth devices.

We now present our metric-based proposal which addresses the aforementioned design aspects.

SOLUTIONS AND RECOMMENDATIONS

For completeness, we now briefly describe inter-AS power reduction technique presented in (Raman, 2012a).

Inter-AS Low-Power Path

At the network core, MPLS label switched paths may be used to carry traffic from a head-end to a tail-end router through an ordered set of AS. The AS use BGP to exchange routing and topology information (Rekhter & Li, 1995). One of the BGP attributes AS-PATH-INFO can be used to deduce the Internet AS level topology (Venkat, 2010). The Constrained Shortest Path First (CSPF) algorithm is run on this AS level topology with the *consumed-power-to-available-bandwidth (PWR)* ratio as a constraint to determine a low-power path from the head-end to the tail-end AS. Note that calculation of such low-power paths can be computationally intensive due to the size of the topology (measured in terms of the AS and their links), and hence certain heuristics may be needed to reduce the computation time. This ratio can be exchanged using BGP. Routing is then made explicit between the head-end and the tail-end AS using the Resource Reservation Protocol with TE extensions (RSVP-TE) (Awduche, 2001). A low-power path connecting the AS is built by using inter-AS Traffic Engineered Label Switched Path (TE-LSP) that spans multiple ASes. The approach consists of three steps namely,

- Constructing the topology.
- Calculating the *PWR* ratio.
- Performing explicit routing using TE-LSPs.

Constructing Network Topology Using BGP Strands

Inter-AS topology can be modeled as a directed graph G = (V, E, f) where the vertices (V) are mapped to AS and the edges (E) map the link that connect the neighboring AS. The direction (f) on the edge, represents the data flow from the head-end to the tail-end AS. To obtain inter-AS topology, the approach proposed in (Venkat, 2010) is used, where it is shown that a sub-graph of the Internet topology, can be obtained by collecting several prefix updates in BGP. Figure 1 shows the different graph strands of AS that are recorded from the BGP messages.

Each vertex in this graph is assigned a weight according to the *PWR* ratio of the AS, as seen by an Autonomous System Border Router (ASBR) that acts as an entry point to the AS.

Figure 2 shows the strands merged together to form the topology sub-graph. In this figure, the weight of the vertex is mapped to the ingress edge. A reference AS level topology derived from 100 strands of AS-PATH-INFO received by an ASBR in the Internet is presented in Figure 3. The head-end router is the top-most node and the tail-end router is the bottom-most node. In this figure, we see that there are redundant paths between the head-end and the tail-end routers. It has been argued that the information based on the strands may only be representative of the Internet topology (Ricardo, 2010). However, the accuracy of the topology can be increased by using other topology discovery mechanisms such as using Simple Network Management Protocol information (SNMP) (Stallings, 1998) or a proprietary protocol like Cisco Discovery Protocol (Cisco, 2007).

PWR Ratio Calculation

In the topology sub-graph, each AS is expected to share its *PWR* ratio. To obtain this ratio we calculate the consumed-power representative of the AS and the maximum bandwidth available

Figure 1. Different strands obtained from BGP updates using AS-PATH-INFO attributes. Vertices A, B, C, D, and G represent the head-end AS. Vertices D, H, and X form the tail-end AS. The vertex weights refer to the PWR ratio of the AS, and the direction of the link shows the next hop neighbor AS.

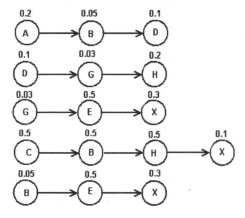

with an ASBR on its egress links into the AS. The maximum available-bandwidth at the ASBR's egress link limits the available paths through the AS. For example, if the available-bandwidth is 5 Gbps and a path is needed with a bandwidth of 6 Gbps then the ASBR might not satisfy the requirement for establishing a path.

The entry point to the AS is through the AS-BRs that advertise the prefixes reachable through the AS. Hence the numerator of the *PWR* ratio is calculated for the AS at each of the ingress ASBRs. We obtain the sum of power consumed

at the Provider (P) and the Provider Edge (PE) routers within an AS. The numerator of the *PWR* ratio is calculated by summing up the consumed-power within the AS and then dividing this sum by the number of routers which gives the *average consumed-power*. Other approaches such as weighted average method by assigning routers to categories and having appropriate co-efficient for each of these categories can also be used. In our discussions we use the average consumed-power.

The amount of consumed-power per bit of information must be low for the shortest path. This average consumed-power is divided by the maximum available-bandwidth at each of the ASBR's egress link into the AS. The highest available-bandwidth among the egress links of the ASBR is used as the denominator in the *PWR* ratio computation. If the entry point to the AS is through a different ASBR then the *PWR* ratio assigned to the ingress link of the ASBR might vary. Hence, a head-end AS might see different *PWR* ratios for an intermediate AS, if the intermediate AS has different ASBRs as its entry point. Further the lesser the power consumed per available bit of bandwidth denotes that routers are more optimal in their power consumption as they accept more traffic. The *PWR* ratio must be computed and disbursed much ahead of time before inter-AS TE-LSP explicit path or route is computed using the CSPF algorithm. The correctness of this ratio is of importance to compute the inter-AS TE-LSP route through a low-power AS.

Figure 2. Combining the strands to obtain the topology of the Internet. The PWR ratio is mapped to the ingress link of the ASBR and not to the AS.

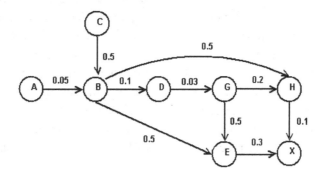

Figure 3. Topology of the Internet obtained using 100 strands of BGP packets from AS-PATH-INFO attribute. Note that the head-end which is the top-most AS is well connected with the tail-end (the bottom-most AS) with redundant paths.

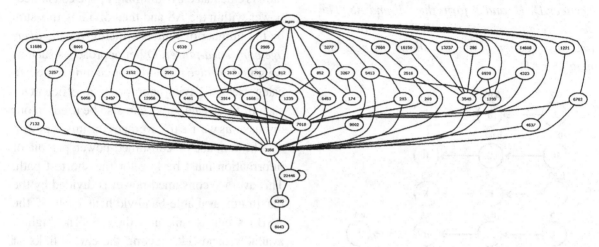

The *PWR* ratio is a mapping function defined for each ingress link of the ASBR associated with an AS. For the head-end AS this mapping function does not exist as there is no ingress link. The *PWR* ratio can then be advertised to the other neighboring AS using BGP control-plane extensions. BGP ensures that the information is percolated to other AS beyond the immediate neighbors. On receipt of these power metrics to the AS at the far-ends of the Internet, the overall AS level *PWR* ratio based Internet topology can be constructed. This view of the Internet is available with each of the routers without using any other complex discovery mechanism. Some sample link weights shown in Figure 2 is obtained by using such a mapping function on the ingress links.

Explicit Routing Using TE-LSPs

We assume that the head-end and the tail-end may reside in different ASes and the path is along multiple intervening ASes. The way to realize the path is to use inter-AS TE-LSPs to influence the exact path at the AS level. This path can be installed by providing a set of low-power consuming AS to a protocol like RSVP-TE which creates TE-LSPs or tunnels, using its label assigning procedure.

The routers use these low-power paths created by the explicit routing method rather than using the conventional shortest path. By this way a number of high power ASes on the way from the head-end to the tail-end AS are excluded. For example, the dotted line in Figure 4 represents the explicit route that is chosen by making use of low-power transit AS from the head-end AS *A* to the tail-end AS *X*. Note that if number of hops was the metric used by CSPF, then the route chosen is the path with three (3) hops.

The details of the algorithm are given as two sub-algorithms: Algorithm 1 and Algorithm 2. The first algorithm is executed by all the ASBRs in the network and the second by all the Path Computation Elements (PCEs) (Farrel, 2006) in their respective AS.

Example: Consider the AS level topology sub-graph in Figure 4 constructed using the strands in Figure 1. The *PWR* ratio calculated at an ASBR is assigned to the ingress link. For example, AS *H* has two edges coming into it: one from *B* and the other from *G*. Note that the power metrics for the two strands are different as *G* to *H* is lower than that of *B* to *H*. This means that the lower power metric into *H* is better if the path from *G* to *H* is chosen rather than the one from *B* to *H*.

To construct a path with *A* as the head-end AS and *X* as the tail-end AS, from the AS level topology we see that the path *A, B, H, X* and *A, B, E, X* have the shortest number of hops. However by using CSPF with the *PWR* ratio as the constraint, we see that the path *A, B, D, G, H, X* is power efficient. The routing choice will however be based on the reservation of the bandwidth on this path. Given that available-bandwidth exists to setup a TE-LSP, the explicit path *A, B, D, G, H, X* is chosen. RSVP adheres to its usual operation and tries to setup a path. If bandwidth is not available in a low-power path thus calculated, then we may fallback to other paths like *A, B, H, X* or *A, B, E, X* provided there is available-bandwidth in these paths. The low-power path algorithm given as Algorithm 2 is executed by the PCE. Algorithm 1 prepares the topology and feeds it as input to the PCE as a weighted topology graph.

Certain issues exist with the proposed algorithms and detail can be found in (Raman, 2012a). These include

1. Use of the CSPF algorithm could be time consuming for large networks. Hence heuristics may be needed to reduce computation time.
2. Use of heuristics might trade-off the optimal low-power path.
3. The topology may be dynamically updated and hence the computation of a low-power path must be triggered based on need otherwise oscillations due to path changes could occur.
4. The power consumed must not be measured as a discrete quantity but in intervals to ensure that the *PWR* ratio update is not triggered frequently thereby flooding the network.
5. BGP needs to be modified to accommodate Algorithms 1 and 2.

We now show that Algorithms 1 and 2 could be extended to derive backup paths in the network.

Application to Building Backup Paths

The method for finding low-power paths described above can also be used to build protection or backup paths for the primary path. Such paths can be used either in case of load-balancing or link failures. We show that primary and backup paths (either in a "1:1" or "1: N" redundancy mode) can be derived based on the *PWR* values. Note that in the discussion below, we have considered the case of *disjoint links* i.e., no link in the primary path is common with any of the links in the backup path that is generated. We could also apply a constraint such that the path must be *node disjoint*. This means that the nodes (or ASes) considered for the primary path must not be used while discovering the backup path. This constraint also includes

Figure 4. Low-power path is A, B, D, G, H, and X. This low-power path has longer number of hops than the shortest path based on hops.

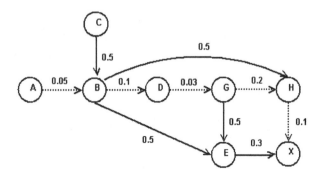

Algorithm 1. ASBR low-power path algorithm

```
Require: Weighted Topology Graph T=(AS, E, f)
1: Begin
2: if ROUTER == ASBR then
3:/* As part of IGP-TE */
4: Trigger exchange of available-bandwidth on bandwidth change, to the AS in-
ternal neighbors;
5: BEGIN PARALLEL PROCESS 1
6: while PWR ratio changes do
7: Assign the PWR ratio to the Ingress links;
8: Exchange the PWR ratio with its external neighbors;
9: Exchange the PWR ratio with AS's (internal) ASBRs;
10: end while
11: END PARALLEL PROCESS 1
12: BEGIN PARALLEL PROCESS 2
13: while RSVP-TE messages arrive do
14: Send and Receive TE-LSP reservations in the explicit path;
15: Update routing table with labels for TE-LSP;
16: end while
17: END PARALLEL PROCESS 2
18: end if
19: End
```

Algorithm 2. PCE low-power path algorithm

```
Require: Weighted Topology Graph T=(AS, E, f)
Require: Source and Destination for inter-AS TE LSP with sufficient bandwidth
1: Begin
2: if ROUTER == PCE then
3: Calculate the shortest paths from the head to the tail-end using CSPF using
PWR ratio as the metric;
4: if no path available then
5: Signal error;
6: end if
7: if path exists then
8: Send explicit path to head-end to construct path;
9: end if
10: Continue passively listening to BGP updates to update T = (AS, E, f);
11: end if
12: End
```

the removal of links incident onto the nodes that were removed.

We extend the ideas presented earlier to build link and node disjoint backup or protection paths. Once the primary path (i.e., a low-power path obtained by applying the CSPF algorithm on *PWR* ratio) is identified we can compute a backup path by applying Algorithms 1 and 2 again. We can obtain either a disjoint path which does not use the primary link or, a path which uses neither the nodes nor the link of the primary path. In case we want link disjoint paths, we need to remove the links corresponding to the primary path, and run Algorithms 1 and 2 on the reduced graph. This exclusion ensures that the backup path is always link disjoint with the primary path. A similar approach can be used for finding a complete disjoint path that does not include any nodes or links from the primary path (except the head-end and the tail-end).

Backup Path Construction

Consider the graph G on which a low-power path is calculated after applying Algorithms 1 and 2. Assume there is a requirement to construct one or more backup paths that are mutually link disjoint with the primary path. Let the set of links in the path formed out of the primary graph be called *P*. It is possible that the graph becomes disconnected in case the primary path is removed, i.e., *G-P* may be disconnected. In case the graph *G-P* is still connected, then a low-power path algorithm could be run on *G-P*. In case the graph *G-P* is disconnected, then there may not be available paths that are completely disjoint with the primary path *P*. In this case only the minimum of the originally used links from *P* in the primary path should be included in the backup path. This procedure is given as Algorithm 3. It should be noted that the graph partition based algorithm given in (Raman, 2012a) could be suitably modified and would reduce the time required for calculating the backup path.

Once the primary path is constructed then the backup paths may be obtained by excluding to the maximum extent possible the links (interconnection links between ASes) of the primary path from the backup paths. It is possible that more than one backup path may be required to be constructed. In that case the process is repeated (through iterations) to construct the required number of backup paths.

Algorithm 3. General algorithm for constructing disjoint back up paths

```
Require: Weighted Topology Graph T=(AS, E, f)
1: Begin
2: Let P be the path obtained by applying the low-power path Algorithms 1 and
2.
3: Construct T' = T-P./* Remove links in low-power path */
4: If (T') is connected run step 1 on T'; return P;/* To get a mutually exclu-
sive link disjoint path */
5: If (T') is disconnected then/* If a mutually exclusive link disjoint path
is not possible */
6: T' = T' + E/* E is minimal number of links from the low-power path that
makes T' connected.*/
7: If more links remain in T' Goto Step 3:
8: End
```

From the algorithm we see that finding a minimal set which makes the graph connected can be NP-Complete. Therefore this calls for the use of heuristic algorithms. If we apply the constraint that we use minimal set of links to construct T', the resulting disjoint path may not be power optimal. This scenario is discussed in the example. Further note that Algorithm 3 could be repeated a number of times to get more backup paths. The regular TE based methods for switching traffic from the primary path to the backup path could be followed for fault tolerance or load-balancing needs.

Example: In Figure 5, the path P from A to X was constructed through A, B, D, G, H and X. Once we remove the links $(A, B), (B, D), (D, G), (G, H)$ and (H, X) from this path, the graph becomes disconnected. We see that we have to include (A, B) and (H, X) for the backup path A, B, H and X. We can include (A, B) alone for the other backup path A, B, E, X. The algorithm chooses this path as it has minimal number of links in common with the primary path. Note that the path A, B, H and X is a better path than A, B, E and X, as it has more low-power links from P. Hence the redundant paths chosen with "maximal link disjoint" constraint may not be a low-power path.

In the next sections, we will extend the metric-based approach for deducting low-power paths

under intra-AS scenarios for both unicast and multicast.

Intra-AS Schemes for Unicast and Multicast

In IGPs (e.g., OSPF) the shortest path to the destination for a backbone or a non-backbone area is computed using the TE-metrics advertised for the area. If we also add an additional constraint of "low-power consumption" it becomes possible to provide a path that reduces the power consumed by the routers and links that make up the network. We produce a topology of the areas starting at the line-card of the router. This topology is constructed by assigning metrics to a link interconnecting the line-cards of adjacent routers. We will call it as the power topology. The metric used is power consumed by the line-cards (and hence their respective ports). We introduce the *POWER* metric which is obtained by including two factors:

1. Power consumed by a line-card on a single/ multi chassis router and consequently a port,
2. Utilization on that port and the link.

Figure 5. Construction of the alternate low-power path. Primary low-power path is A, B, D, G, H, and X and the backup path is A, B, E, and X. Note that A, B, H, and X has much lower power than A, B, E, and X. However it has two links in common with the primary path whereas the A, B, E, and X path has only one link in common with the primary path. Therefore the path A, B, H, and X is rejected.

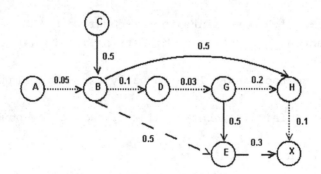

A single/multi chassis router or switch has a set of ports in each line-card. Each of the ports has a designated capacity. A single chassis router uses single chassis and has slots for the Route Processor (typically two cards) and line-cards. The characteristics of the line-card depend on the link layer technology support, port density and the port type (e.g., SONET, Ethernet, and ATM). A multi-chassis system has multiple single chassis interconnected with each other through a switch fabric chassis. Links interconnect ports within line-cards of different systems.

Consider the vendor independent single chassis system topology shown in Figure 6 and the corresponding point to point (P2P) interconnections shown in Table 1. In the table, the last column shows the available link utilization value normalized between 0 and 1, which is used as the denominator in the *POWER* metric computation. We do not consider Broadcast Multi-access links or Non-Broadcast Multi-access link set in our discussions. This proposed low-power path detection scheme can be extended to such networks.

Each line-card consumes certain amount of power. It is assumed that the power consumed by a line-card will be made available by the equipment vendor as a readable value. Consider that *Router A* is a more capable router and has high port density. Assume that *LC1, LC2* on *Router A* consumes more power than the other line-cards. In order to calculate the power consumed on a link by a line-card we normalize the power to *consumed power per port*. If all the links in the topology have 10 Gigabits per second (Gbps) port capacity then the power calculated should be in terms of consumed power per 10 Gbps port. In general all line-cards consume a base power and the link speed determines the operational power. We now calculate the normalized *POWER* metric for each of the ports forming a link as that in Box 1.

Consider link *L1* where both ports are 10 Gbps and the ports are *P5* on *Router A* and *P4* on *Router D*. For calculating the *POWER* metric for a link (*PWRLINK*) we calculate the *POWER* for each side of the link and average them. For example the metric for link *L1* is that in Box 2.

The values in the numerator can also be weighted if there is a multi-capacity port on one side of the link. A multi-capacity link provides multiple bandwidth capabilities such 1 or 10 or 100 Gbps, and auto-negotiates the capacity with the other end. The *PWRLINK* metric that is calculated is filled in a defined OSPF-TE Link State Advertisement (LSA) as an adapted TE-metric and flooded as a link characteristic. Once the LSAs have been flooded, the routers run CSPF on the power topology graph with *PWRLINK* as the metric and calculate the path whose *PWRLINK* sum is minimal. This path can be used for forwarding high bandwidth streams within the area.

The link power is averaged so that even if one end consumes excess power then the *PWRLINK* metric increases and thus less preferred in the CSPF algorithm. If there is no bias in the power usage of the router under high bandwidth, the metric stays low even if it carries more data streams. It is possible that multiple links would have the same *PWRLINK* metric after a computation cycle. In such cases load-balancing techniques can be used to keep the Equal Cost Multi-path (ECMP) (Hopps, 2000) links in a steady state. Depending on the utilization thereafter it is possible that the ECMP links may turn into Unequal Cost Paths.

Example: Consider the topology given in Figure 5 in which the nodes represent routers and weight of the links represents *PWRLINK* values. These values get flooded in the network as an LSA. Node *B* is the Area Border Router (ABR) for Area 1 and the nodes *A* and *C* are the Area 0 core routers. The rest of the nodes are assumed to be Area 1 routers. Once the power topology for Area 1 is obtained, CSPF can be run from the ABR to any of the other routers say *H, E,* or *X*. The CSPF algorithm constructs a low-power path from router *B* to other routers in Area 1.

Figure 6. A typical system which shows router chassis, line-cards and links connected to the ports. "LC"s represent line-card, "P"s represent ports and "L"s represent lines. A single router may have many line-cards and each line-card may have different types of ports.

Table 1. Characteristics and interconnections of the line-cards of the system shown in Figure 7

Links	Routers	Line-card Connectivity	Port Connections	Capacity	Available Utilization
L1	A to D	LC1 to LC1	P5 to P4	10 Gbps	0.75
L2	A to D	LC2 to LC2	P5 to P1	10 Gbps	0.6
L3	A to D	LC2 to LC1	P2 to P1	10 Gbps	0.6
L4	A to B	LC2 to LC1	P4 to P4	10 Gbps	0.2
L5	B to C	LC1 to LC1	P5 to P4	10 Gbps	0.35
L6	B to E	LC1 to LC1	P2 to P5	10 Gbps	0.1
L7	D to E	LC2 to LC1	P3 to P3	10 Gbps	0.6
L8	D to E	LC1 to LC1	P5 to P4	10 Gbps	0.15
L9	E to F	LC1 to LC2	P5 to P5	100 Gbps	0.2
L10	E to F	LC2 to LC1	P4 to P4	10 Gbps	0.15
L11	B to C	LC2 to LC1	P1 to P1	10 Gbps	0.3
L12	E to C	LC2 to LC2	P1 to P5	10 Gbps	0.2
L13	C to F	LC2 to LC1	P1 to P2	10 Gbps	0.1
L14	F to OA	LC2 to OAL	P1 to OAP	10 Gbps	0.2
L15	E to C	LC2 to LC2	P1 to P5	10 Gbps	0.25

Figure 7. Calculation of PWRA for an ABR. Note that in this case since traffic can flow in both the directions the reverse PWRA metric may also apply. The I's and E's assume that the tail-end lies inside Area 1 and hence represented by single head arrows. The traffic flows from Area 0 to Area 1 in this case.

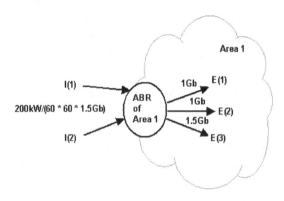

After the path has been computed, we use RSVP-TE to construct the *PWRLINK* based shortest path with appropriate labels for the paths instantiated in a TE-LSP. In Figure 5, if we want to construct a path from *B* to *X* then *B, D, G, H* and *X* can be used. We make use of TE signaling protocols to place the traffic streams from one point to the other.

Our discussion until now considered a low-power path within Area 1. The question remains on how this low-power path can be made known to other areas so that complete low-power paths can be constructed within the AS integrating multiple areas.

Building Low-Power Inter-AREA TE LSPs Using Pre-Computed Paths

In this section, we will discuss a method to build low-power intra-Area TE LSP with pre-computed path, using *selective leak* technique. The proposed technique requires a few modifications to the existing features of the IGPs supporting TE extensions. When link state routing protocols like OSPF or IS-IS are used to discover TE topology, there is a limitation that TE-paths can be set up only if the head and tail-ends of the label switched paths are within the same area. The topology of one area is not revealed to the other in OSPF and IS-IS TE. To overcome this limitation three known solutions exists for inter-area TE:

- Hop expansion at area boundaries where only the head-end can choose the path.
- Centralized or hierarchical PCE attached to all areas which is aware of the entire topology.
- Path stitching by designated ABRs acting as BGP route reflectors.

Box 1.

$$POWER = \frac{Power\ consumed\ per\ "x"\ Gbps\ for\ a\ given\ port\ on\ a\ line\text{-}card}{Available\ utilization\ on\ that\ port}$$

where "x" represents normalized bandwidth.

Box 2.

$$PWRLINK = \frac{POWER\ for\ P5\ on\ LC1\ on\ Router\ A + POWER\ for\ P4\ on\ LC1\ on\ Router\ D}{2}$$

Even though, it is possible to build low-power paths using these techniques connectivity information may not be known a-priori. We propose an alternate approach that uses *selective leaking* of low-power TE path information between areas. In our method we compute a low-power path in the areas a-priori and then leak this information into other areas so that provisioning these paths can be done. It should be noted that in case the tail-end and the head-end are with different ASes then inter-domain traffic engineering techniques must be used.

The AS uses IGP for exchanging routing related information. Similar to the scheme discussed in inter-AS, the CSPF algorithm runs on a specific area with *PWR* ratio as a constraint. We determine "k" (where "k" is a suitable number) low-power paths from the head-end to the tail-end within the same area. We propose that the low power paths that minimize the sum of the *PWR* ratio be exchanged among the collaborating areas using IGP-TE-Type, Length, and Value (TLV). Explicit routing using RSVP-TE (for signaling) is used between the head and the tail-end routers. This low-power path routing information is used to traverse multiple areas using the inter-Area TE-LSP.

Let $\{N\}$ be the set of nodes in a network running link state routing protocol and $\{N'\}$ be the set of nodes that are the endpoints of the TE paths. The topology $\{N, E\}$ where E is the set of edges connecting the nodes is divided into hierarchical areas. The backbone area forms the second level and all the non-backbone areas form the first level. The set of nodes $\{N'\}$ can belong to any non-backbone area or the backbone area. Nodes in $\{N'\}$ may become aware of being potential TE endpoints through offline configuration. Once

the nodes in $\{N'\}$ become aware of being TE endpoints, they advertise themselves in a special TLV in TE link state information called the "TE Endpoint TLV." In OSPF, they define the TLV in a TE LSA and in IS-IS in the TE LSP. The ABRs advertise a new TLV called as "Area Border TLV." We do not discuss the contents of this TLV as the details are beyond the scope of this work. We now discuss how the Area Border Router (ABR) uses this TLV for advertising low-power paths.

Area Border Router Operation

Apart from standard OSPF and IS-IS ABR functions, each ABR should discover the TE end points in every area attached to it. For an ABR, let the set of discovered end points be $\{A_i, N'_j\}$. The ABR should compute a low-power path to every element in $\{A_i, N'_j\}$. The constraint applied here is the minimal *PWRA* ratio which is defined for the intra-area scenario as follows:

For a given router which is either an ABR or a core router within an area, all the egress links that can potentially be used towards a TE endpoint are identified along with the available-bandwidth. The link that has the maximum of the available-bandwidth (at that instant in time) is identified and used. Note that the computation here similar to *PWR* computation.

This *PWRA* metric is assigned to the ingress links in the path leading towards the TE end point. Potentially for all the TE end points that lead to the non-backbone area core router the *PWRA* metric is the same. Note that the egress links becomes the ingress links for the reverse direction and hence a similar procedure applies. For an ABR having part of its links in Area 1 and the

Box 3.

$$PWRA = \frac{Power\ consumed\ by\ the\ area}{Maximum\ of\ available\text{-}bandwidth\ of\ the\ egress\ link}$$

rest in Area 0 (backbone area) the *PWRA* metric would be assigned to the incoming links I(1) and I(2) of the ABR router for the direction of traffic from Area 0 towards Area 1.

Inside Area 1 in the core area router the denominator condition is modified. It is derived from a subset "S" which consists of links with the maximum bandwidth out of the "k" egress links towards the TE endpoint.

In this case, each element is removed per iteration from subset "S" to derive more than one shortest path from the calculating router, provided |S| > 1. If no link exists to the TE endpoint then the algorithm stops. To minimize the computational complexity, |S| can be set to "1", i.e., we assume that there is only one link out of the ABR that connects to the TE end point (see Figure 8). However, the intention is to calculate as many disjoint paths as possible initially. Partially disjoint paths (discussed earlier) can also be found with suitable modifications for the inter-area algorithm. After computing the ingress link *PWRAR* metric in a given step, there is a flooding done within the area through the ingress links of a router with a new TLV called "PWRAR metric TLV." This TLV contains details of the router and the link metrics assigned for the ingress links. This TLV is used to produce various *PWRA* metric assigned topologies such as the one shown in Figure 9.

Example: Consider the topology given in Figure 9, in a non-backbone area obtained after calculating the *PWR* ratio.

Here *B* is an ABR and has two ingress links into it from *C* and *A* which are in the backbone area. Let *C* and *A* be connected with other routers in the backbone area. Routers *D, G, E, H,* and *X* are routers in the non-backbone area. Routers *H, E* and *X* are potential TE endpoints. The *PWRAR* metrics shown on the edges within the area represent metrics for a specific TE endpoint. The metrics on edges *(C, B)* and *(A, B)* are for traffic through *B* into the non-backbone area towards any TE endpoint *H, E* or *X*.

The most widely used constraints in the CSPF algorithms are TE metric, link groups and bandwidth. Our method assumes no restriction on the use of other constraints. We add the *PWRAR* metric of a link as an additional constraint. Once the ABR computes the shortest-paths to every $\{A_i, N'_j\}$ it has the topology information and advertises the shortest-paths as a reachability vector in a newly defined "TE Reachability Vector TLV."

Example: Consider the example network shown in Figure 10. TEhs are the head-ends and TEts are the tail-ends of a TE path, ABR1 and ABR2 are area border routers. ABR1's TE Reachability vector TLV for area 1 and area 0 are given as

```
{ABR1, (<TEh1, <Path info 1>>, <TEh2,
<Path info 2>>)}
{ABR1, ABR2, (<TEt1, <Path info 3>>,
<TEt2, <Path info 4>>)}.
```

The vector TLVs are arranged as per ascending sum of the *PWRAR* metric associated with each path. Similarly ABR2's TE Reachability vector TLV for area 2 and area 0 are given as

```
{ABR2, (<TEt1, <Path info 3>>, <TEt2,
<Path info 4>>)}
```

Box 4.

$$PWRAR = \frac{Power\ consumed\ by\ the\ router}{Maximum\ available\text{-}bandwidth\ of\ the\ subset\ "S"\ that\ lead\ to\ a\ TE\ endpoint}$$

Figure 8. PWRAR ratio calculation in an area. Note that there could be two egress links to the end-point and the available-bandwidth is greater in E (3). Therefore the subset "S"= {E (3)} which has the low-power path within the area will be chosen.

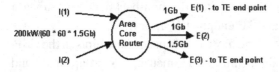

Figure 9. Calculation of the intra-area low-power path

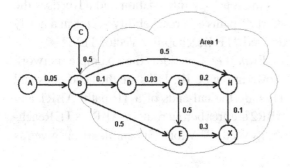

```
{ABR2, ABR1, (<TEh1, <Path info 1>>,
<TEh2, <Path info 2>>)}.
```

A few observations are in order:

1. We see that head-ends are also considered as TE-endpoints. This means that head-end and tail-ends are interchangeable as traffic can flow both directions.

2. The reachability vector advertised by ABR1 also contains the reachability vector of ABR2. If ABR2 is brought up first, then it is likely that ABR1 would have the TE Reachability vector TLV for area 0 before ABR2 computes path to the TE endpoints in area 2. (i.e., {ABR1, ABR2}).

3. The <Path info> TLV would contain the aggregate of link attributes namely cost, bandwidth etc., including the *PWRAR* metric but not the intermediate nodes. For example, <Path info 1> may be a set of <2, admin-group-1|admin-group-2, 1 Gbps> (where 1 Gbps could be the *minimum* bandwidth available along the path).

4. The given topology has only one path from ABRs to TE endpoints. In general, the number of paths to be identified "k" may be configured by the operator on all nodes.

Traffic Engineered Path Head-End Operation

When any TE-enabled application requests TE path to be setup to an endpoint that is not present in the same area, the head-end scans the TE Reachability vector TLVs advertised by ABRs and selects the path using the <Path info> contained in the vector TLVs. We explain this with an example.

Figure 10. The backbone and the non backbone area routers are depicted to show the complete transfer and selective leak of low-power path information.

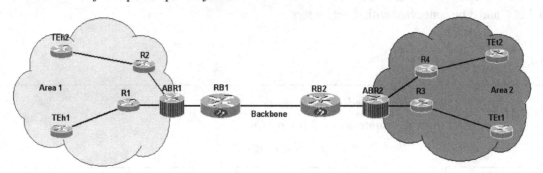

Example: Consider Figure 11 which has multiple paths in area 1, backbone and area 2.

In Figure 11, we consider the tail-ends TEts 1, 2 and 3. TEt3 is reachable through ABRs 4, 6 and 2. The TE reachability TLVs advertised by ABR6 for Area 2 would occur multiple times to each tail-end as there are multiple paths to the destination. The least cost low-power path is listed first.

```
{ABR6, (<TEt3, <Path info 1>>, <TEt3,
<Path info 2>>, <TEt2, <Path Info
3>>, etc.. }
```

For area 0 the TE reachability TLV would be

```
{ABR6, ABR1, (<TEh1, <Path info 4>>,
<TEh1, <Path info 5>>...)}
{ABR6, ABR5, (<TEh1, <Path info 6>>,
<TEh1, <Path info 7>>...)}
{ABR6, ABR3, (<TEh1, <Path info 8>>,
<TEh1, <Path info 9>>...)}
```

For the sake of brevity we do not enumerate all the possible path information.

Numerous variations are possible with respect to advertising the LSPs. We do not go into the details of the implementation but state a few of these variations. These are

1. LSPs already setup for *transit traffic* on the backbone or non-backbone areas could be used.
2. It is also feasible to advertise already set up LSPs in the path info; no additional TLV is required.
3. If existing LSPs are setup along a utilized path, then there can be selective filtering of advertisements to other areas.
4. If we have lower utilization with respect to the *PWRAR* metric then a more favorable metric could be advertised.

Once a path in the TLV has been used for reserving bandwidth for traffic, then it is withdrawn from the advertisements so that it becomes unusable. Another path may be computed over the same path but with possibly a different *PWRAR* sum as the traffic over that path could have changed the *PWRAR* metrics of the links. The proposed scheme has many advantages over conventional schemes:

1. The TE reachability vector TLV contains the aggregate of all link attributes along with TE constraints. So the head-end of the TE path

Figure 11. Multiple paths scenario depicting TLV exchanges in different areas using selective leaks

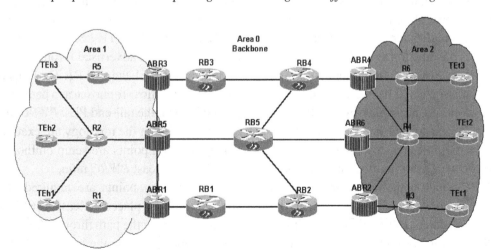

can *explicitly select* the *ABR* that connects the destination area even though it does not know the complete topology of the backbone area.

2. Flooding overhead to support this mechanism is limited as the TE reachability vector contains only the aggregate attributes of low-power paths.

3. The additional overhead of computing additional low-power paths on ABR can be solved by offloading the computation overhead to an additional processor in multi-core platforms.

We now consider some multicast scenarios where we apply the metric for placing multicasting paths.

Intra-AS Multicast Point-to-Multipoint Path Placement

In multicast replication choosing replication points that can decrease overall power consumption is extremely important. *Multicast replication capacity* is an attribute of every line-card of the routers and switches that support multicast replication. Multicast replication points on a Point-to-Multipoint Traffic Engineering Label-Switched-Paths (P2MP-TE-LSPs) consume power as the incoming data has to be replicated through suitable methods before delivering multiple output streams of data. The multicast distribution trees must be constructed with proper placement of the replication points. Improper replication points could affect the overall power consumption as well as unbalanced usage of routers. Some of the routers with high power consumption could be overloaded. In this section, we propose a mechanism by which P2MP TE-LSPs can be constructed for carrying multicast traffic across multiple areas within a given AS.

The metric we use for multicast power reduction is *PWRC* which is the *consumed-power to available-replication capacity* on each of the line-cards of a router. The goal is to minimize the *PWRC* ratio at the replication points in a

multicast path. In routers that carry multicast traffic an advertisement about the *PWRC* metric is sent in the flooding process using protocols such as OSPF-TE or ISIS-TE. A head-end router can generate a TE-LSP using a P2MP TE-LSP between the ingress PE to all egress PEs of a multicast stream. The CSPF algorithm is modified to compute the least cost *PWRC* ratio path from the head-end router. This least cost *PWRC* path would be supplied to the RSVP-TE component of the head-end which would set up the path with appropriate labels to carry traffic. After this, the reduced replication capacity of the routers in the P2MP TE-LSP path would be advertised again. This in turn would be useful for computation of the other paths as replication capacity would have changed on these routers.

Example: Consider the router topology given in Figures 12a and 12b.

1. Initial path through R6 is established with *PWRC* metric.
2. New path is established through R2 due to changes in the metric.

In Figure 12a, the source is connected using multi-homed connection to the same ISP through routers *R1* and *R2*. There are two receiver sites *RcvrA* and *RcvrB* that are multi-homed to two routers. *RcvrB* is multi-homed to *R3* and *R4* and *RcvrA* to R4 and R8. Given that the path calculation engine at the head-end *R1* has the topology and information from TE-LSA packets, the current *PWRC* ratios are advertised through the IGP-TE extensions to the head-end *R1*. The links with the least *PWRC* ratios are chosen as a path from head-end PEs to all the tail-end PEs. *PWRC* ratios that are computed on the topology are examined and the replication points are setup on those routers that have the least *PWRC* ratio.

If branching points are required at certain points, these are placed on least cost *PWRC* ratio routers. Assume the path through *R6, R7, R8* and *R4* is computed using the least *PWRC* ratio. Let the multicast stream occupy 4 Gbps of traffic. Given that the base capacity is 10 Gbps, the available capacity of these routers reduces to 6 Gbps. Subsequent paths that are constructed would have to take into account the new *PWRC* ratio in the topology. If *R6*, *R7*, *R8* and *R4* have exhausted their capacity as a result of them carrying the 4 Gbps stream then a different path would be chosen *R2*, *R3* and *R4*. This is shown in Figure 12b. Since *R4* is the only choice that has connectivity to both receivers the branch point is placed in *R3*. Such policy decisions could guide the placement in case of a tie. Here the only choice is to drive the end replication to *RcvrA* through *R4* and *RcvrB* through *R3* owing to topology constraints.

A few points are worth noting in the proposed method.

1. Our scheme applies to a centralized method for path calculation. The tree is calculated by the PCE at the head-end of the ingress router where the sources connect. The PCE calculates the intra-AS P2MP path (the P2MP TE-LSP within the AS).

2. *PWRC* ratio is assigned to each ingress link of a line-card in a router and the egress links have multicast stream replicated. All ingress links to a router through a line-card are assigned the same *PWRC* ratio. The egress links may have different types of connections such as a unicast tunnel, another branch-point in the tunnel towards the receivers, or other downstream egress routers. This method could be applied for multicast traffic to be transported through Multicast Virtual Private Networks (M-VPNs). The method of egress router discovery can be done with the existing mechanisms. The inputs needed for our technique are an ingress router with its respective egress routers and the router level topology with the *PWRC* metric.

3. Similar to the unicast schemes, a line-card that does not drastically change power consumption even when large bandwidth

streams are added for replication can be recognized for its low-power characteristic. The best case would be a low-power consuming line-card or a router that works at a fixed power irrespective of the replication capacity. This scenario would be of interest to router manufacturers.

In many cases an ingress PE becomes common when several multicast streams get aggregated into a single P2MP-TE-LSP. This P2MP-TE-LSP represents a multicast tree that encompasses the union of all the egress PEs and is commonly used to save the amount of state in the core of the network. By aggregating these streams onto a single P2MP tree, it is possible to amortize the cost of replication between a set of ingress line-cards with the *PWRC* ratio.

The dynamic nature of the multicast tree where the egress PEs joins and leave is based on the multicast listeners attached to the egress PE. Hence it is important to position the replication points such that there we reduce the overall *PWRC* ratios for the AS. The key point is to aggregate multiple streams with a set approach that maximizes overlap of egress PEs and position them on top of a P2MP-TE-LSP to ensure that the *PWRC* sum for the path is minimal.

Building Low-Power Multicast Trees

Multicast traffic across multiple areas can be obtained using multicast distribution trees. The networks usually comprise of multiple areas with several non-backbones interconnected through the backbone. To carry multicast streams it would be useful to have multicast distribution trees constructed that have low *PWRC* ratio on the routers' line-cards (provided there is sufficient replication capacity available).

As before, the key metric we consider is the *consumed-power to available-replication capacity* on each of the line-cards (*PWRMLINE*) of a router. The ports in these routers form part of an

Figure 12. Topology within a given AS showing low-power consuming distribution tree. Once a multicast tree is set up it is possible that newer requests could choose other paths because of the PWRC ratio. Policy decisions could also influence the replication points.

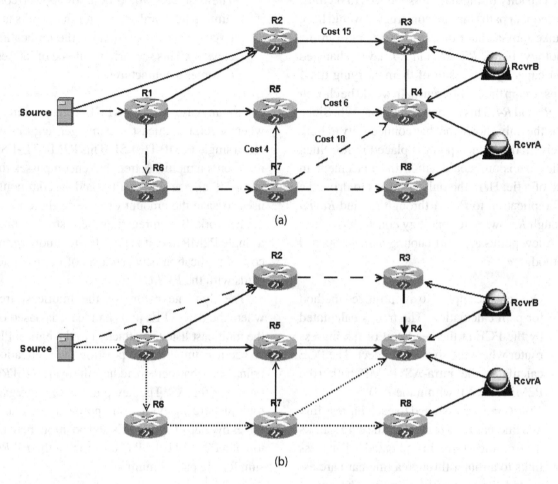

(a)

(b)

ECMP (Hopps, 2000) set of paths to a Protocol Independent Multicast (PIM) (Deering, 1995) upstream neighbor. The ports on the different line-cards that form the ECMP set of links are eligible to be used as a line-card: port combination to carry multicast traffic. When choosing the path from an ECMP set of paths to a PIM upstream neighbor, the downstream PIM neighbor calculates the *PWRMLINE* ratio for each of the line-card: port combination. The lowest ratio decides the line-card to be chosen. If multiple ports exist within the line-card, the one with the smallest *PWRMLINE* ratio is used to select one of those ports. The key proposal here is the use

of the *PWRMLINE* ratio to choose from the different line-cards. The choice of port is left to the standard method.

Example: Assume the router topology given in Figure 13, in the vicinity of the senders.

In Figure 13, we have multi-homed sources connected to routers *R1* and *R2* within an ISP. Similarly there are two multi-homed receiver sites *RcvrA* and *RcvrB* connected to two Routers: *RcvrB* to *R3* and *R4* and *RcvrA* to *R4* and *R8*. *R4* is connected to *R7* through multiple paths. Assuming that both these paths are of equal cost then ECMP paths exist for the PIM downstream router *R4* to the PIM upstream router *R7*. Let *RcvrA* send an

IGMP join to *R4*. *R4* needs to send a PIM join towards the upstream router *R7*. Assume this is a shared tree with rendezvous point being *R7*. There are two equal cost paths to *R7* from *R4* each with cost 10 (*R7, R5, R4* and *R7, R4*). Assume that each of these paths to *R7* is on different line-cards in the chassis *R4*. In the existing schemes one of them would be chosen and *PWRMLINE* ratio would not be considered. We propose that *R4*'s decision be based on this PWRC metric. In the metric comparison the line-card that has the lower value will win and is selected to send a PIM join to *R7*.

In the example shown in Figure 13 we find that the direct link to *R4* and *R7* can be used in the distribution tree. However there is an exception in the case of ECMP. If the Outgoing Interface (OIF) list consists of ports on a line-card "L" in which *R4*'s downstream neighbors have sent their respective PIM joins and if the ECMP set of paths to the router *R7* consists of line-card "L" and "M," then it would be preferable to choose line-card "L" without considering the metric. This is because if majority of the OIF list's port members use line-card "L" and the ingress port were also to be placed on line-card "L" then it would be beneficial for replication. Other such localized conditions must be considered as exceptions to the metric-based rule. Note that in the current case the unicast traffic already on the line-card may also contribute to the consumed-power. If ECMP paths do not exist

then the default selection (send a PIM join to the upstream neighbor) is followed. If the metric is included then we know that the paths in the tree where ECMP links occur consume low-power at the time of computation.

As discussed before, a new path may be computed if the old streams reduce the replication capacity so that routers along the path cannot be used due to high ratio. Such link avoidance applies in ECMP sections of the distribution tree as well. Dynamic changes in multicast trees are important as PIM Prune messages and PIM Join messages may happen at a replication point. Suitable modifications to the algorithm must be done for dynamic conditions without causing major interruption to the multicast flows.

Our scheme applies to PIM-Sparse Mode and PIM-Source Specific Multicast. However, applicability to PIM-Bidirectional (Handley, 2007) is also possible but not discussed in detail.

The pseudo code for the proposed changes is given below:

1. If (there exist ECMP paths to a PIM upstream neighbor) AND (no localized conditions exist)
2. then
3. Calculate *PWR* ratio for each line-card;
4. *PWRMLINE* = power consumed by line-card/available multicast replication capacity;
5. Choose the lowest *PWRMLINE*;

Figure 13. Topology within a given network with an upstream ECMP link from R4 to R7

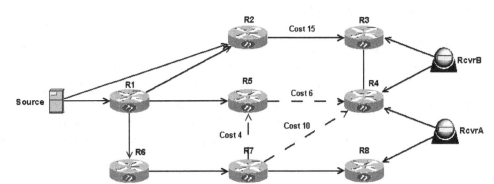

6. Select that line-card for the link to send PIM-Join;
7. Endif

Consider the case where the port choices are on the same line-card. In this case, a tie breaking mechanism is required and the following changes are implemented:

1. If (there exist ports on the same line-card which constitute ECMP paths to a PIM upstream neighbor)
2. AND (no localized conditions exist)
3. then
4. Choose the lowest utilized port;
5. Select that port in line-card for the link to send PIM-Join;
6. Endif

We now present mechanism to handle PIM ECMP redirects when the ports lie in different line-cards.

PIM ECMP Redirect Based on Line-Card Replication Capacity and Power

The previous mechanism can be adapted to scenario where ECMP redirect from a PIM upstream neighbor instructs the PIM downstream neighbor to choose one of its ECMP links. This scheme to redirect PIM ECMP is also based on power consumed in the line-cards and the multicast replication capacity available within the line-cards forming the ECMP links.

We propose that power consumed by the line-cards (if the ECMP links fall on multiple line-cards with respect to their ECMP link ports) be used along with the available replication capacity of the line-cards. This ratio can be a measure for the ECMP link to which the PIM-join is redirected. For example if there exists multiple replication engines within different line-cards then the lightly

loaded replication engine and its corresponding ECMP link can be recommended to the PIM downstream neighbor. This is implemented when the downstream neighbor sends a PIM-Join to the upstream neighbor for a specific (S,G) or (*,G) group, where (S,G) represents source/multicast group and (*,G) represents any source/multicast group.

Let the router ports be used between PIM upstream and downstream such that there are multiple ECMP links on different line-cards on the upstream neighbor called *A*, *B* and *C*. Let line-card *A* carry multiple data streams in the incoming direction and replicate it to multiple outgoing line-cards through a switch fabric. Let line-card *B* be lightly loaded with respect to multicast traffic but heavily loaded with respect to unicast traffic. Let line-card *C* be lightly loaded with respect to unicast and multicast traffic. We see that line-card *C* would be a better point of placement of the replication for the group for which the PIM-join comes from the downstream neighbor. When a request from downstream neighbor arrives, existing mechanisms would choose line-card *A*. We see that it would be power-conservative to send a redirect to the downstream neighbor asking it to choose line-card *C instead* of line-card A. This is done by recommending the neighbor address field as the port IP address of line-card *C*. The existing Protocol Data Unit (PDU) format for the ECMP redirect and the procedures that go along with it can be used. It is also possible to make this decision in combination with the above or solely on a metric which we will call *PWR-REPLIC-CAP* defined as that in Box 5.

The lowest *PWR-REPLIC-CAP* metric is chosen which minimizes the power spent on replication. It is important to note that a line-card may have multiple replication engines and ports assigned to each replication engine. If the ECMP links and their ports fall on the same line-card then it is possible to choose a specific replication engine that has better available replication capacity. This can be done by choosing a neighbor address of the port that belongs to the superior replication engine. If there is no distinction between ports with respect to the multiple replication engines then it actually makes no difference since it would be an internal decision as to where the replication for that port actually happens.

The pseudo code for the steps to be followed to implement this scheme is:

1. if (multiple ECMP links exist to the PIM neighbor from which PIM-join was received) then
2. Get the list of ECMP ports which are members of the ECMP links;
3. Get the list of line-cards on which these ECMP ports are placed;
4. LCA = Consider the least used line-card with respect to the replication capacity;
5. if (port on LCA is the same on which PIM-join was received)
6. break;
7. else if (choice is made on replication capacity)
8. LCA = Consider the least used line-card with respect to replication capacity;
9. else if (choice is to be made on *PWR-REPLIC-CAP*)
10. LCA = Consider the line-card with the lowest *PWR-REPLIC-CAP* metric;
11. end if
12. Send PIM redirect to PIM downstream neighbor recommending LCA ECMP link;
13. end if

We now discuss some implementation issues and further work that can be done to the schemes presented in this chapter.

FUTURE RESEARCH DIRECTIONS

Our approach relies on certain pre-requisites to be enabled in the hardware, such as advertising capability for consumed-power, available-bandwidth of a link and replication capacity of a link-card or device. Today's networking devices provide such capability. There is Management Information Base (MIBs) for gathering such metrics. Using Simple Network Management Protocol and MIBs, we could consider implementing our methods *offline* rather than integrating them with the devices through a Network Management System.

In determining the backup paths, it is possible that low-power criteria may not be satisfied. But we identify backup paths only in the case of load-balancing or link failures. We could explore algorithms which could find combination of redundant paths that effectively consume low-power.

Further work needs to be done to analyze the performance of these algorithms when detecting the backup paths. Note that step 5 in Algorithm 3 in the worst case may lead to |E|! permutations. Hence finding the minimum number of common nodes with the primary path turns out to be computationally intensive. The Internet provides redundancy so that finding an alternate path will involve executing the low-power path algorithm at most twice, in most of the scenarios. However,

Box 5.

$$PWR\text{-}REPLIC\text{-}CAP = \frac{Power \ consumed \ by \ the \ line\text{-}card}{Available \ replication \ capacity}$$

more work needs to be done in order to fully explore and understand any tradeoffs.

In all the schemes discussed a common issue is that the metrics may fluctuate quite frequently due to traffic mix as well as power consumption. Therefore we propose that both the numerator and denominator of the metric values be operated within different ranges rather than discrete values. Any change in these values must be propagated through out the network which could cause flooding effects leading to oscillations while determining low cost paths. Such flooding can be avoided by reducing the frequency of the updates. Determining the optimal frequency of updates given the traffic pattern would lead to some interesting questions on control of such networks.

We propose the addition of some attributes with no change to the protocol implementation for communicating the power information. There may be a time lag when the far ends of the network receive the attribute and the time it originated. This however cannot be avoided as with other attributes and metrics. It would be of interest to see the value addition that could be brought about by modifying existing protocol mechanisms, or proposing new protocols for the power reduction problem.

All our schemes prefer low-power paths and thus more data is transmitted to paths that have low metric values. If an ISP's billing model is based on bandwidth usage, more data will flow to ISPs having a low metric value. The proposed methods require trust between ISPs. Formal governance may have to be in place for implementing any cooperative scheme for power reduction.

In all the methods discussed, we could use the heuristic given in (Raman, 2012a), where we could divide the network into equivalence classes and perform the computations. We will have a single algorithm for finding the low cost path under inter-AS, intra-AS unicast and multicast schemes. We concentrated on wired networks. It would be interesting to see whether the ideas can be extended to wireless and optical domains

as the metric-based proposals discussed in this chapter are independent of the technology used.

We discussed methods to reduce power consumption at the network topology level. However, the power consumed by the AS, as well as the areas, are calculated based on the power consumption of the individual devices. Hence reducing the power consumption of individual devices also assumes significance and complements the proposed approach. For example, using optical technology or removing power consuming components such as buffers inside routers may also be explored (Wischik, 2005). Additionally, the judicious use of feedback from queues, and the design of queue management policies may help routers to enhance performance without a tradeoff in power consumption (Raina, 2005; Raman, 2012b).

CONCLUSION

We presented a metric-based distributed and hierarchical approach to reduce power consumption in core and edge router based networks. The approach aims to reduce the power consumption in both unicast and multicast traffic scenarios. The metrics we considered were *consumed-power to available-bandwidth* in the case of unicast and *consumed-power to available-replication capacity* in the case of multicast. We showed that the metric-based approach could be used with minimal modifications to routing protocols at various levels of the Internet hierarchy to find low-power paths. For the intra-AS unicast scenario, we proposed a new approach of selectively leaking information by ABRs for disseminating low-power path information. We discussed methods to detect low-power multicast path as well as multicast replication points. We also showed that our approach provides incentive to router manufacturers as well as ISPs to opt for low-power high bandwidth devices.

Kilper et. al., (2011) raises an interesting point that today access devices and other associated equipments consume more power than the edge and core routers. The prediction is that this power consumption break-up will continue for the next decade. So it is suggested that research focus should lie on power-saving methods for access devices. This could certainly be true in the short-term. However given the increasing power consumption in the Internet, any reasonable saving in edge and core networks should be welcome by ISPs. Additionally, with rapid changes in technology, it is imperative to have power-saving solutions that do not depend on technology, but are distributed and hierarchical. Our work represents a step in that direction.

ACKNOWLEDGMENT

Shankar Raman would like to acknowledge the support by BT Public Limited (UK) under the BT IITM PhD Fellowship award. Balaji Venkat and Gaurav Raina would like to acknowledge the UK EPSRC Digital Economy Programme and the Government of India Department of Science and Technology (DST) for funding given to the IU-ATC. The authors would like to thank Vasan V. S and Bhargav Bhikkaji for their help while preparing this chapter.

REFERENCES

Adelin, A., Owezarski, P., & Gayraud, T. (2010). On the impact of monitoring router energy consumption for greening the Internet. *11th IEEE/ACM International Conference on Grid Computing-2010* (pp. 298-304). doi: 10.1109/GRID.2010.5697988

Amaldi, E., Capone, A., Gianoli, L. G., & Mascetti, L. (2011). Energy management in IP traffic engineering with shortest path routing. *IEEE International Symposium on a World of Wireless, Mobile and Multimedia Networks-2011* (pp.1-6). doi: 10.1109/WoWMoM.2011.5986482

Awduche, D. O., Berger, L., Srinivasan, V., Li, T., & Gan, D. H. (2001). RSVP-TE: Extensions to RSVP for LSP tunnels. Retrieved Ocotber 22, 2012, from http://tools.ietf.org/html/rfc3209

Baliga, J., Hinton, K., & Tucker, R. S. (2007). Energy consumption of the Internet. *Joint International Conference on Optical Internet 2007 and the 2007 32nd Australian Conference on Optical Fibre Technology-2007* (pp. 1 - 3). doi: 10.1109/COINACOFT.2007.4519173

Bianzino, A. P., Chaudet, C., Moretti, S., Rougier, J. L., Chiaraviglio, L., & Rouzic, E. L. (2012a, June). Enabling sleep mode in backbone IP-networks: A criticality-driven tradeoff. In *Proc. of the ICC Workshop on Green Communications and Networking, Ottawa, Canada.*

Bianzino, A. P., Chiaraviglio, L., Mellia, M., & Rougier, J.-L. (2012). GRiDA: Green distributed algorithm for energy-efficient IP backbone networks. *Computer Networks*, *56*(14), 3219–3232. doi:10.1016/j.comnet.2012.06.11

Bolla, R., Bruschi, R., Davoli, F., & Cucchietti, F. (2011). Energy efficiency in the future Internet: A survey of existing approaches and trends in energy-aware fixed network infrastructures. *IEEE Communications Surveys & Tutorials*, *13*(2), 223–244. doi:10.1109/SURV.2011.071410.00073

Callon, R. W. (1990). *Use of OSI IS-IS for routing in TCP/IP and dual environments*. Retrieved October 22, 2012, from http://tools.ietf.org/html/rfc1195.html

Chabarek, J., Sommers, J., Barford, P., Estan, C., Tsiang, D., & Wright, S. (2008). Power awareness in network design and routing. *The 27th IEEE Conference on Computer Communications-2008* (pp.457-465). doi: 10.1109/INFOCOM.2008.93

Chiaraviglio, L., Mellia, M., & Neri, F. (2009). Energy-aware backbone networks: A case study. *IEEE International Conference on Communications Workshops-2009* (pp.1-5). doi: 10.1109/ICCW.2009.5208038

Chu, H.-W., Cheung, C.-C., Ho, K.-H., & Wang, N. (2011). Green MPLS traffic engineering. *Australasian Telecommunication Networks and Applications Conference, 2011*, 1–4. doi: 10.1109/ATNAC.2011.6096644

Cisco, I. O. S. (2007). *Configuration fundamentals guide configuring cisco discovery protocol* (pp. FC-277–FC-280).

Cisco. (2012). *Website*. Retrieved October 22, 2012, from http://newsroom.cisco.com/press-release-content?type=webcontent&article Id=888280

Deering, S., Estrin, D., Farinacci, D., Jacobson, V., Liu, C. G., Wei, L., & Helmy, A. (1995). Protocol independent multicast (pim): Motivation and architecture: doi=10.1.1.45.4672

Dhamdhere, A., & Dovrolis, C. (2011). Twelve years in the evolution of the internet ecosystem. [TON]. *IEEE/ACM Transactions on Networking*, *19*(5), 1420–1433. doi:10.1109/TNET.2011.2119327

Farrel, A., Vasseur, J. P., & Ash, J. (2006). A path computation element (PCE)-based architecture (RFC 4655). Retrieved October 22, 2012, from http://www.ietf.org/rfc/rfc4655.txt

Gelenbe, E., & Silvestri, S. (2009). Reducing power consumption in wired networks. *24th International Symposium on Computer and Information Sciences-2009* (pp.292-297). doi: 10.1109/ISCIS.2009.5291829

Gupta, M., & Singh, S. (2003, August). Greening of the Internet. In *Proceedings of the 2003 conference on Applications, technologies, architectures, and protocols for computer communications* (pp. 19-26). ACM. doi: 10.1145/863955.863959

Handley, M., Vicisano, L., Kouvelas, I., & Speakman, T. (2007). Bidirectional protocol independent multicast (BIDIR-PIM). Retrieved October 22, 2012, from http://tools.ietf.org/rfc/rfc5015.txt

Hopps, C. E. (2000). *Analysis of an equal-cost multi-path algorithm*. Retrieved October 22, 2012, from http://tools.ietf.org/html/rfc2992

Idzikowski, F., Chiaraviglio, L., & Portoso, F. (2012). Optimal design of green multi-layer core networks. In *Proceedings of the 3rd ACM International Conference on Future Energy Systems: Where Energy, Computing and Communication Meet-2012* (Art. 15). doi: 10.1145/2208828.2208843

Jiang, W., & Prasanna, V. K. (2012). Energy-efficient Internet infrastructure. In Zomaya, A. Y., & Lee, Y. C. (Eds.), *Energy-efficient distributed computing systems*. John Wiley & Sons, Inc. doi:10.1002/9781118342015.ch20

Kilper, D. C., Atkinson, G., Korotky, S. K., Goyal, S., Vetter, P., Suvakovic, D., & Blume, O. (2011). Power trends in communication networks. *IEEE Journal on Selected Topics in Quantum Electronics*, *17*(2), 275–284. doi:10.1109/JSTQE.2010.2074187

Le Roux, J. L., Vasseur, J. P., & Boyle, J. (2005). *Requirements for inter-area MPLS traffic engineering*. Retrieved October 22, 2012, from http://tools.ietf.org/html/rfc4105

Luo, J., Ye, D., Xu, L., & Fan, M. (2009). A survey of multicast routing protocols for mobile ad-hoc networks. *IEEE Communications Surveys & Tutorials*, *11*(1), 78–91. doi:10.1109/SURV.2009.090107

Moy, J. (1997). *OSPF version 2*. Retrieved October 22, 2012, from http://tools.ietf.org/html/rfc2178

Raina, G., Towsley, D., & Wischik, D. (2005). Part II: Control theory for buffer sizing. *SIGCOMM Computer Communications Review, 35*(3), 79–82. doi:10.1145/1070873.1070885

Raman, S., Jain, S., & Raina, G. (2012). Feedback, transport layer protocols and buffer sizing. In *Proceedings of the 11th International Conference on Networks* (pp. 125-131). ISBN: 978-1-61208-183-0.

Raman, S., Venkat, B., & Raina, G. (2012). Reducing power consumption using the border gateway protocol. In *The 2nd International Conference on Smart Grids, Green Communications and IT Energy-aware Technologies* (pp. 83-89). ISBN 978-1-61208-189-2.

Rekhter, Y., & Li, T. (1995). A border gateway protocol 4 (BGP-4). Retrieved October 22, 2012, from http://tools.ietf.org/html/rfc4271

Riacardo, O., Dan, P., Walter, W., Beichuan, Z., & Lixia, Z. (2010). The (In)completeness of the observed Internet AS-level structure. *IEEE/ACM Transactions on Networking, 18*(1), 109–122. doi:10.1109/TNET.2009.2020798

RSVP. (2001). *RSVP-TE: Extensions to RSVP for LSP Tunnels*. Retrieved October 22, 2012, from http://tools.ietf.org/html/rfc3209

RSVP. (2008). *Inter-domain MPLS and GMPLS traffic engineering*. Retrieved October 22, 2012, from http://tools.ietf.org/html/rfc5151

Stallings, W. (1998). *SNMP, SNMPv2, SNMPv3, and RMON 1 and 2*. Addison-Wesley Longman Publishing Co., Inc.

Venkat, B., et al. (2010, July 6). Constructing disjoint and partially disjoint. Inter AS TE LSPs, *USPTO Patent 7751318*. Cisco Systems.

Vereecken, W., Van Heddeghem, W., Deruyck, M., Puype, B., Lannoo, B., & Joseph, W. et al. (2011). Power consumption in telecommunication networks: Overview and reduction strategies. *IEEE Communications Magazine, 49*(6), 62–69. doi:10.1109/MCOM.2011.5783986

Viswanathan, A., Feldman, N., Wang, Z., & Callon, R. (1998). Evolution of multiprotocol label switching. *Communications Magazine, IEEE, 36*(5), 165-173. doi: 10.1.1.124.3180

Wischik, D., & McKeown, N. (2005). Part I: Buffer sizes for core routers. *ACM SIGCOMM Computer Communications Review, 35*(3), 75–78. doi:10.1145/1070873.1070884

Yoo, S. J. B. (2011). Energy efficiency in the future internet: the role of optical packet switching and optical-label switching. *IEEE Journal on Selected Topics in Quantum Electronics, 17*(2), 406–418. doi:10.1109/JSTQE.2010.2076793

Zhang, Y., & Liu, Y-C. (2011). An improved ant colony optimisation and its application on multicast routing problem. *International Journal of Wireless and Mobile Computing, 5*(1/2011), 18-23. doi: 10.1504/IJWMC.2011.044116

ADDITIONAL READING

Aleksic, S. (2008). Power consumption issues in future high-performance switches and routers. In *10th Anniversary International Conference on Transparent Optical Networks-2008* (pp.194-198). doi: 10.1109/ICTON.2008.4598688

Athanasiou, G., Tsagkaris, K., Vlacheas, P., & Demestichas, P. (2011). Introducing energy-awareness in traffic engineering for future networks. In *7th International Conference on Network and Service Management-2011* (pp.1-4). ISBN: 978-3-901882-44-9

Bartczak, T., & Zwierzykowski, P. (2012). Lightweight PIM—a new multicast routing protocol. *International Journal of Communication Systems.* doi:10.1002/dac.2407

Bolla, R. et al. (2012). Cutting the energy bills of Internet service providers and telecoms through power management: An impact analysis. *Computer Networks, 56*(10), 2320–2342. doi:10.1016/j.comnet.2012.04.003

Chiaraviglio, L., Mellia, M., & Neri, F. (2009). Reducing power consumption in backbone networks. *IEEE International Conference on Communications-2009* (pp.1-6). doi: 10.1109/ICC.2009.5199404

CSCI. (2012). *Climate savers computing.* Retrieved October 22, 2012, from http://www.climatesaverscomputing.org/

Fan, J., Hu, C., He, K., Jiang, J., & Bin, L. (2012). Reducing power of traffic manager in routers via dynamic on/off-chip scheduling. *The 32nd IEEE Conference on Computer Communications-2012* (pp.1925-1933). doi: 10.1109/INFCOM.2012.6195569

Gelenbe, E., & Morfopoulou, C. (2012). Gradient optimisation for network power consumption. *Green Communications and Networking, 51,* 125–134. doi:10.1007/978-3-642-33368-2_11

Guo, H., Ngoh, L.-H., & Wong, W.-C. (2008). Optimizing inter-domain Internet multicast. In Freire, M., & Perera, M. (Eds.), *Encyclopedia of Internet technologies* (pp. 391–410). IGI Global.

Herreria-Alonso, S., Rodriguez-Perez, M., Fernandez-Veiga, M., & Lopez-Garcia, C. (2012). Bounded energy consumption with dynamic packet coalescing. *17th European Conference on Networks and Optical Communications-2012* (pp.1-5). doi: 10.1109/NOC.2012.6249925

Hinton, K., Baliga, J., Ayre, R., & Tucker, R. S. (2009). The future Internet - An energy consumption perspective. *14th Opto-Electronics and Communications Conference-2009* (pp.1-2). doi: 10.1109/OECC.2009.5222592

Khan, R., Bolla, R., Repetto, M., Bruschi, R., & Giribaldi, M. (2012). Smart proxying for reducing network energy consumption. *International Symposium on Performance Evaluation of Computer and Telecommunication Systems-2012* (pp.1-8).

Li, G. Y., Zhikun, X., Cong, X., Chenyang, Y., Shunqing, Z., Yan, C., & Shugong, X. (2011). Energy-efficient wireless communications: Tutorial, survey, and open issues. *IEEE Wireless Communications, 18*(6), 28–35. doi:10.1109/MWC.2011.6108331

Mingui, Z., Cheng, Y., Bin, L., & Beichuan, Z. (2010). GreenTE: Power-aware traffic engineering. *18th IEEE International Conference on Network Protocols-2010* (pp. 21-30). doi: 10.1109/ICNP.2010.5762751

Paul, S., Pan, J., & Jain, R. (2011). Architectures for the future networks and the next generation Internet: A survey. *Computer Communications, 34*(1), 2–42. doi:10.1016/j.comcom.2010.08.001.

Pickavet, M., Vereecken, W., Demeyer, S., Audenaert, P., Vermeulen, B., Develder, C., et al. (2008). Worldwide energy needs for ICT: The rise of power-aware networking. *2nd International Symposium on Advanced Networks and Telecommunication Systems-2008* (pp. 1-3). doi: 10.1109/ANTS.2008.4937762

Puype, B., Vereecken, W., Colle, D., Pickavet, M., & Demeester, P. (2009). Power reduction techniques in multilayer traffic engineering. *11th International Conference on Transparent Optical Networks-2009* (pp. 1-4). doi: 10.1109/ICTON.2009.5184981

Reviriego, P., Sivaraman, V., Zhao, Z., Maestro, J. A., Vishwanath, A., Sanchez-Macian, A., & Russell, C. (2012). An energy consumption model for energy efficient ethernet switches. *International Conference on High Performance Computing and Simulation-2012* (pp.98-104). doi: 10.1109/HPCSim.2012.6266897

Rexford, J., & Dovrolis, C. (2010). Future internet architecture: Clean-slate versus evolutionary research. *Communications of the ACM*, *53*(9), 36–40. doi:10.1145/1810891.1810906

Rosenberg, E. (2012). A primer on multicast routing, Springer Briefs. In Computer Science. ISBN: 978-1-4614-1873-3.

Sanso, B., & Mellah, H. (2009). On reliability, performance and Internet power consumption. *7th International Workshop on Design of Reliable Communication Networks-2009* (pp. 259-264). doi: 10.1109/DRCN.2009.5339997

Singh, J., Veeraraghavan, P., & Singh, S. (2006). QoS multicast routing using explore best path. *Computer Communications*, *29*(15), 2881–2894. doi:10.1016/j.comcom.2006.03.011

Uichin, L., Ivica, R., & Volker, H. (2010). Greening the internet with content-centric networking. *ACM Proceedings of the 1st International Conference on Energy-Efficient Computing and Networking-2010* (pp. 179-182). doi:10.1145/1791314.1791342

Vasic, N., & Kostic, D. (2009). Energy-aware traffic engineering. In *Proceedings of the 1st International Conference on Energy-efficient Computing and Networking-2009* (pp. 169-178). doi: 10.1145/1791314.1791341

Vishwanath, A., Zhi, Z., Sivaraman, V., & Russell, C. (2010). An empirical model of power consumption in the NetFPGA Gigabit router. *IEEE 4th International Symposium on Advanced Networks and Telecommunication Systems-2010* (pp.16-18). doi: 10.1109/ANTS.2010.5983514

Yetginer, E., & Rouskas, G. N. (2009). Power efficient traffic grooming in optical WDM networks. *IEEE Global Telecommunications Conference-2009* (pp.1-6). doi: 10.1109/GLOCOM.2009.5425886

Yongjun, L., Wang, J. Z., Wenhui, Z., & Deyu, Q. (2006). Optimizing IP multicast through delayed multicast tree pruning. In *3rd International Conference on Broadband Communications, Networks and Systems-2006* (pp.1-7). doi: 10.1109/BROADNETS.2006.4374383

Yuanyuan, Y., Jianchao, W., & Min, Y. (2008). A service-centric multicast architecture and routing protocol. *IEEE Transactions on Parallel and Distributed Systems*, *19*(1), 35–51. doi:10.1109/TPDS.2007.70711.

KEY TERMS AND DEFINITIONS

All Source, Multicast Group (G): * Refers to all sources and G refers to multicast group.

Area Border Router (ABR): Routers that belong to more than one area.

Autonomous System (AS): A collection of routers under a single administrative authority.

Autonomous System Border Router (ASBR): A high performance router that exchanges routing information with other high performance routers belonging to other Autonomous Systems.

Border Gateway Protocol (BGP): A protocol used for exchanging routing information between gateways in a network of autonomous systems.

Constrained Shortest Path First (CSPF): The shortest path first algorithm designed for fulfilling a given set of constraints.

Equal Cost Multi Path (ECMP): A routing technique for routing packets along multiple paths of equal cost.

Exterior Gateway Protocol (EGP): A protocol for exchanging routing information between two neighbor gateways in a network of autonomous systems.

Interior Gateway Protocol (IGP): A protocol for exchanging routing information between gateways within an autonomous network.

Internet Service Provider (ISP): A company that provides individuals or companies access to the Internet.

Label Switched Path (LSP): The specific path through a network that a packet follows based on its MPLS label.

Link State Advertisement (LSA): A means to share communication between routers about the topology within an OSPF area.

Multi Protocol Label Switching (MPLS): A standards based technology setting up a specific path for a given sequence of packets, identified by a label inserted into each packet.

Open Shortest Path First (OSPF): A router protocol used within autonomous systems.

Path Computation Element (PCE): A network node or in general, any entity capable of computing a network path or route based on a network graph after applying computational constraints.

Point to MultiPoint (P2MP): A communication transmission between single source to multiple destination.

Protocol Data Unit (PDU): A unit of information that is formatted as a distinct element to be exchanged between peers in a network.

Protocol Independent Multicast (PIM): A set of four specifications namely: spare mode, dense mode, source-specific multicast and bidirectional modes of Internet communication to allow one-to-many and many-to-many transmission.

Provider Edge (PE): Provider edge routers are placed at the edge of the carrier network.

Source, Multicast Group (S, G): A service model that identifies session traffic by both source and group address. This model builds shortest-path trees. Such trees are represented by (S, G) pairs, where S refers to the single unicast address and G refers to the specific multicast group address.

Traffic Engineering (TE): Methods used for optimizing the performance of a communication network by analyzing, predicting and regulating the behavior of data transmitted.

Type/Tag, Length, Value (TLV): A way to encode information attributes which can be sent through a protocol.

Virtual Private Network (VPN): A network that uses a public communication infrastructure like the Internet to provide secure access between remote offices or individual users with enterprise network.

Chapter 10
Waveband Switching:
A Scalable and Cost Efficient Solution for the Internet Backbone

Yang Wang
Georgia State University, USA

Vishal Anand
The College at Brockport, USA

Xiaojun Cao
Georgia State University, USA

ABSTRACT

In this chapter, the authors describe and review some of the recent research on WBS, including Multi-Granular optical cross-connect (MG-OXC) architectures that can switch traffic at different granularities. The authors focus on the dynamic online WBS problem, and describe and analyze two reconfigurable MG-OXC architectures in terms of their port count and blocking probabilities. Based on the analyses, the authors then propose a novel dynamic graph-based waveband assignment algorithm in conjunction with adaptive routing. The proposed algorithm employs ant optimization techniques to reduce ports and blocking probability in the network with online traffic in a distributed manner. The authors use simulation experiments to evaluate the effectiveness of the authors' approach under various parameters such as varying number of ants, varying the number of routes and the wavelength assignment algorithm. The authors' simulation results show that their graph-based waveband assignment algorithm combined with adaptive routing can achieve a superior performance when compared to other schemes. Furthermore, the authors' studies shows that even with limited resources, WBS can achieve a low blocking probability and port savings.

DOI: 10.4018/978-1-4666-4305-5.ch010

INTRODUCTION

In recent years, the role and importance of backbone communication networks has significantly increased due to the exponential growth of the Internet and Internet-based services and applications such as IPTV, VoIP and P2P, and more recently large-scale science collaborations and Cloud-based services. Backbone communication networks typically support traffic between large, strategically interconnected networks and core routers in the Internet. Optical fiber networks using wavelength division multiplexing (WDM) technology are the foremost solution to meet this ever-growing traffic demand, and to support higher layer networks such as the Internet Protocol (IP) network. Using WDM each optical fiber can carry more than 100 wavelengths, with each wavelength supporting 100 Gbits/s or higher (Mukherjee, 2006) traffic. While the use of WDM technology has significantly increased the available bandwidth in backbone networks, the rapid advances in dense WDM technologies with hundreds of wavelengths per fiber and world-wide fiber deployment has brought about a tremendous increase in the cost and size of electronic cross-connects or DXCs (e.g., OEO grooming switches).

Optical (photonic) cross-connects (OXCs) that switch bypass traffic all-optically are useful in reducing the cost and size of the OEO grooming switches. However, when the number of wavelengths is large traditional OXCs that switch traffic *only* at the wavelength granularity themselves can become huge (i.e., requiring a large number of wavelength ports), resulting in increased cost and control complexity. Waveband switching (WBS) in conjunction with new multi-granular optical cross-connects (or MG-OXCs) that can switch traffic at fiber, waveband and wavelength granularities has been proposed to reduce this cost and complexity (Lee, Yu, Kim, Kang, & Park (2002); Noirie, Gorgeuille, & Bisson (2002); Cao, Anand, & Qiao (2003)). The main idea of WBS is to group several wavelengths together as a band, and switch the band using a single port whenever

possible (e.g., as long as it carries only bypass or express traffic), and demultiplex it to switch the individual wavelengths only when some traffic needs to be added/dropped. As the bypass traffic accounts for up to 60% to 80% of the total traffic in the backbone, only a limited number of fibers and bands need to be demultiplexed into wavelengths. Thus, not only the size of wavelength cross-connects, but also the overall number of ports and complexity of the MG-OXCs can be reduced by using waveband switching.

In this work, we review the challenges in designing WBS optical networks. We describe our and other related work on designing MG-OXC architectures and algorithms for WBS to accommodate dynamic traffic demands. We also provide mathematical analyses and bounds on the number of required ports and blocking probabilities of various WBS algorithms and architectures. In particular, we develop architectures and algorithms for dynamic WBS to decrease the blocking probability of dynamic traffic. We present our distributive ant-based route optimization and the associated graph-based waveband assignment algorithms to carry dynamic traffic requests in WBS networks so as to minimize the blocking.

BACKGROUND AND RELATED WORK

The concept of WBS based on two stage multiplexing was applied to WDM ring networks in Gerstel, Ramaswami, and Wang (2000), while its merits such as small-scale modularity, crosstalk and complexity reduction were summarized in Harada, Shimizu, Kudou, and Ozeki (1999). A Three-Layer switching fabric consisting of a fiber cross-connect (FXC), a band cross-connect (BXC) and a wavelength crossconnect (WXC) was presented in Noirie, Vigoureux, and Dotaro (2001), and the application of such Three-Layer MG-OXC architectures to metro-area networks was described in Noirie, Gorgeuille, and Bisson (2002). For such multi-Layer MG-OXCs, limited analytic work for some specific traffic patterns in rings was done in Izmailov, Ganguly, Suemura, Nishioka, Maeno, and Araki (2002), Chen, Saengudomlert, and Modiano (2004), and Li, Yao, and Ramamurthy (2005) while Izmailov, Ganguly, Kleptsyn, and Varsou (2003) studied the benefit of non-uniform waveband hierarchy. Hybrid hierarchical switches with all-optical waveband switching and OEO traffic grooming were shown to reduce cost in Cao, Anand, and Qiao (2003), Yao and Mukherjee (2003), and Zhu, Zang, and Mukherjee (2003), while a quantitative investigation on wavelength grouping granularity is presented in Bullock, Ward, and Wang (2003). The authors Lee, Yu, Kim, Kang, and Park (2002), and Huiban, Perennes, and Syska (2002) presented MILP-based approaches for the design of a two-layer MG-OXC network using a simple lightpath grouping strategy, which does not take full advantage of the benefits of wavebanding.

In our prior research (Cao, Xiong, Anand, & Qiao, 2002), the most powerful and flexible lightpath grouping strategy called sub-path grouping was used in conjunction with the Three-Layer MG-OXC architecture. The sub-path grouping strategy maximizes the advantage of waveband switching by allowing the grouping of traffic from any source to any destination, thus maximizing the reduction in port count. In particular, we provided a general Integer Linear Programming (ILP) model, and an efficient heuristic called Balanced Path routing with Heavy-Traffic first waveband assignment (BPHT) for off-line static traffic. The ILP model and the BPHT heuristic were also extended to multi-fiber systems in Cao, Anand, Xiong, and Qiao (2003). The authors Lingampalli and Vengalam (2002) proposed a Single-Layer MG-OXC architecture for WBS but provided no detailed algorithms or comparisons with other architectures. In Cao, Anand, and Qiao (2003), we discussed the differences between WBS and traditional wavelength routed networks (WRN) and provided an overview of the issues related to WBS such as survivability and wavelength/waveband conversion. In this work, we provided a qualitative comparison of the Single-Layer and Multi-Layer MG-OXC architectures, and gave numerical results comparing the two architectures under on-line traffic. Issues related to multi-granular optical switching and waveband grouping under the Generalized Multi-Protocol Label Switching (GMPLS) framework, such as signaling protocols and Link Management Protocols, have been partially addressed in Douville (2003) and Dotaro (2002). While there is a significant amount of research that has focused on wavelength routed networks, many of the works on WBS has been limited to only a specific MG-OXC architecture for the offline traffic case. In Cao, Anand, and Qiao (2007), we quantitatively compared the Single and Three-layer MG-OXCs. We developed an on-line ILP model (On-ILP), which minimizes the used ports and the request blocking probability, given a fixed number of wavelengths and MG-OXC size. We showed that the Three-layer MG-OXC is more suitable for dynamic traffic, while the Single-layer MG-OXC is well suited for static traffic. We also proposed the Waveband Assignment with Path-Graph (WAPG) algorithm that efficiently uses wavelength converter resources and at the same time maximizes the benefit of wavebanding to carry dynamic traffic.

MULTI-GRANULAR OPTICAL CROSS-CONNECT ARCHITECTURES

In this section, we describe two primary multi-granular optical cross-connects based on single and three-layer architectures. We show how these cross-connects can be used to carry dynamic traffic and also compare the two architectures in terms of port counts, which is one of the primary performance metrics.

Optical WDM networks are evolving from interconnected SONET ring to arbitrary-mesh topologies largely due to the development and maturity of optical cross-connects (OXC). In traditional optical networks, wavelengths terminate at, or transparently pass-through a node using an *ordinary-OXC*. Such ordinary-OXCs switch each individual wavelength using one port. On the other hand, in WBS networks several wavelengths are grouped together as a band, and switched as a single entity (i.e., using a single port) whenever possible. A band is demultiplexed into individual wavelengths if and only if necessary, e.g., when the band carries at least one lightpath that needs to be dropped or added. A complementary hardware is an MG-OXC that can not only *switch* traffic at multiple levels (or granularities) such as fiber, waveband, and individual wavelength, but also may *add/drop* traffic at multiple levels, as well as *multiplex/demultiplex* traffic from one level to another.

The MG-OXC is a key element for routing high speed WDM data traffic in a multi-granular optical network. While reducing its size has been a major concern, it is also important to devise node architectures that are flexible (i.e., reconfigurable) yet cost-effective. Two principle MG-OXC architectures: the Three-Layer and Single-Layer have been proposed in literature.

A Three-Layer MG-OXC Architecture

Figure 1 shows a typical Three-Layer MG-OXC, which includes the *FXC*, *BXC* and *WXC* layers. As shown in the figure, the WXC, BXC layers consist of cross-connect(s) and multiplexer(s)/demultiplexer(s). The WXC layer includes a wavelength cross-connect (WXC) that is used to switch bypass lightpaths. To add/drop wavelengths from the WXC layer, we need W_{add}/W_{drop} ports and multiplexers/demultiplexers. At the BXC layer, the waveband crossconnect (BXC), B_{add} and B_{drop} ports are used for bypass wavebands, added wavebands and dropped wavebands, respectively. In addition, *BTW* ports are used to demultiplex wavebands to WXC layer and *WTB* ports are used to multiplex wavelengths from WXC layer to bands. Similarly, fiber cross-connect (FXC)/F_{add}/F_{drop} ports are used to switch/add/drop fibers at the FXC layer. Fiber-to-Band (FTB) and Band-to-Fiber (BTF) ports are used to demultiplex fibers to wavebands, and

multiplex wavebands to fibers, respectively. The demultiplexing is achieved using demultiplexers that enable the separation or extraction (usually by filtering) of the individual bands from its respective fiber, and wavelengths from its respective band. On the other hand the multiplexing is achieved using multiplexers that combine wavelengths into a band, and similarly combine bands into a fiber.

In order to reduce the number of ports, the MG-OXC switches a fiber using one port (space switching) at the FXC cross-connect if none of its wavelengths is used to add or drop a lightpath. Otherwise, it will demultiplex the fiber into bands, and switch an entire band using one port at the BXC cross-connect if none of its wavelengths needs to be added or dropped. In other words, only the band(s) whose wavelengths need to be added or dropped will be demultiplexed, and only the wavelengths in those bands that carry bypass traffic need to be switched using the WXC. This is in contrast to the ordinary-OXCs, which needs to switch every wavelength individually using one port. This multi-layer architecture allows dynamic selection of fibers for multiplexing/demultiplexing from FXC layer to the BXC layer, and bands for multiplexing/demultiplexing from BXC to the WXC layer. For example, at the FXC layer, as long as there is a free FTB port, *any* fiber can be demultiplexed into bands. Similarly, at the BXC layer any band can be demultiplexed to wavelengths using a free BTW port by appropriately configuring the FXC, BXC cross-connects and associated demultiplexers.

Unlike in the off-line case (Cao, Anand, Xiong, & Qiao, 2003) or the case with static traffic demands (i.e., where all the traffic demands are known a priori and the goal is to satisfy all the demands with minimum number of network resources such as cross-connect ports or wavelengths) where the MG-OXC can have as many port as needed to guarantee that all the demands are satisfied, here, the MG-OXC has only a predetermined limited port count to accommodate dynamic traffic. More specifically, let X denote the number of incoming fibers, Y the number of

Figure 1. Three-layer reconfigurable multi-granular photonic optical cross-connect

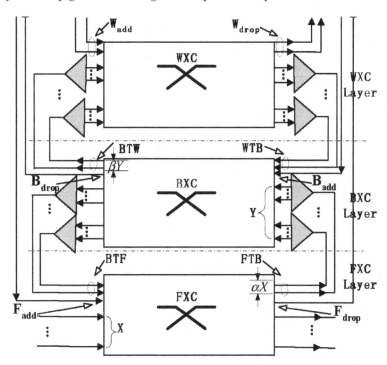

BXC ports from FTB demultiplexers, $\alpha \leq 1$ be the ratio of fibers (to the total number of fibers) that can be demultiplexed into bands using FTB ports, and similarly, $\beta \leq 1$ be the ratio of bands that can be demultiplexed to wavelengths using BTW ports. Such Three-Layer MG-OXC architecture is reconfigurable (and hence flexible) in that *any* $\lceil \alpha X \rceil$ fibers can be demultiplexed into bands and *any* $\lceil \beta X \rceil$ of these bands can be demultiplexed into wavelengths simultaneously by appropriately configuring the MG-OXC. In Cao, Anand, and Qiao (2007), we show that even with limited reconfiguration (i.e., $\alpha < 1$ and $\beta < 1$), we can use an intelligent algorithm to considerably reduce the port count required to satisfy dynamic traffic with an acceptable request blocking probability.

The total number of ports at the input side of node n of such a reconfigurable, Three-Layer MG-OXC can be calculated as in Equation 1 (see Box 1).

Note that when $\alpha = 1, \beta = 1$, there is no limitation on the number of fibers/bands that can be multiplexed/demultiplexed, and hence, the blocking of a lightpath request can only come from the limited number of wavelengths as in an ordinary-OXC network. If we consider single-fiber systems and let δ be the degree of node n, we have $X = \delta$, $Y = \lceil \alpha \times X \times B \rceil$. For an ordinary-OXC that only switches individual wavelengths, the number

Box 1.

$$MG - OXC_n = \left\lceil (1 + \alpha) \times X + (1 + \beta) \times Y + \beta \times Y \times W_{add/drop} \right\rceil \qquad (1)$$

Table 1. Summary of notations used

Notation	Meaning
X	Number of fibers connected to a node.
F	Number of wavelengths per fiber.
B	Number of wavelengths per band.
P	Number of bands per fiber.
α	The ratio of fibers (to the total number of fibers) that can be demultiplexed into bands using FTB ports.
β	The ratio of bands that can be demultiplexed to wavelengths using BTW ports.
D_n	Number of BTW demultiplexers at node n.
M_n	Number of WTB multiplexers at node n.
V	Visited node in a network.
FW	Number of continuous free wavelength(s) along one path.
DM	The minimum number of free demultiplexers among all nodes along one path.
PB_{Li}	The probability of selecting link L_i as the outgoing link.
P_{Li}	The pheromone value of link L_i.
$\lambda_{s,d}$	Arrival rate of the lightpath request from s to d, which follows the Poisson process.
λ_n	Arrival rate of the lightpath request at node n, which follows the Poisson process.
Λ_k	The birth rate of an M/M/C/C Markov chain when k servers are in use.
μ_k	The death rate of an M/M/C/C Markov chain when k servers are in use.
$P_{s,d}$	Routing path for node pair (s,d).
$H_{s,d}$	Number of hops of $P_{s,d}$.

of ports at node n is $OXC_n = \lceil \delta \times B \times W + W_{add/drop} \rceil$. Accordingly, if we ignore the $W_{add/drop}$ ports (which are common to both the Three-Layer reconfigurable MG-OXC and ordinary-OXC), Equation 2 gives the ratio of the port count in a Three-Layer MG-OXC to the port count in an ordinary-OXC, denoted by T_3. In (2) (see Box 2) B and W denote the number of bands in a fiber and number of wavelengths in a band, respectively.

A Single-Layer MG-OXC Architecture

Compared to the previously described Three-Layer MG-OXC, the one shown in Figure 2 is a Single-Layer MG-OXC that has only *one* common switching fabric (Lingampalli & Vengalam, 2002). This switching matrix includes three *logical* divisions corresponding to the FXC, BXC and WXC, respectively. However, the major differences from the Three-Layer MG-OXC are the

Box 2.

$$T_3 = \frac{\left[(1+\alpha) \times \delta + (1+\beta) \times \alpha \times \delta \times B + \alpha \times \beta \times \delta \times B \times W\right]}{\left[\delta \times B \times W\right]} \cong \beta \times \alpha + \frac{(1+\beta) \times \alpha}{W} \qquad (2)$$

Table 2. Ten possible cases to satisfy a new lightpath request

Case	Input Band	Output Band	Additional DEMUX	Additional MUX
A	Empty	Bypass	2	1
B	Empty	Non-bypass	1	0
C	Empty	Empty	0	0
D	New demand in the bypass band from I to O		0	0
E	Bypass	Bypass	2	2
F	Bypass	Non-bypass	1	1
G	Bypass	Empty	1	2
H	Non-bypass	Bypass	1	1
I	Non-bypass	Empty	0	1
J	Non-bypass	Non-bypass	0	0

elimination of FTB/BTW demultiplexers and BTF/WTB multiplexers between the different layers, which results in a simpler architecture to implement, configure and control. Another advantage of this Single-Layer MG-OXC is better signal quality because all lightpaths go through only one switching fabric, whereas in the Three-Layer MG-OXC, some of them may go through as many as three switching fabrics (i.e., FXC, BXC and WXC). As a trade-off, some incoming fibers, e.g., fiber n (see Figure 2), are pre-configured as *designated fibers*. Only these designated fiber(s) can have some of its bands dropped while the remaining bands bypass the node, all other non-designated incoming fibers (e.g., fibers 1 and 2) have to have all the bands either bypass the node entirely or be dropped entirely. Similarly, within these designated fiber(s), only designated band(s) can have some of its wavelengths dropped while the remaining bands bypass the node.

Thus, the Single-Layer MG-OXC is simple, but not flexible in that it does not allow lightpaths to be multiplexed/demultiplexed and grouped into bands arbitrarily, which may result in inefficient utilization of network resources. More specifically, in WBS networks with Single-Layer MG-OXCs, an appropriate WBS algorithm needs to

make sure that the lightpaths to be dropped at a Single-Layer MG-OXC will be assigned wavelengths that belong to a designated fiber/band. Clearly, this may not be always possible if there is only a limited number of designated fibers/bands, especially in the case of on-line traffic where global optimization for all lightpath demands is often difficult (if not impossible) to achieve. For this reason, a network with Three-Layer MG-OXCs may in fact require fewer ports and wavelengths in order to satisfy all the on-line lightpath demands, or result in a better blocking performance (i.e., a lower blocking probability) for a given set of on-line lightpath demands with the same number of wavelength and ports.

Similar to Equation 2, if we limit only $\lceil \alpha X \rceil$ fibers can be demultiplexed into bands and $\lceil \beta Y \rceil$ of these bands can be demultiplexed into wavelengths simultaneously, Equation 3 gives the ratio of the port count in a Single-Layer MG-OXC to the port count in an ordinary-OXC, denoted by T_1. The difference between T_3 and T_1 is due to the fact that there are *no* FTB/BTF and BTW/WTB ports in the Single-Layer MG-OXC architecture, which are present in the Three-Layer MG-OXC architecture.

Figure 2. Single-layer partially-reconfigurable multi-granular optical cross-connect

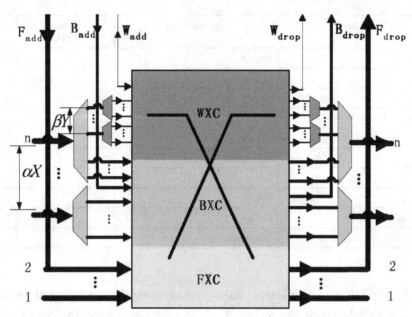

$$T_1 \cong \beta \times \alpha + \frac{(1-\beta) \times \infty}{W} \qquad (3)$$

From Equations 2 and 3, we see that, in order to reduce the port count by using MG-OXCs instead of ordinary-OXCs, the values of α and β need to be constrained so as to ensure that $T_3 < 1$ and $T_1 < 1$. For single-fiber systems, it is necessary to set $\alpha = 1$ to allow any fiber to be demultiplexed to bands (otherwise, the blocking probability is too high). However, we can and should limit the value of β to be less than 1 by allowing only a limited number of bands (i.e., $\lceil \beta Y \rceil$) to be demultiplexed into wavelengths simultaneously.

Port Counts in Three-Layer and Single-Layer MG-OXCs

We use an example to illustrate the differences between the Three-Layer and Single-Layer MG-OXCs. We note that due to the symmetry of the MG-OXC architecture, the number of ports on the input-side and the output-side are equal. Hence, when counting the number of ports, we will only focus on the *input-side* of the MG-OXC. The input-side consists of locally added traffic and traffic coming into the MG-OXC node from all other nodes (i.e., bypass traffic and locally dropped traffic). Assume that there are 10 fibers, each having 100 wavelengths, and one wavelength needs to be dropped and one to be added at a node. The total number of ports required at the node when using an ordinary-OXC is 1000 for incoming wavelengths (including 999 for bypass and 1 for drop wavelength), plus 1 for add wavelength for a total of 1001. However, if the 100 wavelengths in each fiber are grouped into 20 bands, each having 5 wavelengths, then using a MG-OXC as in Figure 1, only one fiber needs to be demultiplexed into 20 bands (using a 11-port FXC). Then, only one of these 20 bands needs to be demultiplexed into 5 wavelengths (using a 21-port BXC). Finally, one wavelength is dropped and added (using a 6-port WXC). Accordingly, the MG-OXC has only 11+21+6 = 38 ports (an almost 30 times reduction). Furthermore, if the single-Layer MG-OXCs as in Figure 2 is used, and if the lightpath to be dropped is assigned to an appropriate fiber (i.e., a designated fiber) and an appropriate (designated) band in the fiber, then even fewer ports are needed. More specifically, only one fiber needs to be demultiplexed into 20 bands so only 9 ports are needed for other non-designated fibers. In addition, only one of 20 bands demultiplexed from the designated fiber needs to be further demultiplexed into wavelengths so only 19 ports are needed for the nondesignated bands in the fiber. Finally, 6 ports are needed for the 5 wavelengths demultiplexed from the designated band and for the add/drop wavelength. Hence, the total number of ports needed is only 9+19+6 = 34, more than 10% less than the three-Layer MG-OXC and 96% less than the ordinary-OXC.

Such a reduction in port count has a direct impact on the scalability and the costs that can be achieved in a waveband switched optical network. In particular, requiring fewer ports reduces the size of the OXCs, which are the main traffic routing and switching elements in the optical network. With WBS the size and the port counts of the OXCs increases only marginally as traffic in the network increases, thus making the network very scalable. In addition, smaller sized OXCs and routing traffic as groups instead of individual wavelengths reduces the overall cost, which is the both the capital expenditures (CAPEX) and operational expenditures (OPEX). Lower CAPEX means lower cost of installing and setting up a new network, while lower OPEX cost means lower operational, management and day-to-day costs. In this work, we show that by using WBS we can achieve lower costs and scalability for static as well as dynamic traffic using dynamic waveband switching as explained next.

DYNAMIC WAVEBAND SWITCHING

In WBS networks, the routing path and wavelength/waveband have to be intelligently selected and assigned to carry the traffic so as to minimize the required cross-connect ports and wavelength resources. This is defined as the routing and wavelength assignment (RWA) problem with the additional complexity of choosing the 'right' band to route the traffic. Based on whether the traffic demands are known a priori or not, RWA problems are categorized as offline or online RWA problems. The offline RWA is generally formulated to satisfy a given set of traffic demands, while incurring the minimum cost or resources in the network, which is proven to be NP-Complete (Cao, Anand, Xiong, & Qiao, 2003; Ramaswami & Sivarajan, 2002; Chlamtac, Ganz, & Karmi, 1992). To solve the RWA problem with offline traffic, the integer linear programming approach is widely adopted to optimally set up lightpaths in a small size network (Lee, Yu, Kim, Kang, & Park, 2002; Cao, Anand, Xiong, & Qiao, 2003), while heuristic algorithms are developed for large scale networks in Cao, Anand, Xiong, and Qiao (2003), Varma and Jue (2004), Todimala and Ramamurthy (2007), and Wang and Cao (2009).

In the case with online traffic, the network topology and the nodal architecture are given, the basic problem is how to minimize the blocking probability or maximize the throughput for dynamic traffic demands. In other words, given the limited amount of available networking resources (e.g., wavelengths, switching ports), how to efficiently accommodate dynamic traffic demands which arrive and depart randomly. There is little work that focuses on how to accommodate online traffic in WBS networks to reduce the blocking probability. We propose a routing scheme based on ant optimization techniques together with a graph-based waveband assignment algorithm to distributively satisfy online traffic while reducing the blocking and used ports in the network. As explained earlier, the Three-Layer MG-OXC architecture has been shown to be flexible and well suited for dynamic traffic, while the Single-Layer MG-OXC is better suited for static traffic. Since we are dealing with dynamic traffic, we will focus on the use of the Three-Layer MG-OXC shown in Figure 1 from now on.

In circuit-switched networks (WRNs or WBS networks), it is not cost-efficient or infeasible to deploy maximum (or unlimited) number of equipments to guarantee successful call connection under all possible circumstances. To provide an acceptable performance, limited equipments and resources are normally allocated in practice. This also leads to the inevitable blocking of some dynamic traffic demands as the future traffic demands are not known a priori. Hence, global optimization for all on-line lightpath demands is often difficult (if not impossible) to achieve (Mukherjee, 2006). Specifically, the blocking in WBS networks can be caused by two factors: limited available wavelengths and the limited number of ports at the MG-OXCs (Cao, Anand, & Qiao, 2004; Escobar & Marshall, 2002). On one hand, the blocking can be due to the lack of free wavelengths (or channels) along the routing path (Ngo, Jiang, Horiguchi, & Guo, 2004; Ngo, Jian, Le, & Horiguchi, 2006). For example, without wavelength conversion, a lightpath request can be blocked as a result of the wavelength continuity constraint which requires the same wavelength to be available along the route from the source to the destination. On the other hand, to accommodate online traffic in WBS networks, a reconfigurable MG-OXC architecture (Figure 1) is generally adopted. Such an MG-OXC may block lightpath requests due to the limited fibers/bands that can be demultiplexed into bands/wavelengths through the FTB/BTW demultiplexers. In other words, the exhaustion of multiplexers/demultiplexers at a certain node along the routing path may trigger the rejection of a new lightpath request.

To optimize the allocation of the resources (e.g., wavelengths) in the network, efficient routing algorithms are necessary. Generally, the routing schemes are broadly classified into three categories: fixed routing, alternative routing, and adaptive routing. In the case with fixed routing, the routes between node pairs are preconfigured and fixed while the alternative routing scheme selects route from a set of candidate routes that are precomputed (e.g., k-shortest paths (Yen, 1971)).

In the case with adaptive routing, the routes can be adapted according to the system status (e.g., resource allocation, congestion) to optimize the routing decision. As an appealing strategy to satisfy online traffic demands with limited resources, adaptive routing schemes based on tabu-search, agent-based or swarm intelligence are proposed to adaptively change the routing table in the network according the network status. For example, ant system is adopted in telecommunication networks to balance the traffic load and adaptively learn the routing tables (Schoonderwoerd, Holland, & Bruten, 1997; Caro & Dorigo, 1998). The techniques based on ant system have also been incorporated to enhance the performance of routing and protection in WRNs (Ngo, Jian, Le, & Horiguchi, 2006; Ngo, Jiang, Horiguchi, & Guo, 2004; Garlick & Barr, 2002). In this work, we apply ant optimization techniques to WBS networks. By defining artificial ants and pheromone, we develop an adaptive routing scheme which is combined with the proposed graph-based waveband algorithm to balance and optimize the allocation of resources such as wavelengths and multiplexers/demultiplexers in WBS networks. We analyze the blocking performance of the reconfigurable Three-layer MG-OXC node discussed previously. We use the notations in Table 1 in our discussion.

Allocation of the Multiplexer and Demultiplexer

As explained earlier the reconfigurable three-layer MG-OXC consists of the FXC, BXC and WXC layers. The FTB/BTW demultiplexers, BTF/WTB multiplexers are used to connect different layers. This MG-OXC architecture only allows $\lceil \alpha X \rceil$ fibers to be demultiplexed into bands and $\lceil \beta Y \rceil$ of these bands (where $\alpha \leq 1$ and $\beta \leq 1$) to be demultiplexed into wavelengths simultaneously. The limited deployment for BTF and WTB multiplexers only allows a limited number of bands and wavelength to be multiplexed to fiber and band layer, respectively. We assume that $\alpha =$

1, which means each MG-OXC node is equipped with the maximum number of FTB/BTF demultiplexers/multiplexers and all fibers can be demultiplexed to the BXC layer simultaneously. However the number of bands that can be demultiplexed to the WXC layer at node n is limited by $D_n = X * P * \beta$. Similarly, the number of bands multiplexed from the WXC layer is limited by $M_n = X * P * \beta$. Hence, we hereafter only focus on the BTW/WTB demultiplexers/multiplexers and ports. We refer to a band without any traffic as an *empty* band. When all the lightpaths within one band go through only the FXC layer at a node, we call this band as *bypass* band. Otherwise, the band is called as *non-bypass* band, which has to be demultiplexed or multiplexed through the BXC layer. Furthermore, we assume that no wavelength conversion is available in the system.

In WBS networks, the allocation of extra demultiplexers/multiplexers is directly related to traffic grouping. Inefficient traffic grouping may lead to the exhaustion of the demultiplexers/multiplexers at an MG-OXC node, which may block future traffic requests going through this node. For a specific lightpath request, we define the input band as the band that contains the wavelength for the lightpath in the input fiber, and the output band as the band that contains the wavelength for the lightpath in the output fiber. Due to the wavelength continuity constraint, input band and output band must have the same band index. Figure 3 shows an example of traffic grouping and the necessary allocation of the demultiplexer/multiplexer (DEMUX/MUX). As shown in the figure, an existing lightpath resides in a bypass band from input band A to output band O. To satisfy a new lightpath request from input band I to output band O, the node has to allocate demultiplexers/multiplexers for the traffic grouping. This is because the bands from A and I have to be demultiplexed first at this node. Then the two lightpaths are multiplexed together to form the band leaving O of this node. Such traffic grouping requires two additional demultiplexers and one multiplexer. If the node has less than two unused demultiplexers

and one unused multiplexer, the new traffic has to be blocked by this node. In fact to accommodate a new lightpath request from input band I to output band O, there are 10 possible cases based on the existing configuration or traffic of this node as shown in Figure 4. The input band I and output band O can be bypass, non-bypass, or empty band, which generate 9 combinations, namely, case (A), (B), (C), (E), (F), (G), (H), (I), and (J) as shown in Figure 4. When both I and O are occupied by a bypass band, case (E) only indicates the bypass band through I and O are different. Hence, we need an additional case (D) to represent the possible bypass band from I directly to O.

The example in Figure 3 corresponds to the case (A). In case (B), the band through I is empty and existing traffic from A to O is non-bypass band (going through DEMUX/MUX). Grouping the new lightpath request to O only requires one more demultiplexer. In cases (C), no extra DEMUXs/MUXs are required since both I and O are empty. When the existing lightpath has the same input and output band as the new request, the wavebanding can be achieved without costing extra DEMUXs/MUXs as shown in case (D). Case (E) uses/costs the most extra DEMUXs/MUXs among all the cases because we have to demultiplex/multiplex two bands for the grouping at this node. The amount of additional DEMUXs/MUXs required for this node to satisfy a new request in other cases can be similarly derived, which is shown in Table 2. Note that among the 10 cases, four cases require 0 additional DEMUXs, two cases require 2 additional DEMUXs, and four cases require 4 additional DEMUXs. Similarly, four cases require 0 additional MUXs, two cases require 2 additional MUXs, and four cases require 4 additional MUXs.

Upper Bound of β

Under the assumption that $\alpha = 1$, the total number of ports, namely TP, required at an MG-OXC node can be calculated as in Equation 4, where X is the number of fibers, F is the number of wavelengths

Figure 3. Allocation of DEMUX/MUX to satisfy a new lightpath

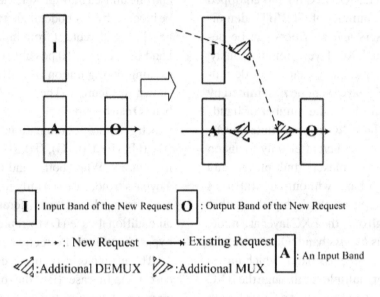

Figure 4. Different cases for accommodation a new lightpath

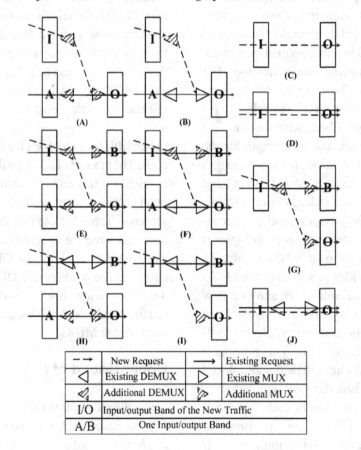

per fiber, and P is the number of bands per fiber. To be cost-efficient, the port number TP for the MG-OXC should be no more than that used in corresponding traditional OXCs (T-OXC) that do not use waveband switching (i.e., $TP \leq 2 * X * F$). Thus based on Equation 4, the upper bound of β can be obtained as in Equation 5. For example, when $X = 1$, $F = 100$, $P = 10$, we have $\beta \leq 0.8$ and $\beta = 0.8$ is the upper bound.

$$TP = 4 * X + 2 * (1 + \beta) * X * P + 2 * X * F * \beta \tag{4}$$

$$\beta <= 1 - 2 * \frac{P+1}{P+F} \tag{5}$$

Lower Bound of β

Having limited number of DEMUXs/MUXs in WBS networks with dynamic traffic request can result in call or connection blocking. Hence, β is also limited with a lower bound based on the allowable blocking probability in the network. Here we propose an analysis model to approximately derive the lower bound of β. To simplify the analysis, we assume that for any node pair (s, d), a fixed routing path is calculated; the traffic arrival follows the Poisson distribution with rate $\lambda_{s,d}$; the service time for the call is exponentially distributed with a mean of 1. Moreover, we assume that the available DEMUXs/MUXs is independent from one node to another. Given the symmetrical traffic demand and DEMUXs/MUXs in the network, only DEMUXs need to be considered in the steady state of the network. If the new lightpath requests are uniformly distributed into the ten cases in Figure 4, the expectancy E of additional DEMUXs for an incoming request is $E = 0.2 * 2 + 0.4 * 1 + 0.4 * 0 = 0.8$, since we have two cases, four cases, and four cases require 2, 1, and 0 additional DEMUXs, respectively. Thus, we can calculate the Poisson rate for DEMUX usage at a specific node n as in Equation 6.

$$\lambda_n = E \times \sum_{n \in P_{s,d}} \lambda_{s,d} \tag{6}$$

We model the consumption of DEMUXs at node n using an M/M/C/C ($C=D_n$) Markov chain (Repairman Model), as shown in Figure 5. The birth rate for this Markov chain is $\Lambda_k = \lambda_n$, for $k = 0, ..., D_n - 1$, and the death rate is $\mu_k = k$, for $k = 1, ..., D_n$, and $\mu_0 = \Lambda_{Dn} = 0$. According to the Erlang's formula, we let $\pi_n(c)$ denote the probability that c DEMUXs are in use at node n. Then the blocking probability at node n is given in Equation 7.

$$\pi_n(D_n) = \frac{(\lambda_n)^{D_n} / D_n!}{\sum\limits_{j \in [0, D_n]} (\lambda_{D_n})^j / j!} \tag{7}$$

If the allowable blocking probability for node pair (s, d) is Q, then the blocking probability along the route should be no more than Q, which constrains the lower bound of β as shown in Equation 8.

$$1 - \Pi \quad (1 - \pi_n(D_n)) <= Q \tag{8}$$

ANT-BASED ADAPTIVE ROUTING

In this section, we describe our algorithm and simulation results for WBS with dynamic traffic that minimizes the blocking probability given an MG-OXC with fixed number of ports. Our solution uses ant-based optimization techniques in conjunction with a dynamic graph-based waveband assignment algorithm.

With ant optimization, individuals (i.e., ant) cooperate through self-organization to find a good solution for a certain problem (e.g., food hunting) (Dorigo, Maniezzo, & Colorni, 1996). Instead of using a central control mechanism, the individuals use *stigmergy*, which is a mechanism of indirect coordination or communication. In particular, ants exchange information by laying down a chemical

Figure 5. The Markov chain for DEMUX usage

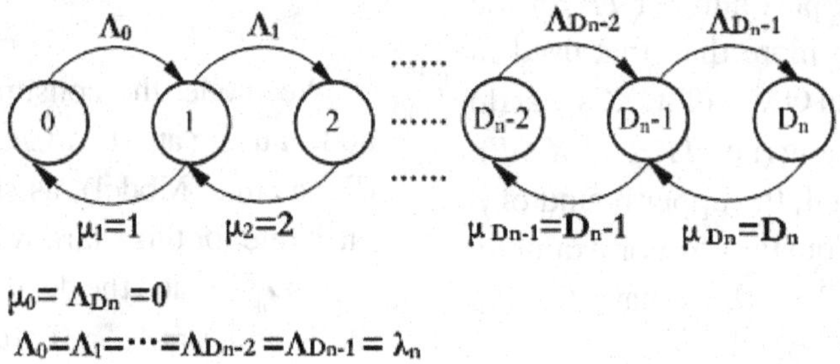

$$\mu_0 = \Lambda_{Dn} = 0$$
$$\Lambda_0 = \Lambda_1 = \cdots = \Lambda_{Dn-2} = \Lambda_{Dn-1} = \lambda_n$$

substance called pheromones that can be sensed by other ants. By following the strong-pheromone route, the ants can quickly converge to the shorter path (or the best path) to the food. Based on this principle, we define artificial ants and pheromone to track the available demultiplexers/multiplexers and free wavelengths in the network distributively. There are three types of ants, *forward* ants, *backward* ants, and *decision* ants. Forward ants are walking in the network to explore good routes. When forward ants reach the destination, they are changed to backward ants. The backward ants trace back along the opposite direction of the original path of corresponding forward ants and update the pheromone table at each node they traversed. After launching a number of ants, the final route is selected along the path which accumulates the highest pheromone value. Subsequently, a decision ant is launched to decide the waveband to accommodate the new lightpath request.

Ant and Node Structure

Each ant carries a stack consisting of the available continuous wavelength(s), demultiplexers/multiplexers, and the visited nodes. As shown in Figure 6(a), the visited nodes are kept for avoiding a route loop. The free wavelengths are recorded by a free wavelength mask. Whenever a new node is visited, the free wavelength(s) mask is updated to record the continuous free wavelength(s). Similarly, information for demultiplexers/multiplexers is recorded using DM and updated hop

by hop until the destination node is reached. We will further elaborate the updating in the following subsection. Each node in the network has a pheromone table containing pheromone value that is calculated based on the free wavelengths and demultiplexers/multiplexers. In this table, each incident link of the node has a pheromone value. For example, as shown in Figure 6(b), node 3 has a pheromone table, which consists of pheromone values for its outgoing links. A higher pheromone value indicates that more available wavelengths and demultiplexers/multiplexers can be accessed by going through this link. The pheromone value is used for ants to make decision on the way to the destination, and also is used for creating the final route for the new lightpath request.

Updating of Ant Stack and Pheromone Table

The available continuous wavelengths are recorded using a mask, which contains multiple bits. Each bit represents a unique wavelength. When a wavelength is available all the way down to the current node from the source node, the corresponding bit is set to be 1. A logical *AND* operation can be conducted to update the mask of the ant stack whenever the forward ant traverses through a link. At the destination node, the number of continuous free wavelength(s) along one path, denoted by FW, can be counted from the mask. Similarly, the demultiplexers/multiplexers information along a path should be updated. We use *DM* to represent

Figure 6. Ant stack and pheromone table

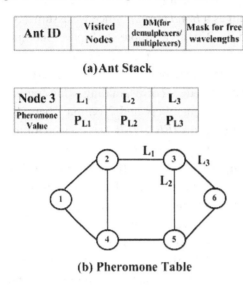

(a) Ant Stack

(b) Pheromone Table

the minimum number of available demultiplexers along one path.

Each forward ant also has to make a decision for next hop if the current node is not the destination. Among all the incident links of the current node, the probability of using one link to next node is calculated as in Equation 9, where V is the set of visited nodes. With Equation 9, the ant will be more likely to take the link with higher pheromone value, which promotes the convergence of the optimized route selection. However, if the ant has visited all the neighbors of the current node, the ant will be killed immediately.

$$PB_{Li} = \frac{P_{Li}}{\sum_{j \notin V} P_{Lj}} \qquad (9)$$

Once the forward ant arrives at the destination node, the ant is changed to be a backward ant and updates the pheromone value for the traversed link at each corresponding incident node according to Equation 10. With Equation 10, the routes having more available continuous wavelength (i.e., larger *FW*), less bottleneck nodes (i.e., larger *DM*), and shorter length (i.e., smaller $H_{s,d}$) are set with

more pheromone value (since these routes have less chances to block the traffic requests). The variable θ is a scalar to tune the impacts of free wavelengths or demultiplexers/multiplexers. Note that for a route with FW = 0, we will not increase the pheromone value along the route.

$$P_{Li} = P_{Li} + \theta * \frac{FW}{H_{s,d}} + (1 - \theta) * DM \qquad (10)$$

When enough backward ants arrive at the source, the source can decide the final routing path for the lightpath request. The routing path is decided hop by hop according to the link that has the highest pheromone value. Specifically, the source selects the next node by using the link that has the highest pheromone. This process is repeated until the destination is reached.

Ant Walking Algorithm

The ant walking algorithm identifies the routing path for the online traffic requests in a distributed (on-demand) manner. To accommodate a new arriving lightpath request, the following process is performed in the WBS networks with reconfigurable MG-OXCs. The algorithm used to decide the waveband will be elaborated in the next section.

1. For the new request from s to d, the source launches multiple forward ants to the destination.
2. Each ant walks distributively until reaching the destination using Algorithm 1.
3. Once the forward ant reach the destination, the ant is changed to backward ant, which follows the reverse path of the original forward ant using Algorithm 1, and updates the pheromone table at the node along the way.
4. When enough backward ants arrive at source, the new path can be generated. The source sends one decision ant along the new path

to the destination for choosing the waveband to use for the lightpath request.

5. The decision ant goes back to the source from the destination.

6. Along the new path and the decided waveband, establish the lightpath for the new request.

A GRAPH-BASED WAVEBAND ASSIGNMENT ALGORITHM

When accommodating a new lightpath request along the selected routing path, additional demultiplexers/multiplexers may be used as enumerated in Figure 4 and Table 2. Instead of randomly choosing or using a first-fit strategy to select the band, we propose a graph-based waveband assignment algorithm to use minimum number of additional demultiplexers/multiplexers in the process of satisfying dynamic traffic requests.

To effectively and cautiously allocate the demultiplexers/multiplexers, in the waveband assignment, we construct an auxiliary graph for each node along the routing path. The edges in the auxiliary graph are assigned weights based on the demultiplexers/multiplexers information. A band corresponding to minimum weight is selected to preserve more demultiplexers/multiplexers for future traffic thus saving ports and reducing blocking probabilities. Figure 7 shows an example in the basic steps of the proposed algorithm constructing the auxiliary graph for waveband assignment. To satisfy a lightpath request for the node pair (S, D) along the path S-W-U-D (Figure 7(a)), we use P *Band Node*, W_0, W_1, ..., W_{P-1} to represent node W, where P is the number of bands per fiber. Similarly, node U is represented by U_0, U_1, ..., U_{P-1} as shown in Figure 7(b). If we assume that each link consists of $\bar{X}$ fibers, a band b may come from any of the $\bar{X}$ input fibers and leave the node through any of the $\bar{X}$ output fibers. Accordingly, we create a bipar-

tite complete graph for each *Band Node*, which we call as a *Band Graph*. Since we assume $\bar{X} = 2$ and $P = 2$ in this example, the bipartite complete graph for W_0 (or W_1) (see Figure 7(c)) contains 2 nodes for each disjoint set of the bipartite graph, and has 2*2 edges corresponding to the combination of 2 input fibers and 2 output fibers. Specifically, vertex $IFB_{0,0}$ ($IFB_{1,0}$) is created for input fiber 0 (1) while vertex $OFB_{0,0}$ ($OFB_{1,0}$) is created for output fiber 0 (1) in the Band Graph of W_0. After the auxiliary Band Graph is constructed, we can assign the weight for each edge to reflect the cost (in terms of additional demultiplexers/multiplexers) for a new lightpath request using the band from the corresponding input fiber to the output fiber. As shown in Figure 4, at a node n any band b can be bypass, non-bypass or an empty band. Hence, we assign weight $BT_{i,o}^{n,b}$ to the edge between $IFB_{i,b}$ and $OFB_{i,b}$ using Equation 11 (see Box 3).

Equation 11 assigns the weight to the edges in Band Graph based on the available demultiplexers/multiplexers and the additional demultiplexers/multiplexers to satisfy a request. For example, in case (E), the weight is set to $2 / D_n + 2 / M_n$ at node n to reflect the two additional demultiplexers and two extra multiplexers. The weight value is set to -1 in case (D) since case (D) is desirable for waveband grouping and no extra demultiplexers/multiplexers are required. Based on the above weight assignment, each Band Node will be given the weight $WT_{n,b}$ for each band, which equals to the minimum value among all $BT_{i,j}^{n,b}$, where $i, j \in \left[0, X-1\right]$. The value of $WT_{n,b}$ represents the minimum weight (i.e., cost) to use band b at node n. Thus, the cost for using band b along the routing path can be obtained using Equation 12 and a band with minimum RT_b will be chosen to accommodate the new lightpath request.

Algorithm 1. Ant walking

```
if (a forward ant) then
     if (current node is not the destination) then
          Update DM and FW
          Make decision for next hop
          if (No next hop) then
               Kill itself
          else
               Move to the next hop
          end if
     else
          Current node is the destination, change itself to backward ant
          Move to the last visited node
     end if
else
     Current ant is a backward ant, update the pheromone value at current node
     if (current node is the source) then
          Kill itself
     else
          Move to the next node towards the source
     end if
end if
```

Box 3.

$$
\begin{cases}
BT_{i,o}^{n,b} = -1; \forall b \subset case(D) & (i) \\
BT_{i,o}^{n,b} = 0; \forall b \in case(C,J) & (ii) \\
BT_{i,o}^{n,b} = 1 / D_n; \forall b \in case(B) & (iii) \\
BT_{i,o}^{n,b} = 1 / M_n; \forall b \in case(I) & (iv) \\
BT_{i,o}^{n,b} = 1 / D_n + 1 / M_n; \forall b \in case(H,F) & (v) \\
BT_{i,o}^{n,b} = 2 / D_n + 1 / M_n; \forall b \in case(A) & (vi) \\
BT_{i,o}^{n,b} = 1 / D_n + 2 / M_n; \forall b \in case(G) & (vii) \\
BT_{i,o}^{n,b} = 2 / D_n + 2 / M_n; \forall b \in case(E) & (viii)
\end{cases}
\tag{11}
$$

$$
RT_b = \sum_{n \in p_{s,d}} WT_{n,b} \tag{12}
$$

To distributively select the waveband for the new lightpath request Algorithm 2 is used for the decision ant to find the minimum weight band when travels along the routing path. The decision ant has a weight field consisting of minimum cost for using each band b along the routing path, denoted by RT_b, as shown in Figure 8. RT_b is

Figure 7. Band node and band graph

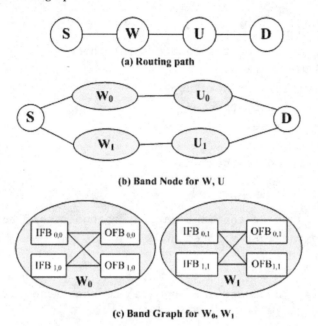

(a) Routing path

(b) Band Node for W, U

(c) Band Graph for W_0, W_1

updated node by node through adding the $WT_{n,b}$ to the current RT_b. Thus, the source node can choose the band with the minimum RT_b to accommodate the lightpath request. As one can see that the proposed waveband assignment algorithm cautiously selects a band that requires minimum number of additional demultiplexers/multiplexers. In this way, we can preserve more demultiplexers/multiplexers for future traffic demands and potentially reduce the blocking probability. In addition, the more the demultiplexers/multiplexers are used at node n, the larger the weight will be as shown in Equation 12, which can balance the demultiplexers/multiplexers usage in the network.

SIMULATION AND PERFORMANCE EVALUATION

We simulate the adaptive routing in conjunction with the graph-based waveband assignment algorithm using the 14-node NSF network as the network topology. We assume that there are two fibers, one in each direction on each network link. We set $F = 25$, $P = 5$, and $\theta = 50\%$. The lightpath requests arrive at the network according to a Poisson process. The traffic arrival rate is λ, and randomly distributed over the network. The request holding time is exponentially distributed with one unit as the mean value. All simulations are conducted with more than 50 thousands dynamic lightpath requests, and results are collected as the mean of multiple running instances of the simulation.

Ant Number and the Blocking Probability

As stated before, for each new arriving lightpath request, a number of ants are launched to explore the optimal (or the near-optimal) route. The number of ants to launch can affect the performance of the blocking probability in the network. As shown in Figure 9, when the network has heavy or light traffic load, the blocking probability can be reduced significantly by increasing the number of ants when the number of ants is no more

Figure 8. Weight field for the decision ant

Algorithm 2. Graph-based waveband assignment

```
if (Current node n is not the destination node) then
    Create the Band-Graph for current node
    Assign the weight in the Band-Graph using Equation 11
    Calculate the value of WT_{n,b} for each band b
    Update the weight field RT_b of the decision ant for each band b
    Move to the next node towards the destination
else
    Current node is the destination, change itself to backward ant
end if
```

than 100. This is because more ants can facilitate identify better paths. However, when the number of ants is large enough (e.g., > 100), the blocking performance almost does not change with the increasing of the number of ants. This is due to the convergence on the best found paths by the ants. In addition, we can also observe that the blocking probability can be improved more significantly by launching more ants in the case with heavy traffic load. This implies that reinforcing learning techniques could be helpful by adjusting the number of ants to be launched under different traffic load.

Comparison between Fixed Routing and Adaptive Routing

Based on our discussion on the calculation of the bounds for β, we can see that the upper bound of

$$\beta = 1 - 2 * \frac{P+1}{P+F} = 1 - 2 \times \frac{5+1}{5+25} = 0.456,$$

which means β should be no more than 0.6 to be cost-efficient. As shown in Figure 10, our algorithm can actually approach the lowest blocking probability when $\beta = 0.5$. When $\beta > 0.5$, further

increasing β (i.e., deploying more demultiplexers/multiplexers) does not help in reducing the blocking probability in the network since the major reason for the blocking is the shortage of wavelengths. A lower bound for β based on the simulation is 0.25 if the allowable blocking probability is 0.05. Hence, WBS network can save ports

Figure 9. Ant number and blocking probability

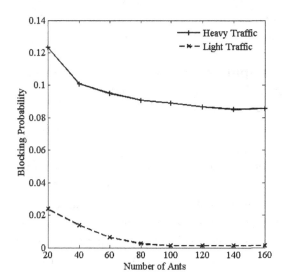

Figure 10. *Variation of the blocking probability for different values of β*

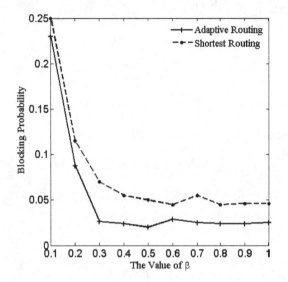

Figure 11. *Variation of the blocking probability for different load values*

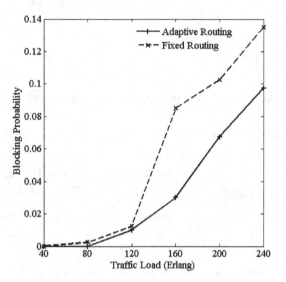

and achieve a low blocking probability when accommodating dynamic traffic requests.

Furthermore, it can be seen that the proposed adaptive routing scheme outperforms the fixed (shortest path) routing under various β and traffic load as shown in Figure 10 and Figure 11. This is because the adaptive routing efficiently takes the limited resources into consideration and the route selection based on the availability of demultiplexers/multiplexers and free wavelengths. The advantage of the proposed scheme is even more obvious when very limited resources are deployed (e.g., β < 0.3 and traffic load > 120).

Comparison between First-Fit and the Graph-Based Waveband Assignment Algorithm

To study the performance of the proposed graph-based waveband assignment algorithm (GWB), we compare the GWB and first-fit waveband assignment scheme (FF) together with adaptive or fixed (shortest path) routing schemes. Figure 12 shows the results of the comparison between the schemes using adaptive routing and GWB

Figure 12. *Variation of the blocking probability of the different schemes for different load values*

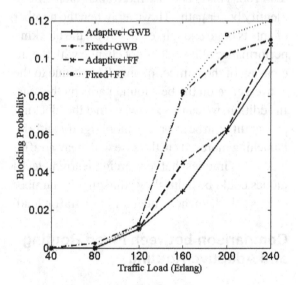

(Adaptive+GWB), and adaptive routing and FF (Adaptive+FF). From our simulations we note that the Adaptive+GWB scheme outperforms the Adaptive+FF scheme because the former scheme tries to balance and minimize the usage of demultiplexers/multiplexers, which can avoid

the exhaustion of demultiplexers/multiplexers at a single node thus reducing the blocking probability. For the same reason, we can see that the scheme using fixed routing and GWB (Fixed+GWB) outperforms the scheme using fixed routing and first-fit scheme Fixed+FF. Note that the advantage of GWB under fixed routing is even more significant since demultiplexers/multiplexers are more likely be unevenly used in the network with the fixed routing scheme.

CONCLUSION

The rapid increase in number of wavelengths per fiber, and the number of fibers per link increases the number of ports and complexity of the optical cross-connects (OXC) that switch these wavelengths. Waveband Switching (WBS) using multi-granular optical cross-connect (MG-OXC) can be used to reduce the increasing cost and complexity of optical cross-connects (OXC). In this paper, we have studied the dynamic WBS problem, and analyzed the Three-Layer and Single-Layer MG-OXC architecture. More specifically, we have analyzed the port counts of the MG-OXCs and the blocking probability when using the Three-Layer MG-OXC architecture. We derive upper and lower bounds on β, which is the ratio or the percentage of the number of bands that can be demultiplexed. Parameter β is important as it directly impacts the number of ports in the MG-OXC and the blocking probability. We have proposed an adaptive routing scheme that distributively selects optimum routing paths for dynamic traffic demands based on the ant optimization techniques. In addition, we have described a new graph-based waveband assignment algorithm. We have demonstrated the effectiveness of our routing and waveband assignment algorithms by using detailed simulations. Our simulation results have shown that our approach can reduce active ports and achieve lower blocking probability compared to the traditional fixed routing scheme and first-fit waveband assignment algorithm.

In our future work we plan to further study adaptive routing and dynamic waveband assignment in WBS networks as follows: (i) Analyzing the signaling protocols in WBS networks based on the GMPLS plane, (ii) Applying reinforcement learning techniques to further improve the intelligence of the ants for better routes discovery, and (iii) Study of the blocking and port usage performance in the WBS networks with proactive computation of the routes and periodical update of the paths.

REFERENCES

Bullock, P., Ward, C., & Wang, Q. (2003). Optimizing wavelength grouping granularity for optical add-drop network architectures. *Optical Fiber Conference (OFC)* (p. WH2).

Cao, X., Anand, V., & Qiao, C. (2003). Waveband switching in optical networks. *IEEE Communications Magazine*, *41*(4), 105–112. doi:10.1109/MCOM.2003.1193983.

Cao, X., Anand, V., & Qiao, C. (2004). *Multi-layer versus single-layer optical cross-connect architectures for waveband switching* (pp. 1830–1840). IEEE Infocom.

Cao, X., Anand, V., & Qiao, C. (2007). Waveband switching for dynamic traffic demands in multi-granular optical networks. *IEEE/ACM Transactions on Networking*, *15*(1), 957–968. doi:10.1109/TNET.2007.896234.

Cao, X., Anand, V., Xiong, Y., & Qiao, C. (2003). A study of waveband switching with multi-layer multi-granular optical cross-connects. *IEEE Journal on Selected Areas in Communications*, *21*(7), 1081–1095. doi:10.1109/JSAC.2003.815907.

Cao, X., Xiong, Y., Anand, V., & Qiao, C. (2002). Wavelength band switching in multi-granular all-optical networks. *OptiComm, 4874*, 198–210.

Caro, G., & Dorigo, M. (1998). Antnet: Distributed stigmergetic control for communications networks. *Journal of Artificial Intelligence*, 317-365.

Chen, L., Saengudomlert, P., & Modiano, E. (2004). *Optimal waveband switching in WDM networks* (pp. 1604–1608). IEEE ICC.

Chlamtac, I., Ganz, A., & Karmi, G. (1992). Lightpath communications: An approach to high bandwidth optical WANs. *IEEE Transactions on Communications, 40*(7), 1171–1182. doi:10.1109/26.153361.

Ciaramella, E. (2000). Introducing wavelength granularity to reduce the complexity of optical cross connects. *IEEE Photonics Technology Letters*, 699–701. doi:10.1109/68.849089.

Dorigo, M., Maniezzo, V., & Colorni, A. (1996). The ant system: Optimization by a colony of co-operating agents. *IEEE Transactions on Systems*, 1-13.

Dotaro, E. et al. (2002). Optical multi-granularity architectural framework.

Douville, R. et al. (2003). Extensions to generalized MPLS in support of waveband switching.

Escobar, H. E., & Marshall, L. R. (2002). All-optical wavelength band conversion enables new scalable and efficient optical network. *Optical Fiber Conference (OFC)* (p. WH2).

Garlick, R. M., & Barr, R. S. (2002). *Dynamic wavelength routing in WDM networks via ant colony optimization* (pp. 250–255). IEEE ANTS. doi:10.1007/3-540-45724-0_23.

Gerstel, O., Ramaswami, R., & Wang, W. (2000). Making use of a two stage multiplexing scheme in a WDM network. *Optical Fiber Conference (OFC)* (p. ThD1).

Harada, K., Shimizu, K., Kudou, T., & Ozeki, T. (1999). Hierarchical optical path cross-connect systems for large scale WDM networks. *Optical Fiber Conference (OFC)* (p. WM55).

Huiban, G., Perennes, S., & Syska, M. (2002). *Traffic grooming in WDM networks with multi-layer switches* (pp. 2896–2901). IEEE ICC. doi:10.1109/ICC.2002.997370.

Izmailov, R., Ganguly, S., Kleptsyn, V., & Varsou, A. (2003). *Non-uniform waveband hierarchy in hybrid optical networks* (pp. 1344–1354). IEEE Infocom.

Izmailov, R., Ganguly, S., Suemura, Y., Nishioka, I., Maeno, Y., & Araki, S. (2002). *Waveband routing in optical networks* (pp. 2727–2733). IEEE ICC.

Lee, M., Yu, J., Kim, Y., Kang, C., & Park, J. (2002). Design of hierarchical crossconnect WDM networks employing a two-stage multiplexing scheme of waveband and wavelength. *IEEE Journal on Selected Areas in Communications, 20*(1), 166–171. doi:10.1109/49.974670.

Li, M., & Ramamurthy, B. (2004). *A graph model for dynamic waveband switching in WDM mesh networks* (pp. 1821–1825). IEEE ICC. doi:10.1109/ICC.2004.1312822.

Li, M., & Ramamurthy, B. (2006). heterogeneous waveband switching in wavelength division multiplexed networks based on autonomous clustering architecture. [JoN]. *OSA Journal of Optical Networking, 5*(9), 667–680. doi:10.1364/JON.5.000667.

Li, M., Yao, W., & Ramamurthy, B. (2005). *Same-destination-intermediate grouping vs. End-to-end grouping for waveband switching in WDM mesh networks* (pp. 1807–1812). IEEE ICC.

Lingampalli, R., & Vengalam, P. (2002). Effect of wavelength and waveband grooming on all-optical networks with single layer photonic. *Optical Fiber Conference (OFC)* (p. ThP4).

Mukherjee, B. (2006). *Optical WDM Networks.* New York: Springer.

Ngo, S.-H., Jian, X., Le, V. T., & Horiguchi, S. (2006). Ant-based survivable routing in dynamic WDM networks with shared backup paths. *The Journal of Supercomputing*, 297–307. doi:10.1007/s11227-006-8299-9.

Ngo, S.-H., Jiang, X., Horiguchi, S., & Guo, M. (2004). Dynamic routing and wavelength assignment in WDM networks with ant-based agents. *International Conference on Embedded and Ubiquitous Computing (EUC)* (pp. 584-593).

Noirie, L., Gorgeuille, F., & Bisson, A. (2002). 32x10 Gbit/s DWDM metropolitan network demonstration with 10 waveband- ADMs and 155Km teralight metro fiber. *Optical Fiber Conference (OFC)* (p. ThH4).

Noirie, L., Vigoureux, M., & Dotaro, E. (2001). Impact of intermediate grouping on the dimensioning of multi-granularity optical networks. *Optical Fiber Conference (OFC)* (p. TuG3).

Ramaswami, R., & Sivarajan, K. N. (2002). *Optical networks: A practical perspective.* San Francisco: Morgan Kaufmann.

Schoonderwoerd, R., Holland, O., & Bruten, J. (1997). Ant-like agents for load balancing in telecommunications networks. *International Conference of Autonomous Agents* (pp. 209-216).

Todimala, A., & Ramamurthy, B. (2007). *Algorithms for intermediate waveband switching in optical WDM mesh networks* (pp. 21–25). IEEE Infocom. doi:10.1109/HSNW.2007.4290539.

Varma, S., & Jue, J. (2004). *Protection in multigranular waveband networks* (pp. 1759–1763). IEEE Globecom.

Wang, Y., & Cao, X. (2009). *A new hierarchical waveband assignment algorithm for multigranular optical networks* (pp. 1–6). ICCCN. doi:10.1109/ICCCN.2009.5235374.

Xu, D., Xiong, Y., Qiao, C., & Li, G. (2003). Trap avoidance and protection schemes in networks with shared risk links groups. *Journal of Lightwave Technology*, 2683–2693.

Yao, S., & Mukherjee, B. (2003). Design of hybrid waveband-switched networks with OEO traffic grooming. *Optical Fiber Conference* (p. WH3).

Yen, J. (1971). Finding the k shortest loopless paths in a network. *Management Science, 17*(11), 712–716. doi:10.1287/mnsc.17.11.712.

Zhu, K., Zang, H., & Mukherjee, B. (2003). A comprehensive study on next-generation optical grooming switches. *IEEE Journal on Selected Areas in Communications, 21*(7), 1173–1186. doi:10.1109/JSAC.2003.815683.

Glossary

Address (or IP Address): An object which was initially defined to be used as a "Locator" but in practice an "Address" combines both identification information and host attachment information.

Default Free Zone (DFZ): A portion of the Internet where involved routers maintain full routing tables (i.e., routes for all reachable destinations). In particular, routers in the DFZ are not configured with default routes.

Egress Tunnel Router (ETR): Denotes a functional entity responsible for handling encapsulated packets received from an ITR. Precisely, an ETR is responsible for de-capsulating received packets before forwarding them to their ultimate destinations.

Host: Refers to a device that can send and receive packets but, unlike a router, it does not forward packets.

Identifier: A topology-independent object bound to a node, one of its interfaces or even a software instance. An "Identifier" is generally structured as a "name", e.g., FQDN (Fully Qualified Domain Name) or URI (Unique Resource Identifier). "Identifier" objects must not be used for forwarding purposes. Early IP specification documents adopt the following definition: "name" (i.e., "Identifier") of a resource indicates "what" we seek, an "address" indicates "where" it is, and a "route" tells us "how to get there".

Ingress Tunnel Router (ITR): Denotes a functional entity responsible for encapsulating received packets (from a "Host") to an ETR (identified by an RLOC). The source is not aware of the presence of ITRs/ETRs in the forwarding path. An ITR is likely to be close to the source while the ETR is close to the ultimate destination.

IP Connectivity Provider (ICP): An administrative entity which offers IP connectivity service to customers. "Nodes" connected to a network owned by an "IP Connectivity Provider" can send and receive packets to/from destinations reachable in the Internet.

Locator: A topology-dependent object used to identify a topological attachment of a "Host" or an interface belonging to a "Host". A "Locator" is also referred to as host attachment information. A "Host" identified by an "Identifier" can be reached using a "Locator" as input to invoke the underlying IP transfer capabilities.

Node: Refers to a "Host" or a "Router".

Provider Assigned or Provider Aggregatable (PA): Refers to an address space belonging to an "IP Connectivity Provider". Addresses belonging to this space can be aggregated as part of the IP Connectivity Provider's routing advertisements.

Provider Independent (PI): Refers to an address space independent of any IP Connectivity Provider. This space meets the portability requirement of some networks (e.g., owned by administrative entities which want to avoid renumbering when re-homing for instance).

Router: Refers to a device that forwards packets at the network layer of the OSI (Open Systems Interconnection) model.

Routing Locator (RLOC): A flavor of "Locator". An RLOC is not assigned to a "Host" (or one of its interfaces) but it is used by intermediary nodes for forwarding purposes. The mapping between the actual host identification and an RLOC is not perceived by the "Host" or the application running on the "Host". The mapping function between the RLOC and "Identifiers" is part of the underlying routing and forwarding system.

Compilation of References

Li, T. (Ed.). (2011, February). Recommendation for a routing architecture.

(Kent, 2005) Kent, S. (2005, December). IP Encapsulating Security Payload (RFC4303). Retrieved from http://www.ietf.org

973. Project. (2006). *Website.* Retrieved from http://www.most.gov.cn/bstd/bstdbsfw/bstdfxzxk/bstdfxz973/bstdfxz973jg/200608/t20060810_35340.htm

Abley, J., Lindqvist, K., Davies, E., Black, B., & Gill, V. (2005, July). IPv4 multihoming practices and limitations.

Adan, J. (2006, December). Tunneled inter-domain routing (TIDR).

Adelin, A., Owezarski, P., & Gayraud, T. (2010). On the impact of monitoring router energy consumption for greening the Internet. *11th IEEE/ACM International Conference on Grid Computing-2010* (pp. 298-304). doi: 10.1109/GRID.2010.5697988

Advanced Network Technology Center at University of Oregon. (n.d.). *The routeviews project.* Retrieved from http://www.routeviews.org

Amaldi, E., Capone, A., Gianoli, L. G., & Mascetti, L. (2011). Energy management in IP traffic engineering with shortest path routing. *IEEE International Symposium on a World of Wireless, Mobile and Multimedia Networks-2011* (pp.1-6). doi: 10.1109/WoWMoM.2011.5986482

Antonov, V. (1995). BGP AS path metrics.

Applegate, D., & Cohen, E. (2003). Making intra-domain routing robust to changing and uncertain traffic demands: Understanding fundamental tradeoffs. *Conference on Applications, technologies, architectures, and protocols for computer communications* (pp. 313-324). doi: 10.1145/863955.863991

Arends, R., Austein, R., Larson, M., Massey, D., & Rose, S. (2005). Internet engineering task force. *DNS Security Introduction and Requirements.* AT&T. (n.d.). *U.S. network latency.* Retrieved from http://ipnetwork.bgtmo.ip.att.net/pws/network_delay.html

Arends, R., Austein, R., Larson, M., Massey, D., & Rose, S. (2005, March). Protocol modifications for the DNS security extensions (RFC 4035). Retrieved from http://www.ietf.org

Atkinson, R. (2011, February). *ILNP Concept of Operations.*

Atkinson, R. J., & Bhatti, S. N. (2012). *ILNP architectural description.* Retrieved from http://www.ietf.org

Atkinson, R., Bhatti, S., & Hailes, S. (2009). ILNP: Mobility, multi-homing, localised addressing and security through naming. *Telecommunication Systems, 42*(3-4), 273–291. doi:10.1007/s11235-009-9186-5.

Aura, T. (2005, March). Cryptographically generated addresses (CGA) (RFC3972). Retrieved from http://www.ietf.org

Awduche, D. O., Berger, L., Srinivasan, V., Li, T., & Gan, D. H. (2001). RSVP-TE: Extensions to RSVP for LSP tunnels. Retrieved Ocotber 22, 2012, from http://tools.ietf.org/html/rfc3209

Bagnulo, M., García-Martínez, A., & Azcorra, A. (2005, April). Efficient security for ipv6 multi-homing. *ACM SIGCOMM Computer Communication Review, 35.*

Baker, F., & Savola, P. (2004, March). Ingress filtering for multihomed networks (RFC 3704). Retrieved from http://www.ietf.org/rfc/rfc3704.txt

Balakrishnan, H., Lakshminarayanan, K., Ratnasamy, S., Shenker, S., Stoica, I., & Walfish, M. (2004, September). A layered naming architecture for the internet. In *Proc. ACM SIGCOMM*.

Baliga, J., Hinton, K., & Tucker, R. S. (2007). Energy consumption of the Internet. *Joint International Conference on Optical Internet 2007 and the 2007 32nd Australian Conference on Optical Fibre Technology-2007* (pp. 1 - 3). doi: 10.1109/COINACOFT.2007.4519173

Ballani, H., Francis, P., Tuan, C., & Wang, J. (2009). Making routers last longer with ViAggre. In *Proceedings of NSDI*.

Bao, C., Huitema, C., Bagnulo, M., Boucadair, M., & Li, X. (2010, October). IPv6 addressing of IPv4/IPv6 translators (RFC6052). Retrieved from http://www.ietf.org

BGP. (n.d.). *BGP routing table analysis report*. Retrieved from http://bgp.potaroo.net

BGP. (n.d.). *Border gateway protocol*. Retrieved from http://tools.ietf.org/html/rfc4271

BGP4.net. (n.d.). *IPv4 route servers*. Retrieved from http://www.bgp4.net/rs

Bianzino, A. P., Chaudet, C., Moretti, S., Rougier, J. L., Chiaraviglio, L., & Rouzic, E. L. (2012a, June). Enabling sleep mode in backbone IP-networks: A criticality-driven tradeoff. In *Proc. of the ICC Workshop on Green Communications and Networking, Ottawa, Canada*.

Bianzino, A. P., Chiaraviglio, L., Mellia, M., & Rougier, J.-L. (2012). GRiDA: Green distributed algorithm for energy-efficient IP backbone networks. *Computer Networks*, *56*(14), 3219–3232. doi:10.1016/j.comnet.2012.06.011.

Bolla, R., Bruschi, R., Davoli, F., & Cucchietti, F. (2011). Energy efficiency in the future Internet: A survey of existing approaches and trends in energy-aware fixed network infrastructures. *IEEE Communications Surveys & Tutorials*, *13*(2), 223–244. doi:10.1109/SURV.2011.071410.00073.

Bonaventure, O. (2011, November). Recent Internet research results.

Bonaventure, O., De Cnodder, S., Haas, J., Quoitin, B., & White, R. (2003). Controlling the redistribution of BGP routes.

Bos, H., Jonsson, E., Djambazova, E., Dimitrov, K., Ioannidis, S., Kirda, E., & Kruegel, C. (2009, March). Anticipating security threats of a future internet (Whitepaper). EU FP7 Project FORWARD.

Bradner, S., & Mankin, A. (1995, January). The recommendation for the IP next generation protocol.

Brim, S., Chiappa, N., Farinacci, D., Fuller, V., Lewis, D., & Meyer, D. (2008). *LISP-CONS: A content distribution overlay network service for LISP*. Retrieved from http://tools.ietf.org/html/draft-fuller-lisp-cons-04

Bullock, P., Ward, C., & Wang, Q. (2003). Optimizing wavelength grouping granularity for optical add-drop network architectures. *Optical Fiber Conference (OFC)* (p. WH2).

Bush, R., & Mayer, D. (2002, December). Some internet architectural guidelines and philosophy.

Bu, T., Gao, L., & Towsley, D. (2002). *On routing table growth*. INFOCOM.

Bu, T., Gao, L., & Towsley, D. (2004). On characterizing BGP routing table growth. *Computer Networks*, *45*(1), 45–54. doi:10.1016/j.comnet.2004.02.003.

Caesar, M., Condie, T., Kannan, J., Lakshminarayanan, K., Stoica, I., & Shenker, S. (2006). ROFL: Routing on Flat Labels. In *Proc. of the ACM SIGCOMM*.

CAIDA. (2012). *Website*. Retrieved from http://www.caida.org/home/

Cain, B. (2002). *Auto aggregation method for IP prefix/length pairs*. Retrieved from http://www.freepatentsonline.com/6401130.html

Callon, R. W. (1990). *Use of OSI IS-IS for routing in TCP/IP and dual environments*. Retrieved October 22, 2012, from http://tools.ietf.org/html/rfc1195.html

Cao, X., Anand, V., & Qiao, C. (2003). Waveband switching in optical networks. *IEEE Communications Magazine*, *41*(4), 105–112. doi:10.1109/MCOM.2003.1193983.

Cao, X., Anand, V., & Qiao, C. (2004). *Multi-layer versus single-layer optical cross-connect architectures for waveband switching* (pp. 1830–1840). IEEE Infocom.

Cao, X., Anand, V., & Qiao, C. (2007). Waveband switching for dynamic traffic demands in multigranular optical networks. *IEEE/ACM Transactions on Networking*, *15*(1), 957–968. doi:10.1109/TNET.2007.896234.

Cao, X., Anand, V., Xiong, Y., & Qiao, C. (2003). A study of waveband switching with multi-layer multi-granular optical cross-connects. *IEEE Journal on Selected Areas in Communications*, *21*(7), 1081–1095. doi:10.1109/JSAC.2003.815907.

Cao, X., Xiong, Y., Anand, V., & Qiao, C. (2002). Wavelength band switching in multi-granular all-optical networks. *OptiComm*, *4874*, 198–210.

Caro, G., & Dorigo, M. (1998). Antnet: Distributed stigmergetic control for communications networks. *Journal of Artificial Intelligence*, 317-365.

Carpenter, B. (1996, June). Architectural principles of the Internet.

Carpenter, B., Atkinson, R., & Flinck, H. (2010, May). Renumbering still needs work.

Carpenter, B., Boucadair, M., Halpern, J., Jiang, S., & Moore, K. (2011, October). A generic referral object for Internet entities.

Castineyra, I., Chiappa, N., & Steenstrup, M. (1996, August). The Nimrod routing architecture.

Chabarek, J., Sommers, J., Barford, P., Estan, C., Tsiang, D., & Wright, S. (2008). Power awareness in network design and routing. *The 27th IEEE Conference on Computer Communications-2008* (pp.457-465). doi: 10.1109/INFOCOM.2008.93

Chandra, R., Traina, P., & Li, T. (1997). BGP Communities Attribute. ISSN 2070-1721

Chen, E., & Bates, T. (1996). Destination Preference Attribute for BGP.

Chen, J., Dong, P., Zhang, H., & Zeng, Y. (2011). A routing scalability model for core-edge separation internet with hybrid routing. *IEEE Communications Letters*, *10*(15), 1142–1144. doi:10.1109/LCOMM.2011.080811.111285.

Chen, L., Saengudomlert, P., & Modiano, E. (2004). *Optimal waveband switching in WDM networks* (pp. 1604–1608). IEEE ICC.

Chiappa, N. (1991). *A new IP routing and addressing architecture*. Retrieved from http://ana-3.lcs.mit.edu/~jnc/nimrod/overview.txt

Chiaraviglio, L., Mellia, M., & Neri, F. (2009). Energy-aware backbone networks: A case study. *IEEE International Conference on Communications Workshops-2009* (pp.1-5). doi: 10.1109/ICCW.2009.5208038

Chlamtac, I., Ganz, A., & Karmi, G. (1992). Lightpath communications: An approach to high bandwidth optical WANs. *IEEE Transactions on Communications*, *40*(7), 1171–1182. doi:10.1109/26.153361.

Chu, H.-W., Cheung, C.-C., Ho, K.-H., & Wang, N. (2011). Green MPLS traffic engineering. *Australasian Telecommunication Networks and Applications Conference*, *2011*, 1–4. doi: doi:10.1109/ATNAC.2011.6096644.

Ciaramella, E. (2000). Introducing wavelength granularity to reduce the complexity of optical cross connects. *IEEE Photonics Technology Letters*, 699–701. doi:10.1109/68.849089.

Cisco. (2012). *Website*. Retrieved October 22, 2012, from http://newsroom.cisco.com/press-release-content?type=webcontent&articleId=888280

Cisco, I. O. S. (2007). *Configuration fundamentals guide configuring cisco discovery protocol* (pp. FC-277–FC-280).

Cittadini, L., Muehlbauer, W., Uhlig, S., Bush, R., Francois, P., & Maennel, O. (2010). Evolution of Internet address space deaggregation: Myths and reality. *IEEE Journal on Selected Areas in Communications*, *28*(8), 1238–1249. doi:10.1109/JSAC.2010.101002.

Clark, D. et al. (1991, Decmber). *Towards the future internet architecture*.

Cuda, D., et al. (2011). *Getting routers out of the core: Building an optical wide area network with multipaths*. Retrieved from http://arxiv.org/PS_cache/arxiv/pdf/1110/1110.1245v1.pdf

Deering, S. (1996). *The map & encap scheme for scalable IPv4 routing with portable site prefixes*. Retrieved from http://arneill-py.sacramento.ca.us/ipv6mh/map-n-encap.pdf

Deering, S., Estrin, D., Farinacci, D., Jacobson, V., Liu, C. G., Wei, L., & Helmy, A. (1995). Protocol independent multicast (pim): Motivation and architecture.

Delauney-Triangulation. (n.d.). In *Wikipedia*. Retrieved from http://en.wikipedia.org/wiki/Delaunay_triangulation

Dhamdhere, A., & Dovrolis, C. (2006). ISP and egress path selection for multihomed networks. *25th IEEE International Conference on Computer Communications* (pp. 1-12). doi: 10.1109/INFOCOM.2006.280

Dhamdhere, A., & Dovrolis, C. (2008). Ten years in the evolution of the internet ecosystem. *8th ACM SIGCOMM conference on Internet measurement* (pp. 183-196). doi: 10.1145/1452520.1452543

Dhamdhere, A., & Dovrolis, C. (2011). Twelve years in the evolution of the internet ecosystem.[TON]. *IEEE/ACM Transactions on Networking, 19*(5), 1420–1433. doi:10.1109/TNET.2011.2119327.

Dong, P., Qin, Y., & Zhang, H. (2007). Research on universal network supporting pervasive services[in Chinese]. *Acta Electronica Sinica, 35*(4), 599–606.

Dong, P., Wang, H., Qin, Y., Zhang, H., & Kuo, S.-K. (2009). *Evaluation of scalable routing architecture based on locator/identifier separation.* IEEE Globecom. doi:10.1109/GLOCOMW.2009.5360746.

Donnet, B., Iannone, L., & Bonaventure, O. (2008). Interdomain traffic engineering in a locator/identifier separation context. In *Proc. of Internet Network Management Workshop 2008 (INM)*(pp. 1-6).

Dorigo, M., Maniezzo, V., & Colorni, A. (1996). The ant system: Optimization by a colony of cooperating agents. *IEEE Transactions on Systems*, 1-13.

Dotaro, E. et al. (2002). Optical multi-granularity architectural framework.

Douville, R. et al. (2003). Extensions to generalized MPLS in support of waveband switching.

Draves, R., King, C., Venkatachary, S., & Zill, B. D. (1999). Constructing optimal IP routing tables. In Proceedings of IEEE INFOCOM..

Elmokashfi, A., Kvalbein, A., & Dovrolis, C. (2010). On the scalability of BGP: The role of topology growth. *IEEE Journal on Selected Areas in Communications, 28*(8), 1250–1261. doi:10.1109/JSAC.2010.101003.

Escobar, H. E., & Marshall, L. R. (2002). All-optical wavelength band conversion enables new scalable and efficient optical network. *Optical Fiber Conference (OFC)* (p. WH2).

Farinacci, D. Fuller, Oran, V., D., Meyer, D., & Brim, S. (2012). *Locator/ID Separation Protocol (LISP).* Retrieved from http://www.ietf.org

Farinacci, D., Fuller, V., & Meyer, D. (2011). *LISP alternative topology (LISP-ALT).* Retrieved from http://tools.ietf.org/html/draft-fuller-lisp-alt-10

Farinacci, D., Fuller, V., Meyer, D., & Lewis, D. (2010, October). Locator/ID Separation Protocol (LISP).

Farinacci, D., Fuller, V., Meyer, D., & Lewis, D. (2012). *LISP alternative topology (LISP+ALT).* Retrieved from http://www.ietf.org

Farrel, A., Vasseur, J. P., & Ash, J. (2006). A path computation element (PCE)-based architecture (RFC 4655). Retrieved October 22, 2012, from http://www.ietf.org/rfc/rfc4655.txt

Feamster, N., Balakrishnan, H., Rexford, J., Shaikh, A., & Van Der Merwe, J. (2004). The case for separating routing from routers. In *ACM SIGCOMM Workshop on Future Directions in Network Architecture*.

Feamster, N., Borkenhagen, J., & Rexford, J. (2003). Guidelines for interdomain traffic engineering. *ACM SIGCOMM Computer Communications Review, 33*(5), 19–30. doi:10.1145/963985.963988.

Floyd, S. (2002, November). General architectural and policy considerations.

Fonseca, R., Porter, R., Katz, R., Shenker, S., & Stoica, I. (2005). *IP options are not an option.* Retrieved from http://www.eecs.berkeley.edu/Pubs/TechRpts/2005/EECS-2005-24.html

Ford, A., Raiciu, C., Handley, M., Barre, S., & Iyengar, J. R. (2011). Architectural guidelines for multipath TCP development (RFC 6182). Retrieved from http://www.ietf.org

Ford, M., Boucadair, M., Durand, A., Levis, P., & Roberts, P. (2011, June). Issues with IP address sharing.

Francis, P., Xu, X., Ballani, H., Jen, D., Raszuk, R., & Zhang, L. (2012). *FIB Suppression with virtual aggregation*. Internet Draft. Retrieved from http://tools.ietf.org/html/draft-ietf-grow-va-06

Frejborg, P. (2011, July). Hierarchical IPv4 framework (RFC 6306). Retrieved from http://www.ietf.org/rfc/rfc6306.txt

Fuller, V. (2006). Scaling issues with routing+multihoming. In *Proceedings of the Sixty Seventh Internet Engineering Task Force*. Retrieved from http://www.ietf.org/proceedings/67/slides/v6ops-13.pdf

Fuller, V., & Farinacci, D. (2012). *LISP map server interface*. Retrieved from http://tools.ietf.org/html/draft-ietf-lisp-ms-16

Fuller, V., & Li, T. (2006, August). Classless inter-domain routing (CIDR): The internet address assignment and aggregation plan.

Fuller, V., Farinacci, D., Meyer, D., & Lewis, D. (2010, October). LISP alternative topology (LISP+ALT). Internet Engineering Task Force.

Fuller, V., Lewis, D., & Farinacci, D. (2012, March). LISP delegated database tree. Retrieved from http://www.ietf.org

Fuller, V., Li, T., Yu, J., & Varadhan, K. (1993). *Classless inter-domain routing (CIDR): an address assignment and aggregation strategy*. Retrieved from http://www.ietf.org/rfc/rfc1519.txt

Gao, L., & Rexford, J. (2001). Stable internet routing without global coordination. *IEEE/ACM Transactions on Networking, 9*(6), 681–692. doi:10.1109/90.974523.

Gao, R., Dovrolis, C., & Zegura, E. W. (2005). *Interdomain ingress traffic engineering through optimized AS-path prepending. 4th IFIP-TC6 international conference on Networking Technologies, Services, and Protocols; Performance of Computer and Communication Networks* (pp. 647–658). Mobile and Wireless Communication Systems.

García-Martínez, A., Bagnulo, M., & van Beijnum, I. (2010, September). The shim6 architecture for ipv6 multihoming. *IEEE Communications Magazine*. doi:10.1109/MCOM.2010.5560599.

Garlick, R. M., & Barr, R. S. (2002). *Dynamic wavelength routing in WDM networks via ant colony optimization* (pp. 250–255). IEEE ANTS. doi:10.1007/3-540-45724-0_23.

Gelenbe, E., & Silvestri, S. (2009). Reducing power consumption in wired networks. *24th International Symposium on Computer and Information Sciences-2009* (pp.292-297). doi: 10.1109/ISCIS.2009.5291829

Gerstel, O., Ramaswami, R., & Wang, W. (2000). Making use of a two stage multiplexing scheme in a WDM network. *Optical Fiber Conference (OFC)* (p. ThD1).

Gross, P., & Almquist, P. (1992, November). IESG deliberations on routing and addressing.

Gupta, M., & Singh, S. (2003, August). Greening of the Internet. In *Proceedings of the 2003 conference on Applications, technologies, architectures, and protocols for computer communications* (pp. 19-26). ACM. doi: 10.1145/863955.863959

Gurtov, A. (2008). Host identity protocol (HIP) – Towards the secure mobile internet.

Haldane, J. B. S. (1928). *Being the right size*. Retrieved on May 12, 2008, from http://irl.cs.ucla.edu/papers/right-size.html

Handley, M., Vicisano, L., Kouvelas, I., & Speakman, T. (2007). Bidirectional protocol independent multicast (BIDIR-PIM). Retrieved October 22, 2012, from http://tools.ietf.org/rfc/rfc5015.txt

Handley, M. (2006, July). Why the Internet only just works. *BT Technology Journal, 24*(3). doi:10.1007/s10550-006-0084-z.

Harada, K., Shimizu, K., Kudou, T., & Ozeki, T. (1999). Hierarchical optical path cross-connect systems for large scale WDM networks. *Optical Fiber Conference (OFC)* (p. WM55).

Heiner, H. (2010, September). Topology aggregating routing architecture.

Herrin, W. (2008). *Opportunistic topological aggregation in the RIB-FIB calculation?* Retrieved from http://psg.com/lists/rrg/2008/msg01880.html

Herrin, W. (2008). *Tunneling route reduction protocol (TRRP)*. Retrieved from http://bill.herrin.us/network/trrp.html

Hinden, R. (1996). New Scheme for Internet Routing and Addressing (ENCAPS) for IPNG. *RFC 1955*. Retrieved from http://www.ietf.org/rfc/rfc1955.txt

HIPL. (n.d.). *Website*. Retrieved from http://hipl.hiit.fi/hipl/release/

Honda, M., Nishida, Y., Raiciu, C., Greenhalgh, A., Handley, M., & Tokuda, H. (2011, November). Is it still possible to extend TCP? In *Internet Measurement Conference*.

Hopps, C. E. (2000). *Analysis of an equal-cost multi-path algorithm*. Retrieved October 22, 2012, from http://tools.ietf.org/html/rfc2992

Houston, G. (2001). Commentary on inter-domain routing in the Internet. ISSN 2070-1721.

Huiban, G., Perennes, S., & Syska, M. (2002). *Traffic grooming in WDM networks with multi-layer switches* (pp. 2896–2901). IEEE ICC. doi:10.1109/ICC.2002.997370.

Huston, G. (2001, December). Commentary on inter-domain routing in the Internet.

Huston, G. (2011, November). *BGP growth revisited*. Retrieved from http://www.potaroo.net/ispcol/2011-11/bgp2011.pdf

Huston, G. (2011, November). *The BGP world is flat*. Retrieved from http://www.potaroo.net/ispcol/2011-12/flat.pdf

Huston, G. (2012). *Growth of the BGP table - 1994 to present*. Retrieved from http://bgp.potaroo.net/

Iannone, L., & Bonaventure, O. (2007). On the cost of caching locator/ID mappings. In *Proceedings of the CoNext Conference*.

Iannone, L., Saucez, D., & Bonaventure, O. (2012, March). Lisp map-versioning. Retrieved from http://www.ietf.org

Iannone, L., & Levä, T. (2010, May). Modeling the economics of Loc/ID split for the future internet. In *Towards the Future Internet – Emerging Trends from the European Research*. IOS Press.

Idzikowski, F., Chiaraviglio, L., & Portoso, F. (2012). Optimal design of green multi-layer core networks. In *Proceedings of the 3rd ACM International Conference on Future Energy Systems: Where Energy, Computing and Communication Meet-2012* (Art. 15). doi: 10.1145/2208828.2208843

IETF. (2011). The internet routing overlay network (IRON) (RFC6179). Retrieved from http://tools.ietf.org/html/rfc6179

IETF. (2012). *IETF locator/ID separation protocol*. Retrieved from http://datatracker.ietf.org/wg/lisp/

IETF. (2012). *IRTF routing research group*. Retrieved from http://tools.ietf.org/group/irtf/trac/wiki/RoutingResearchGroup

Igure, V., & Williams, R. (2008, 1st Quarter). Taxonomies of attacks and vulnerabilities in computer systems. *IEEE Communications Surveys & Tutorials, 10*(1).

Instability Report, B. G. P. (n.d.). *Website*. Retrieved from http://bgpupdates.potaroo.net/instability/bgpupd.html

Internet Architecture Board (IAB). (1992, July). IP Version 7.

IRTF Routing Research Group. (n.d.). *Website*. Retrieved from http://www.irtf.org/charter?gtype=rg&group=rrg

isc.org. (n.d.). *Website*. Retrieved from https://www.isc.org

Iyengar, J. R., Amer, P. D., & Stewart, R. (2006). Concurrent multipath transfer using SCTP multihoming over independent end-to-end paths. *IEEE/ACM Transactions on Networking, 14*(5), 951–964. doi:10.1109/TNET.2006.882843.

Izmailov, R., Ganguly, S., Kleptsyn, V., & Varsou, A. (2003). *Non-uniform waveband hierarchy in hybrid optical networks* (pp. 1344–1354). IEEE Infocom.

Izmailov, R., Ganguly, S., Suemura, Y., Nishioka, I., Maeno, Y., & Araki, S. (2002). *Waveband routing in optical networks* (pp. 2727–2733). IEEE ICC.

Jakab, L., Cabellos-Aparicio, A., Coras, F., Saucez, D., & Bonaventure, O. (2010). LISP-TREE: A DNS hierarchy to support the LISP mapping system. *IEEE Journal on Selected Areas in Communications, 28*(8), 1332–1343. doi:10.1109/JSAC.2010.101011.

Jen, D., Meisel, M., Massey, D., Wang, L., Zhang, B., & Zhang, L. (2007, November). APT: A practical transit mapping service.

Jen, D., Meisel, M., Massey, D., Wang, L., Zhang, B., & Zhang, L. (2008). *APT: A practical tunneling architecture for routing scalability.* Technical Report No. 080004. UCLA. Retrieved from http://www.cs.ucla.edu/~meisel/apt-tech.pdf

Jen, D., Meisel, M., Yan, H., Massey, D., Wang, L., Zhang, B., & Zhang, L. (2008). Towards a future internet routing architecture: Arguments for separating edges from transit core. In *Proceedings of ACM workshop on Hot Topics in Networks.*

Jiang, W., & Prasanna, V. K. (2012). Energy-efficient Internet infrastructure. In Zomaya, A. Y., & Lee, Y. C. (Eds.), *Energy-efficient distributed computing systems.* John Wiley & Sons, Inc. doi:10.1002/9781118342015.ch20.

Kandula, S., Katabi, D., Davie, B., & Charny, A. (2005). Walking the tightrope: Responsive yet stable traffic engineering. *Conference on Applications, technologies, architectures, and protocols for computer communications* (pp. 253-264). doi: 10.1145/1080091.1080122

Kent, S., & Seo, K. (2005, December). Security architecture for the internet protocol (RFC 4301). Retrieved from http://www.ietf.org/rfc/rfc4301.txt

Kent, S., Lynn, C., & Seo, K. (2000). Secure border gateway protocol. *IEEE Journal on Selected Areas in Communications, 18*(4). doi:10.1109/49.839934.

Keynote Systems. (n.d.). *Internet health report.* Retrieved from http://www.internethealthreport.com/

Khare, V. et al. (2009, October). Evolution towards global routing scalability. *IEEE Journal on Selected Areas in Communications, 28*(8).

Kilper, D. C., Atkinson, G., Korotky, S. K., Goyal, S., Vetter, P., Suvakovic, D., & Blume, O. (2011). Power trends in communication networks. *IEEE Journal on Selected Topics in Quantum Electronics, 17*(2), 275–284. doi:10.1109/JSTQE.2010.2074187.

Kohler, E., Handley, M., & Floyd, S. (2006, March). Datagram congestion control protocol (DCCP).

Krioukov, D., Claffy, K. C., Fall, K., & Brady, A. (2007, July). On compact routing for the Internet. *ACM SIGCOMM CCR, 37*(3), 43–52. doi:10.1145/1273445.1273450.

Krishnan, S., Thaler, D., & Hoagland, J. (2011, April). Security concerns with IP tunneling (RFC 6169). Retrieved from http://www.ietf.org/rfc/rfc6169.txt

Le Roux, J. L., Vasseur, J. P., & Boyle, J. (2005). *Requirements for inter-area MPLS traffic engineering.* Retrieved October 22, 2012, from http://tools.ietf.org/html/rfc4105

Lear, E. (2012). *NERD: A not-so-novel EID to RLOC database.* Retrieved from http://www.ietf.org

Lee, M., Yu, J., Kim, Y., Kang, C., & Park, J. (2002). Design of hierarchical crossconnect WDM networks employing a two-stage multiplexing scheme of waveband and wavelength. *IEEE Journal on Selected Areas in Communications, 20*(1), 166–171. doi:10.1109/49.974670.

Li, L., Alderson, D., Willinger, W., & Doyle, J. (2004). A first-principles approach to understanding the Internet's router-level topology. In *Proceedings of ACM SIGCOMM.*

Li, T. (2007, July). Design goals for scalable internet routing (RFC6227). Retrieved from http://www.ietf.org

Li, T. (2009). *Preliminary recommendation for a routing architecture.* Retrieved from http://tools.ietf.org/html/draft-irtf-rrg-recommendation-02

Li, T. (2011). Internet research task force. *RFC 6115: Recommendation for a Routing Architecture.*

Li, T. (2011). Recommendation for a routing architecture (RFC 6115). Retrieved from http://www.ietf.org

Li, T. (2011, May). Design goals for scalable internet routing.

Li, M., & Ramamurthy, B. (2004). *A graph model for dynamic waveband switching in WDM mesh networks* (pp. 1821–1825). IEEE ICC. doi:10.1109/ICC.2004.1312822.

Li, M., & Ramamurthy, B. (2006). heterogeneous waveband switching in wavelength division multiplexed networks based on autonomous clustering architecture. [JoN]. *OSA Journal of Optical Networking*, 5(9), 667–680. doi:10.1364/JON.5.000667.

Li, M., Yao, W., & Ramamurthy, B. (2005). *Same-destination-intermediate grouping vs. End-to-end grouping for waveband switching in WDM mesh networks* (pp. 1807–1812). IEEE ICC.

Lingampalli, R., & Vengalam, P. (2002). Effect of wavelength and waveband grooming on all-optical networks with single layer photonic. *Optical Fiber Conference (OFC)* (p. ThP4).

LISP4. (n.d.). *Website*. Retrieved from http://www.lisp4.net/

Luo, H. B., Qin, Y. J., & Zhang, H. K. (2009). A DHT-based Identifier-to-locator mapping approach for a scalable internet. *IEEE Transactions on Parallel and Distributed Systems*, 20(12), 1790–1802. doi:10.1109/TPDS.2009.30.

Luo, H., Zhang, H., & Qiao, C. (2011). Efficient mobility support by indirect mapping innetworks with locator/identifier separation. *IEEE Transactions on Vehicular Technology*, 60(5), 2265–2279. doi:10.1109/TVT.2011.2152867.

Luo, H., Zhang, H., & Zukerman, M. (2011). Decoupling the design of identifier-to-locator mapping services from identifiers. *Computer Networks*, 55(4), 959–974. doi:10.1016/j.comnet.2010.12.009.

Luo, J., Ye, D., Xu, L., & Fan, M. (2009). A survey of multicast routing protocols for mobile ad-hoc networks. *IEEE Communications Surveys & Tutorials*, 11(1), 78–91. doi:10.1109/SURV.2009.090107.

Maino, F., Ermagan, V., Cabellos, A., Saucez, D., & Bonaventure, O. (2012, March). LISP-security (LIS-SEC).

Massey, D., Wang, L., Zhang, B., & Zhang, L. (2007, August). A scalable routing system design for future Internet. In *Proceedings of the ACM SIGCOMM Workshop on IPv6 and the Future of the Internet*.

Mathy, L., & Iannone, L. (2008). LISP-DHT: Towards a DHT to Map Identifiers onto Locators. *In Proc. of the ACM ReArch Conference.*

Medina, A., Taft, N., Salamatian, K., Bhattacharyya, S., & Diot, C. (2002). Traffic matrix estimation: Existing techniques and new directions. *ACM SIGCOMM Computer Communication Reviews*, 32(4), 161–174. doi:10.1145/964725.633041.

Menth, M., Hartmann, M., & Klein, D. (2010, April). Global locator, local locator, and identifier split (GLI-Split). Technical Report No. 470, University of Wuerzburg.

Meyer, D., Zhang, L., & Fall, K. (2007). Internet engineering task force. *RFC 4984: Report from the IAB Workshop on Routing and Addressing.*

Meyer, D., Zhang, L., & Fall, K. (2007). Report from the IAB Workshop on Routing and Addressing (RFC 4984). Retrieved from http://www.ietf.org

Meyer, D. (2008, March). The locator identifier separation protocol (LISP). *Internet Protocol Journal*, 11(1), 23–36.

Moore, K. (2002). On the use of HTTP as a substrate.

Morris, R., Kohler, E., Jannotti, J., & Kaashoek, M. F. (1999). The click modular router. *SIGOPS Operating Systems Review*, 33(5), 217–231. doi:10.1145/319344.319166.

Moskowitz, R., & Nikander, P. (2006, May). *Host Identity Protocol (HIP) Architecture* (RFC 4423). Retrieved from http://www.ietf.org

Moskowitz, R., Nikander, P., Jokela, P., & Henderson, T. (2008). Host identity protocol (RFC 5201). Retrieved from http://www.ietf.org

Moy, J. (1997). *OSPF version 2*. Retrieved October 22, 2012, from http://tools.ietf.org/html/rfc2178

Moy, J. (1998). *OSPF version 2*. Retrieved from http://www.ietf.org/rfc/rfc2328.txt

MRTD. The multi-threaded routing toolkit. (n.d.). *Website*. Retrieved from http://mrt.sourceforge.net/

Mukherjee, B. (2006). *Optical WDM Networks*. New York: Springer.

Narten, T. (2010, February). On the scalability of Internet routing.

Net-Patricia Perl Module. (n.d.). *Website*. Retrieved from http://search.cpan.org/dist/Net-Patricia/

Ngo, S.-H., Jiang, X., Horiguchi, S., & Guo, M. (2004). Dynamic routing and wavelength assignment in WDM networks with ant-based agents. *International Conference on Embedded and Ubiquitous Computing (EUC)* (pp. 584-593).

Ngo, S.-H., Jian, X., Le, V. T., & Horiguchi, S. (2006). Ant-based survivable routing in dynamic WDM networks with shared backup paths. *The Journal of Supercomputing*, 297–307. doi:10.1007/s11227-006-8299-9.

Noirie, L., Gorgeuille, F., & Bisson, A. (2002). 32x10 Gbit/s DWDM metropolitan network demonstration with 10 waveband- ADMs and 155Km teralight metro fiber. *Optical Fiber Conference (OFC)* (p. ThH4).

Noirie, L., Vigoureux, M., & Dotaro, E. (2001). Impact of intermediate grouping on the dimensioning of multi-granularity optical networks. *Optical Fiber Conference (OFC)* (p. TuG3).

Nordmark, E., & Bagnulo, M. (2009). Shim6: Level 3 multihoming shim protocol for IPv6 (RFC 5533). Retrieved from http://www.ietf.org

Nordmark, E., Bagnulo, M., & Levy-Abegnoli, E. (2012, May). FCFS SAVI: First- come, first-served source address validation improvement for locally assigned IPv6 addresses (RFC 6620). Retrieved from http://www.ietf.org/rfc/rfc6620.txt

O'Dell, M. (1997). *GSE - An alternate addressing architecture for IPv6*. Retrieved from http://tools.ietf.org/html/draft-ietf-ipngwg-gseaddr-00

Oliveira, R., Pei, D., Willinger, W., Zhang, B., & Zhang, L. (2010). The (in) completeness of the observed internet AS-level structure. *IEEE/ACM Transactions on Networking*, *18*(1), 109–122. doi:10.1109/TNET.2009.2020798.

Pelsser, C., Maennel, O., Mohapatra, P., Bush, R., & Patel, K. (2011, March). *Route flap damping made usable*. Passive and Active Measurement (PAM).

Quoitin, B., Iannone, L., de Launois, C., & Bonaventure, O. (2007, August). Evaluating the benefits of the locator/identifier separation. In the *2nd ACM/IEEE workshop on mobility in the evolving internet architecture* (mobiarch'07).

Quoitin, B., Pelsser, C., Bonaventure, O., & Uhlig, S. (2005). A performance evaluation of BGP-based traffic engineering. *International Journal of Network Management*, *15*(3), 177–191. doi:10.1002/nem.559.

Quoitin, B., Pelsser, C., Swinnen, L., Bonaventure, O., & Uhlig, S. (2003). Interdomain traffic engineering with BGP. *IEEE Communications Magazine*, *41*(5), 122–128. doi:10.1109/MCOM.2003.1200112.

Quoitin, B., & Uhlig, S. (2005). Modeling the routing of an autonomous system with C-BGP. *IEEE Network*, *19*(6), 12–19. doi:10.1109/MNET.2005.1541716.

Raina, G., Towsley, D., & Wischik, D. (2005). Part II: Control theory for buffer sizing. *SIGCOMM Computer Communications Review*, *35*(3), 79–82. doi:10.1145/1070873.1070885.

Raman, S., Jain, S., & Raina, G. (2012). Feedback, transport layer protocols and buffer sizing. In *Proceedings of the 11th International Conference on Networks* (pp. 125-131). ISBN: 978-1-61208-183-0.

Raman, S., Venkat, B., & Raina, G. (2012). Reducing power consumption using the border gateway protocol. In *The 2nd International Conference on Smart Grids, Green Communications and IT Energy-aware Technologies* (pp. 83-89). ISBN 978-1-61208-189-2.

Ramaswami, R., & Sivarajan, K. N. (2002). *Optical networks: A practical perspective*. San Francisco: Morgan Kaufmann.

Raszuk, R., Heitz, J., Lo, A., Zhang, L., & Xu, X. (2012). *Simple virtual aggregation (S-VA)*. Retrieved from http://tools.ietf.org/html/draft-ietf-grow-simple-va-12

Re: (RRG, n.d.) Arguments in favour of Core-Edge Elimination vs. Separation? (n.d.). *Website*. Retrieved from http://www.ietf.org/mail-archive/web/rrg/current/msg05801.html

Rekhter, Y., & Li, T. (1995). A border gateway protocol 4 (BGP-4). Retrieved October 22, 2012, from http://tools.ietf.org/html/rfc4271

Rekhter, Y., Li, T., & Hares, S. (2006). A border gateway protocol (BGP-4).

Rekhter, Y., Li, T., & Hares, S. (2006). Internet engineering task force. *RFC 4271: A Border Gateway Protocol.*

Retana, A., & White, R. (2011). BGP custom decision process.

Riacardo, O., Dan, P., Walter, W., Beichuan, Z., & Lixia, Z. (2010). The (In)completeness of the observed Internet AS-level structure. *IEEE/ACM Transactions on Networking*, *18*(1), 109–122. doi:10.1109/TNET.2009.2020798.

Richardson, S. J. (1996). *Vertical aggregation: A strategy for FIB reduction.* Retrieved from http://tools.ietf.org/html/draft-richardson-fib-reduction-00

RIPE. (2006). *RIPE routing working group recommendations on route-flap damping.* Retrieved from http://www.ripe.net/ripe/docs/ripe-378

Rosen, E., Viswanathan, A., & Callon, R. (2001). Multiprotocol label switching architecture (RFC 3031). Retrieved from http://www.ietf.org

RouteViews.org. (2012). RouterViews Project. Retrieved from http://www.routeviews.org/

RRG. (n.d.). *IRTF Routing Research Group Home Page.* Retrieved from http://tools.ietf.org/group/irtf/trac/wiki/RoutingResearchGroup

RSVP. (2001). *RSVP-TE: Extensions to RSVP for LSP Tunnels.* Retrieved October 22, 2012, from http://tools.ietf.org/html/rfc3209

RSVP. (2008). *Inter-domain MPLS and GMPLS traffic engineering.* Retrieved October 22, 2012, from http://tools.ietf.org/html/rfc5151

Saucez, D., Donnet, B., Iannone, L., & Bonaventure, O. (2008, October). Inter-domain traffic engineering in a locator/identifier separation context. In *Proc. of Internet Network Management Workshop* (INM'08).

Saucez, D., Iannone, L., & Bonaventure, O. (2012, March). LISP threats analysis.

Schoonderwoerd, R., Holland, O., & Bruten, J. (1997). Ant-like agents for load balancing in telecommunications networks. *International Conference of Autonomous Agents* (pp. 209-216).

Shoch, J. (1978, January). *A note on inter-network naming, addressing, and routing. Internet Experiment Note 19.* Retrieved from http://www.rfc-editor.org/ien/ien19.txt

Sriram, K., Gleichmann, P., Young-Tak, K., & Montgomery, D. (2010, August). Enhanced efficiency of mapping distribution protocols in scalable routing and addressing architectures. In *Computer Communications and Networks (ICCCN), 2010 Proceedings of 19th International Conference.*

Stallings, W. (1998). *SNMP, SNMPv2, SNMPv3, and RMON 1 and 2.* Addison-Wesley Longman Publishing Co., Inc..

Stewart, R. (2007, September). Stream control transmission protocol.

Subramanian, L., Caesar, M., & Ee, C. T., Handley, M., Mao, Z. M., Shenker, S., & Stoica, I. (2005). HLP: A next generation inter-domain routing protocol. In ACM SIGCOMM.

Teixeira, R., Griffin, G., Resende, M., & Rexford, J. (2007). TIE breaking: Tunable interdomain egress selection. *IEEE/ACM Transactions on Networking*, *15*(4), 761 774. doi:10.1109/TNET.2007.893877.

Templin, F. (2010, February). Routing and addressing in networks with global enterprise recursion (RANGER).

Templin, F. (2011, March). The internet routing overlay network (IRON).

Thaler, D. (2011, May). Evolution of the IP model.

Todimala, A., & Ramamurthy, B. (2007). *Algorithms for intermediate waveband switching in optical WDM mesh networks* (pp. 21–25). IEEE Infocom. doi:10.1109/HSNW.2007.4290539.

Tree, S. (n.d.). In *Wikipedia.* Retrieved from http://en.wikipedia.org/wiki/Steiner_tree_problem

Turner, S., & Chen, L. (2011, March). Updated security considerations for the MD5 message-digest and the HMAC-MD5 algorithms (RFC 6151). Retrieved from http://www.ietf.org/rfc/rfc6151.txt

Uhlig, S. (2004). *Implications of the traffic characteristics on interdomain traffic engineering*. (Doctoral thesis). Université catholique de Louvain.

Uhlig, S., Quoitin, B., Lepropre, J., & Balon, S. (2006). Providing public intradomain traffic matrices to the research community. *ACM SIGCOMM Computer Communication Review, 36*(1), 83–86. doi:10.1145/1111322.1111341.

Ullmann, R. (1993, June). TP/IX: The Next Internet.

Van Beijnum, I. (2002). BGP: Building reliable networks with the border gateway protocol. *O'Reilly*. Retrieved from http://oreilly.com/catalog/bgp/chapter/ch06.html

Van Beijnum, I., & Winter, R. (2009). A BGP Inter-AS Cost Attribute.

Varma, S., & Jue, J. (2004). *Protection in multi-granular waveband networks* (pp. 1759–1763). IEEE Globecom.

Venkat, B., et al. (2010, July 6). Constructing disjoint and partially disjoint. Inter AS TE LSPs, *USPTO Patent 7751318*. Cisco Systems.

Vereecken, W., Van Heddeghem, W., Deruyck, M., Puype, B., Lannoo, B., & Joseph, W. et al. (2011). Power consumption in telecommunication networks: Overview and reduction strategies. *IEEE Communications Magazine, 49*(6), 62–69. doi:10.1109/MCOM.2011.5783986.

Villamizar, C., Chandra, R., & Govindan, R. (1998, November). BGP route flap damping.

Viswanathan, A., Feldman, N., Wang, Z., & Callon, R. (1998). Evolution of multiprotocol label switching. *Communications Magazine, IEEE, 36*(5), 165-173. doi: 10.1.1.124.3180

Vixie, P., Gudmundsson, O., Eastlake, D., & Wellington, B. (2000, May). Secret key transaction authentication for DNS (TSIG).

Vogt, C. (2008). Six/one router: A scalable and backwards-compatible solution for provider-independent addressing. In ACM SIGCOMM MobiArch Workshop.

Vogt, C. (2009, December). *Simplifying Internet applications development with a name-based sockets interface*. Retrieved from http://www.sics.se/nbs-project

Vohra, Q., & Chen, E. (2007, May). BGP support for four-octet AS number space.

Voronoi diagram. (n.d.). In *Wikipedia*. Retrieved from http://en.wikipedia.org/wiki/Voronoi_diagram

Wang, Y., Bi, J., & Wu, J. (2010). Empirical analysis of core-edge separation by decomposing Internet topology graph. In *Proceedings of GLOBECOM*, 1-5.

Wang, Z. (1992, November). EIP: The extended internet protocol.

Wang, Z., & Crowcroft, J. (1992, May). A two-tier address structure for the internet.

Wang, Y., & Cao, X. (2009). *A new hierarchical waveband assignment algorithm for multi-granular optical networks* (pp. 1–6). ICCCN. doi:10.1109/ICCCN.2009.5235374.

Wasserman, M., & Baker, F. (2011, June). IPv6-to-IPv6 network prefix translation.

Wellington. (2000, November). Secure domain name system (DNS) dynamic update (RFC3007). Retrieved from http://www.ietf.org

Whittle, R. (2010). *Ivip (Internet vastly improved plumbing) architecture*. Retrieved from http://tools.ietf.org/html/draft-whittle-ivip-arch-04

Williams, N., & Richardson, M. (2008, November). Better-than-nothing security: An unauthenticated mode of IPsec (RFC 5386). Retrieved from http://www.ietf.org/rfc/rfc5386.txt

Winick, J., Jamin, S., & Rexford, J. (2002). *Traffic engineering between neighboring domains*. Retrieved August 31, 2012, from http://www.cs.princeton.edu/~jrex/papers/interAS.pdf

Winter, R., & Van Beijnum, I. (2012). Explicitly accommodating origin preference for inter-domain traffic engineering. *27th Annual ACM Symposium on Applied Computing*. doi: 10.1145/2245276.2245389

Wischik, D., & McKeown, N. (2005). Part I: Buffer sizes for core routers. *ACM SIGCOMM Computer Communications Review, 35*(3), 75–78. doi:10.1145/1070873.1070884.

Wood, P., Nisbet, M., Egan, G., Johnston, N., Haley, K., Krishnappa, B.,..., Watson, A. (2012, April). Internet security threat report – trends (Vol. 17; Tech. Rep.). Symantec Corporation.

Xiaoliang, Z., Dante, J. P., & Jason, S. (2010). Routing scalability: An operator's view. *IEEE Journal on Selected Areas in Communications*, 28(8), 1262–1270. doi:10.1109/JSAC.2010.101004.

Xu, X. (2009, July). Transition mechanisms for routing architecture for the next generation internet (RANGI).

Xu, X. (2010, August). Routing architecture for the next generation internet (RANGI).

Xu, C., Liu, T., Guan, J., Zhang, H., & Muntean, G.-M. (2012). CMT-QA: Quality-aware adaptive concurrent multipath data transfer in heterogeneous wireless networks. *IEEE Transactions on Mobile Computing*, 99.

Xu, C., Zhao, F., Guan, J., Zhang, H., & Muntean, G.-M. (2012). QoE-driven user-centric VoD services in urban multi-homed P2P-based vehicular networks. *IEEE Transactions on Vehicular Technology*, 99.

Xu, D., Xiong, Y., Qiao, C., & Li, G. (2003). Trap avoidance and protection schemes in networks with shared risk links groups. *Journal of Lightwave Technology*, 2683–2693.

Yao, S., & Mukherjee, B. (2003). Design of hybrid waveband-switched networks with OEO traffic grooming. *Optical Fiber Conference* (p. WH3).

Yen, J. (1971). Finding the k shortest loopless paths in a network. *Management Science*, 17(11), 712–716. doi:10.1287/mnsc.17.11.712.

Yoo, S. (n.d.). Energy efficiency in the future internet: The role of optical packet switching and optical-label switching.

Yoo, S. J. B. (2011). Energy efficiency in the future internet: the role of optical packet switching and optical-label switching. *IEEE Journal on Selected Topics in Quantum Electronics*, 17(2), 406–418. doi:10.1109/JSTQE.2010.2076793.

Zhang, L. (2006). An overview of multihoming and open issues in GSE. *IETF Journal*, 2.

Zhang, L., Wakikawa, R., & Zhu, Z. (2009). Support mobility in the global Internet. In *Proceedings of the 1st ACM Workshop on Mobile Internet through Cellular Networks*.

Zhang, X., Francis, P., Wang, J., & Yoshida, K. (2006). Scaling IP routing with the core router-integrated overlay. In *Proceedings of ICNP*.

Zhang, Y., & Liu, Y-C. (2011). An improved ant colony optimisation and its application on multicast routing problem. *International Journal of Wireless and Mobile Computing*, 5(1/2011), 18-23. doi: 10.1504/IJWMC.2011.044116

Zhang, H., & Su, W. (2007). Fundamental research on the architecture of new network---Universal network and pervasice services[in Chinese]. *Acta Electronica Sinica*, 35(4), 593–598.

Zhao, X., Liu, Y., Wang, L., & Zhang, B. (2010). On the aggregatability of router forwarding tables. In *Proceedings of IEEE INFOCOM* (pp. 848–856). Piscataway, NJ, USA: IEEE Press. doi:10.1109/INFCOM.2010.5462137.

Zhu, K., Zang, H., & Mukherjee, B. (2003). A comprehensive study on next-generation optical grooming switches. *IEEE Journal on Selected Areas in Communications*, 21(7), 1173–1186. doi:10.1109/JSAC.2003.815683.

Related References

Abawajy, J. H., Pathan, M., Rahman, M., Pathan, A. K., & Deris, M. M. (2012). *Internet and distributed computing advancements: Theoretical frameworks and practical applications*. Hershey, PA: IGI Global.

Abdel Hady, A. Abd El-kader, S. M., Eissa, H. S., Salem, A., & Fahmy, H. M. (2012). A comparative analysis of hierarchical routing protocols in wireless sensor networks. In J. Abawajy, M. Pathan, M. Rahman, A. Pathan, & M. Deris (Eds.), Internet and Distributed Computing Advancements: Theoretical Frameworks and Practical Applications (pp. 212-246). Hershey, PA: Information Science Reference. doi: doi:10.4018/978-1-4666-0161-1.ch009.

Abu-Samaha, A. M., & Al-Salem, L. S. (2010). Focused requirements engineering method for web application development. In Tatnall, A. (Ed.), *Web Technologies: Concepts, Methodologies, Tools, and Applications* (pp. 344–354). Hershey, PA: Information Science Reference.

Achilleos, A., Yang, K., & Papadopoulos, G. A. (2013). Addressing device-based adaptation of services: a model driven web service oriented development approach. In Ortiz, G., & Cubo, J. (Eds.), *Adaptive Web Services for Modular and Reusable Software Development: Tactics and Solutions* (pp. 278–301). Hershey, PA: Information Science Reference.

Adda, M. (2010). A pattern language for knowledge discovery in a semantic web context. [IJITWE]. *International Journal of Information Technology and Web Engineering*, 5(2), 16–31. doi:10.4018/jitwe.2010040102.

Adda, M. (2012). A pattern language for knowledge discovery in a semantic web context. In Alkhatib, G. (Ed.), *Models for Capitalizing on Web Engineering Advancements: Trends and Discoveries* (pp. 59–74). Hershey, PA: Information Science Publishing. doi:10.4018/978-1-4666-0023-2.ch004.

Ahmed, M. D., & Sundaram, D. (2010). A lifecycle approach for scenario driven decision systems. In Alkhatib, G., & Rine, D. (Eds.), *Web Engineering Advancements and Trends: Building New Dimensions of Information Technology* (pp. 259–268). Hershey, PA: Information Science Reference. doi:10.4018/978-1-60566-719-5.ch015.

Aishah, A. R., Abidin Mohamad, I. Z., & Komiya, R. (2010). Voice driven emotion recognizer mobile phone: Proposal and evaluations. In Alkhatib, G., & Rine, D. (Eds.), *Web Engineering Advancements and Trends: Building New Dimensions of Information Technology* (pp. 144–159). Hershey, PA: Information Science Reference. doi:10.4018/978-1-60566-719-5.ch008.

Aklouf, Y., Pierra, G., Ait Ameur, Y., & Drias, H. (2005). PLIB ontology: A mature solution for products characterization in B2B electronic commerce. [IJITSR]. *International Journal of IT Standards and Standardization Research, 3*(2), 66–81. doi:10.4018/jitsr.2005070106.

Aktas, M. S., Fox, G. C., & Pierce, M. (2012). A federated approach to information management in grids. In Hung, P. (Ed.), *Web Service Composition and New Frameworks in Designing Semantics: Innovations* (pp. 71–103). Hershey, PA: Information Science Reference. doi:10.4018/978-1-4666-1942-5.ch004.

Al-Ahmad, A., Abu Ata, B., & Wahbeh, A. (2012). Pen testing for web applications. [IJITWE]. *International Journal of Information Technology and Web Engineering, 7*(3), 1–13. doi:10.4018/jitwe.2012070101.

Al-Bahadili, H., Maqousi, A., & Naoum, R. S. (2012). Analyzing the effect of node density on the performance of the LAR-1P algorithm. [IJITWE]. *International Journal of Information Technology and Web Engineering, 7*(2), 16–29. doi:10.4018/jitwe.2012040102.

Al-Oqily, I., Subaih, B., Bani-Mohammad, S., Alshaer, J. J., & Refai, M. (2012). Autonomic healing for service specific overlay networks. [IJITWE]. *International Journal of Information Technology and Web Engineering, 7*(2), 46–59. doi:10.4018/jitwe.2012040104.

Al-Raisi, A., Amin, S., & Tahir, S. (2013). E-performance systems: A method of measuring performance. In Polgar, J., & Adamson, G. (Eds.), *Web Portal Design, Implementation, Integration, and Optimization* (pp. 50–57). Hershey, PA: Information Science Reference. doi:10.4018/978-1-4666-2779-6.ch004.

Al-Zoubi, K. (2009). Hierarchical scheduling in heterogeneous grid systems. In Alkhatib, G., & Rine, D. (Eds.), *Integrated Approaches in Information Technology and Web Engineering: Advancing Organizational Knowledge Sharing* (pp. 143–157). Hershey, PA: Information Science Reference.

Alam, M., Nauman, M., Zhang, X., Ali, T., Hung, P., & Alam, Q. (2012). Behavioral attestation for web services based business processes. In Hung, P. (Ed.), *Web Service Composition and New Frameworks in Designing Semantics: Innovations* (pp. 308–329). Hershey, PA: Information Science Reference. doi:10.4018/978-1-4666-1942-5.ch014.

Albalas, F. W., Abu-Alhaija, B. A., Awajan, A., Awajan, A., & Al-Begain, K. (2012). Quality of service for multimedia and real-time services. In Alkhatib, G. (Ed.), *Models for Capitalizing on Web Engineering Advancements: Trends and Discoveries* (pp. 241–262). Hershey, PA: Information Science Publishing. doi:10.4018/978-1-4666-0023-2.ch013.

Alchieri, E. A., Bessani, A. N., & Fraga, J. D. (2012). A dependable infrastructure for cooperative web services coordination. In Hung, P. (Ed.), *Web Service Composition and New Frameworks in Designing Semantics: Innovations* (pp. 27–49). Hershey, PA: Information Science Reference. doi:10.4018/978-1-4666-1942-5.ch002.

Ali, H. A., & Farrag, T. A. (2009). High performance scheduling mechanism for mobile computing based on self-ranking algorithm (SRA). In Alkhatib, G., & Rine, D. (Eds.), *Integrated Approaches in Information Technology and Web Engineering: Advancing Organizational Knowledge Sharing* (pp. 127–142). Hershey, PA: Information Science Reference.

Alkhatib, G. (2011). *Web engineered applications for evolving organizations: Emerging knowledge.* Hershey, PA: IGI Global. doi:10.4018/978-1-60960-523-0.

Alkhatib, G. (2012). *Models for capitalizing on web engineering advancements: Trends and discoveries.* Hershey, PA: IGI Global. doi:10.4018/978-1-46660-023-2.

Alkhatib, G. I., & Rine, D. C. (2009). *Integrated approaches in information technology and web engineering: Advancing organizational knowledge sharing.* Hershey, PA: IGI Global.

Alkhatib, G. I., & Rine, D. C. (2010). *Web engineering advancements and trends: Building new dimensions of information technology.* Hershey, PA: IGI Global. doi:10.4018/978-1-60566-719-5.

Alsumait, A., & Habib, S. J. (2012). SPACots: A software tool for selecting COTS components. In Alkhatib, G. (Ed.), *Models for Capitalizing on Web Engineering Advancements: Trends and Discoveries* (pp. 263–275). Hershey, PA: Information Science Publishing. doi:10.4018/978-1-4666-0023-2.ch014.

Alves, C., Caceres, E., Dehne, F., & Song, S. (2010). Communication issues in scalable parallel computing. In Li, K., Hsu, C., Yang, L., Dongarra, J., & Zima, H. (Eds.), *Handbook of Research on Scalable Computing Technologies* (pp. 378–395). Hershey, PA: Information Science Reference.

Alwan, A. A., Ibrahim, H., & Udzir, N. I. (2012). A model for ranking and selecting integrity tests in a distributed database. In Alkhatib, G. (Ed.), *Models for Capitalizing on Web Engineering Advancements: Trends and Discoveries* (pp. 138–157). Hershey, PA: Information Science Publishing. doi:10.4018/978-1-4666-0023-2.ch008.

AlZahrani, S., Ayesh, A., & Zedan, H. (2011). Multi-agent based dynamic e-learning environment. In Alkhatib, G. (Ed.), *Web Engineered Applications for Evolving Organizations: Emerging Knowledge* (pp. 142–158). Hershey, PA: Information Science Reference. doi:10.4018/978-1-60960-523-0.ch009.

Anbar, M., & Vidyarthi, D. P. (2012). A comparative study of evolutionary algorithms for maximizing reliability of a flow in cellular IP network. In Prakash Vidyarthi, D. (Ed.), *Technologies and Protocols for the Future of Internet Design: Reinventing the Web* (pp. 247–257). Hershey, PA: Information Science Reference. doi:10.4018/978-1-4666-0203-8.ch013.

Anbar, M., & Vidyarthi, D. P. (2012). Optimizing path reliability in IPTV systems using genetic algorithm. In Prakash Vidyarthi, D. (Ed.), *Technologies and Protocols for the Future of Internet Design: Reinventing the Web* (pp. 179–190). Hershey, PA: Information Science Reference. doi:10.4018/978-1-4666-0203-8.ch009.

Andrei, D. M., & Guran, A. M. (2011). A framework for early usability integration in web applications development process. In Alkhatib, G. (Ed.), *Web Engineered Applications for Evolving Organizations: Emerging Knowledge* (pp. 292–314). Hershey, PA: Information Science Reference. doi:10.4018/978-1-60960-523-0.ch017.

Andrés, I. (2010). A new framework for intelligent semantic web services based on GAIVAs. In Alkhatib, G., & Rine, D. (Eds.), *Web Engineering Advancements and Trends: Building New Dimensions of Information Technology* (pp. 38–62). Hershey, PA: Information Science Reference. doi:10.4018/978-1-60566-719-5.ch003.

Anticoli, L., & Toppano, E. (2011). How culture may influence ontology co-design: A qualitative study. [IJITWE]. *International Journal of Information Technology and Web Engineering, 6*(2), 1–17. doi:10.4018/jitwe.2011040101.

Ardagna, C. A., Frati, F., & Gianini, G. (2009). Open source in web-based applications: A case study on single sign-on. In Alkhatib, G., & Rine, D. (Eds.), *Integrated Approaches in Information Technology and Web Engineering: Advancing Organizational Knowledge Sharing* (pp. 83–97). Hershey, PA: Information Science Reference.

Ardissono, L., Bosio, G., Goy, A., Petrone, G., & Segnan, M. (2012). Integration of cloud services for web collaboration: A user-centered perspective. In Alkhatib, G. (Ed.), *Models for Capitalizing on Web Engineering Advancements: Trends and Discoveries* (pp. 1–19). Hershey, PA: Information Science Publishing. doi:10.4018/978-1-4666-0023-2.ch001.

Ashish, N., & Maluf, D. A. (2009). Intelligent information integration: Reclaiming the intelligence. [IJIIT]. *International Journal of Intelligent Information Technologies, 5*(3), 28–54. doi:10.4018/jiit.2009070102.

Atanasov, I., & Pencheva, E. (2012). Quality of service management by third party in the evolved packet system. In Alkhatib, G. (Ed.), *Models for Capitalizing on Web Engineering Advancements: Trends and Discoveries* (pp. 276–305). Hershey, PA: Information Science Publishing. doi:10.4018/978-1-4666-0023-2.ch015.

Azam, N., Curcin, V., Guo, L., & Ghanem, M. (2010). Towards automatic service composition within ARGUGRID. In K. Ragab, T. Helmy, & A. Hassanien (Eds.), Developing Advanced Web Services through P2P Computing and Autonomous Agents: Trends and Innovations (pp. 49-68). Hershey, PA: Information Science Reference. doi: doi:10.4018/978-1-61520-973-6.ch004.

Baarah, A., Mouttham, A., & Peyton, L. (2012). Architecture of an event processing application for monitoring cardiac patient wait times. [IJITWE]. *International Journal of Information Technology and Web Engineering, 7*(1), 1–16. doi:10.4018/jitwe.2012010101.

Babiker, S. F., Ahmed, A. A., & Yasin, M. A. (2012). Web navigation tool for visually impaired people. [IJITWE]. *International Journal of Information Technology and Web Engineering, 7*(1), 31–45. doi:10.4018/jitwe.2012010103.

Bagui, S., & Loggins, A. (2011). Automating the generation of joins in large databases and web services. In Alkhatib, G. (Ed.), *Web Engineered Applications for Evolving Organizations: Emerging Knowledge* (pp. 123–140). Hershey, PA: Information Science Reference. doi:10.4018/978-1-60960-523-0.ch008.

Bai, X., Gao, J. Z., & Tsai, W. (2013). Cloud scalability measurement and testing. In Tilley, S., & Parveen, T. (Eds.), *Software Testing in the Cloud: Perspectives on an Emerging Discipline* (pp. 356–381). Hershey, PA: Information Science Reference.

Baloglu, A., Wyne, M. F., & Bahcetepe, Y. (2010). Web 2.0 based intelligent software architecture for photograph sharing. [IJIIT]. *International Journal of Intelligent Information Technologies, 6*(4), 17–29. doi:10.4018/jiit.2010100102.

Barbero, J. M. (2012). Remote delivery of video services over video links. In Fortino, G., & Palau, C. (Eds.), *Next Generation Content Delivery Infrastructures: Emerging Paradigms and Technologies* (pp. 230–250). Hershey, PA: Information Science Reference. doi:10.4018/978-1-4666-1794-0.ch010.

236

Barth, A., Kleis, M., Klenk, A., Radier, B., El-moumouhi, S., Carle, G., & Salaun, M. (2010). Context dissemination in peer-to-peer networks. In K. Ragab, T. Helmy, & A. Hassanien (Eds.), Developing Advanced Web Services through P2P Computing and Autonomous Agents: Trends and Innovations (pp. 69-90). Hershey, PA: Information Science Reference. doi: doi:10.4018/978-1-61520-973-6.ch005.

Basu, K., Zeadally, S., & Siddiqui, F. (2012). Quality of service (QoS) in WiMAX. In Prakash Vidyarthi, D. (Ed.), *Technologies and Protocols for the Future of Internet Design: Reinventing the Web* (pp. 143–161). Hershey, PA: Information Science Reference. doi:10.4018/978-1-4666-0203-8.ch007.

Belalem, G., Benotmane, Z., & Benhallou, K. (2009). Self adjustable negotiation mechanism for convergence and conflict resolution of replicas in data grids. [IJCINI]. *International Journal of Cognitive Informatics and Natural Intelligence, 3*(1), 95–110. doi:10.4018/jcini.2009010106.

Belalem, G., Yagoubi, B., & Bouamama, S. (2010). An approach based on market economy for consistency management in data grids with optorsim simulator. In Alkhatib, G., & Rine, D. (Eds.), *Web Engineering Advancements and Trends: Building New Dimensions of Information Technology* (pp. 269–280). Hershey, PA: Information Science Reference. doi:10.4018/978-1-60566-719-5.ch016.

Ben Djemaa, R., Amous, I., & Ben Hamadou, A. (2011). Adaptability and adaptivity in the generation of web applications. In Alkhatib, G. (Ed.), *Web Engineered Applications for Evolving Organizations: Emerging Knowledge* (pp. 99–122). Hershey, PA: Information Science Reference. doi:10.4018/978-1-60960-523-0.ch007.

Berger, O., Bac, C., & Hamet, B. (2009). Integration of libre software applications to create a collaborative work platform for researchers at GET. In Alkhatib, G., & Rine, D. (Eds.), *Integrated Approaches in Information Technology and Web Engineering: Advancing Organizational Knowledge Sharing* (pp. 1–17). Hershey, PA: Information Science Reference. doi:10.4018/978-1-60566-060-8.ch175.

Blake, M. B. (2012). Semi-automated lifecycles for eliciting requirements for service-oriented environments. In Lee, J., Ma, S., & Liu, A. (Eds.), *Service Life Cycle Tools and Technologies: Methods, Trends and Advances* (pp. 22–34). Hershey, PA: Information Science Reference.

Blake, M. B., Singh, L., Williams, A. B., Norman, W., & Sliva, A. L. (2009). Experience report: A component-based data management and knowledge discovery framework for aviation studies. In Alkhatib, G., & Rine, D. (Eds.), *Integrated Approaches in Information Technology and Web Engineering: Advancing Organizational Knowledge Sharing* (pp. 244–256). Hershey, PA: Information Science Reference.

Blanco, E., Cardinale, Y., & Vidal, M. (2011). Aggregating functional and non-functional properties to identify service compositions. In Milanovic, N. (Ed.), *Engineering Reliable Service Oriented Architecture: Managing Complexity and Service Level Agreements* (pp. 145–174). Hershey, PA: Information Science Reference. doi:10.4018/978-1-60960-493-6.ch008.

Blind, K. (2007). Factors influencing the lifetime of telecommunication and information technology standards: results of an explorative analysis of the PERINORM database. [IJITSR]. *International Journal of IT Standards and Standardization Research, 5*(1), 1–24. doi:10.4018/jitsr.2007010101.

Booth, D., & Jansen, B. J. (2010). A Review of Methodologies for Analyzing Websites. In Tatnall, A. (Ed.), *Web Technologies: Concepts, Methodologies, Tools, and Applications* (pp. 145–166). Hershey, PA: Information Science Reference.

Bosin, A., Dessì, N., Madusudhanan, B., & Pes, B. (2013). A SOA-based environment supporting collaborative experiments in e-science. In Polgar, J., & Adamson, G. (Eds.), *Web Portal Design, Implementation, Integration, and Optimization* (pp. 122–136). Hershey, PA: Information Science Reference. doi:10.4018/978-1-4666-2779-6.ch011.

Bravetti, M., & Zavattaro, G. (2013). Service discovery and composition based on contracts and choreographic descriptions. In Ortiz, G., & Cubo, J. (Eds.), *Adaptive Web Services for Modular and Reusable Software Development: Tactics and Solutions* (pp. 60–88). Hershey, PA: Information Science Reference.

Bravo, M., & Alvarado, M. (2012). Similarity measures for substituting web services. In Hung, P. (Ed.), *Web Service Composition and New Frameworks in Designing Semantics: Innovations* (pp. 143–170). Hershey, PA: Information Science Reference. doi:10.4018/978-1-4666-1942-5.ch007.

Bryant, S. C. (2010). A strategic framework for integrating web 2.0 into the marketing mix. In Tatnall, A. (Ed.), *Web Technologies: Concepts, Methodologies, Tools, and Applications* (pp. 909–923). Hershey, PA: Information Science Reference.

Buchwald, S., Bauer, T., & Reichert, M. (2012). Bridging the gap between business process models and service composition specifications. In Lee, J., Ma, S., & Liu, A. (Eds.), *Service Life Cycle Tools and Technologies: Methods, Trends and Advances* (pp. 124–153). Hershey, PA: Information Science Reference.

Cardellini, V., Di Valerio, V., Iannucci, S., & Lo Presti, F. (2013). Service-oriented systems for adaptive management of service composition. In Ortiz, G., & Cubo, J. (Eds.), *Adaptive Web Services for Modular and Reusable Software Development: Tactics and Solutions* (pp. 161–195). Hershey, PA: Information Science Reference.

Caus, T., Christmann, S., & Hagenhoff, S. (2010). Mobile social web: Opportunities and drawbacks. In Tatnall, A. (Ed.), *Web Technologies: Concepts, Methodologies, Tools, and Applications* (pp. 11–21). Hershey, PA: Information Science Reference.

Caviglione, L., & Coccoli, M. (2012). Enhancement of e-learning systems and methodologies through advancements in distributed computing technologies. In Abawajy, J., Pathan, M., Rahman, M., Pathan, A., & Deris, M. (Eds.), *Internet and Distributed Computing Advancements: Theoretical Frameworks and Practical Applications* (pp. 45–69). Hershey, PA: Information Science Reference. doi:10.4018/978-1-4666-0161-1.ch002.

Cheikh, F. (2011). Web services composition problem: Model and complexity. In Milanovic, N. (Ed.), *Engineering Reliable Service Oriented Architecture: Managing Complexity and Service Level Agreements* (pp. 175–198). Hershey, PA: Information Science Reference. doi:10.4018/978-1-60960-493-6.ch009.

Chen, I., Ni, G., & Lee, R. C. (2012). A QoS-aware service bus with WSLA-based monitor for media production systems. In Lee, J., Ma, S., & Liu, A. (Eds.), *Service Life Cycle Tools and Technologies: Methods, Trends and Advances* (pp. 80–99). Hershey, PA: Information Science Reference.

Choi, B. (2013). Multiagent social computing. In Polgar, J., & Adamson, G. (Eds.), *Web Portal Design, Implementation, Integration, and Optimization* (pp. 229–242). Hershey, PA: Information Science Reference. doi:10.4018/978-1-4666-2779-6.ch018.

Chollet, S., & Lalanda, P. (2012). A model-driven approach to service composition with security properties. In Lee, J., Ma, S., & Liu, A. (Eds.), *Service Life Cycle Tools and Technologies: Methods, Trends and Advances* (pp. 154–174). Hershey, PA: Information Science Reference.

Chollet, S., Lalanda, P., & Bardin, J. (2012). Service-oriented computing: From web services to service-oriented components. In Lee, J., Ma, S., & Liu, A. (Eds.), *Service Life Cycle Tools and Technologies: Methods, Trends and Advances* (pp. 1–20). Hershey, PA: Information Science Reference.

Conte, T., Vaz, V. T., Massolar, J., Bott, A., Mendes, E., & Travassos, G. H. (2010). Applying the WDP technique to usability inspections in web development organizations. In Spiliotopoulos, T., Papadopoulou, P., Martakos, D., & Kouroupetroglou, G. (Eds.), *Integrating Usability Engineering for Designing the Web Experience: Methodologies and Principles* (pp. 324–344). Hershey, PA: Information Science Reference. doi:10.4018/978-1-60566-896-3.ch017.

Corazza, L. (2010). ICT and interculture opportunities offered by the web. In Tatnall, A. (Ed.), *Web Technologies: Concepts, Methodologies, Tools, and Applications* (pp. 1–10). Hershey, PA: Information Science Reference.

Creaner, G., & Pahl, C. (2013). Flexible coordination techniques for dynamic cloud service collaboration. In Ortiz, G., & Cubo, J. (Eds.), *Adaptive Web Services for Modular and Reusable Software Development: Tactics and Solutions* (pp. 239–252). Hershey, PA: Information Science Reference.

Cubo, J., & Pimentel, E. (2013). Reusing services through context-aware discovery and adaptation in pervasive systems. In Ortiz, G., & Cubo, J. (Eds.), *Adaptive Web Services for Modular and Reusable Software Development: Tactics and Solutions* (pp. 90–147). Hershey, PA: Information Science Reference.

Dahlem, N. (2011). OntoClippy: A user-friendly ontology design and creation methodology. [IJIIT]. *International Journal of Intelligent Information Technologies*, 7(1), 15–32. doi:10.4018/jiit.2011010102.

Dai, X., Chaudhary, K., & Grundy, J. (2012). NetPay: A micro-payment system for peer-to-peer networks. In Alkhatib, G. (Ed.), *Models for Capitalizing on Web Engineering Advancements: Trends and Discoveries* (p. 2P). Hershey, PA: Information Science Publishing. doi:10.4018/978-1-4666-0023-2.ch009.

Das, N. (2012). Pervasive internet via wireless infrastructure-based mesh networks. In Prakash Vidyarthi, D. (Ed.), *Technologies and Protocols for the Future of Internet Design: Reinventing the Web* (pp. 274–288). Hershey, PA: Information Science Reference. doi:10.4018/978-1-4666-0203-8.ch015.

Decker, M. (2011). Location-aware access control for mobile workflow systems. In Alkhatib, G. (Ed.), *Web Engineered Applications for Evolving Organizations: Emerging Knowledge* (pp. 44–62). Hershey, PA: Information Science Reference. doi:10.4018/978-1-60960-523-0.ch004.

Delgado, J. C. (2012). The user as a service. In Prakash Vidyarthi, D. (Ed.), *Technologies and Protocols for the Future of Internet Design: Reinventing the Web* (pp. 37–59). Hershey, PA: Information Science Reference. doi:10.4018/978-1-4666-0203-8.ch003.

Delgado, J. C. (2013). Structural interoperability as a basis for service adaptability. In Ortiz, G., & Cubo, J. (Eds.), *Adaptive Web Services for Modular and Reusable Software Development: Tactics and Solutions* (pp. 33–59). Hershey, PA: Information Science Reference.

Deng, S., Wu, Z., & Wu, J. (2012). An efficient service discovery method and its application. In Jie-Zhang, L. (Ed.), *Innovations, Standards and Practices of Web Services: Emerging Research Topics* (pp. 382–404). Hershey, PA: Information Science Reference.

Deroussi, L., & Lemoine, D. (2013). Discrete particle swarm optimization for the multi-level lot-sizing problem. In Yin, P. (Ed.), *Trends in Developing Metaheuristics, Algorithms, and Optimization Approaches* (pp. 99–113). Hershey, PA: Information Science Reference.

Dhingra, V., & Bhatia, K. (2012). Comparative analysis of ontology ranking algorithms. [IJITWE]. *International Journal of Information Technology and Web Engineering, 7*(3), 55–66. doi:10.4018/jitwe.2012070104.

di. M. T., & Gennari, R. (2010). A usability guide to intelligent web tools for the literacy of deaf people. In T. Spiliotopoulos, P. Papadopoulou, D. Martakos, & G. Kouroupetroglou (Eds.), Integrating Usability Engineering for Designing the Web Experience: Methodologies and Principles (pp. 210-224). Hershey, PA: Information Science Reference. doi: doi:10.4018/978-1-60566-896-3. ch011.

Di Modica, G., & Tomarchio, O. (2011). Flexible and dynamic SLAs management in service oriented architectures. In Milanovic, N. (Ed.), *Engineering Reliable Service Oriented Architecture: Managing Complexity and Service Level Agreements* (pp. 22–40). Hershey, PA: Information Science Reference. doi:10.4018/978-1-60960-493-6.ch002.

Dingli, A., & Seychell, D. (2012). Blending augmented reality with real world scenarios using mobile devices. In Prakash Vidyarthi, D. (Ed.), *Technologies and Protocols for the Future of Internet Design: Reinventing the Web* (pp. 258–273). Hershey, PA: Information Science Reference. doi:10.4018/978-1-4666-0203-8.ch014.

dos Reis, J. C., Bonacin, R., & Baranauskas, M. C. (2013). A semiotic-based approach for search in social network services. In Polgar, J., & Adamson, G. (Eds.), *Web Portal Design, Implementation, Integration, and Optimization* (pp. 137–151). Hershey, PA: Information Science Reference. doi:10.4018/978-1-4666-2779-6.ch012.

Dourlens, S., & Ramdane-Cherif, A. (2011). Cognitive memory for semantic agents architecture in robotic interaction. [IJCINI]. *International Journal of Cognitive Informatics and Natural Intelligence, 5*(1), 43–58. doi:10.4018/jcini.2011010103.

Downey, E., & Jones, M. A. (2012). *Public service, governance and web 2.0 technologies: Future trends in social media*. Hershey, PA: IGI Global. doi:10.4018/978-1-46660-071-3.

Du, X., Xing, C., Zhou, L., & Han, K. (2013). Modeling control flow in WS-BPEL with Chu spaces. In Wang, J. (Ed.), *Implementation and Integration of Information Systems in the Service Sector* (pp. 184–204). Hershey, PA: Business Science Reference.

Dustdar, S., Leitner, P., Nardini, F. M., Silvestri, F., & Tolomei, G. (2013). Mining lifecycle event logs for enhancing service-based applications. In Ortiz, G., & Cubo, J. (Eds.), *Adaptive Web Services for Modular and Reusable Software Development: Tactics and Solutions* (pp. 196–206). Hershey, PA: Information Science Reference.

El-Basioni, B. M., El-Kader, S. M., Eissa, H. S., & Zahra, M. M. (2012). Low loss energy-aware routing protocol for data gathering applications in wireless sensor network. In Abawajy, J., Pathan, M., Rahman, M., Pathan, A., & Deris, M. (Eds.), *Internet and Distributed Computing Advancements: Theoretical Frameworks and Practical Applications* (pp. 272–302). Hershey, PA: Information Science Reference. doi:10.4018/978-1-4666-0161-1.ch011.

El-Ghalayini, H., Odeh, M., & McClatchey, R. (2009). Engineering conceptual data models from domain ontologies: A critical evaluation. In Alkhatib, G., & Rine, D. (Eds.), *Integrated Approaches in Information Technology and Web Engineering: Advancing Organizational Knowledge Sharing* (pp. 304–316). Hershey, PA: Information Science Reference.

Eljinini, M. A. (2011). The medical semantic web: Opportunities and issues. [IJITWE]. *International Journal of Information Technology and Web Engineering, 6*(2), 18–28. doi:10.4018/jitwe.2011040102.

Erickson, J., & Siau, K. (2010). Web services, service-oriented computing, and service-oriented architecture: Separating hype from reality. In Tatnall, A. (Ed.), *Web Technologies: Concepts, Methodologies, Tools, and Applications* (pp. 1786–1798). Hershey, PA: Information Science Reference. doi:10.4018/978-1-61520-967-5.ch006.

Ezenwoye, O., & Sadjadi, S. M. (2011). Applying concept reuse for adaptive service composition. In Milanovic, N. (Ed.), *Engineering Reliable Service Oriented Architecture: Managing Complexity and Service Level Agreements* (pp. 212–235). Hershey, PA: Information Science Reference. doi:10.4018/978-1-60960-493-6.ch011.

Ezumah, B., & Adekunle, S. O. (2012). A review of privacy, internet security threat, and legislation in Africa: A case study of Nigeria, South Africa, Egypt, and Kenya. In Abawajy, J., Pathan, M., Rahman, M., Pathan, A., & Deris, M. (Eds.), *Internet and Distributed Computing Advancements: Theoretical Frameworks and Practical Applications* (pp. 115–136). Hershey, PA: Information Science Reference. doi:10.4018/978-1-4666-0161-1.ch005.

Ferguson, J. D., & Miller, J. (2009). Modeling defects in e-projects. In Alkhatib, G., & Rine, D. (Eds.), *Integrated Approaches in Information Technology and Web Engineering: Advancing Organizational Knowledge Sharing* (pp. 317–330). Hershey, PA: Information Science Reference.

Fernando, H. S., & Abawajy, J. H. (2012). A security framework for networked RFID. In Abawajy, J., Pathan, M., Rahman, M., Pathan, A., & Deris, M. (Eds.), *Internet and Distributed Computing Advancements: Theoretical Frameworks and Practical Applications* (pp. 85–114). Hershey, PA: Information Science Reference. doi:10.4018/978-1-4666-0161-1.ch004.

Folmer, E., & Bosch, J. (2010). Experiences with software architecture analysis of usability. In Alkhatib, G., & Rine, D. (Eds.), *Web Engineering Advancements and Trends: Building New Dimensions of Information Technology* (pp. 177–202). Hershey, PA: Information Science Reference. doi:10.4018/978-1-60566-719-5.ch010.

Fomin, V. V. (2012). Standards as hybrids: An essay on tensions and juxtapositions in contemporary standardization. [IJITSR]. *International Journal of IT Standards and Standardization Research, 10*(2), 59–68. doi:10.4018/jitsr.2012070105.

Fortino, G., Calafate, C., & Manzoni, P. (2012). Robust broadcasting of media content in urban environments. In Fortino, G., & Palau, C. (Eds.), *Next Generation Content Delivery Infrastructures: Emerging Paradigms and Technologies* (pp. 105–120). Hershey, PA: Information Science Reference. doi:10.4018/978-1-4666-1794-0.ch005.

Fortino, G., & Palau, C. E. (2012). *Next generation content delivery infrastructures: Emerging paradigms and technologies*. Hershey, PA: IGI Global. doi:10.4018/978-1-4666-1794-0.

Francisco de Souza, J., Siqueira, S. W., & Melo, R. N. (2012). Applying ontology similarity functions to improve software agent communication. In Alkhatib, G. (Ed.), *Models for Capitalizing on Web Engineering Advancements: Trends and Discoveries* (pp. 43–57). Hershey, PA: Information Science Publishing. doi:10.4018/978-1-4666-0023-2.ch003.

Fudzee, M. F., & Abawajy, J. (2010). Request-driven cross-media content adaptation technique. In K. Ragab, T. Helmy, & A. Hassanien (Eds.), Developing Advanced Web Services through P2P Computing and Autonomous Agents: Trends and Innovations (pp. 91-113). Hershey, PA: Information Science Reference. doi: doi:10.4018/978-1-61520-973-6.ch006.

Georgiakakis, P., & Retalis, S. (2010). DEPTH: A method and a web-based tool for designing and executing scenario-based usability inspections of e-systems. In Spiliotopoulos, T., Papadopoulou, P., Martakos, D., & Kouroupetroglou, G. (Eds.), *Integrating Usability Engineering for Designing the Web Experience: Methodologies and Principles* (pp. 309–323). Hershey, PA: Information Science Reference. doi:10.4018/978-1-60566-896-3.ch016.

Ghaleb-Seddik, A., Ghamri-Doudane, Y., & Senouci, S. M. (2012). TCP for wireless internet: Solutions and challenges. In Abawajy, J., Pathan, M., Rahman, M., Pathan, A., & Deris, M. (Eds.), *Internet and Distributed Computing Advancements: Theoretical Frameworks and Practical Applications* (pp. 1–44). Hershey, PA: Information Science Reference. doi:10.4018/978-1-4666-0161-1.ch001.

Ghose, A. K. (2012). The foundations of service eco-systems. In Lee, J., Ma, S., & Liu, A. (Eds.), *Service Life Cycle Tools and Technologies: Methods, Trends and Advances* (pp. 65–78). Hershey, PA: Information Science Reference.

Giallonardo, E., & Zimeo, E. (2011). Adding semantics to QoS requirements. In Milanovic, N. (Ed.), *Engineering Reliable Service Oriented Architecture: Managing Complexity and Service Level Agreements* (pp. 104–124). Hershey, PA: Information Science Reference. doi:10.4018/978-1-60960-493-6.ch006.

Gil, V. (2012). Virtual java service container. In Vaquero, L., Cáceres, J., & Hierro, J. (Eds.), *Open Source Cloud Computing Systems: Practices and Paradigms* (pp. 155–177). Hershey, PA: Information Science Reference. doi:10.4018/978-1-4666-0098-0.ch008.

Ginsburg, M. (2004). Unified citation management and visualization using open standards: The open citation system. [IJITSR]. *International Journal of IT Standards and Standardization Research, 2*(1), 23–41. doi:10.4018/jitsr.2004010102.

Gomez, J., Bia, A., & Parraga, A. (2009). Tool support for model-driven development of web applications. In Alkhatib, G., & Rine, D. (Eds.), *Integrated Approaches in Information Technology and Web Engineering: Advancing Organizational Knowledge Sharing* (pp. 331–344). Hershey, PA: Information Science Reference.

Gönczy, L., & Varró, D. (2011). Design and deployment of service oriented applications with non-functional requirements. In Milanovic, N. (Ed.), *Engineering Reliable Service Oriented Architecture: Managing Complexity and Service Level Agreements* (pp. 315–339). Hershey, PA: Information Science Reference. doi:10.4018/978-1-60960-493-6.ch015.

González, L., & Ruggia, R. (2013). Adaptive ESB infrastructure for service based systems. In Ortiz, G., & Cubo, J. (Eds.), *Adaptive Web Services for Modular and Reusable Software Development: Tactics and Solutions* (pp. 1–32). Hershey, PA: Information Science Reference.

González-Calleros, J. M., Vanderdonckt, J., & Muñoz-Arteaga, J. (2010). A structured methodology for developing 3D web applications. In Spiliotopoulos, T., Papadopoulou, P., Martakos, D., & Kouroupetroglou, G. (Eds.), *Integrating Usability Engineering for Designing the Web Experience: Methodologies and Principles* (pp. 15–43). Hershey, PA: Information Science Reference. doi:10.4018/978-1-60566-896-3.ch002.

Grady, J. P., Spring, M. B., & Rotondi, A. J. (2010). Designing medical research web sites. In Tatnall, A. (Ed.), *Web Technologies: Concepts, Methodologies, Tools, and Applications* (pp. 291–309). Hershey, PA: Information Science Reference.

Grandinetti, L., & Pisacane, O. (2012). Web services for healthcare management. In Prakash Vidyarthi, D. (Ed.), *Technologies and Protocols for the Future of Internet Design: Reinventing the Web* (pp. 60–94). Hershey, PA: Information Science Reference. doi:10.4018/978-1-4666-0203-8.ch004.

Grigg, A., & Guan, L. (2010). A scalable approach to real-time system timing applications. In Li, K., Hsu, C., Yang, L., Dongarra, J., & Zima, H. (Eds.), *Handbook of Research on Scalable Computing Technologies* (pp. 606–644). Hershey, PA: Information Science Reference.

Grigoras, D., Doolan, D. C., & Tabirca, S. (2010). Scalability of mobile ad hoc networks. In Li, K., Hsu, C., Yang, L., Dongarra, J., & Zima, H. (Eds.), *Handbook of Research on Scalable Computing Technologies* (pp. 705–717). Hershey, PA: Information Science Reference.

Guidi, D., Gaspari, M., & Profiti, G. (2010). Web services integration in multi-agent systems. In K. Ragab, T. Helmy, & A. Hassanien (Eds.), Developing Advanced Web Services through P2P Computing and Autonomous Agents: Trends and Innovations(pp. 1-17). Hershey, PA: Information Science Reference. doi: doi:10.4018/978-1-61520-973-6.ch001.

Gupta, N., Saini, D., & Saini, H. (2010). Class level test case generation in object oriented software testing. In Alkhatib, G., & Rine, D. (Eds.), *Web Engineering Advancements and Trends: Building New Dimensions of Information Technology* (pp. 203–211). Hershey, PA: Information Science Reference. doi:10.4018/978-1-60566-719-5.ch011.

Han, J., & Lee, S. T. (2012). Impact of vendor selection on firms' IT outsourcing: The Korea experience. [JGIM]. *Journal of Global Information Management*, 20(2), 25–43. doi:10.4018/jgim.2012040102.

Hanh, H. H., Tho, M. N., & A., M. T. (2010). A semantic web-based approach for context-aware user query formulation and information retrieval. In G. Alkhatib, & D. Rine (Eds.), *Web Engineering Advancements and Trends: Building New Dimensions of Information Technology* (pp. 1-23). Hershey, PA: Information Science Reference. doi:10.4018/978-1-60566-719-5.ch001

Haque, E., & Yoshida, N. (2012). Clustering in wireless sensor networks: Context-aware approaches. In Abawajy, J., Pathan, M., Rahman, M., Pathan, A., & Deris, M. (Eds.), *Internet and Distributed Computing Advancements: Theoretical Frameworks and Practical Applications* (pp. 197–211). Hershey, PA: Information Science Reference. doi:10.4018/978-1-4666-0161-1.ch008.

Harney, J., & Doshi, P. (2011). Selective querying for adapting hierarchical web service compositions. In Milanovic, N. (Ed.), *Engineering Reliable Service Oriented Architecture: Managing Complexity and Service Level Agreements* (pp. 125–144). Hershey, PA: Information Science Reference. doi:10.4018/978-1-60960-493-6.ch007.

Hassan, O. A., Ramaswamy, L., & Miller, J. (2012). The MACE approach for caching mashups. In Hung, P. (Ed.), *Web Service Composition and New Frameworks in Designing Semantics: Innovations* (pp. 261–284). Hershey, PA: Information Science Reference. doi:10.4018/978-1-4666-1942-5.ch012.

Hellmann, S., Lehmann, J., & Auer, S. (2009). Learning of OWL class descriptions on very large knowledge bases. [IJSWIS]. *International Journal on Semantic Web and Information Systems*, 5(2), 25–48. doi:10.4018/jswis.2009040102.

Helmy, T. (2010). Adaptive ensemble multi-agent based intrusion detection model. In K. Ragab, T. Helmy, & A. Hassanien (Eds.), Developing Advanced Web Services through P2P Computing and Autonomous Agents: Trends and Innovations (pp. 36-48). Hershey, PA: Information Science Reference. doi: doi:10.4018/978-1-61520-973-6.ch003.

Helmy, T., & Al-Nazer, A. (2010). Personalized web services selection. In K. Ragab, T. Helmy, & A. Hassanien (Eds.), Developing Advanced Web Services through P2P Computing and Autonomous Agents: Trends and Innovations (pp. 114-132). Hershey, PA: Information Science Reference. doi: doi:10.4018/978-1-61520-973-6.ch007.

Hofer, W., Sincero, J., Schröder-Preikschat, W., & Lohmann, D. (2011). Configuration of non-functional properties in embedded operating systems: The CiAO approach. In Milanovic, N. (Ed.), *Engineering Reliable Service Oriented Architecture: Managing Complexity and Service Level Agreements* (pp. 84–103). Hershey, PA: Information Science Reference. doi:10.4018/978-1-60960-493-6.ch005.

Hogan, A., Harth, A., & Polleres, A. (2009). Scalable authoritative OWL reasoning for the web. [IJSWIS]. *International Journal on Semantic Web and Information Systems*, 5(2), 49–90. doi: doi:10.4018/jswis.2009040103.

Hogg, S., Holt, P. O., & Aitchison, J. (2010). A case study of usability engineering in the defence industry. In Spiliotopoulos, T., Papadopoulou, P., Martakos, D., & Kouroupetroglou, G. (Eds.), *Integrating Usability Engineering for Designing the Web Experience: Methodologies and Principles* (pp. 44–57). Hershey, PA: Information Science Reference. doi:10.4018/978-1-60566-896-3.ch003.

Howison, J., Conklin, M., & Crowston, K. (2009). FLOSSmole: A collaborative repository for FLOSS research data and analyses. In Alkhatib, G., & Rine, D. (Eds.), *Integrated Approaches in Information Technology and Web Engineering: Advancing Organizational Knowledge Sharing* (pp. 18–27). Hershey, PA: Information Science Reference. doi:10.4018/978-1-60566-060-8.ch009.

Hu, Y., & Li, R. (2012). Energy-efficient MAC protocols in distributed sensor networks. In Abawajy, J., Pathan, M., Rahman, M., Pathan, A., & Deris, M. (Eds.), *Internet and Distributed Computing Advancements: Theoretical Frameworks and Practical Applications* (pp. 247–271). Hershey, PA: Information Science Reference. doi:10.4018/978-1-4666-0161-1.ch010.

Huang, K., Geller, J., Halper, M., Elhanan, G., & Perl, Y. (2013). Scalability of piecewise synonym identification in integration of SNOMED into the UMLS. In Gangopadhyay, A. (Ed.), *Methods, Models, and Computation for Medical Informatics* (pp. 170–188). Hershey, PA: Medical Information Science Reference.

Igelnik, B., & Zurada, J. M. (2013). *Efficiency and scalability methods for computational intellect*. Hershey, PA: IGI Global. doi:10.4018/978-1-4666-3942-3.

Isaías, P., Pífano, S., & Miranda, P. (2012). Web 2.0: Harnessing democracy's potential. In Downey, E., & Jones, M. (Eds.), *Public Service, Governance and Web 2.0 Technologies: Future Trends in Social Media* (pp. 223–236). Hershey, PA: Information Science Reference. doi:10.4018/978-1-4666-0071-3.ch014.

Islam, M. S., Morshed, M. N., Islam, S. S., & Azam, M. M. (2012). Random early discard (RED) queue evaluation for congestion control. In Prakash Vidyarthi, D. (Ed.), *Technologies and Protocols for the Future of Internet Design: Reinventing the Web* (pp. 229–246). Hershey, PA: Information Science Reference. doi:10.4018/978-1-4666-0203-8.ch012.

Issa, T., West, M., & Turk, A. (2010). Development and evaluation of a methodology for developing marketing websites. In Spiliotopoulos, T., Papadopoulou, P., Martakos, D., & Kouroupetroglou, G. (Eds.), *Integrating Usability Engineering for Designing the Web Experience: Methodologies and Principles* (pp. 103–123). Hershey, PA: Information Science Reference. doi:10.4018/978-1-60566-896-3.ch006.

Jacobsen, R. H., Toftegaard, T. S., & Kjærgaard, J. K. (2012). IP connected low power wireless personal area networks in the future internet. In Prakash Vidyarthi, D. (Ed.), *Technologies and Protocols for the Future of Internet Design: Reinventing the Web* (pp. 191–213). Hershey, PA: Information Science Reference. doi:10.4018/978-1-4666-0203-8.ch010.

Jegadeesan, H., & Balasubramaniam, S. (2012). Service flavors: Differentiating service offerings in a services marketplace. In Hung, P. (Ed.), *Web Service Composition and New Frameworks in Designing Semantics: Innovations* (pp. 171–193). Hershey, PA: Information Science Reference. doi:10.4018/978-1-4666-1942-5.ch008.

Jie-Zhang, L. (2012). *Innovations, standards and practices of web services: Emerging research topics*. Hershey, PA: IGI Global.

Jijun, L., & Swapna, S. G. (2010). Performance analysis of a web server. In Alkhatib, G., & Rine, D. (Eds.), *Web Engineering Advancements and Trends: Building New Dimensions of Information Technology* (pp. 230–242). Hershey, PA: Information Science Reference. doi:10.4018/978-1-60566-719-5.ch013.

Kacprzyk, J., & Zadrozny, S. (2010). Linguistic data summarization: A high scalability through the use of natural language? In Laurent, A., & Lesot, M. (Eds.), *Scalable Fuzzy Algorithms for Data Management and Analysis: Methods and Design* (pp. 214–237). Hershey, PA: Information Science Reference.

Kamthan, P. (2010). A perspective on the credibility engineering of web applications. In Alkhatib, G., & Rine, D. (Eds.), *Web Engineering Advancements and Trends: Building New Dimensions of Information Technology* (pp. 243–258). Hershey, PA: Information Science Reference. doi:10.4018/978-1-60566-719-5.ch014.

Kamthan, P. (2010). On the prospects and concerns of pattern-oriented web engineering. In Alkhatib, G., & Rine, D. (Eds.), *Web Engineering Advancements and Trends: Building New Dimensions of Information Technology* (pp. 97–128). Hershey, PA: Information Science Reference. doi:10.4018/978-1-60566-719-5.ch006.

Kareem, S., & Bajwa, I. S. (2012). Virtual telemedicine and virtual telehealth: A natural language based implementation to address time constraint problem. In Alkhatib, G. (Ed.), *Models for Capitalizing on Web Engineering Advancements: Trends and Discoveries* (pp. 183–195). Hershey, PA: Information Science Publishing. doi:10.4018/978-1-4666-0023-2.ch010.

Khader, O. H. (2009). FSR evaluation using the suboptimal operational values. In Alkhatib, G., & Rine, D. (Eds.), *Integrated Approaches in Information Technology and Web Engineering: Advancing Organizational Knowledge Sharing* (pp. 203–211). Hershey, PA: Information Science Reference.

Khosravifar, B., Bentahar, J., Moazin, A., & Thiran, P. (2012). Analyzing communities of web services using incentives. In Hung, P. (Ed.), *Web Service Composition and New Frameworks in Designing Semantics: Innovations* (pp. 330–351). Hershey, PA: Information Science Reference. doi:10.4018/978-1-4666-1942-5.ch015.

Kilfoil, M., & Ghorbani, A. (2011). SWAMI: A multiagent, active representation of a user's browsing interests. In Alkhatib, G. (Ed.), *Web Engineered Applications for Evolving Organizations: Emerging Knowledge* (pp. 171–195). Hershey, PA: Information Science Reference. doi:10.4018/978-1-60960-523-0.ch011.

Kim, Y., Park, M., & Lee, K. (2012). Autonomous web services migration in mobile and wireless environments. In Jie-Zhang, L. (Ed.), *Innovations, Standards and Practices of Web Services: Emerging Research Topics* (pp. 117–131). Hershey, PA: Information Science Reference.

Kona, S., Bansal, A., Simon, L., Mallya, A., Gupta, G., & Hite, T. D. (2012). USDL: A service-semantics description language for automatic service discovery and composition1. In Jie-Zhang, L. (Ed.), *Innovations, Standards and Practices of Web Services: Emerging Research Topics* (pp. 23–53). Hershey, PA: Information Science Reference.

Kumar, S., Kumar, K., & Jain, A. (2010). An agent-enabled semantic web service composition framework. In Alkhatib, G., & Rine, D. (Eds.), *Web Engineering Advancements and Trends: Building New Dimensions of Information Technology* (pp. 63–82). Hershey, PA: Information Science Reference. doi:10.4018/978-1-60566-719-5.ch004.

Kuppuswami, S., & Chithralekha, T. (2010). A new behavior management architecture for language faculty of an agent for task delegation. [IJIIT]. *International Journal of Intelligent Information Technologies*, 6(2), 44–64. doi:10.4018/jiit.2010040103.

Laurent, A., & Lesot, M. (2010). *Scalable fuzzy algorithms for data management and analysis: Methods and design*. Hershey, PA: IGI Global.

Laws, R. D., Howell, S. L., & Lindsay, N. K. (2009). Ten scalability factors in distance education. In Rogers, P., Berg, G., Boettcher, J., Howard, C., Justice, L., & Schenk, K. (Eds.), *Encyclopedia of Distance Learning* (2nd ed., pp. 2095–2102). Hershey, PA: Information Science Reference. doi:10.4018/978-1-60566-198-8.ch309.

Le, D. X., Rahayu, J. W., & Taniar, D. (2009). Web data warehousing convergence: From schematic to systematic. In Alkhatib, G., & Rine, D. (Eds.), *Integrated Approaches in Information Technology and Web Engineering: Advancing Organizational Knowledge Sharing* (pp. 278–303). Hershey, PA: Information Science Reference. doi:10.4018/978-1-60566-058-5.ch041.

Lecue, F., & Mehandjiev, N. (2012). Satisfying end user constraints in service composition by applying stochastic search methods. In Hung, P. (Ed.), *Web Service Composition and New Frameworks in Designing Semantics: Innovations* (pp. 238–260). Hershey, PA: Information Science Reference. doi:10.4018/978-1-4666-1942-5.ch011.

Lee, C. L., Liu, A., & Shr, A. (2012). A goal-driven approach for service-oriented systems design. In Lee, J., Ma, S., & Liu, A. (Eds.), *Service Life Cycle Tools and Technologies: Methods, Trends and Advances* (pp. 101–122). Hershey, PA: Information Science Reference.

Lee, S. C. (2009). Modeling variant user interfaces for web-based software product lines. In Alkhatib, G., & Rine, D. (Eds.), *Integrated Approaches in Information Technology and Web Engineering: Advancing Organizational Knowledge Sharing* (pp. 212–242). Hershey, PA: Information Science Reference.

Lee, Y., Chu, P., & Tseng, H. (2012). Cross-national and cross-industrial comparison of ICT-enabled business process management and performance. [JGIM]. *Journal of Global Information Management*, 20(2), 44–66. doi:10.4018/jgim.2012040103.

Leong, I., Si, Y., & Biuk-Aghai, R. P. (2012). Predicting temporal exceptions in concurrent workflows. In Alkhatib, G. (Ed.), *Models for Capitalizing on Web Engineering Advancements: Trends and Discoveries* (pp. 196–218). Hershey, PA: Information Science Publishing. doi:10.4018/978-1-4666-0023-2.ch011.

Li, K., Hsu, C., Yang, L., Dongarra, J., & Zima, H. (2010). *Handbook of research on scalable computing technologies*. Hershey, PA: IGI Global.

Li, L., Niu, C., Chen, N., Wei, J., & Huang, T. (2012). High performance approach for server side SOAP processing. In Jie-Zhang, L. (Ed.), *Innovations, Standards and Practices of Web Services: Emerging Research Topics* (pp. 189–215). Hershey, PA: Information Science Reference.

Li, M., Yu, B., Sahota, V., & Qi, M. (2010). Web services discovery with rough sets. In Tatnall, A. (Ed.), *Web Technologies: Concepts, Methodologies, Tools, and Applications* (pp. 830–847). Hershey, PA: Information Science Reference.

Li, M., Yu, B., Sahota, V., & Qi, M. (2012). Web services discovery with rough sets. In Jie-Zhang, L. (Ed.), *Innovations, Standards and Practices of Web Services: Emerging Research Topics* (pp. 74–91). Hershey, PA: Information Science Reference.

Liu, M., Wu, X., Zhao, J. L., & Zhu, L. (2010). Outsourcing of community source: Identifying motivations and benefits. [JGIM]. *Journal of Global Information Management*, 18(4), 36–52. doi:10.4018/jgim.2010100103.

Liu, X., & Georgalas, N. (2011). Specification of non-functional requirements and their trade-offs in service contracts in the NGOSS framework. In Milanovic, N. (Ed.), *Engineering Reliable Service Oriented Architecture: Managing Complexity and Service Level Agreements* (pp. 199–211). Hershey, PA: Information Science Reference. doi:10.4018/978-1-60960-493-6.ch010.

Looker, N., & Munro, M. (2011). Dependability assessment of service-oriented architectures using fault injection. In Milanovic, N. (Ed.), *Engineering Reliable Service Oriented Architecture: Managing Complexity and Service Level Agreements* (pp. 340–359). Hershey, PA: Information Science Reference. doi:10.4018/978-1-60960-493-6.ch016.

Lopes, R., Votis, K., Carriço, L., Likothanassis, S., & Tzovaras, D. (2010). A service oriented ontological framework for the semantic validation of web accessibility. In Tatnall, A. (Ed.), *Web Technologies: Concepts, Methodologies, Tools, and Applications* (pp. 522–540). Hershey, PA: Information Science Reference. doi:10.4018/978-1-60960-100-3.ch201.

López-Fernández, L., Robles, G., Gonzalez-Barahona, J. M., & Herraiz, I. (2009). Applying social network analysis techniques to community-driven libre software projects. In Alkhatib, G., & Rine, D. (Eds.), *Integrated Approaches in Information Technology and Web Engineering: Advancing Organizational Knowledge Sharing* (pp. 28–50). Hershey, PA: Information Science Reference. doi:10.4018/978-1-60566-060-8.ch112.

Loucky, J. P. (2010). Improving online readability in a web 2.0 context. In Tatnall, A. (Ed.), *Web Technologies: Concepts, Methodologies, Tools, and Applications* (pp. 1411–1436). Hershey, PA: Information Science Reference.

Lucia, D. K., & Restyandito,. (2010). Localized user interface for improving cell phone users' device competency. In G. Alkhatib, & D. Rine (Eds.), *Web Engineering Advancements and Trends: Building New Dimensions of Information Technology* (pp. 129-143). Hershey, PA: Information Science Reference. doi:10.4018/978-1-60566-719-5.ch007

Mahdin, H., & Abawajy, J. H. (2012). An approach to faulty reader detection in RFID reader network. In Abawajy, J., Pathan, M., Rahman, M., Pathan, A., & Deris, M. (Eds.), *Internet and Distributed Computing Advancements: Theoretical Frameworks and Practical Applications* (pp. 70–84). Hershey, PA: Information Science Reference. doi:10.4018/978-1-4666-0161-1.ch003.

Mahmood, A., & Homeed, T. S. (2009). Object grouping and replication on a distributed web server system. In Alkhatib, G., & Rine, D. (Eds.), *Integrated Approaches in Information Technology and Web Engineering: Advancing Organizational Knowledge Sharing* (pp. 158–173). Hershey, PA: Information Science Reference.

Malinen, S., & Ojala, J. (2013). Perceptions of trust between online auction consumers. In Polgar, J., & Adamson, G. (Eds.), *Web Portal Design, Implementation, Integration, and Optimization* (pp. 186–197). Hershey, PA: Information Science Reference. doi:10.4018/978-1-4666-2779-6. ch015.

Malizia, A., De Angeli, A., Levialdi, S., & Aedo Cuevas, I. (2010). Exploiting collaborative tagging systems to unveil the user-experience of web contents: An operative proposal. In Tatnall, A. (Ed.), *Web Technologies: Concepts, Methodologies, Tools, and Applications* (pp. 1374–1387). Hershey, PA: Information Science Reference.

Manaseer, S. S., Ould-Khaoua, M., & Mackenzie, L. M. (2009). On the logarithmic backoff algorithm for MAC protocol in MANETs. In Alkhatib, G., & Rine, D. (Eds.), *Integrated Approaches in Information Technology and Web Engineering: Advancing Organizational Knowledge Sharing* (pp. 174–184). Hershey, PA: Information Science Reference.

Mansour, N., & Baba, N. (2010). Ripple effect in web applications. [IJITWE]. *International Journal of Information Technology and Web Engineering*, 5(2), 1–15. doi:10.4018/jitwe.2010040101.

Mansour, N., & Baba, N. (2012). Ripple effect in web applications. In Alkhatib, G. (Ed.), *Models for Capitalizing on Web Engineering Advancements: Trends and Discoveries* (pp. 97–111). Hershey, PA: Information Science Publishing. doi:10.4018/978-1-4666-0023-2.ch006.

Margaritis, D., Faloutsos, C., & Thrun, S. (2009). NetCube: Fast, approximate database queries using bayesian networks. In Erickson, J. (Ed.), *Database Technologies: Concepts, Methodologies, Tools, and Applications* (pp. 2011–2036). Hershey, PA: Information Science Reference. doi:10.4018/978-1-60566-058-5.ch120.

Maria, I., & Seng, L. (2010). The impact of ontology on the performance of information retrieval: A case of WordNet. In Alkhatib, G., & Rine, D. (Eds.), *Web Engineering Advancements and Trends: Building New Dimensions of Information Technology* (pp. 24–37). Hershey, PA: Information Science Reference. doi:10.4018/978-1-60566-719-5.ch002.

Mariño, P., Fontán, F., Domínguez, M., & Otero, S. (2011). Viticulture zoning by an experimental WSN. In Alkhatib, G. (Ed.), *Web Engineered Applications for Evolving Organizations: Emerging Knowledge* (pp. 13–26). Hershey, PA: Information Science Reference. doi:10.4018/978-1-60960-523-0.ch002.

Marquezan, C. C. Metzger, Pohl, Engen, Boniface, Phillips, & Zlatev. (2013). Adaptive future internet applications: Opportunities and challenges for adaptive web services technology. In Adaptive Web Services for Modular and Reusable Software Development: Tactics and Solutions, (pp. 333-353). Hershey, PA: IGI Global. doi: doi:10.4018/978-1-4666-2089-6.ch014.

Martino, L., & Bertino, E. (2012). Security for web services: Standards and research issues. In Jie-Zhang, L. (Ed.), *Innovations, Standards and Practices of Web Services: Emerging Research Topics* (pp. 336–362). Hershey, PA: Information Science Reference.

Massarelli, M., Raibulet, C., Cammareri, D., & Perino, N. (2011). Design of quality aspects in service oriented architecture through service level agreements: The streaming case study. In Milanovic, N. (Ed.), *Engineering Reliable Service Oriented Architecture: Managing Complexity and Service Level Agreements* (pp. 1–21). Hershey, PA: Information Science Reference. doi:10.4018/978-1-60960-493-6.ch001.

Matei, S. A., Faiola, A., Wheatley, D. J., & Altom, T. (2012). The role of physical affordances in multifunctional mobile device design. In Alkhatib, G. (Ed.), *Models for Capitalizing on Web Engineering Advancements: Trends and Discoveries* (pp. 306–324). Hershey, PA: Information Science Publishing. doi:10.4018/978-1-4666-0023-2.ch016.

Matei, S. A., Madsen, L., & Bruno, R. (2012). Information acquisition and recall in location-aware and search engine retrieval systems. In Alkhatib, G. (Ed.), *Models for Capitalizing on Web Engineering Advancements: Trends and Discoveries* (pp. 20–42). Hershey, PA: Information Science Publishing. doi:10.4018/978-1-4666-0023-2.ch002.

Matsuo, T., & Fujimoto, T. (2011). *E-activity and intelligent web construction: Effects of social design.* Hershey, PA: IGI Global. doi:10.4018/978-1-61520-871-5.

McDonald, M., McDonald, J. S., Merwin, G. A., Merwin, K. A., & Richardson, M. (2012). Assessment of web 2.0 applications employed by human resource departments in U.S. cities. In Downey, E., & Jones, M. (Eds.), *Public Service, Governance and Web 2.0 Technologies: Future Trends in Social Media* (pp. 122–138). Hershey, PA: Information Science Reference. doi:10.4018/978-1-4666-0071-3.ch008.

Meng, S. K., & Chatwin, C. R. (2010). Ontology-based shopping agent for e-marketing. [IJIIT]. *International Journal of Intelligent Information Technologies*, 6(2), 21–43. doi:10.4018/jiit.2010040102.

Mergel, I. A., & Schweik, C. M. (2012). The paradox of the interactive web in the U.S. public sector. In Downey, E., & Jones, M. (Eds.), *Public Service, Governance and Web 2.0 Technologies: Future Trends in Social Media* (pp. 266–289). Hershey, PA: Information Science Reference. doi:10.4018/978-1-4666-0071-3.ch017.

Michlmayr, A., Rosenberg, F., Leitner, P., & Dustdar, S. (2012). Selective service provenance in the VRESCo runtime. In Hung, P. (Ed.), *Web Service Composition and New Frameworks in Designing Semantics: Innovations* (pp. 372–394). Hershey, PA: Information Science Reference. doi:10.4018/978-1-4666-1942-5.ch017.

Milanovic, N., & Milic, B. (2011). Model-based methodology and framework for assessing service and business process availability. In Milanovic, N. (Ed.), *Engineering Reliable Service Oriented Architecture: Managing Complexity and Service Level Agreements* (pp. 257–291). Hershey, PA: Information Science Reference. doi:10.4018/978-1-60960-493-6.ch013.

Miller, J., Zhang, L., Ofuonye, E., & Smith, M. (2010). Towards automated bypass testing of web applications. In Alkhatib, G., & Rine, D. (Eds.), *Web Engineering Advancements and Trends: Building New Dimensions of Information Technology* (pp. 212–229). Hershey, PA: Information Science Reference. doi:10.4018/978-1-60566-719-5.ch012.

Mirante, D. P., & Ammari, H. M. (2012). Wireless sensor network security attacks: A survey. In Abawajy, J., Pathan, M., Rahman, M., Pathan, A., & Deris, M. (Eds.), *Internet and Distributed Computing Advancements: Theoretical Frameworks and Practical Applications* (pp. 162–196). Hershey, PA: Information Science Reference. doi:10.4018/978-1-4666-0161-1.ch007.

Mirbel, I., & Crescenzo, P. (2013). Improving collaborations in the neuroscientist community. In Polgar, J., & Adamson, G. (Eds.), *Web Portal Design, Implementation, Integration, and Optimization* (pp. 33–49). Hershey, PA: Information Science Reference. doi:10.4018/978-1-4666-2779-6.ch003.

Molina, B., Palau, C. E., & Esteve, M. (2012). CDN modeling and performance. In Fortino, G., & Palau, C. (Eds.), *Next Generation Content Delivery Infrastructures: Emerging Paradigms and Technologies* (pp. 1–28). Hershey, PA: Information Science Reference. doi:10.4018/978-1-4666-1794-0.ch001.

Monfort, V., Cherif, S., & Chaabani, R. (2013). A service-based approach to connect context-aware platforms and adaptable android for mobile users. In Ortiz, G., & Cubo, J. (Eds.), *Adaptive Web Services for Modular and Reusable Software Development: Tactics and Solutions* (pp. 302–332). Hershey, PA: Information Science Reference.

Najjar, F., & Slimani, H. (2011). A linked neighboring leaves n-tree to support distance range search. In Alkhatib, G. (Ed.), *Web Engineered Applications for Evolving Organizations: Emerging Knowledge* (pp. 27–43). Hershey, PA: Information Science Reference. doi:10.4018/978-1-60960-523-0.ch003.

Nanda, P., & He, X. (2010). Scalable internet architecture supporting quality of service (QoS). In Li, K., Hsu, C., Yang, L., Dongarra, J., & Zima, H. (Eds.), *Handbook of Research on Scalable Computing Technologies* (pp. 739–759). Hershey, PA: Information Science Reference.

Nauerz, A., & Thompson, R. (2010). Adaptation and recommendation in modern web 2.0 portals. In Tatnall, A. (Ed.), *Web Technologies: Concepts, Methodologies, Tools, and Applications* (pp. 404–416). Hershey, PA: Information Science Reference.

Neff, F., Kehoe, A., & Pitt, I. (2010). Considering the perceptual implications of auditory rich content on the web. In Spiliotopoulos, T., Papadopoulou, P., Martakos, D., & Kouroupetroglou, G. (Eds.), *Integrating Usability Engineering for Designing the Web Experience: Methodologies and Principles* (pp. 191–209). Hershey, PA: Information Science Reference. doi:10.4018/978-1-60566-896-3.ch010.

Nepal, S., & Zic, J. (2012). Issues on the compatibility of web service contracts. In Jie-Zhang, L. (Ed.), *Innovations, Standards and Practices of Web Services: Emerging Research Topics* (pp. 154–188). Hershey, PA: Information Science Reference.

Oh, S., & Lee, D. (2012). Complex network theory based web services composition benchmark toolkit. In Jie-Zhang, L. (Ed.), *Innovations, Standards and Practices of Web Services: Emerging Research Topics* (pp. 1–22). Hershey, PA: Information Science Reference.

Okyere-Benya, J., Exarchakos, G., Menkovski, V., Liotta, A., & Giaccone, P. (2012). Mechanisms for parallel data transport. In Fortino, G., & Palau, C. (Eds.), *Next Generation Content Delivery Infrastructures: Emerging Paradigms and Technologies* (pp. 172–198). Hershey, PA: Information Science Reference. doi:10.4018/978-1-4666-1794-0.ch008.

Ortiz, G., & Bordbar, B. (2012). Quality of service and extra-functional properties for web services: A model-driven approach. In Lee, J., Ma, S., & Liu, A. (Eds.), *Service Life Cycle Tools and Technologies: Methods, Trends and Advances* (pp. 35–64). Hershey, PA: Information Science Reference.

Ortiz, G., Boubeta-Puig, J., García de Prado, A., & Medina-Bulo, I. (2013). Towards event-driven context-aware web services. In Ortiz, G., & Cubo, J. (Eds.), *Adaptive Web Services for Modular and Reusable Software Development: Tactics and Solutions* (pp. 148–159). Hershey, PA: Information Science Reference.

Ortiz, G., & Cubo, J. (2013). *Adaptive web services for modular and reusable software development: Tactics and solutions*. Hershey, PA: IGI Global.

Page, G. A., & Ali, R. (2010). The power and promise of web 2.0 tools. In Tatnall, A. (Ed.), *Web Technologies: Concepts, Methodologies, Tools, and Applications* (pp. 188–200). Hershey, PA: Information Science Reference.

Palomo-Duarte, M. (2012). Service composition verification and validation. In Lee, J., Ma, S., & Liu, A. (Eds.), *Service Life Cycle Tools and Technologies: Methods, Trends and Advances* (pp. 200–219). Hershey, PA: Information Science Reference.

Parkin, M., Kuo, D., & Brooke, J. (2012). A framework and protocols for service contract agreements based on international contract law. In Jie-Zhang, L. (Ed.), *Innovations, Standards and Practices of Web Services: Emerging Research Topics* (pp. 216–231). Hershey, PA: Information Science Reference.

Parkinson, C. M., & Olphert, C. W. (2010). Website accessibility and the role of accessibility statements. In Spiliotopoulos, T., Papadopoulou, P., Martakos, D., & Kouroupetroglou, G. (Eds.), *Integrating Usability Engineering for Designing the Web Experience: Methodologies and Principles* (pp. 166–190). Hershey, PA: Information Science Reference. doi:10.4018/978-1-60566-896-3.ch009.

Pathan, M., Broberg, J., & Buyya, R. (2012). On the performance of content delivery clouds. In Fortino, G., & Palau, C. (Eds.), *Next Generation Content Delivery Infrastructures: Emerging Paradigms and Technologies* (pp. 29–54). Hershey, PA: Information Science Reference. doi:10.4018/978-1-4666-1794-0.ch002.

Pathan, M., Palmer, D., & Salehi, A. (2012). A walk through sensor network programming models. In Abawajy, J., Pathan, M., Rahman, M., Pathan, A., & Deris, M. (Eds.), *Internet and Distributed Computing Advancements: Theoretical Frameworks and Practical Applications* (pp. 138–161). Hershey, PA: Information Science Reference. doi:10.4018/978-1-4666-0161-1.ch006.

Patiniotiakis, I., Papageorgiou, N., Verginadis, Y., Apostolou, D., & Mentzas, G. (2013). A framework for situation-aware adaptation of service-based applications. In Ortiz, G., & Cubo, J. (Eds.), *Adaptive Web Services for Modular and Reusable Software Development: Tactics and Solutions* (pp. 253–262). Hershey, PA: Information Science Reference.

Payrits, S., Dornbach, P., & Zólyomi, I. (2012). XML data binding for C++ using metadata. In Jie-Zhang, L. (Ed.), *Innovations, Standards and Practices of Web Services: Emerging Research Topics* (pp. 232–249). Hershey, PA: Information Science Reference.

Pelet, J. (2010). The influence of e-commerce website colors on usability. In Spiliotopoulos, T., Papadopoulou, P., Martakos, D., & Kouroupetroglou, G. (Eds.), *Integrating Usability Engineering for Designing the Web Experience: Methodologies and Principles* (pp. 264–288). Hershey, PA: Information Science Reference. doi:10.4018/978-1-60566-896-3.ch014.

Peng, D., Wang, X., & Zhou, A. (2012). Managing the replaceability of web services using underlying semantics. In Hung, P. (Ed.), *Web Service Composition and New Frameworks in Designing Semantics: Innovations* (pp. 124–142). Hershey, PA: Information Science Reference. doi:10.4018/978-1-4666-1942-5.ch006.

Pérez-Llopis, I., Palau, C. E., & Esteve, M. (2012). Wireless multimedia content distribution architecture. In Fortino, G., & Palau, C. (Eds.), *Next Generation Content Delivery Infrastructures: Emerging Paradigms and Technologies* (pp. 78–104). Hershey, PA: Information Science Reference. doi:10.4018/978-1-4666-1794-0.ch004.

Petry, F., Ladner, R., Gupta, K. M., Moore, P., Aha, D., Lin, B., & Sween, R. (2011). Discovery and mediation approaches for management of net-centric web services. In Alkhatib, G. (Ed.), *Web Engineered Applications for Evolving Organizations: Emerging Knowledge* (pp. 233–254). Hershey, PA: Information Science Reference. doi:10.4018/978-1-60960-523-0.ch014.

Pipan, M., Arh, T., & Blažic, B. J. (2010). The evaluation cycle management - Method applied to the evaluation of learning management systems. In Spiliotopoulos, T., Papadopoulou, P., Martakos, D., & Kouroupetroglou, G. (Eds.), *Integrating Usability Engineering for Designing the Web Experience: Methodologies and Principles* (pp. 58–80). Hershey, PA: Information Science Reference. doi:10.4018/978-1-60566-896-3.ch004.

Pitariu, H. D., Andrei, D. M., & Guran, A. M. (2010). Social research methods used in moving the traditional usability approach towards a user-centered design approach. In Spiliotopoulos, T., Papadopoulou, P., Martakos, D., & Kouroupetroglou, G. (Eds.), *Integrating Usability Engineering for Designing the Web Experience: Methodologies and Principles* (pp. 225–242). Hershey, PA: Information Science Reference. doi:10.4018/978-1-60566-896-3.ch012.

Poggi, A., & Tomaiuolo, M. (2010). Extending the JADE framework for semantic peer-to-peer service based applications. In K. Ragab, T. Helmy, & A. Hassanien (Eds.), Developing Advanced Web Services through P2P Computing and Autonomous Agents: Trends and Innovations (pp. 18-35). Hershey, PA: Information Science Reference. doi: doi:10.4018/978-1-61520-973-6.ch002.

Polgar, J., & Adamson, G. (2013). *Web portal design, implementation, integration, and optimization.* Hershey, PA: IGI Global. doi:10.4018/978-1-4666-2779-6.

Pontelli, E., Son, T. C., & Baral, C. (2010). A logic programming based framework for intelligent web service composition. In Tatnall, A. (Ed.), *Web Technologies: Concepts, Methodologies, Tools, and Applications* (pp. 355–378). Hershey, PA: Information Science Reference.

Povalej, R., & Weiß, P. (2010). Basics to develop web services for human resources. In Tatnall, A. (Ed.), *Web Technologies: Concepts, Methodologies, Tools, and Applications* (pp. 167–176). Hershey, PA: Information Science Reference.

Power, C., Freire, A. P., & Petrie, H. (2010). Integrating accessibility evaluation into web engineering processes. In Spiliotopoulos, T., Papadopoulou, P., Martakos, D., & Kouroupetroglou, G. (Eds.), *Integrating Usability Engineering for Designing the Web Experience: Methodologies and Principles* (pp. 124–148). Hershey, PA: Information Science Reference. doi:10.4018/978-1-60566-896-3.ch007.

Prakash Vidyarthi, D. (2012). *Technologies and protocols for the future of internet design: Reinventing the web*. Hershey, PA: IGI Global.

Prasolova-Forland, E., & Hov, O. Ø. (2013). Eidsvoll 1814: Creating educational historical reconstructions in 3D collaborative virtual environments. In Polgar, J., & Adamson, G. (Eds.), *Web Portal Design, Implementation, Integration, and Optimization* (pp. 171–185). Hershey, PA: Information Science Reference. doi:10.4018/978-1-4666-2779-6.ch014.

Pruski, C., Guelfi, N., & Reynaud, C. (2013). Adaptive ontology-based web information retrieval: The TARGET framework. In Polgar, J., & Adamson, G. (Eds.), *Web Portal Design, Implementation, Integration, and Optimization* (pp. 152–170). Hershey, PA: Information Science Reference. doi:10.4018/978-1-4666-2779-6.ch013.

Purohit, N. (2012). The physical layer aspects of wireless networks. In Prakash Vidyarthi, D. (Ed.), *Technologies and Protocols for the Future of Internet Design: Reinventing the Web* (pp. 95–113). Hershey, PA: Information Science Reference. doi:10.4018/978-1-4666-0203-8.ch005.

Ragab, K., Helmy, T., & Hassanien, A. (2010). Developing advanced web services through P2P computing and autonomous agents: Trends and innovations. Hershey, PA: IGI Global. doi:doi:10.4018/978-1-61520-973-6.

Raghuwanshi, S. K. (2012). Optical networking: Current issues and review. In Prakash Vidyarthi, D. (Ed.), *Technologies and Protocols for the Future of Internet Design: Reinventing the Web* (pp. 4–36). Hershey, PA: Information Science Reference. doi:10.4018/978-1-4666-0203-8.ch002.

Rahman, W. N., & Meziane, F. (2011). A generic QoS model for web: Services design. [IJITWE]. *International Journal of Information Technology and Web Engineering*, 6(3), 15–38. doi:10.4018/jitwe.2011070102.

Raj, E. D., Prakash, S. J., & Raja, S. (2011). Analysis of quality of service routing algorithms. In Alkhatib, G. (Ed.), *Web Engineered Applications for Evolving Organizations: Emerging Knowledge* (pp. 159–169). Hershey, PA: Information Science Reference. doi:10.4018/978-1-60960-523-0.ch010.

Ramachandra, M., & Pattabhirama, P. (2012). Analysis of the high-speed network performance through a prediction feedback based model. In Prakash Vidyarthi, D. (Ed.), *Technologies and Protocols for the Future of Internet Design: Reinventing the Web* (pp. 162–178). Hershey, PA: Information Science Reference. doi:10.4018/978-1-4666-0203-8.ch008.

Ramachandra, M., & Pattabhirama, P. (2012). Information feedback based architecture for handling the scalability issues in the reusable cloud components. In Yang, H., & Liu, X. (Eds.), *Software Reuse in the Emerging Cloud Computing Era* (pp. 186–202). Hershey, PA: Information Science Reference. doi:10.4018/978-1-4666-0897-9.ch008.

Ramirez, E. H., & Brena, R. F. (2006). Multi-agent systems integration in enterprise environments using web services. [IJIIT]. *International Journal of Intelligent Information Technologies, 2*(3), 72–88. doi:10.4018/jiit.2006070105.

Ranaldo, N., & Zimeo, E. (2012). Optimizing content delivery in QoS-aware multi-CDNs. In Fortino, G., & Palau, C. (Eds.), *Next Generation Content Delivery Infrastructures: Emerging Paradigms and Technologies* (pp. 147–171). Hershey, PA: Information Science Reference. doi:10.4018/978-1-4666-1794-0.ch007.

Ringelstein, C., & Staab, S. (2012). DiALog: A distributed model for capturing provenance and auditing information. In Hung, P. (Ed.), *Web Service Composition and New Frameworks in Designing Semantics: Innovations* (pp. 352–371). Hershey, PA: Information Science Reference. doi:10.4018/978-1-4666-1942-5.ch016.

Robert, L., & Nadarajan, R. (2011). Fault-tolerant text data compression algorithms. In Alkhatib, G. (Ed.), *Web Engineered Applications for Evolving Organizations: Emerging Knowledge* (pp. 80–98). Hershey, PA: Information Science Reference. doi:10.4018/978-1-60960-523-0.ch006.

Rosario, S., Benveniste, A., & Jard, C. (2012). Flexible probabilistic QoS management of orchestrations. In Hung, P. (Ed.), *Web Service Composition and New Frameworks in Designing Semantics: Innovations* (pp. 195–217). Hershey, PA: Information Science Reference. doi:10.4018/978-1-4666-1942-5.ch009.

Rouached, M., Fdhila, W., & Godart, C. (2012). Web services compositions modelling and choreographies analysis. In Hung, P. (Ed.), *Web Service Composition and New Frameworks in Designing Semantics: Innovations* (pp. 1–26). Hershey, PA: Information Science Reference. doi:10.4018/978-1-4666-1942-5.ch001.

Saab, C. B., Coulibaly, D., Haddad, S., Melliti, T., Moreaux, P., & Rampacek, S. (2012). An integrated framework for web services orchestration. In Jie-Zhang, L. (Ed.), *Innovations, Standards and Practices of Web Services: Emerging Research Topics* (pp. 306–335). Hershey, PA: Information Science Reference.

Sadeghi, L., Ressler, S., & Krzmarzick, A. (2012). Using web 2.0 to reconceptualize e-government: The case for GovLoop. In Downey, E., & Jones, M. (Eds.), *Public Service, Governance and Web 2.0 Technologies: Future Trends in Social Media* (pp. 153–166). Hershey, PA: Information Science Reference. doi:10.4018/978-1-4666-0071-3.ch010.

Sadi, M. S., Myers, D. G., & Sanchez, C. O. (2011). Complexity analysis at design stages of service oriented architectures as a measure of reliability risks. In Milanovic, N. (Ed.), *Engineering Reliable Service Oriented Architecture: Managing Complexity and Service Level Agreements* (pp. 292–314). Hershey, PA: Information Science Reference. doi:10.4018/978-1-60960-493-6.ch014.

Saini, H., Mishra, B. K., & Panda, T. C. (2013). Computing the spreading power of a business portal to propagate the malicious information in the network. In Polgar, J., & Adamson, G. (Eds.), *Web Portal Design, Implementation, Integration, and Optimization* (pp. 71–79). Hershey, PA: Information Science Reference. doi:10.4018/978-1-4666-2779-6.ch006.

Sajeev, G., & Sebastian, M. (2011). Analyzing the traffic characteristics for evaluating the performance of web caching. In Alkhatib, G. (Ed.), *Web Engineered Applications for Evolving Organizations: Emerging Knowledge* (pp. 196–210). Hershey, PA: Information Science Reference. doi:10.4018/978-1-60960-523-0.ch012.

Santos, R. O., Oliveira, F. F., Gomes, R. L., Martinello, M., & Guizzardi, R. S. (2013). Lightweight collaborative web browsing. In Polgar, J., & Adamson, G. (Eds.), *Web Portal Design, Implementation, Integration, and Optimization* (pp. 17–32). Hershey, PA: Information Science Reference. doi:10.4018/978-1-4666-2779-6.ch002.

Sarker, B. K., Descottes, J., Sohail, M., & Kosaraju, R. K. (2012). Smart rooms: A framework for inferencing using semantic web technology in ambient intelligent network. In Prakash Vidyarthi, D. (Ed.), *Technologies and Protocols for the Future of Internet Design: Reinventing the Web* (pp. 289–303). Hershey, PA: Information Science Reference. doi:10.4018/978-1-4666-0203-8.ch016.

Saxon, A., Walker, S., & Prytherch, D. (2010). Whose questionnaire is it, anyway? In Spiliotopoulos, T., Papadopoulou, P., Martakos, D., & Kouroupetroglou, G. (Eds.), *Integrating Usability Engineering for Designing the Web Experience: Methodologies and Principles* (pp. 289–308). Hershey, PA: Information Science Reference. doi:10.4018/978-1-60566-896-3.ch015.

Saxon, A., Walker, S., & Prytherch, D. (2011). Measuring the unmeasurable? Eliciting hard to measure information about the user experience. In Alkhatib, G. (Ed.), *Web Engineered Applications for Evolving Organizations: Emerging Knowledge* (pp. 256–277). Hershey, PA: Information Science Reference. doi:10.4018/978-1-60960-523-0.ch015.

Scacchi, W., Jensen, C., Noll, J., & Elliott, M. (2009). Multi-modal modeling, analysis, and validation of open source software development processes. In Alkhatib, G., & Rine, D. (Eds.), *Integrated Approaches in Information Technology and Web Engineering: Advancing Organizational Knowledge Sharing* (pp. 51–65). Hershey, PA: Information Science Reference.

Scowen, G., & Regenbrecht, H. (2011). Increased popularity through compliance with usability guidelines in e-learning web sites. In Alkhatib, G. (Ed.), *Web Engineered Applications for Evolving Organizations: Emerging Knowledge* (pp. 211–232). Hershey, PA: Information Science Reference. doi:10.4018/978-1-60960-523-0.ch013.

Serpeloni, F., Moraes, R., & Bonacin, R. (2013). Ontology mapping validation: Dealing with an NP-complete problem. In Polgar, J., & Adamson, G. (Eds.), *Web Portal Design, Implementation, Integration, and Optimization* (pp. 111–121). Hershey, PA: Information Science Reference. doi:10.4018/978-1-4666-2779-6.ch010.

Shadlou, S., Kai, N. J., & Hajmoosaei, A. (2013). Online payment via PayPal API case study event registration management system (ERMS). In Polgar, J., & Adamson, G. (Eds.), *Web Portal Design, Implementation, Integration, and Optimization* (pp. 87–95). Hershey, PA: Information Science Reference. doi:10.4018/978-1-4666-2779-6.ch008.

Shadlou, S., Solaymani, H., & Hajmoosaei, A. (2013). Advanced content management system in murdoch research institute. In Polgar, J., & Adamson, G. (Eds.), *Web Portal Design, Implementation, Integration, and Optimization* (pp. 80–86). Hershey, PA: Information Science Reference. doi:10.4018/978-1-4666-2779-6.ch007.

Sharma, D. K., & Sharma, A. K. (2010). Deep web information retrieval process: A technical survey. [IJITWE]. *International Journal of Information Technology and Web Engineering*, 5(1), 1–22. doi:10.4018/jitwe.2010010101.

Sharma, D. K., & Sharma, A. K. (2011). A novel architecture for deep web crawler. [IJITWE]. *International Journal of Information Technology and Web Engineering*, 6(1), 25–48. doi:10.4018/jitwe.2011010103.

Sharma, D. K., & Sharma, A. K. (2012). Deep web information retrieval process: A technical survey. In Alkhatib, G. (Ed.), *Models for Capitalizing on Web Engineering Advancements: Trends and Discoveries* (pp. 75–96). Hershey, PA: Information Science Publishing. doi:10.4018/978-1-4666-0023-2.ch005.

She, W., Yen, I., & Thuraisingham, B. (2012). Enhancing security modeling for web services using delegation and pass-on. In Hung, P. (Ed.), *Web Service Composition and New Frameworks in Designing Semantics: Innovations* (pp. 286–307). Hershey, PA: Information Science Reference. doi:10.4018/978-1-4666-1942-5.ch013.

Shen, P., Tang, M., Liu, V., & Caelli, W. (2012). Performance and scalability assessment for non-certificate-based public key management in VANETs. [IJISP]. *International Journal of Information Security and Privacy*, 6(1), 33–56. doi:10.4018/jisp.2012010103.

Shi, J., Yang, S., & Huang, T. (2012). SOA designed health care system for Taiwan government. In Lee, J., Ma, S., & Liu, A. (Eds.), *Service Life Cycle Tools and Technologies: Methods, Trends and Advances* (pp. 245–271). Hershey, PA: Information Science Reference. doi:10.4018/978-1-4666-1740-7.ch032.

Sikder, I. U., Gangopadhyay, A., & Shampur, N. V. (2010). Web-based geospatial services: Implementing interoperability specifications. In Alkhatib, G., & Rine, D. (Eds.), *Web Engineering Advancements and Trends: Building New Dimensions of Information Technology* (pp. 281–297). Hershey, PA: Information Science Reference. doi:10.4018/978-1-60566-719-5.ch017.

Silva Souza, V. E., de Almeida Falbo, R., & Guizzardi, G. (2010). Designing web information systems for a framework-based construction. In Tatnall, A. (Ed.), *Web Technologies: Concepts, Methodologies, Tools, and Applications* (pp. 310–343). Hershey, PA: Information Science Reference.

Singh, J. (2013). Research essay: Challenges and considerations of modern day portal tooling. In Polgar, J., & Adamson, G. (Eds.), *Web Portal Design, Implementation, Integration, and Optimization* (pp. 96–110). Hershey, PA: Information Science Reference. doi:10.4018/978-1-4666-2779-6.ch009.

Singh, M., & Tapaswi, S. (2012). Token based mutual exclusion in peer-to-peer systems. In Prakash Vidyarthi, D. (Ed.), *Technologies and Protocols for the Future of Internet Design: Reinventing the Web* (pp. 214–228). Hershey, PA: Information Science Reference. doi:10.4018/978-1-4666-0203-8.ch011.

Singh, N., Spillan, J. E., & Little, J. P. (2010). Web site localization practices: Some insights into the localization industry. In Tatnall, A. (Ed.), *Web Technologies: Concepts, Methodologies, Tools, and Applications* (pp. 229–243). Hershey, PA: Information Science Reference.

Singh, S. (2010). Usability techniques for interactive software and their application in e-commerce. In Spiliotopoulos, T., Papadopoulou, P., Martakos, D., & Kouroupetroglou, G. (Eds.), *Integrating Usability Engineering for Designing the Web Experience: Methodologies and Principles* (pp. 81–102). Hershey, PA: Information Science Reference. doi:10.4018/978-1-60566-896-3.ch005.

Singhera, Z., Horowitz, E., & Shah, A. (2010). A graphical user interface (GUI) testing methodology. In Alkhatib, G., & Rine, D. (Eds.), *Web Engineering Advancements and Trends: Building New Dimensions of Information Technology* (pp. 160–176). Hershey, PA: Information Science Reference. doi:10.4018/978-1-60566-719-5.ch009.

Skov, M. B. (2010). Supporting web developers in evaluating usability and identifying usability problems. In Spiliotopoulos, T., Papadopoulou, P., Martakos, D., & Kouroupetroglou, G. (Eds.), *Integrating Usability Engineering for Designing the Web Experience: Methodologies and Principles* (pp. 1–14). Hershey, PA: Information Science Reference. doi:10.4018/978-1-60566-896-3.ch001.

Skov, M. B., & Stage, J. (2011). A conceptual tool for usability problem identification in website development. In Alkhatib, G. (Ed.), *Web Engineered Applications for Evolving Organizations: Emerging Knowledge* (pp. 278–291). Hershey, PA: Information Science Reference. doi:10.4018/978-1-60960-523-0.ch016.

Spiliotopoulos, D., & Kouroupetroglou, G. (2010). Usability methodologies for spoken dialogue web interfaces. In Spiliotopoulos, T., Papadopoulou, P., Martakos, D., & Kouroupetroglou, G. (Eds.), *Integrating Usability Engineering for Designing the Web Experience: Methodologies and Principles* (pp. 149–165). Hershey, PA: Information Science Reference. doi:10.4018/978-1-60566-896-3.ch008.

Spiliotopoulos, D., Kouroupetroglou, G., & Stavropoulou, P. (2011). VoiceWeb: Spoken dialogue interfaces and usability. In Alkhatib, G. (Ed.), *Web Engineered Applications for Evolving Organizations: Emerging Knowledge* (pp. 340–359). Hershey, PA: Information Science Reference. doi:10.4018/978-1-60960-523-0.ch019.

Spiliotopoulos, T., Papadopoulou, P., Martakos, D., & Kouroupetroglou, G. (2010). *Integrating usability engineering for designing the web experience: Methodologies and principles*. Hershey, PA: IGI Global. doi:10.4018/978-1-60566-896-3.

Sticklen, D. J., & Issa, T. (2013). An initial examination of free and proprietary software-selection in organizations. In Polgar, J., & Adamson, G. (Eds.), *Web Portal Design, Implementation, Integration, and Optimization* (pp. 198–215). Hershey, PA: Information Science Reference. doi:10.4018/978-1-4666-2779-6.ch016.

Stieglitz, S., & Fuchß, C. (2011). Message-based routing in mobile networks. In Alkhatib, G. (Ed.), *Web Engineered Applications for Evolving Organizations: Emerging Knowledge* (pp. 1–12). Hershey, PA: Information Science Reference. doi:10.4018/978-1-60960-523-0.ch001.

Stober, T., & Hansmann, U. (2010). WebSphere portal 6.1: An agile development approach. In Tatnall, A. (Ed.), *Web Technologies: Concepts, Methodologies, Tools, and Applications* (pp. 394–403). Hershey, PA: Information Science Reference.

Stoilos, G., Pan, J. Z., & Stamou, G. (2010). Scalable reasoning with tractable fuzzy ontology languages. In Laurent, A., & Lesot, M. (Eds.), *Scalable Fuzzy Algorithms for Data Management and Analysis: Methods and Design* (pp. 130–158). Hershey, PA: Information Science Reference.

Tang, L., Dong, J., & Zhao, Y. (2012). SLA-aware enterprise service computing. In Cardellini, V., Casalicchio, E., Castelo Branco, K., Estrella, J., & Monaco, F. (Eds.), *Performance and Dependability in Service Computing: Concepts, Techniques and Research Directions* (pp. 26–52). Hershey, PA: Information Science Reference.

Tappenden, A. F., Huynh, T., Miller, J., Geras, A., & Smith, M. (2009). Agile development of secure web-based applications. In Alkhatib, G., & Rine, D. (Eds.), *Integrated Approaches in Information Technology and Web Engineering: Advancing Organizational Knowledge Sharing* (pp. 257–277). Hershey, PA: Information Science Reference.

Targowski, A. (2011). The architecture of service systems as the framework for the definition of service science scope. In Wang, J. (Ed.), *Information Systems and New Applications in the Service Sector: Models and Methods* (pp. 55–75). Hershey, PA: Business Science Reference.

Tariq, F. B., & Korrapati, S. (2013). F-DRARE: A framework for deterministic runtime adaptation of cyber physical systems. In *Adaptive Web Services for Modular and Reusable Software Development: Tactics and Solutions* (pp. 263–276). Hershey, PA: IGI Global.

Tatnall, A. (2010). *Web technologies: Concepts, methodologies, tools, and applications*. Hershey, PA: IGI Global.

Taweel, A., & Tyson, G. (2011). Prediction of non-functional properties of service-based systems: A software reliability model. In Milanovic, N. (Ed.), *Engineering Reliable Service Oriented Architecture: Managing Complexity and Service Level Agreements* (pp. 236–256). Hershey, PA: Information Science Reference. doi:10.4018/978-1-60960-493-6.ch012.

Tekli, J., Damiani, E., & Chbeir, R. (2012). Using XML-based multicasting to improve web service scalability. [IJWSR]. *International Journal of Web Services Research, 9*(1), 1–29. doi:10.4018/jwsr.2012010101.

Tiwari, S., Singh, A., Singh, R. S., & Singh, S. K. (2012). Internet security using biometrics. In Prakash Vidyarthi, D. (Ed.), *Technologies and Protocols for the Future of Internet Design: Reinventing the Web* (pp. 114–142). Hershey, PA: Information Science Reference. doi:10.4018/978-1-4666-0203-8.ch006.

Torres-Coronas, T., Monclús-Guitart, R., Rodríguez-Merayo, A., Vidal-Blasco, M. A., & Simón-Olmos, M. J. (2010). Web 2.0 technologies: Social software applied to higher education and adult learning. In Tatnall, A. (Ed.), *Web Technologies: Concepts, Methodologies, Tools, and Applications* (pp. 794–804). Hershey, PA: Information Science Reference.

Touseau, L., Gama, K., Donsez, D., & Rudametkin, W. (2012). Adaptive and dynamic service compositions in the OSGi service platform. In Lee, J., Ma, S., & Liu, A. (Eds.), *Service Life Cycle Tools and Technologies: Methods, Trends and Advances* (pp. 175–198). Hershey, PA: Information Science Reference.

Tsou, M. (2012). Geographic information retrieval and text mining on chinese tourism web pages. In Alkhatib, G. (Ed.), *Models for Capitalizing on Web Engineering Advancements: Trends and Discoveries* (pp. 219–239). Hershey, PA: Information Science Publishing. doi:10.4018/978-1-4666-0023-2.ch012.

Udzir, N. I., Ibrahim, H., & Demesie, S. (2012). Finer garbage collection in lindacap. In Alkhatib, G. (Ed.), *Models for Capitalizing on Web Engineering Advancements: Trends and Discoveries* (pp. 112–137). Hershey, PA: Information Science Publishing. doi:10.4018/978-1-4666-0023-2.ch007.

Ueno, K., & Tatsubori, M. (2012). Early capacity testing of an enterprise service bus. In Jie-Zhang, L. (Ed.), *Innovations, Standards and Practices of Web Services: Emerging Research Topics* (pp. 288–305). Hershey, PA: Information Science Reference.

Urban, S. D., Gao, L., Shrestha, R., Xiao, Y., Friedman, Z., & Rodriguez, J. (2012). The assurance point model for consistency and recovery in service composition. In Jie-Zhang, L. (Ed.), *Innovations, Standards and Practices of Web Services: Emerging Research Topics* (pp. 250–287). Hershey, PA: Information Science Reference.

van der Aalst, W. M., & Nikolov, A. (2008). Mining e-mail messages: Uncovering interaction patterns and processes using e-mail logs. [IJIIT]. *International Journal of Intelligent Information Technologies*, *4*(3), 27–45. doi:10.4018/jiit.2008070102.

Vaquero, L. M., Cáceres, J., & Morán, D. (2011). The challenge of service level scalability for the cloud. [IJCAC]. *International Journal of Cloud Applications and Computing*, *1*(1), 34–44. doi:10.4018/ijcac.2011010103.

Vaquero, L. M., Cáceres, J., & Morán, D. (2013). The challenge of service level scalability for the cloud. In Aljawarneh, S. (Ed.), *Cloud Computing Advancements in Design, Implementation, and Technologies* (pp. 37–48). Hershey, PA: Information Science Reference.

Vassilopoulou, K., Keeling, K. K., & Macaulay, L. A. (2010). A theoretical framework measuring the usability of retail sites. In Spiliotopoulos, T., Papadopoulou, P., Martakos, D., & Kouroupetroglou, G. (Eds.), *Integrating Usability Engineering for Designing the Web Experience: Methodologies and Principles* (pp. 243–263). Hershey, PA: Information Science Reference. doi:10.4018/978-1-60566-896-3.ch013.

Vidyarthi, D. P. (2012). Historical evolution in internet: An introduction. In Prakash Vidyarthi, D. (Ed.), *Technologies and Protocols for the Future of Internet Design: Reinventing the Web* (pp. 1–3). Hershey, PA: Information Science Reference. doi:10.4018/978-1-4666-0203-8.ch001.

Viroli, M., Zambonelli, F., Stevenson, G., & Dobson, S. (2013). From SOA to pervasive service ecosystems: An approach based on semantic web technologies. In Ortiz, G., & Cubo, J. (Eds.), *Adaptive Web Services for Modular and Reusable Software Development: Tactics and Solutions* (pp. 207–237). Hershey, PA: Information Science Reference.

Wang, G., Wang, C., Wang, H., Santiago, R. A., Jin, J., & Shaw, D. (2011). Quality of service monitoring, diagnosis, and adaptation for service level management. In Milanovic, N. (Ed.), *Engineering Reliable Service Oriented Architecture: Managing Complexity and Service Level Agreements* (pp. 41–58). Hershey, PA: Information Science Reference. doi:10.4018/978-1-60960-493-6.ch003.

Wang, P., Jin, Z., Liu, L., & Wu, B. (2012). Specifying and composing web services with an environment ontology-based approach. In Hung, P. (Ed.), *Web Service Composition and New Frameworks in Designing Semantics: Innovations* (pp. 105–123). Hershey, PA: Information Science Reference. doi:10.4018/978-1-4666-1942-5.ch005.

Wang, S., Brown, K. P., Lu, J., & Capretz, M. (2013). A reference ontology based approach for service oriented semantic interoperability. In Polgar, J., & Adamson, G. (Eds.), *Web Portal Design, Implementation, Integration, and Optimization* (pp. 1–16). Hershey, PA: Information Science Reference. doi:10.4018/978-1-4666-2779-6.ch001.

Wang, X., & Rine, D. (2009). Secure online DNS dynamic updates: Architecture and implementation. In Alkhatib, G., & Rine, D. (Eds.), *Integrated Approaches in Information Technology and Web Engineering: Advancing Organizational Knowledge Sharing* (pp. 185–202). Hershey, PA: Information Science Reference.

Warner, A. G., & Fairbank, J. F. (2008). Integrating real option and dynamic capability theories of firm boundaries: The logic of early acquisition in the ICT industry. [IJITSR]. *International Journal of IT Standards and Standardization Research, 6*(1), 39–54. doi:10.4018/jitsr.2008010102.

Weber, I., & Evans, P. (2013). E = mportfolios2? Challenges and opportunities in creating mobile electronic portfolio systems for lifelong learning. In Polgar, J., & Adamson, G. (Eds.), *Web Portal Design, Implementation, Integration, and Optimization* (pp. 58–70). Hershey, PA: Information Science Reference. doi:10.4018/978-1-4666-2779-6.ch005.

Wei, S., David, T., & Torab, T. (2010). Image mining: A case for clustering shoe prints. In Alkhatib, G., & Rine, D. (Eds.), *Web Engineering Advancements and Trends: Building New Dimensions of Information Technology* (pp. 83–96). Hershey, PA: Information Science Reference. doi:10.4018/978-1-60566-719-5.ch005.

Welicki, L., Juan, J. P., Martin, F. L., & de Vega Hernandez, V. (2010). Employee life-cycle process management improvement with web-enabled workflow systems. In Tatnall, A. (Ed.), *Web Technologies: Concepts, Methodologies, Tools, and Applications* (pp. 1708–1723). Hershey, PA: Information Science Reference.

Weng, T., Lin, Y., & Stu, J. (2012). Case study on SOA implementation framework and applications. In Lee, J., Ma, S., & Liu, A. (Eds.), *Service Life Cycle Tools and Technologies: Methods, Trends and Advances* (pp. 272–302). Hershey, PA: Information Science Reference.

Werth, D., Emrich, A., & Chapko, A. (2013). Prosumerization of mobile service provision: A conceptual approach. In Polgar, J., & Adamson, G. (Eds.), *Web Portal Design, Implementation, Integration, and Optimization* (pp. 216–228). Hershey, PA: Information Science Reference. doi:10.4018/978-1-4666-2779-6.ch017.

Wigand, F. D. (2012). Communication and collaboration in a web 2.0 world. In Downey, E., & Jones, M. (Eds.), *Public Service, Governance and Web 2.0 Technologies: Future Trends in Social Media* (pp. 1–18). Hershey, PA: Information Science Reference. doi:10.4018/978-1-4666-0071-3.ch001.

Woerndl, W., Brocco, M., & Eigner, R. (2011). Context-aware recommender systems in vehicular networks and other mobile domains. In Alkhatib, G. (Ed.), *Web Engineered Applications for Evolving Organizations: Emerging Knowledge* (pp. 63–79). Hershey, PA: Information Science Reference. doi:10.4018/978-1-60960-523-0.ch005.

Wu, Z., & Weaver, A. C. (2012). Privacy-preserving trust establishment with web service enhancements. In Jie-Zhang, L. (Ed.), *Innovations, Standards and Practices of Web Services: Emerging Research Topics* (pp. 54–73). Hershey, PA: Information Science Reference.

Xanthidis, D., Nicholas, D., & Argyrides, P. (2010). A proposed template for the evaluation of web design strategies. In Tatnall, A. (Ed.), *Web Technologies: Concepts, Methodologies, Tools, and Applications* (pp. 119–144). Hershey, PA: Information Science Reference.

Xiong, P., Pu, C., & Zhou, M. (2012). Protocol-level service composition mismatches: A petri net siphon based solution. In Hung, P. (Ed.), *Web Service Composition and New Frameworks in Designing Semantics: Innovations* (pp. 50–70). Hershey, PA: Information Science Reference. doi:10.4018/978-1-4666-1942-5.ch003.

Yadamsuren, B., Paul, A., Erdelez, S., & Moore, J. L. (2010). Multiple-user simultaneous testing: Experience with two methods. In Spiliotopoulos, T., Papadopoulou, P., Martakos, D., & Kouroupetroglou, G. (Eds.), *Integrating Usability Engineering for Designing the Web Experience: Methodologies and Principles* (pp. 345–356). Hershey, PA: Information Science Reference. doi:10.4018/978-1-60566-896-3.ch018.

Yan, Y., Dague, P., Pencolé, Y., & Cordier, M. (2012). A model-based approach for diagnosing fault in web service processes. In Jie-Zhang, L. (Ed.), *Innovations, Standards and Practices of Web Services: Emerging Research Topics* (pp. 92–116). Hershey, PA: Information Science Reference.

Yan, Y., Liang, Y., Roy, A., & Du, X. (2012). Web service enabled online laboratory. In Jie-Zhang, L. (Ed.), *Innovations, Standards and Practices of Web Services: Emerging Research Topics* (pp. 363–381). Hershey, PA: Information Science Reference.

Yee, G. (2012). Estimating the privacy protection capability of a web service provider. In Jie-Zhang, L. (Ed.), *Innovations, Standards and Practices of Web Services: Emerging Research Topics* (pp. 132–153). Hershey, PA: Information Science Reference.

Yi, J., Jang, Y. J., Oh, D., & Ro, W. W. (2010). Programmability and scalability on multi-core architectures. In Li, K., Hsu, C., Yang, L., Dongarra, J., & Zima, H. (Eds.), *Handbook of Research on Scalable Computing Technologies* (pp. 276–294). Hershey, PA: Information Science Reference.

Zhang, T., Cheng, X., & Shi, W. (2012). P2P streaming content delivery systems. In G. Fortino, & C. Palau (Eds.), Next Generation Content Delivery Infrastructures: Emerging Paradigms and Technologies (pp. 55-77). Hershey, PA: Information Science Reference. doi: doi:10.4018/978-1-4666-1794-0.ch003.

Zhao, Y., Dong, J., Huang, J., Zhang, Y., Yen, I., & Bastani, F. (2012). Abstract service for cyber physical service composition. In Lee, J., Ma, S., & Liu, A. (Eds.), *Service Life Cycle Tools and Technologies: Methods, Trends and Advances* (pp. 303–322). Hershey, PA: Information Science Reference.

Zhao, Z., Grosso, P., van der Ham, J., & de Laat, C. T. (2012). Quality guaranteed media delivery over advanced network. In Fortino, G., & Palau, C. (Eds.), *Next Generation Content Delivery Infrastructures: Emerging Paradigms and Technologies* (pp. 121–146). Hershey, PA: Information Science Reference. doi:10.4018/978-1-4666-1794-0.ch006.

Zheng, Z., & Lyu, M. R. (2012). Optimal fault tolerance strategy selection for web services. In Hung, P. (Ed.), *Web Service Composition and New Frameworks in Designing Semantics: Innovations* (pp. 218–237). Hershey, PA: Information Science Reference. doi:10.4018/978-1-4666-1942-5.ch010.

Zisman, A. (2011). Supporting service level agreement with service discovery. In Milanovic, N. (Ed.), *Engineering Reliable Service Oriented Architecture: Managing Complexity and Service Level Agreements* (pp. 59–83). Hershey, PA: Information Science Reference. doi:10.4018/978-1-60960-493-6.ch004.

About the Contributors

Mohamed Boucadair is an IP Networking Strategist at France Telecom. Mohamed worked as a Senior IP Architect within France Telecom. He worked at the France Telecom corporate division responsible for making recommendations on the evolution of IP/MPLS core networks. He has worked for France Telecom R&D and has been part of the team working on VoIP services. He has been involved in IST research projects, working on dynamic provisioning and inter-domain traffic engineering. He has also worked as an R&D engineer in charge of dynamic provisioning, QoS, multicast and intra/inter-domain traffic engineering. He has published many journal articles and written extensively on these subject areas. Mr. Boucadair holds several patents on VoIP, IPv4 service continuity, IPv6, etc.

David Binet graduated from Telecom-Lille 1 and senior expert on inter access mobility technologies in France Telecom. He first worked on IPv6 technologies for Home Networking services. He has contributed on several French and European collaborative projects in mobility area and convergence issues. Involved in Research and pre-deployment projects, he is the author of several patents and he has contributed to the writing of papers for international conferences. Besides the leading of IPv6 projects, he was responsible for several research contracts with universities and contribute to IETF activities on seamless mobility topics. He participated in several collaborative projects funded by French government and European commission. He currently chairs Mobile WG in France Telecom IPv6 program and is an IP architect involved in IP/MPLS core networks architectures deployment in Orange affiliates.

* * *

Vishal Anand is an associate professor at The College at Brockport, SUNY. He received his B.S. degree in Computer Science and Engineering from the University of Madras, Madras (Chennai), India in 1996, and the M.S. and Ph.D. degrees in Computer Science and Engineering from the University at Buffalo, SUNY in 1999 and 2003. He has worked as a research scientist at Bell Labs, Lucent technologies and Telcordia Technologies (ex-Bellcore), where he investigated issues relating to traffic routing and survivability in optical networks. He is the co-inventor of a patent that cost-effectively improves the switching speed of traffic in the Internet backbone and is the recipient of the "Rising Star" and the "Promising Inventor Award" award from the Research Foundation of The State University of New York (SUNY), and the recipient of the "Visionary Innovator" award from the University of Buffalo (SUNY). His research interests are in the area of wired and wireless computer communication networks and protocols including optical networking, cloud and grid computing.

Iljitsch van Beijnum received the Bachelor of Information and Communication Technology degree from the Haagse Hogeschool in The Hague in 2005 and the Master of Telematics Engineering degree from UC3M in Madrid in 2008. He has worked in the Internet service provider business since 1995 and wrote books about BGP and IPv6 and many articles in the trade press. He is currently pursuing the Ph.D. degree at UC3M.

Olivier Bonaventure is currently Professor at Université catholique de Louvain. He obtained his Ph.D from the University of Liege in 1999. He spent one year at the Alcatel Alsthom Corporate Research Center in Antwerp and became professor at the Facultés Universitaires Notre-Dame de la Paix in Namur until 2002. He is now Professor at Université catholique de Louvain where he leads the network research group composed of ten researchers. He is also vice- president of the Institute of Information and Communication Technologies, Electronics and Applied Mathematics (ICTEAM), a research institute that gathers more than 200 researchers. He received the Wernaers and the Alcatel Bell prizes in 2001 and the INFOCOM best paper award in 2007. He has published more than hundred articles in international conferences and journals and contributes to standardization. His research interests are Internet protocols in general, routing, traffic engineering and network measurements. He was TPC co-chair of SIGCOMM's CoNEXT 2007 and serves on CoNEXT's steering committee. He currently serves on the editorial board of IEEE/ACM Transactions on Networking and is Education Director of ACM SIGCOMM.

Xiaojun (Matt) Cao is an Associate Professor in the Department of Computer Science at Georgia State University, where he leads the Advanced Network Research Group (aNet). Prior to joining Georgia State University, he was an assistant professor in the College of Computing and Information Sciences at Rochester Institute of Technology. He received the B.S. degree from Tsinghua University in 1996, the M.S. degree from Chinese Academy of Sciences in 1999, and the Ph.D. degree in Computer Science from the State University of New York at Buffalo in 2004. Dr. Cao is the co-author of the book, "Wireless Sensor Networks: Principles and Practice," CRC Press, 2010. His primary research interests include protocols design in wireless networks, modeling optical networks and network security. He is a recipient of the National Science Foundation CAREER Award.

Heiner Hummel studied mathematics and computer science at the Technical University Munich and acquired there the masters degree in 1974. In his professional carrier he worked for Siemens AG, both in Germany and the U.S., took part in the software development for several telecommunication systems as well as in the standardization process at the ATM Forum, MPLS Forum, ITU-T, IETF, IRTF. His special expertise is the design of recursive algorithms for mainly routing purposes. This includes, apart from Dijkstra's classical (all- nodes-) spanning tree, the computation of all-links-spanning-trees, cascade trees and minimal Steiner trees. He has been a critical observer of the activities by the IETF/ IRTF routing community especially with respect to the so-called scalability problem as well as to its most sacrosanct paradigms.

Luigi Iannone is currently an Associate Professor at Telecom ParisTech, in Paris, since May 2012. He was previously Senior Research Scientist at Deutsche Telekom Innovation Laboratories (T-Labs), in Berlin, between September 2008 and April 2012. Before that, he worked as post-doc researcher at Université catholique de Louvain (UCL - Belgium) in 2007/2008. From 2002 to 2007, he worked at the

Université Pierre et Marie Curie (Paris VI - France), first as Ph.D. candidate until 2006, when he has got his Ph.D. in Computer Science, and later as post-doc. Before that, he got a degree in Computer Engineering from the Università degli Studi di Pisa (Italy). His current research interests include intra- and inter- domain routing, Future Internet architectures, as well as mobility, wireless networks, and wired/wireless convergence. He is currently serving on the editorial board of Elsevier Computer Networks Journal and he is editor-in-chief of Network Communication Technologies published by the Canadian Center of Science and Education.

Daniel Jen is a research analyst for the Advanced Technology and Systems Analysis division at CNA. He specializes in command, control, communications, computers, collaboration, and intelligence (c5i) issues, with particular expertise in computer networks and cyber security. He has worked with the DoD to improve systems such as the Global Broadcast Service, the Host Based Security System, and the Enterprise Network Management System.

Yaoqing Liu is a research assistant and PhD candidate supervised by Dr. Lan Wang at the University of Memphis. His research interests mainly include networked systems (routing, security, algorithm, measurement, and protocol), Software Defined Networking, and Future Internet Architecture. He holds a B.S. degree (2005) in Computer Science from Dalian Maritime University, China and M.S. degree (2011) in Computer Science from The University of Memphis. He won the first prize of National Mathematical Modeling Contest of 2003 in China and Morton Dissertation Award Nomination from The University of Memphis in 2013.

Meilian Lu is a staff member of State Key Lab. of Networking and Switching Tech., and an associate professor at Beijing University of Posts and Telecommunications. Her current research interests include: architecture of network and service, mobile Internet service, data mining and information distribution.

Hongbin Luo received his M.S. (with honors) and Ph.D. degrees in Communications and Information Science from University of Electronic Science and Technology of China (UESTC), in June 2004 and March 2007, respectively. In June 2007, he joined the School of Electronic and Information Engineering, Beijing Jiaotong University, where he is a full professor. From Sep. 2009 to Sep. 2010, he was a visiting scholar at Purdue University. He is the first author of more than 30 peer-reviewed papers published in leading journals (such as *IEEE/ACM Transactions on Networking* and *IEEE Journal on Selected Areas in Communications*) and conference proceedings. He is an editor of *IEEE Communications Letters* and *KSII Transactions on Internet and Information Systems*. He has served on the technical program committee (TPC) of several international conferences such as IEEE GLOBECOM'08-11, IEEE ICC'08-12, IEEE HPSR'13, ITC 2013. He was a TPC vice-chair of the 2009 IEEE International Conference on Future Information Networks (ICFIN'09) in Beijing. His research interests are in the areas of Internet routing, Internet architecture, and optical networking.

Dan Massey is an associate professor in the Computer Science Department at Colorado State University. Dr. Massey received his doctorate from UCLA and is a senior member of the IEEE, IEEE Communications Society, and IEEE Computer Society. His research interests include robustness and security for large scale network infrastructures. As one of the editors of the DNS Security Extensions

(DNSSEC), he has been working to develop and deploy security in the DNS. In the area of network routing, his works includes BGP monitoring and analysis as well as security enhancements such as the Route Origin Verifier (ROVER). Looking forward to future architectures, Dr. Massey is a member of the Named Data Networking (NDN) team developing a new information centric architecture. He has served as the principal investigator on research projects funded by the National Science Foundation and Department of Homeland Security and the author of over 75 papers.

Michael Meisel received his Ph.D. in computer science at the University of California, Los Angeles in 2011. His dissertation was on unifying mobile networks with Named Data Networking (NDN). He is currently Chief Architect at ThousandEyes. He previously served as Senior Software Engineer for Inveneo, a non-profit that develops and deploys information and communications technology for rural and remote areas in the developing world. He received a B.A. in computer science from UC Berkeley in 2003.

Gaurav Raina is Faculty in the Department of Electrical Engineering, Indian Institute of Technology Madras, India and a Visiting Research Fellow in the Department of Pure Mathematics and Mathematical Statistics, University of Cambridge, U.K. His research interests are in the design and control of communication networks, non-linear systems and mobile commerce.

Shankar Raman is a BT-IITM PhD fellow at Indian Institute of Technology Madras. Prior to this, he worked with service companies like Wipro Technologies and HCL Technologies India in their Research and Development division. At HCL Technologies, he worked with the Cisco Offshore Development Center for a decade in the areas of Network Security and Management. His areas of interest include network protocols, network security, network power reduction and management.

Damien Saucez received his master degree in Computer Science engineering from Université catholique de Louvain in 2007 and his Ph.D. thesis entitled Mechanisms for Interdomain Traffic Engineering with LISP from the same university in 2011, under the supervision of Prof. Olivier Bonaventure. His research interests are related to the Future Internet and routing scalability in general. Damien Saucez actively contributes to the IETF LISP working group and is now post-doctoral researcher at Inria Sophia Antipolis where he works on routing and congestion control for Information-Centric Network and Software Defined Networking.

Wei Su received his Ph.D. degree in Communication and Information Systems from Beijing Jiaotong University (BJTU) in January 2008. He joined the School of Electronic and Information Engineering, BJTU in 2008, and was an assistant professor from November 2011. He participated in many national projects such as National Basic Research Program of China ("973 Program"), the National High-Tech Research and Development Program of China ("863 Program"), and the National Natural Science Foundation of China. His research interests include wireless networking and next generation Internet technology.

Balaji Venkat Venkataswami is a Senior Engineer in the DELL Networking CTO team working out of Chennai, India. He has prior experience with IIT Madras and Indian Service Companies like Tata Unisys, HCL where he worked in the Cisco Offshore Development Center for 14 years. Subsequent to the HCL stint he worked at Juniper for a year. His interest areas include Routing and Switching and in technologies such as MPLS.

Lan Wang is an associate professor in the Computer Science Department at the University of Memphis. She holds a B.S. degree (1997) in Computer Science from Peking University, China and a Ph.D. degree (2004) in Computer Science from University of California, Los Angeles. Dr. Wang's research interests include Internet architecture, Internet routing, network security, network performance measurement and sensor networks.

Yang Wang received his Ph.D degree from from Georgia State University (GSU) in 2012. He obtained a M.E. degree from Beijing University of Posts and Telecommunications (BUPT) in 2007, and a M.S degree in Computer Science from GSU in 2011. His research interests mainly focus on the protocol/algorithm design in optical networks, where he has published over 20 papers in waveband switching networks, OBS networks and spectrum elastic optical networks. He received the Outstanding Graduate Research Award from GSU in both 2010, and 2011, and Ph.D Disseration Grant in 2012. Currently, he is with the Cloud Computing team of Internap Network Infrastructure Service Corporation. Before that, he was with the Research&Innovation Center of FutureWei Technology.

Rolf Winter is Professor for Data Networks at the University of Applied Sciences Augsburg (HSA). He received his PhD from the Freie University Berlin in 2006. Before joining the HSA, he was a Senior Researcher at the NEC Laboratories Europe where he was active in research projects and standardization. His research interests are in the areas of routing and switching, energy management, transport protocols, and network measurement. He is very involved in the Internet Engineering Task Force, where he chaired the recently closed LEDBAT working group. He is also a member of the IETF transport area directorate and co-author of a number of standards documents.

Changqiao Xu received his Ph.D. degree from Institute of Software, Chinese Academy of Sciences (ISCAS) in Jan. 2009. He was an assistant research fellow in ISCAS from 2002 to 2007, where he was research and development project manager in the area communication networks. During 2007-2009, he worked as a researcher in the Software Research Institute at Athlone Institute of Technology, Ireland. He joined Beijing University of Posts and Telecommunications (BUPT) in Dec. 2009, and was an assistant professor from 2009 to 2011. He is currently an associate professor with the Institute of Network Technology at BUPT. His research interests include wireless networking, multimedia communications and next generation Internet technology.

Xiaohu Xu has been working in the telecom industry for more than 10 years and now is a senior staff engineer at IP Advanced Technology Research Department of Huawei Technologies Co., Ltd. Prior to joining Huawei, he was the chief engineer at Technical Support Department and the manager at Router OS Test Team of Harbor Networks, Inc, which was acquired by Huawei later. His current research interests include but not limited to: scalable routing and addressing architecture; id/locator split architecture; data center network and data center interconnection architecture.

Beichuan Zhang is an Associate Professor in the Department of Computer Science at the The University of Arizona. His research interest is in Internet routing architectures and protocols, including information-centric networking, green networking, routing dynamics and security, and overlay multicast. He received the first Applied Networking Research Prize in 2011 by the Internet Society and the Internet Research Task Force, and the best paper award at ICDCS in 2005. Dr. Zhang received Ph.D. in Computer Science from the University of California, Los Angeles (2003) and B.S. in Chemistry from Peking University, China (1995).

Hongke Zhang received his Ph.D. degrees in electrical and communication systems from the University of Electronic Science and Technology of China in 1992. From 1992 to 1994, he was a postdoctoral research associate at Beijing Jiaotong University, and in July 1994, he became a professor there. He has published more than 150 research papers in the areas of communications, computer networks, and information theory. He is the author of eight books written in Chinese and the holder of more than 40 patents. He is now the director of National Engineering Lab for Next Generation Internet Interconnection Devices at Beijing Jiaotong University. He is also the head of the Institute of Network Technology at Beijing University of Posts and Telecommunications, and the chief scientist of a National Basic Research Program of China ("973 Program").

Lixia Zhang received her Ph.D in computer science from MIT and joined Xerox Palo Alto Research Center as a member of research staff. She is now a professor in the Computer Science Department of UCLA. In the past she served as the vice chair of ACM SIGCOMM, member of the editorial board for the IEEE/ACM Transactions on Networking, member of the Internet Architecture Board, and co-chair of the Routing Research Group under IRTF. She is a fellow of ACM and IEEE. She received IEEE Internet Award in 2009 and holds UCLA Jon Postel Chair in Computer Science.

Xin Zhao is a software engineer at Google. He was a master student in the Department of Computer Science at the The University of Arizona under professor Beichuan Zhang. His research interest was in Internet routing architectures and protocols, including routing scalability and stability. He graduated from University of Arizona in 2011. He received master/B.S. in Computer Science from Nankai University, China (2002 and 2005).

Index